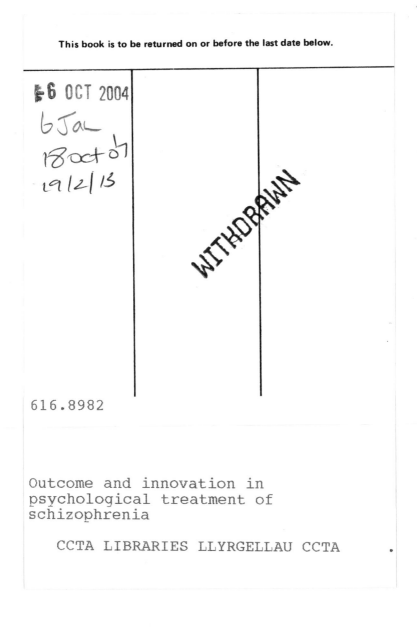

Outcome and innovation in
psychological treatment of
schizophrenia

OUTCOME AND INNOVATION IN PSYCHOLOGICAL TREATMENT OF SCHIZOPHRENIA

Edited by

Til Wykes
Institute of Psychiatry, London, UK

Nicholas Tarrier
University of Manchester, UK

and

Shôn Lewis
University of Manchester, UK

JOHN WILEY & SONS
Chichester • New York • Weinheim • Brisbane • Singapore • Toronto

Other Wiley Editorial Offices

John Wiley & Sons, Inc., 605 Third Avenue,
New York, NY 10158-0012, USA

WILEY-VCH Verlag GmbH, Pappelallee 3,
D-69469 Weinheim, Germany

Jacaranda Wiley Ltd, 33 Park Road, Milton,
Queensland 4064, Australia

John Wiley & Sons (Asia) Pte Ltd, Clementi Loop #02
Jin Xing Distripark, Singapore 129809

John Wiley & Sons (Canada) Ltd, 22 Worcester Road,
Rexdale, Ontario M9W 1L1, Canada

Library of Congress Cataloging-in-Publication Data

Outcome and innovation in psychological treatment of schizophrenia / edited by Til Wykes, Nick Tarrier and Shôn Lewis.
    p.   cm.
  Includes bibliographical references and index.
  ISBN 0-471-97659-8—ISBN 0-471-97842-6 (pbk).
  1. Schizophrenia—Treatment.   2. Psychotherapy.   I. Wykes, Til.
II. Tarrier, Nicholas.   III. Lewis, Shôn.
  RC514.094   1998
  616.89'8206—dc21   97-18366

                                                              CIP

British Library Cataloguing in Publication Data

A catalogue record for this book is available from the British Library

ISBN 0-471-97659-8 (cased)
ISBN 0-471-97842-6 (paper)

Typeset in 10/12pt Palatino by Mackreth Media Services, Hemel Hempstead, Herts.
Printed and bound in Great Britain by Biddles Ltd, Guildford and King's Lynn.
This book is printed on acid-free paper responsibly manufactured from sustainable forestry, in which at least two trees are planted for each one used for paper production.

CONTENTS

About the Editors   v
Contributors   vi
Preface   x

Chapter 1   Innovation and Outcome in Psychological Treatments
             for Schizophrenia: The Way ahead?   1
             Til Wykes, Nicholas Tarrier and Shôn Lewis

Chapter 2   The Cognitive Origins of Schizophrenia and Prospects
             for Intervention   17
             Keith H. Nuechterlein and Kenneth L. Subotnik

Chapter 3   The Measurement of Outcome in Schizophrenia   43
             *Richard Drake, Gillian Haddock, Richard Hopkins and
             Shôn Lewis*

Chapter 4   Cognitive Behaviour Therapy of Schizophrenia   59
             David Kingdon and Douglas Turkington

Chapter 5   Depression and Suicidal Thinking in Psychosis:
             A Cognitive Approach   81
             Max Birchwood and Zaffer Iqbal

Chapter 6   The Evaluation of Cognitive Behavioural Therapy
             for Psychosis   101
             *Philippa Garety, Graham Dunn, David Fowler and Elizabeth
             Kuipers*

Chapter 7   Psychological Processes and Delusional Beliefs:
             Implications for the Treatment of Paranoid States   119
             Richard Bentall and Peter Kinderman

Chapter 8   The Effects of a Remediational Approach to Cognitive
             Therapy for Schizophrenia   145
             *William Spaulding, Dorie Reed, Daniel Storzback, Mary
             Sullivan, Martin Weiler and Charles Richardson*

Chapter 9   Coercion, Adherence or Collaboration? Influences on
             Compliance with Medication   161
             Michael McPhillips and Tom Sensky

Chapter 10   Biobehavioural Therapy: Interactions Between
             Pharmacotherapy and Behavior Therapy in
             Schizophrenia   179
             *Robert Liberman, Stephen Marder, B. D. Marshall, Jim Mintz
             and Timothy Kuehnel*

Chapter 11   Working with Carers: Interventions for Relative and
             Staff Carers of Those who have Psychosis   201
             Elizabeth Kuipers

Chapter 12   Training and Dissemination: Research to Practice in
             Innovative Psychosocial Treatments for Schizophrenia   215
             Nicholas Tarrier, Gillian Haddock and Christine Barrowclough

Chapter 13   Outcome and Costs of Psychological Therapies in
             Schizophrenia   237
             H. D. Brenner and M. Pfammatter

Chapter 14   Economic Evaluation of Psychological Treatments for
             Schizophrenia   259
             Martin Knapp and Andrew Healey

Index   283

ABOUT THE AUTHORS

Dr Til Wykes is a Reader in the Department of Psychology at the Institute of Psychiatry. She is also an Honorary Consultant Clinical Psychologist in The Maudsley. She has been involved in research on services and treatments for patients with a diagnosis of schizophrenia for many years. In 1995 she was presented with the May Davidson Award by the British Psychological Society for her contribution to clinical psychology research and practice. She is currently investigating the efficacy of treatments for alleviating the cognitive deficits associated with schizophrenia.

Professor Shôn Lewis is Professor of Psychiatry in the Department of Psychiatry and Behavioural Sciences, University of Manchester and an Honorary Consultant Psychiatrist in the South Manchester University Hospitals Trust. He has wide-ranging research interests in schizophrenia, from causal factors and the functioning brain imaging of cognition, to evaluating new treatments, particularly the interface between new psychological and new pharmacological treatments.

Professor Nicholas Tarrier is the Professor of Clinical Psychology in the Department of Clinical Psychology, University of Manchester and an Honorary Consultant Clinical Psychologist at the South Manchester University Hospitals NHS Trust. He has been involved in research in schizophrenia since 1974. His main interests have been the influence of psychosocial factors on the development of psychological and psychiatric disorders, and the evaluation of cognitive behavioural interventions. He was chair of the British Association of Behavioural and Cognitive Psychotherapy in 1995–96.

CONTRIBUTORS

Dr Christine Barrowclough
Department of Clinical Psychology, Academic Department of Clinical Psychology, Department of Psychiatry, Thameside General Hospital, Ashton-under-Lyne OL6 9RW, UK

Professor Richard Bentall
Department of Clinical Psychology, University of Liverpool, Whelan Building, PO Box 147, Liverpool, L69 3BX, UK

Professor Max Birchwood
Northern Birmingham Mental Health NHS Trust, Archer Centre, All Saints Hospital, Lodge Road, Winson Green, Birmingham, B18 5SD, UK

Professor H D Brenner
Director, Psychiatry University Services Bern, Mid West Sectors, Laupenstrasse 49, CH-3010 Bern, Switzerland

Dr Richard Drake
Clinical Research Fellow, The University of Manchester, School of Psychiatry and Behavioural Sciences, The Department of Psychiatry, Withington Hospital, West Didsbury, Manchester, M20 8LR, UK

Professor Graham Dunn
Professor of Biomedical Statistics, School of Epidemiology and Health Sciences, University of Manchester, Oxford Road, Manchester, M13 9PT, UK

Mr David Fowler
Lecturer, School of Health Policy and Practice, University of East Anglia, Health Policy and Practice Unit, UEA, Norwich, NR4 7TJ, UK

Professor Philippa Garety
UMDS, Division of Psychiatry and Psychology, St Thomas's Hospital,
Lambeth Palace Road, London, SE1 7EH, UK

Dr Gillian Haddock
The University of Manchester, School of Psychiatry and Behavioural
Sciences, The Department of Clinical Psychology, Withington Hospital,
West Didsbury, Manchester, M20 8LR, UK

Dr Andrew Healey
Lecturer, Institute of Psychiatry, Centre for the Economics of Mental
Health, 7 Windsor Walk, Denmark Hill, London, SE5 8BB, UK

Dr Richard Hopkins
The University of Manchester, School of Psychiatry and Behavioural
Sciences, Department of Psychiatry and Behavioural Sciences, Withington
Hospital, West Didsbury, Manchester, M20 8LR, UK

Dr Zaffer Iqbal
Research Fellow, Northern Birmingham Mental Health NHS Trust, Archer
Centre, All Saints Hospital, Lodge Road, Winson Green, Birmingham, B18
5SD, UK

Dr Peter Kinderman
Lecturer in Clinical Psychology, The University of Manchester, Department
of Psychiatry and Behavioural Sciences, Withington Hospital, West
Didsbury, Manchester, M20 8LR, UK

Dr David Kingdon
Medical Director, Nottingham Health Centre, Duncan Macmillan House,
Porchester Road, Nottingham, NG3 6AA, UK

Professor Martin Knapp
Institute of Psychiatry, Centre for the Economics of Mental Health, 7
Windsor Walk, Denmark Hill, London, SE5 8BB, UK

Dr Timothy Kuehnel
UCLA Research Center for Severe Mental Illnesses, Las Posadas Treatment
Center, Lewis Road, Camarillo, CA 93011, USA

Dr Elizabeth Kuipers
Institute of Psychiatry, Department of Psychology, De Crespigny Park,
Denmark Hill, London, SE5 8AF, UK

Professor Shôn Lewis
The University of Manchester, School of Psychiatry and Behavioural Sciences, Department of Psychiatry and Behavioural Sciences, Withington Hospital, West Didsbury, Manchester, M20 8LR, UK

Professor Robert Liberman
UCLA Research Center for Severe Mental Illnesses, Las Posadas Treatment Center, Lewis Road, Camarillo, CA 93011, USA

Dr Michael McPhillips
Imperial College School of Medicine, Horton Hospital, Long Grove Road, Epsom, Surrey, KT19 8PZ, UK

Professor Stephen Marder
Chief Psychiatry Service, Department of Veterans Affairs, Medical Center, West Los Angeles, 11301 Wilshire Boulevard, Los Angeles, CA 90073, USA

Dr B D Marshall
UCLA Research Center for Severe Mental Illnesses, Las Posadas Treatment Center, Lewis Road, Camarillo, CA 93011, USA

Dr Jim Mintz
UCLA Research Center for Severe Mental Illnesses, Las Posadas Treatment Center, Lewis Road, Camarillo, CA 93011, USA

Professor Keith Nuechterlein
Department of Psychiatry and Biobehavioral Sciences, UCLA School of Medicine, 300 UCLA Medical Plaza, Los Angeles, CA, USA

Dr M Pfammatter
Psychiatrische Universitats Klinic, Bern 3072 Ostermundigen, Bern, Switzerland

Dr Dorie Reed
Department of Psychology, University of Nebraska, Lincoln, USA

Dr Charles Richardson
Department of Psychology, University of Nebraska, Lincoln, USA

Dr Tom Sensky
West Middlesex University Hospital, Isleworth, Middlesex, TW7 6AF, UK

Professor William Spaulding
Department of Psychology, University of Nebraska, Lincoln, USA

Dr Daniel Storzback
Department of Psychology, University of Nebraska, Lincoln, USA

Dr Kenneth Subotnik
Department of Psychiatry and Biobehavioral Sciences, UCLA School of Medicine, 300 UCLA Medical Plaza, Los Angeles, USA

Dr Mary Sullivan
Department of Psychology, University of Nebraska, Lincoln, USA

Professor Nicholas Tarrier
The University of Manchester, School of Psychiatry and Behavioural Sciences, Department of Clinical Psychology, Withington Hospital, West Didsbury, Manchester, M20 8LR, UK

Dr Douglas Turkington
Newcastle Mental Health NHS Trust, UK

Dr Martin Weiler
Department of Psychology, University of Nebraska, Lincoln, USA

Dr Til Wykes
Institute of Psychiatry, Department of Psychology, De Crespigny Park, Denmark Hill, London, SE5 8AF, UK

PREFACE

New psychological treatments for schizophrenia have attracted a burgeoning interest in recent years. These exciting new developments have received considerable publicity in the academic journals in both psychiatry and psychology, but until a year or two ago had been less scrutinised by practitioners. The idea for this book arose from a conference in Cambridge, England, in September 1995, which provided a forum for a critical discussion about the utility of these different approaches, and suggested an agenda for future clinical research and practice.

This book provides a review of the evidence and considered discussion of the utility and effectiveness of psychological treatments of schizophrenia and also describes the need for further research to identify specific treatment effects. We would like to thank all the participants for stimulating such useful discussion, and also our sponsors, The Wellcome Trust and the UK Department of Health, for their support.

TIL WYKES

Chapter 1

INNOVATION AND OUTCOME IN PSYCHOLOGICAL TREATMENTS FOR SCHIZOPHRENIA: THE WAY AHEAD?

Til Wykes, Nicholas Tarrier and Shôn Lewis

There is no doubt that psychological treatments do have utility in relieving the symptoms and distress associated with schizophrenia. But until we can define the specific therapeutic effects of these treatments it is unlikely that they will be widely disseminated. This introductory chapter summarises the issues which we believe are important in our assessment of psychological treatments. We also suggest the direction for future research whose outcome is to improve the quality of life of our patients.

BACKGROUND FACTORS IN THE DEVELOPMENT OF TREATMENTS

(i) The move away from diagnosis

Over the past 10 years there has been a move away from concentrating on traditional psychiatric diagnostic classes. This has been particularly evident in schizophrenia treatment research. The focus is now on the wide spectrum of

Outcome and Innovation in Psychological Treatment of Schizophrenia. Edited by T. Wykes, N. Tarrier and S. Lewis.
© 1998 John Wiley & Sons Ltd

symptoms and experiences which may or may not be of diagnostic relevance. Several authors have developed a single theory to explain this diversity of symptoms—e.g. Hemsley (1994)—and Frith (1992) but others have argued for a more radical account. For instance, Bentall, Jackson and Pilgrim (1988) and Boyle (1990) have argued that the cluster of symptoms associated with schizophrenia do not represent evidence for a single diagnostic entity and therefore theories should be developed to explain individual symptoms rather than trying to explain the development of the syndrome as a whole. One synthesis of the two approaches, the single syndrome and the symptom approach is suggested in this volume by Kingdon and Turkington. They emphasise the complicated nature of the phenomenology and have argued on clinical grounds for the existence of separate syndromes within the schizophrenia spectrum. They have also captured a number of different single symptom interventions under one general therapeutic endeavour with adaptations to fit their suggested sub-syndromes.

The individual symptom approach has been received sympathetically by the scientific community mainly because of its pragmatic appeal. It has proved to be fruitful for the development of psychological interventions, particularly cognitive treatments (e.g. Bentall and Kinderman, Garety et al. and Spaulding). These single symptom interventions have been woven into global treatment strategies to produce cognitive behaviour therapy and neurocognitive therapy.

Despite the differences in views, all researchers agree that diagnosis and the overall severity of symptomatology now have to be replaced by more sophisticated notions of the experiential and behavioural phenomena associated with schizophrenia. The multidimensional nature of the new treatments which follow from this approach have encouraged researchers to construct new scales which can reflect their subtle effects. Much previous research has depended solely on broad-brush outcome measures, for example relapse rates, which are known to be affected by a variety of different and fluctuating variables including family structure, bed availability and community support as well as the specific intervention adopted (Harrison, Barrow and Creed, 1995; Lelliot and Wing, 1994). Although broader categories of outcomes will still be necessary because they are implicated in quality of life, health cost analyses and routine service evaluation, more detailed assessments will show subtle clinical changes. New assessments now need to be targeted if they are to reveal the differential effects of each treatment They will not only allow the measurement of treatment-specific gains but may also influence theoretical speculations. Within treatment-changes may indicate some of the relationships between different symptoms and experiences as well as their development and maintenance.

Previous treatment studies have generally adopted the global severity of illness as an outcome measure which is a total score across a range of different symptoms. But the treatments described in this volume are aimed at particular aspects of symptoms, including hallucinations, delusions and cognitive impairment. For example Garety and colleagues (Chapter 6) aim to change the conviction in a delusional belief whereas Spaulding and colleagues aim to change a person's concentration and attention. Both these interventions may produce a reduction in overall illness severity but this would be achieved via very different routes and these routes need to be specified by particular assessment procedures.

Previously the symptoms associated with schizophrenia have been measured either on dichotomous scales (e.g. PSE; Wing, Cooper and Sartorius, 1974) or on severity continua with frequency and severity being measured on a single scale (e.g. Extended BPRS; Lukoff, Neuchterlein and Ventura, 1986). But newer scales now allow a range of ratings separately for frequency and severity as well as permitting both objective and subjective ratings. For example, the distress associated with a particular symptom can be measured alongside its frequency and severity. These more detailed analyses allow individual symptom profiles to be drawn on which to base treatment. This is emphasised for case formulation in the new cognitive behaviour therapies (Kingdon, Chapter 4).

The initial assessment phase has implications for psychological treatment but there are other factors too which have influenced the development of scales. Purchasers and users of mental health services want to define outcome to include quality of life and level of social disability as well as symptomatic relief. There is also now a new emphasis on evidence-based medicine and pressure on clinicians to audit their own practice. New psychological treatments have therefore focused clinicians and researchers alike on the development of appropriate scales which in turn have influenced the development of detailed treatment packages which have led to the recognition of factors in symptom maintenance. One example of this process is given by Bentall and Kinderman (Chapter 7). They concentrated on developing treatments for persecutory delusions They developed a specific instrument to measure attributional style in the normal population. This questionnaire not only provided detail on the thinking processes associated with paranoid ideation but it also furnished the means for testing changes in these processes over time. The information gleaned from their experiments allowed them to develop a theory of the mechanism of maintenance of persecutory delusions which is currently being further tested. It also allowed them to develop a psychological treatment which seems to provide some promise for symptom relief (Kinderman and Bentall, 1997).

Psychological themes in psychological treatment developments

In the 1940s and 1950s psychological treatments for schizophrenia were based on psychodynamic theories. But these interventions were never shown to be effective (Mueser and Berenbaum, 1990; Heinrichs and Carpenter, 1981). Since 1960 treatments for schizophrenia have arisen from biological and biochemical research. Psychological and psychosocial treatments were accepted as appropriately addressing the problems of institutionalism and the rehabilitation of life skills but little else. However, developments in psychological theory have led to a number of novel psychological treatments as well as providing theory-driven rehabilitation approaches. These new treatments have drawn on a number of different areas of human experimental psychology. These include: information processing, cognitive science, behavioural psychology, developmental psychology and social psychology. All the themes rely on the basic assumption that people with schizophrenia are vulnerable to a number of stressors although the nature of this vulnerability and the specification of stressors differs (see Strauss and Carpenter, 1981; Perris, 1989; Nuechterlein and Dawson, 1984; Chapter 27). For example family approaches focus on the social relationships between family members. The stressors include the level of expressed emotion (EE) which reflects the behaviour and attitudes of carers towards the person with schizophrenia (see Tarrier et al., (Chapter 12); Kuipers, Chapter 11). The emphasis in family treatments is on changing the carer's behaviour towards the patient through educational and practical assistance but using a linguistic indicator, EE, to reflect these behavioural changes. The rehabilitation of cognitive deficits, however, uses theories of information processing. For example, theories of executive functioning (Baddeley,1992) and cognitive science have suggested possible treatments for deficits as well as alternative methods of skills enhancement.

Different approaches clearly operate in different psychological domains and produce theoretically driven, testable (and useful) hypotheses of clinical phenomena. The hypotheses then stimulate the process of deriving measurements of these same phenomena which are always couched in the same terms. For those developments based on cognitive science, these are tests of cognitive abilities, or they may be more general measures of thinking which can throw light on changes in thinking style.

Developments based on different fields are discussed in the various chapters in this book. Information processing and cognitive science have fuelled the work on cognitive remediation (Chapter 8). Cognitive behaviour therapy is also grounded on these approaches together with theories on the psychology of behaviour (Chapters 4 and 6). Hypotheses derived from a mixture of behavioural and social psychological theories have produced family approaches to schizophrenia (Chapter 11).

Phases of the disorder

Irrespective of whether there is an acceptance of a particular diagnostic classification system there is a widely held belief in a phasic structure to the experience of the disorder of schizophrenia. It can be categorised into several distinct stages depending on three factors: time, disability and symptom severity. These stages may warrant different approaches to treatment. The most useful differentiation is in a time sequence from an initial prodromal stage through to remission or a residual state (see Figure 1.1). The prodromal period is often experienced in adolescence or early adulthood and results in a noticeable functional decline in both vocational and social areas. Some time after the prodromal phase there is the onset of psychotic symptoms, usually referred to as an acute phase which often includes both delusions and hallucinations. Following this acute phase there is a decline in symptoms following specific pharmacological treatment. This reduction in symptoms may lead to full recovery or it may lead to a continued but reduced presence of either positive and/or negative symptoms frequently accompanied by a level of social and functional impairment. Symptoms fluctuate over time resulting in further acute phases as their severity increases to a point where the person is unable to safely function without increased assistance. There is also evidence of improvements and decrements in functioning even when the disorder is severe. For example, Harding and colleagues report that different aspects of functioning, including vocational achievement, fluctuated over a 30-year follow-up of the most severely affected patients in a rehabilitation service (Harding, Zubin and Strauss, 1987).

Psychological interventions need to accommodate to the changes in frequency and severity of symptoms and social behaviour problems in order to maximise the effectiveness of such interventions. It is now known that the shorter the periods of untreated illness the less chance there is of a relapse within two years (Macmillan, Crow, Johnson and Johnson, 1986; Loebel, Liberman, Alvir, Mayerhoff, Geisler and Szmanski, 1992). Studies of the EPPIC project in Australia have shown that early interventions also

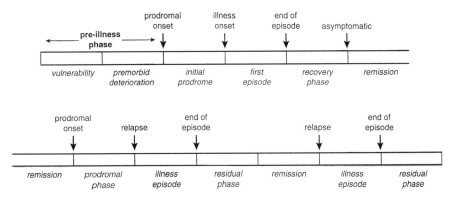

Figure 1.1   Phases of psychotic disorders

reduce negative symptoms and the number of hospitalisations, and improve quality of life (McGorry, Edwards, Mihalopolous, Harrison and Jackson,1996). Even after taking into account the association between an insidious onset and poor outcome it is obvious that this initial prodromal phase is a critical period and its reduction is a priority. The prodromes for further episodes of illness too may be a focus for intervention as these constitute phases when it may be possible to engage the clients themselves in the process of early recognition of crucial signs and symptoms of an episode.

The focus for intervention in the acute stage may be the levels of distress experienced by the patient and the experience of hallucinations and other symptoms. Following the first onset there are additional issues related to the stigma associated with mental illness and with the loss of self-esteem which often follows the recognition of a disabling psychiatric illness. In particular there are depressive symptoms which may lead to suicide, a known risk for people with schizophrenia (Johnson, 1981). These later effects together with the underlying deficits associated with the disorder and adverse social circumstances can produce secondary social disability handicaps (Wing, 1983). Because of the early onset of the disorder the person with schizophrenia may also miss opportunities for practising social skills or beginning work. This social decline can be targeted in a number of ways, including social skills training, life skills assessment and specific vocational interventions.

Different stages in the disorder inevitably interact with the age of the clients themselves. The prodromal and first onset stages usually occur in late adolescence to early adulthood. The therapies which are appropriate at this stage of the client's life may be very different to those which are appropriate to older clients. The clinical issues at each stage interact with other important factors in the person's life, such as the presence of a supportive family as well as their own aspirations and lifestyle. Together these factors will define the aims of treatment and the design of assessments for outcome.

CURRENT ISSUES FOR PSYCHOLOGICAL TREATMENT

What is the target for intervention?

The possible targets for therapeutic intervention include both vulnerabilities and environmental stressors, as well as the symptoms and deficits associated with the disorder. Vulnerabilities include the deficits in social and/or information processing which increase the likelihood of occurrence of an environmental stressor or amplify its effects. For example, social skills deficits are likely to affect the availability of family support. External stressors may be life events or merely normal social expectations which to an individual who has lost or never gained such skills provide a constant reminder of social inadequacy. Some of these expectation come from the client's family whose degree of criticism, hostility and/or overinvolvement constitute the concept of expressed emotion.

The choice for intervention may be individuals or the naturally (or unnaturally) occurring stressors in the environment. For individual-focused work there are two main options- to provide therapy for the client or their carers. Interventions with carers are either aimed at providing coping skills for dealing with the client's behaviour or are general education programmes which aim to support families and reduce their burden. Staff too, particularly those working in hostels, who are long-term carers are also the subject of the same sorts of intervention (Ball, Moore and Kuipers, 1992). But the therapeutic focus for most mental health services is the user of those services. The targets for intervention are reductions in symptoms, cognitive and social deficits, improvements in self-esteem, as well as increased quality of life.

But interventions can also take place in the environments themselves. Patients with schizophrenia may reach their optimal level of coping with the maximal increase in quality of life when they are provided with a certain amount of shelter. This can be provided within their residence or their work or leisure environment. There is already indirect evidence that increasing the unpredictability of environments has an effect on a patient's well-being. This evidence comes from two sorts of studies. The first is the behaviour of high and low EE relatives. High EE relatives produce many different responses to the same behaviours of the client whereas low EE relatives tend to use coping behaviours more consistently (McCarthy, Hemsley, Shrank-Fernandez, Kuipers and Katz, 1986). It is possible that one reason for effective interventions for high EE is to reduce the uncertainty in the environment for the client either by reducing the amount of contact with the relative or by directly changing the behaviour of the relative. The second set of studies shows that patients with more cognitive deficits derive little benefit and may be disadvantaged in unpredictable community settings (Wykes, 1994). The mechanism of this effect is probably the interaction of vulnerabilities with environmental stressors.

Increasing environmental predictability may therefore be an alternative or addition to the therapeutic armamentarium. However, this possibility is difficult to implement as we have very little agreement on how to measure this aspect of the environment. But we do have the building blocks of such a measure which include developments in life events measurement, EE, and the measurement of support (e.g. provision of meals, sheltered work etc). These assessments, together with a cognitive ergonomic assessment of the expectations of any environment, would permit a classification of environments which would then allow studies of the interaction between these environments and vulnerability factors.

Previous research has also focused on single stressors rather than on the interaction between different stressors. These data are particularly important for psychological interventions because it is not clear whether interventions for different targets would have additive effects. For example, if social skills deficits were ameliorated would this have the same or greater effect if family therapy was added to the treatment package? It is also easy to envisage a situation where it would be counter-productive to try to alleviate two targets simultaneously even if they were aimed separately at clients and carers.

Finally, many psychological therapies were developed for clients with severe and chronic disorders who not only had some social disability but who also continued to experience both hallucinations and delusions. These same therapies are now being extended for people with shorter histories who are generally younger. In their extension they will have to undergo some further development to make them acceptable to a younger clientele with different expectations and slightly different needs.

Which intervention?

The list of useful psychological interventions increases at an encouraging rate. As well as different targets for these interventions there are different types of intervention for the same targets. The choice of intervention is therefore an extremely difficult one to make. What would be helpful is a causative model which identifies the relationships between the different intrinsic and extrinsic factors associated with the appearance of the disorder which would enable researchers and clinicians to identify key points for intervention. If intervention targets are the immediate precursors of symptoms the outcome would be measured as the lack of development of the symptom. If the link between the factor and symptoms is more distant the immediate effects of the intervention are assessed differently, although the long-term aspects of the treatment may be the same (i.e. a reduction in relapse). This global approach has been attempted by Nuechterlein and Subotnik (Chapter 2), who have identified both protective and stressor factors. The approach is different from that taken by most UK researchers who have generally been interested in detailed descriptions of single symptoms. But although the global approach may indicate where the effect of intervention will take place it does not prescribe the intervention which should take precedence. It is unlikely that either the client's resources or those of the mental health services would stretch to simultaneous treatments for a variety of problems, so it is left to the clinical skill of the mental health professional to decide on the most appropriate target. What is needed is more information on the rehabilitation readiness of individuals which will be affected by the client's own aspirations as well as the development of a comprehensive structure for interventions that suggests particular sequences which can be tested.

One comprehensive rehabilitation system was devised for patients with chronic disorders and involves the remediation of both cognitive and social deficits. The system is called Integrated Psychological Therapy (IPT, Brenner, Roden, Hodel, Kienzle, Reed and Liberman, 1994) and is a programme presented in a group format. The programme is divided into a number of separate modules each concentrating on a micro-deficit, e.g. cognitive disability. These micro-deficits were hypothesised to affect the molar behaviours involved in social skills. The system was therefore based on a hierarchy of rehabilitation with the basic underlying skills being treated first followed by the more general skills higher up the model. In their model the basic deficits were of information processing and so their theory would suggest that rehabilitation aimed at these skills would be the most profitable. Unfortunately the only study to test this assumption has not supported this temporal approach. Hodel and Brenner (1994) report a study of two interventions, social problem solving and cognitive remediation. Their hypothesis was that the most benefit would be gained if cognitive rehabilitation was presented first followed by social problem solving. However, the opposite result was found—bigger benefits even for cognitive functioning when the social problem-solving module was presented first. The researchers suggest that this may be due to the ecological validity of the social problem solving-intervention which appealed to patients because it dealt with the everyday problems faced by people with schizophrenia and therefore they were more motivated to take part in such rehabilitation. However, they do not provide data in support of this hypothesis. An alternative interpretation may be that their group approach favoured the social problem-solving therapy because it dealt with issues which were more common to the group as a whole. Cognitive deficits probably show individual profiles (Shallice, Burgess and Frith, 1991) and it may be particularly difficult to provide therapy for these deficits in a group format. Despite this there is evidence that cognitive remediation therapy is effective when compared to a control group not receiving such therapy (Brenner, Hodel, Roder and Corrigan, 1992).

Because there is no comprehensive structure for the introduction of psychological therapies and since there is no literature on the relative contributions of different types of therapy, clinicians will have to rely on their judgement in introducing particular therapies. There are a number of factors which may guide their judgement. For example, the face validity of a particular treatment alluded to by Hodel and Brenner may affect the engagement in therapy. It is directly considered in cognitive behaviour therapies (CBT). In the first stages of these therapies when the case is formulated, the client contributes to the treatment plan and negotiates the goals of treatment. This formulation is stressed as a vital component of cognitive behaviour therapy although the ability of skilled clinicians to formulate a case in the same way is questionable (Persons, Mooney and Padesky, 1995).

The type of treatment also covaries with the mode of treatment. Both cognitive therapies, cognitive remediation and family therapy have been devised for both single case and group formats. Some individuals may benefit from a group format, particularly when therapy involves the normalisation of particular problems such as the occurrence of voices or those therapies which have a social theme.

But the choice of therapy is not only between categories of treatments, it is also between the different formulations of specific therapies. This is an important problem to address because it is not clear what are the specific components of therapy which are important to outcome. This is obvious in the descriptions of the elements of cognitive behaviour therapy. From the authors' last count there were 15 possible options, some of which are used with different individuals in the same trial, but there are also differences between trials. For example, Tarrier, Beckett, Harwood, Baker, Yusupoff and Ugartebru (1993) used a problem-solving approach as a control condition whereas Garety, Kuipers, Fowler, Dunn and Chamberlain (1994) included this in their experimental condition. This lack of standardisation has made it difficult to interpret data on the effectiveness of this form of treatment between studies. This evolution of cognitive behavioural therapies is another obstacle to the evaluation of its relative effectiveness.

A further problem has been the measurements adopted as outcome assessments. Although there is general agreement that more sophisticated measures are needed, otherwise the subtle effects of different forms of cognitive behaviour therapies may not be captured, there is no agreement on what these should be. Garety and colleagues make this same point with suggestions in this volume.

As with cognitive behaviour therapy, family therapy too suffers from a lack of general definition (Soloman, 1996). It has recently been divided into psychoeducation in which there are both therapeutic and educational aims, and family education which focuses on the reduction of family burden rather than reducing relapse in the key relative. Psychoeducation has been shown to be variously effective using relapse as an outcome measure (Mari and Streiner, 1994; Anderson and Adams, 1996). But the elements of different treatments often do not overlap. It is therefore essential for both theory and practice that we identify the different pathways in which elements have their effect on outcome. Identifying different routes to change is of great theoretical value as it will lead to the development of more refined treatment alternatives with the greatest cost effectiveness.

It may be that there is too much concentration on the mode of action of a treatment. Pragmatically many different treatments have an effect on the same outcome measures. It is possible that this occurs because many treatments work on the same underlying processes. For example, cognitive deficits therapies and cognitive behaviour therapies both aim to increase self esteem by encouraging the recognition of success. They also concentrate on encouraging people to identify evidence and evaluate it and particularly to discourage the 'jumping to conclusions' style of thinking evident in people with delusions (Huq, Garety and Hemsley, 1988) and impulsiveness. Both attain these goals using different methods.

Methodological issues

The issues of relative treatment efficacy, comprehensive rehabilitation and the specification of treatment effective elements need to be high on the research agenda for the next decade. But there are a number of methodological problems which militate against outcome research. In many different trials there has been the problem of representativeness of the samples. In the UK the mental health services provide for defined geographical areas and so it is possible to choose an epidemiologically unbiased sample. But in the USA and some European countries, the mental health services are provided differently to different income brackets and determined to some extent by the health insurance of the individual or their family. The likelihood of acquiring a biased sample is therefore high, which makes it difficult to compare data across both countries and studies.

Shapiro (1996), in a review of psychotherapy research, commented on the difficulty of making comparisons of different sorts of therapy. The list includes such problems as missing data, patient attrition over time, drop-outs as well as assessors remaining blind to the treatment condition. All of these difficulties are mentioned in the following chapters. Patients with schizophrenia do realise when they are receiving the "active" therapy condition and unless the comparison condition is also seen as important to them there will be many problems of drop-out over the course of the study. Although there may be statistical methods which can be adopted to allow clinically relevant conclusions to be drawn from the data (see Garety et al. Chapter 6). It is important that psychological treatments are subjected to as rigorous assessment as any other treatment even if this is difficult to do practically, ethically and statistically (Shulz,1996).

The choice of outcome measure is affected by many vested interests. Clinical research grant agencies are often concerned about the reduction in health costs which come from savings in inpatient care rather than improvements in quality of life which may have negligible effects on the nation's mental health costs. The adoption of a common currency of outcome has meant that less effort has been given to the identification of process measures in psychological therapy. These process measures are essential to the evolution of psychological therapies. Outcome assessment needs to have conceptual links to the intervention itself.

Cost-effectiveness

The complications of a cost-effectiveness analysis of psychological therapy are explained by Knapp and Healey (Chapter 14). This analysis is essential if psychological therapies are to be implemented on a wider scale in the mental health services. There is now a world wide-acceptance of evidence based practice but despite this many psychological therapies, e.g. family therapy, do not get implemented (Anderson and Adams, 1996). One possibility is that they do not have a product champion or the marketing budget of alternative therapies. One possible strategy is to show their worth in monetary terms as well as in therapeutic outcome, which may attract cost-conscious mental health purchasers.

The major differences in costs between psychological therapies is accounted for by the amount of therapist contact per patient involved in treatment. Some therapies have been delivered only to individuals whereas other have been developed for groups. Individual therapy is clearly more expensive but for some types of treatment it may not be possible to carry out effective therapy in a group. However, there are some aspects of treatment which may be amenable to a group setting. What has not been investigated is whether the treatments can begin with group involvement followed by specific interventions or vice versa.

Psychological therapies have also been devised and implemented by "expert practitioners" who are generally expensive. The efficacy of trials of psychological therapy will therefore be measured using these expert costs. The dissemination of skills to less expert therapists as in the studies of the Thorn Nurse Training Scheme (Lancashire, Haddock, Tarrier, Baguley, Butterworth and Brooker, 1997, Tarrier et al., Chapter 12) may make a substantial reduction in the costs, especially if therapists are diverted from less to more effective treatments. On the other hand there may be reductions in the efficacy of treatment which will reduce treatments benefits.

Research questions for the next decade

Even though it is clear that psychological treatments are effective in alleviating symptoms, improving skills, continuing supportive family contact and reducing relapse, more data on the effects and effectiveness of individual therapies are needed. Table 1.1 sets out a number of possible questions which need to be addressed. The list is not exhaustive.

The remainder of this volume will show that often the same outcomes can be achieved through a variety of different therapeutic routes. The specificity of particular treatments as well as general categories of therapies is therefore questionable. The research endeavour should therefore shift from deciding which is the most efficacious treatment to the identification

Table 1.1 Research issues for the next decade

(1) What constitutes a psychological therapy?—comprehensive descriptions of therapies to identify the similarities and differences between treatments
(2) What are the treatment elements? Which effect change and which are peripheral?
(3) What are the links to basic psychological theory?—particularly to cognitive, social and applied sciences?
(4) Is there fidelity of interventions when transferred to other settings and other professionals?
(5) What are the standardised and relevant outcome measures?
(6) What is the relative cost-effectiveness of different treatments when delivered by experts and in pragmatic studies?
(7) Can we develop a comprehensive structured rehabilitation programme to identify treatment precedence?
(8) What are the longer-term benefits of psychological treatment?
(9) What is the nature of the relationship between new psychological treatments and pharmacological treatments?

of factors which will predict the acceptability of treatment to a particular client in addition to discovering which treatment skills are the most easily transmissible to mental health professionals.

For mental health service providers the easiest option is to target the client who is using the service by providing sheltered environments and short-term treatments, but this is rarely the client's preference. Clients are more interested in interventions which enable them to blend into normal environments and therefore increase their choices and quality of life. They are therefore more likely to favour psychological interventions which increase their coping skills and decrease their deficits and symptoms.

As Anderson and Adams (1996) point out, even when they have proven worth, psychological therapies may not be implemented in mental health services. One variable which is important is the dissemination of research data about these treatments to mental health professionals. We hope this volume will contribute to this dissemination as well as encouraging further research into novel psychological treatments and promoting their use in clinical practice.

REFERENCES

Anderson, J. and Adams, C. (1996) Family interventions in schizophrenia: An effective but underused treatment. *British Medical Journal*, **313**, 505.

Baddeley, A. (1992) Working Memory, *Science*, **255**, 556–559.

Ball, R., Moore, E. and Kuipers, E. (1992) EE in community carefacilities: a comparison of patient outcome in a 9 month follow-up of two residential care hostels. *Social Psychiatry and Psychiatric Epidemiology*, **27**, 35–39.

Bentall, R., Jackson, H. and Pilgrim, D. (1988) "Abandoning the concept of schizophrenia": Some implications of validity arguments for psychological research into psychotic phenomena, *British Journal of Clinical Psychology*, **27**, 303–324.

Boyle, M. (1990) *Schizophrenia: a Scientific Delusion*. Routledge, London.

Brenner, H., Hodel, B. Roder V. and Corrigan P.(1992) Treatment of cognitive dysfunctions and behavioural deficits in schizophrenia. *Schizophrenia Bulletin*, **18**, 21–26.

Brenner, H., Roder, V., Hodel, B., Kienzle, N., Reed, D. and Liberman, R. (1994) *Integrated Psychological Therapy for Schizophrenia Patients*. Hogrefe and Huber, Toronto.

Frith C.D. (1992) *The Cognitive Neuropsychology of Schizophrenia*. Lawrence Erlbaum Associates, Hove.

Garety, P.A., Kuipers, L. Fowler, D., Dunn, G. and Chamberlain, F. (1994) Cognitive behaviour therapy for drug resistant psychosis. *British Journal of Medical Psychology*, **67**, 59–271.

Harding, C., Zubin, J. and Strauss, J. (1987) Chronicity in schizophrenia: Fact, partical fact or artifact. *Hospital and Community Psychiatry*, **38**, 477–486.

Harrison, J., Barrow, S. and Creed, F. (1995) Social deprivation and psychiatric admission rates among different diagnostic groups. *British Journal of Psychiatry*, **167**, 456–462.

Heinrichs, D.W. and Carpenter, W.T. (1981) The efficacy of psychotherapy: A perspective and review emphasising controlled outcome studies. In S. Arieti and H.K. Brodie (eds) *The American Handbook of Psychiatry*, Basic Books, New York.

Hemsley, D. (1994) Perceptual and cognitive abnormalities as the bases for schizophrenia symptoms. In A. David and J. Cutting (eds) *The Neuropsychology of Schizophrenia* (pp. 97–116), Lawrence Erlbaum Associates, Hove.

Hodel, B. and Brenner, H.D. (1994) Cognitive therapy with schizophrenic patients: conceptual basis, present state and future directions. *Acta Psychiatrica Scandinavica*, **384**, 108–115.

Huq, S.F., Garety, P.A. and Hemsley, D.R. (1988) Probabilistic judgements in deluded and non-deluded subjects. *Quarterly Journal of Experimental Psychology*, **40A**, 801–812.

Johnson, D.A.W. (1981) Studies of depressive symptoms in schizophrenia. The prevalence of depression and its possible causes. *British Journal of Psychiatry*, **139**, 89–101.

Kinderman P. and Bentall R. (1997) Attributional therapy for paranoid delusions: a case study. *Cognitive and Behavioural Therapy*, in press.

Lancashire, S. Haddock, G., Tarrier, Baguley, I., Butterworth, G. and Brooker, C. (1997) Effects of psychosocial interventions for community nurses in England. *Psychiatric Services*, **48**, 39–41.

Lelliott, P. and Wing, J.K. (1994) A national audit of new long stay patients: Impact on services. *British Journal of Psychiatry*, **165**, 170–178.

Loebel, A.D., Liberman, J.A., Alvir, J.M., Mayerhoff, D., Geisler, S.H., and Szmanski, S.R. (1992) Duration of psychosis and outcome in first episode schizophrenia. *American Journal of Psychiatry*, **149**, 1183–1188.

Lukoff, D., Neuchterlein, K.H. and Ventura, J.(1986) Manual for the brief expanded psychiatric rating scale. *Schizophrenia Bulletin*, **12**, 584–602.

MacCarthy, B., Hemsley, D., Shrank-Fernandez, C., Kuipers, E. and Katz, R. (1986) Unpredictability as a correlate of expressed emotion in the relatives of schizophrenics. *British Journal of Psychiatry*, **140**, 727–731.

McGorry, P., Edwards, S., Mihalopolous, M., Harrison, S. and Jackson, H. (1996) EPPIC: an evolving system of early detection and optimal management, *Schizophrenia Bulletin*, **22**, 305–326.

Macmillan, J.F., Crow, T.J., Johnson, A.L. and Johnstone, E. (1986) The Northwick Park first episodes of schizophrenia study. *British Journal of Psychiatry*, **148**, 128–133.

Mari, J.J. and Streiner, D. (1994) An overview of family interventions and relapse in schizophrenia: meta-analysis of research findings. *Psychological Medicine*, **24**, 565–578. (BMJ editorial).

Mueser, K. and Berenbaum, H. (1990) Psychodynamic treatment of schizophrenia. Is there a futuere? (Editorial) *Psychological Medicine*, **20**, 253–262.

Nuechterlein, K.H. and Dawson, M.E. (1984) A heuristic vulnerability/stress model of schizophrenic episodes. *Schizophrenia Bulletin*, **10**, 300–312.

Perris, (1989) *Cognitive Therapy for Patients with Schizophrenia*. Cassell, New York.

Persons, J., Mooney, K. and Padesky, C. (1995) Inter-rater relaibility of cognitive-behavioral case formulations. *Cognitive Therapy and Research*, **19**, 21–34.

Shallice, T., Burgess, P. and Frith, C.D. (1991) Can the neuropsychological case-study approach be applied to schizophrenia? *Psychological Medicine*. **21**, 661–673.

Shapiro, D. (1996) Outcome research. Chapter 10 in G. Parry and F.N. Watts (eds) *Behavioural and Mental Health Research*, 2nd edition. Lawrence Erlbaum Associates, Hove.

Shulz, K.F. (1996) Randomised trials, human nature and reporting guidelines. *Lancet*, **348**, 596–598.

Soloman, P. (1996) Moving from psychoeducation to family eduction for families of adults with serious mental illness. *Psychiatric Services*, **47**, 1364–1370.

Strauss, J. S. and Carpenter, W.T. (1981) *Schizophrenia*. Plenum, New York.

Tarrier, N., Beckett, R., Harwood, S., Baker, A., Yusupoff, L. and Ugartebru, I. (1993) A trial of two cognitive behavioural methods of treating drug resistant psychotic symptoms in schizophrenic patients. I Outcome, *British Journal of Psychiatry*, **162**, 524–532.

Wing, J.K. (1983) Schizophrenia. In F.N. Watts and D.H. Bennett (eds) *Theory and Practice of Rehabilitation*. Wiley, Chichester, pp. 45–64.

Wing, J.K. Cooper, J. and Sartorius, N. (1974) *The Measurement and Classification of Psychiatric Symptoms*. Cambridge University Press, Cambridge.

Wykes, T. (1994) Predicting symptomatic and behavioural outcomes of community care. *British Journal of Psychiatry*, **165**, 486–492.

Chapter 2

THE COGNITIVE ORIGINS OF SCHIZOPHRENIA AND PROSPECTS FOR INTERVENTION

Keith H. Nuechterlein and Kenneth L. Subotnik

KEY COGNITIVE AND PERCEPTUAL SYMPTOMS IN SCHIZOPHRENIA

Marked abnormalities in cognitive and perceptual realms are the most striking symptoms of schizophrenic episodes and are at the core of most diagnostic criteria for schizophrenia (American Psychiatric Association, 1994; World Health Organization, 1992). Characteristic hallucinations in schizophrenia are fully formed perceptions in a state of full consciousness that have no related external sensory basis, typically involving hearing of voices but sometimes also involving other sensory modalities. Delusions involve patently false, fixed beliefs held with full conviction that do not have cultural or educational validation and that are sustained despite obvious, incontrovertible evidence to the contrary. Although delusions occur in several neurological and psychiatric disorders, delusions with bizarre content are particularly characteristic of schizophrenia. A third major class of psychotic symptoms shown by some persons with

Outcome and Innovation in Psychological Treatment of Schizophrenia. Edited by T. Wykes,
N. Tarrier and S. Lewis.

schizophrenia involves incoherence, derailment, and other forms of marked disorganization of speech that make it extremely difficult or impossible to understand the verbal communication of an individual. This marked disorganization of speech is usually conceptualized as reflecting an underlying disorder in the organization of thinking rather than a language disorder *per se.*

Given these characteristic psychotic symptoms, it is not surprising that numerous clinical researchers have focused on abnormalities in elementary processes of perception, cognition, and attention as probable critical links in causal chains leading to schizophrenic episodes. We will use the term "information-processing" abnormalities in this chapter to encompass anomalies within any of these domains, referring to the same domain that we and others also refer to as cognitive neuropsychological abnormalities or neurocognitive abnormalities. The psychotic symptoms of schizophrenia are presumably the product of dysfunctions in the normal processes by which external stimuli are linked to internal codes, transformed, abstracted, interpreted, and acted upon (stimulus-driven processes), and/or in the normal processes through which a person's goals are translated into intentions and actions (goal-driven processes).

In contrast to the so-called positive symptoms of schizophrenia, the negative symptoms of schizophrenia are not as obviously tied to abnormalities in information processing. However, symptoms such as affective flattening, alogia, and avolition appear to involve the interface of emotional processes with cognitive processes. As we will see later in this chapter, information-processing models of schizophrenia that have emphasized either the top-down influences of goals and plans or the role of processing resource allocation have hypothesized that negative symptoms of schizophrenia may be linked to information-processing abnormalities that integrate planning with action.

CLINICAL OBSERVATIONS AND SUBJECTIVE EXPERIENCES OF SCHIZOPHRENIA

In addition to broad conceptual linkages between characteristic schizophrenic symptoms and disordered processing of information, more detailed clinical observations and patients' subjective reports have also been sources of hypotheses regarding abnormalities in information processing in schizophrenia. Some of these accounts have emphasized various attentional abnormalities, whereas others emphasize anomalies of thinking or perception. A deficit in sustaining focused attention was noted very early by Emil Kraepelin (1913/1919) who remarked on "the disorder of attention which we very frequently find conspicuously developed in our patients. It is quite common for them to lose both inclination and ability on their own initiative to keep their attention fixed for any length of time" (pp. 5–6). Using a systematic interview, Freedman and Chapman (1973) also found that schizophrenic patients, more frequently than nonpsychotic psychiatric patients, reported difficulty in concentration that was not attributed to preoccupation with their problems or with daydreams.

Possibly related to some of the problems in sustaining focused attention to relevant stimuli is the "irresistible attraction of the attention to casual external impressions" that Kraepelin also observed (1913/1919, pp. 6–7). This tendency for attention to be captured by stimulus elements that are irrelevant to the current task was emphasized by McGhie and Chapman (1961), who collected subjective accounts from schizophrenic patients. For example, one patient reported:

> If I am reading I may suddenly get bogged down at a word. It may be any word, even a simple word that I know well. When this happens I can't get past it. ...It's as if I am seeing the word for the first time and in a different way from anyone else. It's not so much that I absorb it, it's more like it absorbing me (McGhie and Chapman, 1961, p. 109).

Drawing on such subjective accounts and the information-processing model of Broadbent (1958), McGhie and Chapman (1961) hypothesized that a defective filtering mechanism was a primary defect in schizophrenia, thereby emphasizing the role of impaired selective attention. In a more contemporary integration of such subjective reports, Anscombe (1987) has suggested that this capturing of attention by incidental details and low-level perceptual processes may be due to the absence of, or overriding of, an intentionally imposed focus of attention. As Anscombe (1987, p. 247) cogently argues, "The patient is not able to assert his own purpose and to overcome the power of such low-level processes to attract attention to what they have detected, and so he finds himself staring at something of no particular importance."

This latter theme, weakened influence of an overarching purpose or goal on the focusing of attention, may be related to Eugen Bleuler's influential conceptualization of schizophrenic thinking. Bleuler noted that schizophrenic patients were "incapable of holding the train of thought in the proper channels" (1924/1976, p. 377) and emphasized a thought disorder rather than a perceptual disorder as the primary disturbance. Bleuler attributed this lack of goal-directedness in thinking to a "disconnecting of associative threads" between ideas (1911/1950, p. 21), which led to the common description of schizophrenic thought disorder as being characterized by "loosening of associations". Although Bleuler emphasized these weakened associative connections in his explanation and thereby apparently ascribed the primary dysfunction to associative memory, we can easily see that his view is also highly compatible with the notion that an overarching goal is not playing its normally strong role in directing attention and providing continuity to thought.

Somewhat in contrast to these accounts that emphasize anomalies in attention or thinking, Cutting and Dunne (1989) concluded that qualitative perceptual alterations are the features that best discriminated the subjective experience of schizophrenia from that of depression. They examined subjective reports of stable, remitted patients who were early in the course of their disorders and who were asked to describe alterations in mental processes that had occurred "when they first became ill or experienced a change in the way things were" (Cutting and Dunne, 1989, p. 226). Although Cutting and Dunne found that changes in concentration, thinking, and emotion were very commonly reported, these features did not distinguish schizophrenia from depression. The most distinctive feature reported retrospectively by these remitted schizophrenic patients was a qualitative change in perception, particularly a change in the way that people looked and an indefinable strangeness in visual perceptions. As these were retrospective accounts, we cannot really know whether these perceptual changes occurred prodromally or during the period of active psychosis. Furthermore, Freedman and Chapman (1973), who examined reports of schizophrenic patients in an acute episode rather than recall by remitted schizophrenic patients, found that problems in focusing attention and in thought blocking that disrupts speech were about equally discriminating of schizophrenic self-reports as were visual and auditory misperceptions. Despite these limitations of the Cutting and Dunne (1989) results, it is noteworthy that the subjective accounts of subtle perceptual changes during the early phases of schizophrenia raise the question of whether perceptual dysfunctions play a primary role in the causal chains leading to psychotic symptoms, rather than the secondary role attributed to them by theorists such as Eugen Bleuler (1911/1950).

Given the wide range of abnormalities in perception, thinking, and attentional processes that have been reported in schizophrenia, development of cognitive–behavioral interventions that target these abnormalities is a very logical step and one that has been surprisingly under-represented until recent years. Although many attentional and other information-processing abnormalities in schizophrenia are likely to be under substantial genetic influence or otherwise tied to core biological processes in schizophrenia (Bartfai, Pedersen, Asarnow, and Schalling, 1991; Cornblatt, Risch, Faris, Friedman, and Erlenmeyer-Kimling, 1988; Frith, 1992; Hemsley, 1994a; Kendler, Ochs, Gorman, Hewitt, Ross, and Mirsky, 1991; Nuechterlein, Asarnow, Cantor, Spence, and Subotnik, 1993), this is not a sufficient reason to conclude that they are not modifiable by specialized treatments nor that only psychopharmacologic treatments might be able to modify them. Despite the effectiveness of typical antipsychotic medications in reducing psychotic symptoms, their ability to improve the basic attentional, perceptual, and cognitive processing abnormalities of schizophrenia has been quite limited (Cassens, Inglis, Appelbaum, and Gutheil, 1990). Thus, there is a critical need for development of both cognitive–behavioral and pharmacological treatments that could modify these core processing deficits or, alternatively, that would help patients to compensate optimally for these processing deficits. However, which information-processing abnormalities should be given highest priority for attempts at cognitive-behavioral intervention?

THE MULTIPLE ROLES OF VULNERABILITY FACTORS IN SCHIZOPHRENIA

One strategy for selection of targets for cognitive-behavioral interventions in schizophrenia would be to focus on abnormalities in information processing that are most likely to serve as vulnerability factors for development of episodes or of specific symptoms. Vulnerability or liability factors in schizophrenia are conceptualized as characteristics of individuals that precede development of schizophrenic symptoms and that are associated with continuing proneness to symptoms and schizophrenia-associated functional disability (Garmezy and Streitman, 1974; Gottesman and Shields, 1972; Nuechterlein and Dawson, 1984a; Strauss and Carpenter, 1981; Zubin and Spring, 1977). To the extent that an intervention seeks to reduce schizophrenic symptoms or related functional disability, it would presumably benefit from targeting key links in causal chains that lead to these outcomes. Targeting a cognitive abnormality that was produced by a symptom within an episode, rather than one that is a precursor to a symptom, will not result in successful symptom reduction.

Although causal chains that lead to schizophrenic symptoms are at this point hypothesized rather than known, vulnerability-stress models of schizophrenia offer a useful overall orientation when considering potential interventions to improve the course of schizophrenia. Vulnerability-stress models point to possible contributing factors in the individual, in the environment, and in the interplay between individual and environment. They also highlight the temporal dimension, which is often ignored in cognitive explanations of schizophrenic symptoms and functional impairments. One of the more detailed vulnerability-stress models of schizophrenia was developed at the UCLA Clinical Research Center for the Study of Schizophrenia (Nuechterlein and Dawson, 1984a; Nuechterlein, 1987) and is shown in Figure 2.1.

As shown in this version of the vulnerability-stress model that was developed in 1985, prominent candidates for personal vulnerability factors that are hypothesized to precede development of schizophrenia include dopaminergic dysregulation, information-processing limitations conceptualized as reductions in available processing resources, instability

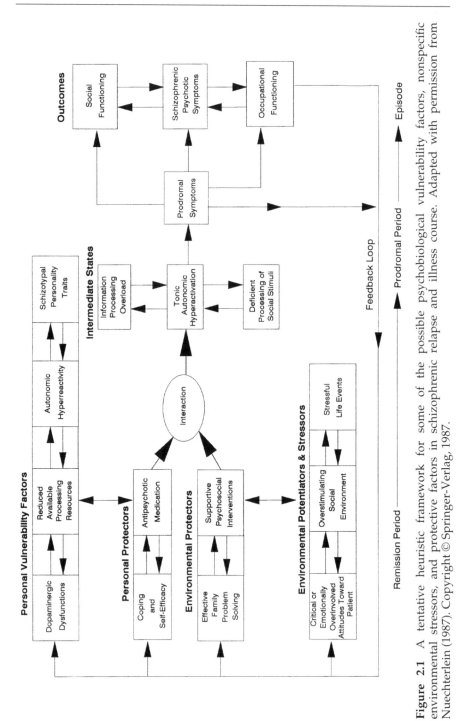

Figure 2.1 A tentative heuristic framework for some of the possible psychobiological vulnerability factors, nonspecific environmental stressors, and protective factors in schizophrenic relapse and illness course. Adapted with permission from Nuechterlein (1987). Copyright © Springer-Verlag, 1987.

and particularly hyperreactivity in autonomic nervous system responses, and schizotypal personality characteristics. Empirical research from biological relatives of schizophrenic patients and from schizophrenic patients in clinically remitted states that supports the choice of these vulnerability candidates is summarized elsewhere (Dawson and Nuechterlein, 1984; Erlenmeyer-Kimling and Cornblatt, 1987; Nuechterlein, 1987; Nuechterlein and Dawson, 1984b). These are broad heuristic categories of vulnerability factors; subsequent developments have already and will continue to refine greatly the nature of these vulnerability factors in neurotransmitter, information processing, and personality trait domains. Some vulnerability factors are probably strongly influenced by genes, because it is estimated that 60–70% of the liability or vulnerability to schizophrenia is attributable to genetic sources (McGuffin, 1991). Neurobiological vulnerability to schizophrenia may also be influenced by intrauterine environment and other early neurodevelopmental factors (Barr, Mednick, and Munk-Jorgenson, 1990; Torrey, Taylor, Bracha, Bowler, McNeil, Rawlings, Quinn, Bigelow, Rickler, Sjostrom, Higgins, and Gottesman, 1994). The extent to which some vulnerability factors, such as schizotypal personality traits, might be modified by typical post-natal environments remains unknown.

In this model, neurobiological vulnerability factors are viewed as establishing a level of proneness to the initial development of schizophrenia and also a level of individual proneness for schizophrenic episodes to return, although not all vulnerability factors necessarily contribute equally to initial onset and to illness course. Environmental factors that appear to affect the likelihood of psychotic exacerbation or relapse after initial onset are also shown, based on the empirical literature (Bebbington and Kuipers, 1994; Kavanagh, 1992; Lukoff, Snyder, Ventura, and Nuechterlein, 1984; Ventura, Nuechterlein, Lukoff, and Hardesty, 1989). The environmental factors in Figure 2.1 focus on social variables that may serve as protective factors or potentiating factors due to the extensive scientific literature on such variables, but street drug usage is certainly another major contributing factor to course of illness in the current era (Linzen, Dingemans, and Lenior, 1994; Shaner, Eckman, Roberts, Wilkins, Tucker, Tsuang, and Mintz, 1995). Although this chapter will focus on possible targets for intervention in the cognitive vulnerability domain, another productive avenue highlighted by such models is to intervene by reducing stressors or bolstering the personal or family strategies for coping with stressors (Liberman, Wallace, Blackwell, Eckmann, and Kuehnel, 1994; Tarrier, Beckett, Harwood, Baker, Yusupoff, and Ugarteburu, 1993).

A conceptual distinction between two types of vulnerability factors (Nuechterlein and Dawson, 1984a) has important implications for cognitive–behavioral and other psychosocial interventions. "Stable vulnerability indicators" are trait-like characteristics of individuals that mark proneness to schizophrenia but remain unchanged across premorbid, acute psychotic, and clinical remitted periods of schizophrenia. The prototype of these vulnerability factors would be stable structural or biochemical brain anomalies that are immediate products of schizophrenia-relevant alleles of genes or early neurodevelopmental deviations, but some information-processing abnormalities that are relatively closely tied to such stable neurobiological factors might also share this characteristic of being independent of symptom state. This form of schizophrenia-related trait is the type that is typically sought by investigators trying to identify schizophrenia "markers" (e.g., Holzman, 1994; Iacono, 1983). Stable vulnerability indicators could be extremely useful for identifying individuals with proneness to schizophrenia and as extended phenotypes for studies of genetic transmission. By virtue of the fact that these factors are unchanged across clinical states, however, stable vulnerability indicators are likely to be several steps away from clinical symptoms in any causal chain leading to symptoms. Some stable vulnerability indicators might not even be components of causal chains leading to symptoms, but might instead be simply associated with factors that are direct components of the causal chains. However, such a lack of contribution to causal chains would seem less likely for information-processing abnormalities than for variables such as immediate biochemical products of genes (genetic markers for specific locations on individual chromosomes). The characteristic pattern of stable vulnerability factors across clinical states in schizophrenia is shown in Figure 2.2.

Another type of schizophrenia vulnerability factor, which we have called a "mediating vulnerability factor" (Nuechterlein and Dawson, 1984a), would also be characterized by levels during premorbid and clinically remitted states that are abnormal relative to general population values, but would be distinguished from stable vulnerability indicators by becoming significantly more deviant immediately before and during exacerbation of at least one type of characteristic schizophrenic symptom (see Figure 2.2). The increased level of abnormality for these variables prior to and during the exacerbation of a schizophrenic symptom would be expected if these factors were proximal links in causal chains for that symptom. In other words, this type of vulnerability factor is hypothesized not only to identify individuals who are prone to develop a schizophrenic symptom, but is also viewed as being near the symptom end of the causal chain and as a direct mediator of symptom development. At least some mediating vulnerability factors would be hypothesized to differ across the distinct dimensions of schizophrenic symptoms, as they would be conceptualized as being determinants of the nature of the schizophrenic symptoms that develop in a given person. Successful normalization of a key mediating vulnerability factor should result in less symptom

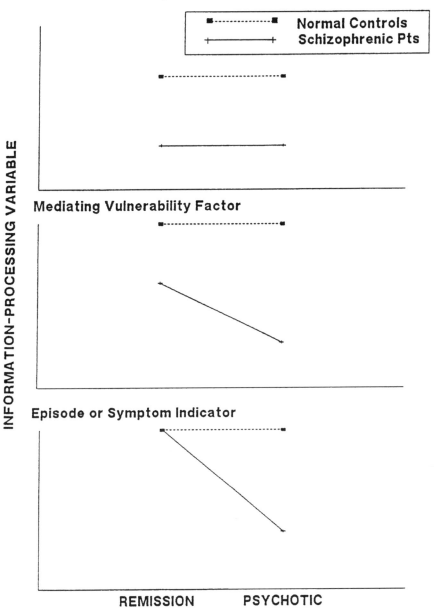

Figure 2.2 Characteristic patterns of information-processing performance across clinical states for stable vulnerability indicators, mediating vulnerability factors, and episode indicators. Reprinted with permission from Nuechterlein et al., (1991). Copyright © Springer-Verlag, 1991.

development or in resolution of any existing symptom of the relevant type. Thus, such mediating vulnerability factors in information processing would seem to be particularly good targets for initial cognitive–behavioral intervention attempts, as the effects on symptoms would be expected to be relatively clear.

It is important to consider a third type of information-processing abnormality that might be an excellent target for cognitive-behavioral interventions, despite not necessarily being a vulnerability factor for schizophrenia. As Green (1993) has pointed out, certain information-processing functions might serve as "rate-limiting factors" in the response of an individual to a type of rehabilitation. A prominent example is verbal learning, which may be a factor that limits the rate at which interventions that involve processing verbal information have an impact (Green, 1993). Thus, even if verbal learning skills did not appear to be a vulnerability factor for schizophrenia, it might be useful to improve verbal learning skills in order to make verbally conveyed interventions more effective. (Actually, though, recent evidence (Cannon, Zorrilla, Shtasel, Gur, Gur, Marco, Moberg, and Price, 1994; Faraone, Seidman, Kremen, Pepple, Lyons, and Tsuang, 1995) does suggest that impaired verbal learning and verbal memory is also a vulnerability factor for schizophrenia.)

A MODEL OF NORMAL INFORMATION PROCESSING

To describe the nature of information-processing abnormalities hypothesized to be prominent in schizophrenia, it is useful to introduce a model of normal information processing. We will use the model of Cowan (1988), as we have elsewhere (Nuechterlein, Dawson, and Green, 1994), to distinguish several alternative types of information-processing dysfunction in schizophrenia. This model is particularly useful for our present purposes because it not only specifies the roles of the functional modules termed brief sensory store, long-term store, activated memory, and central executive, but it also describes the nature of selective attention in relationship to these functional modules. Consistent with many other current models of human information processing, in Cowan's model the functional modules interact extensively with each other during processing of a stimulus. Activation of differing functional modules overlaps temporally (as shown from left to right in Figure 2.3), so that the bottom-up processing (from sensory registration to perception to higher-level problem-solving processes) can be affected in a top-down fashion (higher-level processes influence perception).

Stimuli from the environment enter a brief sensory store that is modality-specific and that represents the physical characteristics of stimuli for a few hundred milliseconds. This brief sensory store has unlimited capacity. The features of incoming stimuli activate corresponding codes in long-term store even without attention being directed to them. The short-term store is a portion of long-term store that is activated at any given time rather than a separate functional module. Thus, the codes activated by features of recent incoming stimuli are shown in Figure 2.3 as part of the activated memory or short-term store. Short-term storage is limited in capacity.

Entry of incoming stimuli into consciousness corresponds to their becoming part of the focus of attention, which involves only a portion of activated memory (see Figure 3). In normal information processing, external stimuli become the focus of attention in one of two ways. The first way is illustrated by the stimulus labelled "a" in Figure 2.3. This stimulus is intentionally selected by the central executive module (or central processor), which directs attention and controls voluntary (or effortful) processing. The central executive operates to facilitate entry into consciousness whenever codes related to this stimulus are activated. The second path of entry into consciousness is illustrated by stimulus "d" in Figure 2.3. Because this stimulus activates codes that are distinctive from those of other recent stimuli (i.e. is novel), it captures the focus of attention and enters awareness.

Two additional ways in which information from long-term memory can enter consciousness do not necessarily involve external stimulation. First, voluntary processing directed by the central executive module can activate stored information without an external stimulus, which corresponds to attention being directed inward to long-term memories in Figure 2.3. Second, associations in long-term memory are spontaneously activated and may enter consciousness when a primary memory is activated by an incoming novel stimulus or by voluntary processing.

Perception involves two phases, a passive phase and an active phase. In the initial passive (or automatic) phase, basic stimulus features activate a set of codes in the long-term storage network and also some potential semantic categories associated with these features. In the active phase, a directed search of long-term storage is made that includes consideration of the context in which the stimulus has occurred and that processes combinations of features. The second phase is particularly important when the identity or meaning of the stimulus is very ambiguous based on the initial passive activation of codes. The final perception is the product of these two perceptual processes.

Two types of actions are distinguished. Controlled actions are those that involve voluntary direction through the central executive module. Automatic actions, as shown in Figure 2.3, do not involve the central executive module or entry into the focus of attention. Automatic actions are typically responses that are part of fixed stimulus-response sequences that have been so highly practiced that attention and the central executive

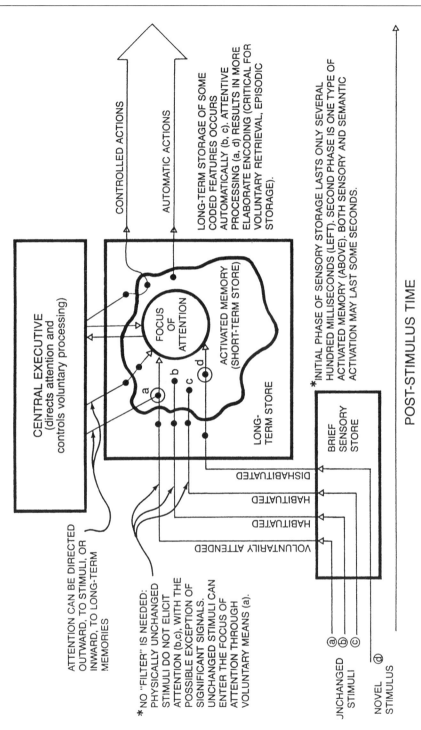

CONTROLLED ACTIONS

AUTOMATIC ACTIONS

LONG-TERM STORAGE OF SOME CODED FEATURES OCCURS AUTOMATICALLY (b, c). ATTENTIVE PROCESSING (a, d) RESULTS IN MORE ELABORATE ENCODING (CRITICAL FOR VOLUNTARY RETRIEVAL, EPISODIC STORAGE).

CENTRAL EXECUTIVE
(directs attention and controls voluntary processing)

FOCUS OF ATTENTION

ACTIVATED MEMORY (SHORT-TERM STORE)

LONG-TERM STORE

BRIEF SENSORY STORE

DISHABITUATED

HABITUATED

HABITUATED

VOLUNTARILY ATTENDED

*INITIAL PHASE OF SENSORY STORAGE LASTS ONLY SEVERAL HUNDRED MILLISECONDS (LEFT). SECOND PHASE IS ONE TYPE OF ACTIVATED MEMORY (ABOVE). BOTH SENSORY AND SEMANTIC ACTIVATION MAY LAST SOME SECONDS.

POST-STIMULUS TIME

ATTENTION CAN BE DIRECTED OUTWARD, TO STIMULI, OR INWARD, TO LONG-TERM MEMORIES

*NO "FILTER" IS NEEDED: PHYSICALLY UNCHANGED STIMULI DO NOT ELICIT ATTENTION (b,c), WITH THE POSSIBLE EXCEPTION OF SIGNIFICANT SIGNALS. UNCHANGED STIMULI CAN ENTER THE FOCUS OF ATTENTION THROUGH VOLUNTARY MEANS (a).

UNCHANGED STIMULI
ⓐ
ⓑ
ⓒ

NOVEL STIMULUS ⓓ

module are no longer required for their execution (Shiffrin and Schneider, 1977).

SOME PROMINENT INFORMATION-PROCESSING VULNERABILITY FACTORS

With this conception of normal information processing in mind, let us now consider several different recent conceptions of fundamental information-processing abnormalities in schizophrenia. First, we will consider the evolving conception at our Clinical Research Center at UCLA and then contrast this view with the conceptualizations of three prominent British investigators.

Theoretical conception developed within the UCLA Clinical Research Center

Our Los Angeles group started from a conception of information-processing deficits in schizophrenia that emphasized the possible role of reduced availability of attentional resources or processing resources (Nuechterlein and Dawson, 1984b), being strongly influenced by the view that attention is best conceptualized as a pool of nonspecific processing resources that normally can be allocated voluntarily to any specific information-processing task (Beatty, 1982; Kahneman, 1973; Shiffrin and Schneider, 1977). We have been primarily interested in identifying information-processing anomalies that are enduring vulnerability factors for schizophrenia, rather than the information-processing abnormalities that may be immediate precursors or accompanying components of an individual schizophrenic symptom (e.g., Nuechterlein and Dawson, 1984b; Nuechterlein, Dawson, Gitlin, Ventura, Goldstein, Snyder, Yee, and Mintz, 1992; Nuechterlein, Dawson, and Green, 1994). Thus, we have focused on studies of schizophrenic patients in remitted states and on studies of

---

Figure 2.3 Cowan's revised model of the information-processing system. The time since stimulus reception is represented ordinally along the x-axis. The components are arranged in real time, and stimulus information can be present in more than one component at the same time. Short-term storage is represented as an activated subset of long-term storage, and the focus of attention is represented as a subset of short-term storage. Habituated stimuli do not enter the focus of attention. The arrows represent the transfer of information from one form to another; these are discrete approximations to continuous processes that can occur in parallel or cascade. Pathways leading to awareness can come from three sources: changed stimuli for which there is dishabituation, items selected through effortful processing (whether of sensory origin or not), and the spontaneous activation of long-term memory information based on associations. Reprinted with permission from Cowan (1988). Copyright © American Psychological Association, 1988

biological relatives of schizophrenia, seeking to demonstrate that certain subtle information-processing anomalies are present in individuals who are prone to schizophrenic episodes even when schizophrenic symptoms are absent. To the extent that we have examined direct symptom correlates, we have found that visual-motor tasks that emphasize rapid processing of very briefly presented letter or numeral stimuli are associated with schizophrenic negative symptoms (Nuechterlein, Edell, Norris, and Dawson, 1986), consistent with the findings of Green and Walker (1986). Within a processing resource conception of schizophrenic cognitive deficits, we hypothesized that negative symptoms of schizophrenia may be linked to deficits in situations that place high momentary demands on active, effortful processing (Nuechterlein et al., 1986). Inadequate allocation of the processing resources that would typically energize activity would presumably lead to a dampening of normal emotional responsivity and actions.

Over time, through the influence of data from our own studies and those of others, we have increasingly emphasized the view that at least two different basic information-processing abnormalities relevant to vulnerability to schizophrenia should be differentiated (Nuechterlein, Dawson, Ventura, Fogelson, Gitlin, and Mintz, 1991; Nuechterlein et al., 1992; Nuechterlein, Dawson, and Green, 1994). One abnormality involves a subtle deficit in early components of perceptual processing, which is evident in perceptual discrimination tasks such as the degraded stimulus version of the Continuous Performance Test (Nuechterlein, Parasuraman, and Jiang, 1983), the forced-choice span of apprehension task (Asarnow and MacCrimmon, 1978), and conditions of visual backward masking in which intervals between target and mask are very short (Green, Nuechterlein, and Mintz, 1994a, 1994b). All of these information-processing situations require identification of basic visual perceptual configurations (letters or numerals) under difficult tachistoscopic conditions in which initial feature extraction and stimulus encoding and analysis processes play a very prominent role. The Degraded Stimulus CPT, for example, entails identification of each presentation of a predesignated single, highly blurred target numeral within a series of single, highly blurred numerals presented very briefly at a pace of one per second. In Cowan's (1988) information-processing model (see Figure 3), these early perceptual processes are represented by passive registration in brief sensory store, activation of corresponding stimulus feature codes in long-term store, and active search for any additional features necessary for character recognition. Because these tasks typically involve search for certain predesignated stimulus feature combinations (individual letters or numerals), they entail use of active central executive functions to facilitate the entry of certain feature codes into the focus of attention and to facilitate detection of certain combinations of features.

Data to date suggest that deficits on these tasks that burden early perceptual discrimination processes characterize remitted schizophrenic patients (Asarnow and MacCrimmon, 1978; Miller, Saccuzzo, and Braff, 1979; Nuechterlein et al., 1992) as well as a disproportionate number of first-degree relatives of schizophrenic patients (Asarnow, Steffy, MacCrimmon, and Cleghorn, 1977; Grove, Lebow, Clementz, Cerri, Medus, and Iacono, 1991; Maier, Franke, Hain, Kopp, and Rist, 1992; Nuechterlein, 1983; Green, Nuechterlein, and Breitmeyer, 1997). Data from specialized backward masking conditions indicate that a deficit in initial perceptual discrimination processes can be detected in schizophrenic patients and their siblings when a visual mask follows a target letter by as little as 20 ms (Green, Nuechterlein, and Mintz, 1994a, 1994b; Green, Nuechterlein, and Breitmeyer, 1997). Furthermore, data from the degraded stimulus version of the Continuous Performance Test and the forced-choice span of apprehension task suggest that an abnormality in early perceptual processes is stable across psychotic and remitted periods within schizophrenic patients (Nuechterlein et al., 1991). Thus, evidence to date indicates that an abnormality in early perceptual discrimination processes is likely to be a stable vulnerability indicator relevant to schizophrenia (Nuechterlein et al., 1992).

A second form of information-processing abnormality in schizophrenia that we and others have increasingly emphasized is an impairment in the use of activated memory or working memory to cue the relevance of current stimuli. In our work with versions of the Continuous Performance Test, this information-processing demand is represented by specifying that the target stimulus, within a quasi-random series of single numerals presented one per second in clear focus, is the numeral 7 only when it is immediately preceded by the numeral 3 (Nuechterlein et al., 1986). This particular memory-load CPT (3-7 CPT) is a variant of the original A-X CPT (Rosvold, Mirsky, Sarason, Bransome, and Beck, 1956). In these sequential-target CPT versions, a preceding stimulus must be used as a cue to determine whether the current stimulus is a target. Adding this working memory component and presenting the numeral stimuli in clear focus yields a different pattern of performance across clinical states in schizophrenia than does the Degraded Stimulus CPT (Nuechterlein et al., 1992). The significant deficit in discriminating targets from nontargets is again present in a clinically remitted state, but the extent of this deficit becomes much more striking during a psychotic state, yielding a highly significant interaction between diagnostic group and test occasion.

This memory-load CPT (3-7 CPT), compared to the Degraded Stimulus CPT, emphasizes selection of target stimuli through temporary storage of the prior stimulus in activated memory and de-emphasizes the role of initial feature extraction and stimulus encoding processes. In terms of Cowan's model, the 3-7 CPT entails the activation of long-term memory by incoming stimuli. identification of certain stimuli (3s) as cues, differential allocation of attention to stimuli following these cues, and activation of a voluntary response if the next stimulus is a particular one (7). It also entails suppression of responses to some current stimuli (some 7s) when the stored cue is absent. These behavioral sequences would all be guided by central executive processes in interaction with activated (short-term) memory. Some theorists, such as Baddeley (1986), refer to such central executive processing of activated memory contents as working memory, a construct that has much in common with the concepts of effortful processing and attention (Baddeley, 1993). Thus, the 3-7 CPT results (Nuechterlein et al., 1992) can be taken to suggest that an abnormality in the use of activated memory to cue target selection is significantly more prominent during psychotic periods than during remitted periods, thereby fitting the pattern of a potential mediating vulnerability factor. We hypothesize that this increased impairment in use of activated, working memory to cue relevance of current stimuli is a precursor of, and contributor to, schizophrenic episodes and not a secondary effect of the psychotic state, but we do not have direct evidence of such a role at this point.

The emphasis on a schizophrenic deficit in use of activated, working memory to guide behavior is also prominent in the recent views of American researchers Goldman-Rakic (1991), Park and Holzman (1992), and Cohen and Servan-Schreiber (1993), so we are certainly not alone in postulating such a role. Goldman-Rakic (1991) has provided a persuasive argument for the relevance to schizophrenia of the neural circuitry of working memory, particularly the interconnections between the prefrontal cortex and the hippocampus. Cohen and Servan-Schreiber (1993) have focused on dopaminergic modulation of a prefrontal module that allows preceding context to be used in processing current stimuli and have used a sequential-target CPT as one example. These recent neurocognitive formulations might also be viewed as important extensions of earlier work that emphasized the abnormal focus of schizophrenic patients on the immediate details of stimuli rather than on the broader relevant context (e.g., Salzinger, Portnoy, and Feldman, 1978). We summarize the roles of two forms of information-processing abnormality hypothesized to be relevant to vulnerability to schizophrenic symptoms in Table 2.1.

Theoretical conception of David Hemsley, Jeffrey Gray, and colleagues

Our view that one of two key cognitive deficits in vulnerability to schizophrenia involves decreased use of activated or working memory to cue relevance of current stimuli is compatible with, and was influenced by, the proposal by Hemsley (1987) that "it is a weakening of the influence of stored memories of regularities of previous input on current perception which is basic to the schizophrenic condition" (p. 182). This proposal has

Table 2.1   Some Proposed Cognitive Factors in Schizophrenia

Proponents	Stable vulnerability indicator	Mediating vulnerability factor
Nuechterlein et al. (1992)	Early perceptual discrimination abnormality	Impaired use of activated or working memory to cue relevance of current stimulus
Hemsley (1987, 1994a)		Reduced influence of regularities of past experience on current perception
Frith (1987, 1992)		Failures in self monitoring of willed intentions and failure of goals to generate willed intentions
Bentall (1994)		Strongly biased attributional processes for threat-related information leads to persecutory delusions

been further elaborated and related to hypothesized neural underpinnings in Gray, Feldon, Rawlins, Hemsley, and Smith (1991), Hemsley (1994a), and Hemsley (1994b). The key element of this model is that the normally rapid, automatic assessment of the significance of current sensory input is hypothesized to be impaired due to reduced influence of past regularities of personal experience. Storage of memories of past stimulus regularities experienced by the individual is assumed to occur, and these memories are believed to remain accessible through controlled processing (Hemsley, 1994a). In Cowan's (1988) terms, this model emphasizes a deficit in the initial passive (or automatic) phase of perception in which basic stimulus features activate corresponding codes in long-term memory. However, it might also involve a deficit in Cowan's second phase of perception, the active search for additional key stimulus features and semantic categories that would normally take stimulus context into account, as some of the evidence cited in favor of this model would appear to involve context effects (Hemsley, 1994b).

For the present purposes, one of the most instructive aspects of the Hemsley-Gray cognitive model is the hypothesized chain of processes linking this basic abnormality to schizophrenic hallucinations and delusions. As shown in Figure 2.4, the reduced influence of stored past experiences on current perception is hypothesized to lead to unstructured, ambiguous sensory input and heightened awareness of irrelevant aspects of stimuli, which in turn will lead to intrusion into consciousness of unintended material from long-term memory that is normally inhibited. This combination of phenomena is hypothesized to set the stage for hallucinations (perceiving uninhibited material from long-term memory as

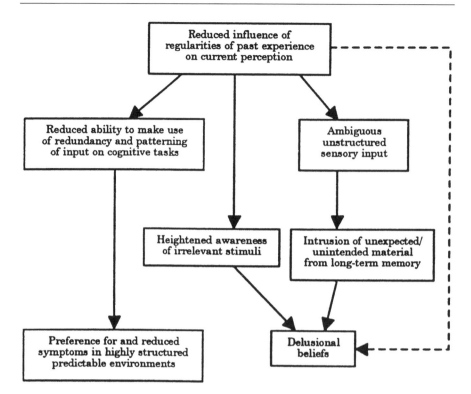

Figure 2.4 Hemsley's model of cognitive abnormalities and symptoms of schizophrenia. Reprinted with permission from Hemsley (1994b). Copyright © Lawrence Erlbaum Associates, Ltd.

if it were due to external stimulation) and for delusions (markedly faulty inferences based on the prominence of irrelevant features in perceptual experiences and on unexpected intrusions from long-term memory). Hemsley, Gray and colleagues apparently conceive of this reduced influence of stored past experiences on current perception as what we would term a mediating vulnerability factor, as their model hypothesizes its role in causal chains leading to hallucinations and delusions. Furthermore, their studies suggest that this cognitive abnormality occurs primarily among acute schizophrenic patients with active positive symptoms and not among chronic patients whose positive symptoms have abated.

Theoretical conception of Christopher Frith

A detailed neuropsychological model of the cognitive abnormalities underlying schizophrenia that was developed by Frith (1987, 1992) is even more specific in its focus on analysis of individual schizophrenic symptoms. He places the source of most schizophrenic symptoms closer to the output end of information-processing sequences than most other current theorists. Frith (1992) notes that one common element of many characteristic schizophrenic psychotic symptoms, particularly those that were considered by Schneider (1959) to be first-rank symptoms, is that a person's perceptions, thoughts, or actions are experienced as though they originated from a source outside of the self. He cites evidence that a self-monitoring system in normal conscious experience provides feedback on willed intentions that result from our plans in any given situation. In schizophrenia, Frith postulates that a disconnection occurs between willed intentions and the self-monitoring system, so that the individual no longer is aware that perceptions, thoughts, and actions were self-generated and instead attributes these activities to forces outside the self. In accounting for negative signs such as poverty of speech and of action, Frith (1987, 1992) argues that another fundamental cognitive defect is the source, in this case a disconnection between goals/plans and the generation of willed intentions.

Frith (1992) also posits particular brain functional systems that are likely to be linked to these symptoms and signs. The positive symptoms of schizophrenia are hypothesized to involve disconnections between certain prefrontal brain structures (e.g., anterior cingulate cortex) that normally send corollary discharges regarding willed intentions and posterior parts of the brain that manage perception, whereas negative features are believed to be linked to disconnections between prefrontal brain structures that generate plans for action and subcortical structures (basal ganglia) that control action.

In Cowan's (1988) terms, Frith emphasizes the interactions between the central executive module and controlled actions, with emphasis on a self-monitoring function that Cowan does not explicitly include. The lack of awareness of self-generated thoughts and perceptions (as opposed to actions) may also be seen as involving failure in self-monitoring of interactions between the central executive module and activated memory.

Frith does not focus on the time course of these cognitive deficits before schizophrenia develops nor on whether they are hypothesized to be present during remitted states. In Table 2.1 we have placed these cognitive deficits in the category of mediating vulnerability factors because Frith proposes a relatively immediate causal linkage between types of cognitive defects and characteristic types of schizophrenic symptoms and signs.

Theoretical conception of Richard Bentall

A final example of a British investigator who posits specific cognitive origins of schizophrenic symptoms is Richard Bentall (Bentall, Kaney, and

Dewey, 1991; Bentall, 1994). Like Frith, Bentall focuses on hypothesized immediate cognitive sources of individual schizophrenic symptoms, although Bentall prefers social psychological to neuropsychological explanatory constructs. Thus, in our terms, Bentall is concerned with mediating vulnerability factors, rather than stable vulnerability indicators that are likely to play more distant roles in causal chains.

Here we will focus on Bentall's hypothesis that persecutory delusions stem from abnormal cognitive attributional biases in response to information that is personally threatening (Bentall, 1994), although Bentall has also examined hallucinations in detail (Bentall, 1990). Bentall and his collaborators have gathered evidence to support the hypothesis that persecutory delusions occur in persons with a cognitive bias to attribute the source of negative events to others in an excessively global and stable way, and also to attribute positive events to internal control in an excessive fashion. Bentall hypothesizes that this abnormal cognitive bias serves the function of preventing any thoughts related to low self-esteem from becoming conscious, thereby maintaining positive self-regard during periods in which threatening information is present.

Although many of the cognitive concepts employed by Bentall (1994) are not the primary focus of Cowan's (1988) information-processing model, we would view Bentall's social attribution hypotheses as emphasizing the top-down influences of central executive processes on the focus of attention. Bentall appears to posit that persons with persecutory delusions fail to move certain aspects of self-threatening information from activated memory into the focus of conscious attention. Bentall argues against the view that delusions are mainly the result of basic stimulus-driven abnormalities in perception, so his emphasis is on abnormal reasoning processes that lead to delusions even when the registration of stimuli in brief sensory store and the passive activation of stimulus features in long-memory is essentially intact. Although Bentall does not directly specify the time course of these abnormal attributional biases, presumably he would hypothesize that they would be subtly present even in clinical remission and would be particularly strong just before and during persecutory delusions, consistent with the pattern that we posit for a mediating vulnerability factor.

TARGETS FOR COGNITIVE–BEHAVIORAL INTERVENTIONS

As the prior section illustrates, current theoretical conceptions of the key cognitive deficits in schizophrenia differ substantially in their specific emphasis, but do provide a number of promising targets for development of cognitive–behavioral interventions. Because cognitive abnormalities probably play several different roles in the complex causal network that is likely to underlie schizophrenia, one needs to consider whether the target of psychological intervention is likely to be an immediate precursor of symptom formation or a somewhat more distant link in the causal chain. In addition, some cognitive abnormalities may be caused by symptoms and would not be an appropriate target for interventions that hope to change symptoms. Studies of schizophrenic patients in remission and of the biological relatives of schizophrenic patients are helping to identify cognitive abnormalities that are likely to be part of the causal chain contributing to schizophrenic symptoms.

From our perspective, one striking difference between typical American and British cognitive theories of schizophrenia at this time is that several British investigators are focusing on a detailed cognitive analysis of individual symptoms of schizophrenia within patients with these active symptoms, while most American investigators are concentrating on cognitive anomalies in remitted schizophrenic patients and biological relatives of patients in hopes of identifying genetic or other biological vulnerability factors relevant to the broad and heterogeneous complex of symptoms known as schizophrenia. In the search for appropriate targets for cognitive–behavioral interventions, both perspectives have their strengths and weaknesses. In the short term, perhaps a focus on cognitive–behavioral attempts to normalize the most immediate cognitive precursors of individual symptoms would be most productive, as successful attempts to modify these precursors would presumably result in less severe symptoms of these specific types. Although the necessary longitudinal data to identify such immediate cognitive precursors empirically do not exist at this point, we have listed in Table 1 some prominent examples of proposed cognitive mediating vulnerability factors in schizophrenic symptom formation.

Psychological interventions that focus on specific cognitive deficits in schizophrenia may be of great benefit to both individual patients and a better scientific understanding of the causal chains leading to schizophrenic symptoms. Since available psychopharmacological treatments have only limited impact on core cognitive deficits in schizophrenia, innovative attempts to change these cognitive abnormalities are critically needed. Successful targeted cognitive interventions that reduced the likelihood of specific symptoms would provide critical support for the hypothesized causal role of the targeted cognitive deficit. More importantly, if new cognitive–behavioral interventions are found to be successful in changing key cognitive deficits, the benefits to the patient might be much more direct and substantial than those produced by broader supportive therapies.

REFERENCES

American Psychiatric Association (1994) *Diagnostic and Statistical Manual of Mental Disorders: DSM-IV (Fourth Edition)*. Washington, D.C.: American Psychiatric Association.

Anscombe, R. (1987) The disorder of consciousness in schizophrenia. *Schizophrenia Bulletin*, **13**, 241–260.

Asarnow, R.F. and MacCrimmon, D.J. (1978) Residual performance deficit in clinically remitted schizophrenics: A marker of schizophrenia? *Journal of Abnormal Psychology*, **87**, 597–608.

Asarnow, R.F., Steffy, R.A., MacCrimmon, D.J. and Cleghorn, J.M. (1977) An attentional assessment of foster children at risk for schizophrenia. *Journal of Abnormal Psychology*, **86**, 267–275.

Baddeley, A.D. (1986) *Working Memory*. Oxford: Oxford University Press.

Baddeley, A.D. (1993) Working memory or working attention? In A. Baddeley and L. Weiskrantz (Eds.), *Attention: Selection, Awareness, and Control. A Tribute to Donald Broadbent* (pp.152–170). Oxford: Clarendon Press.

Barr, C.E., Mednick, S.A. and Munk-Jorgenson, P. (1990) Maternal influenza and schizophrenic births. *Archives of General Psychiatry*, **47**, 869–874.

Bartfai, A., Pedersen, N.L., Asarnow, R.F. and Schalling, D. (1991) Genetic factors for the span of apprehension test: A study of normal twins. *Psychiatry Research*, **38**, 115–124.

Beatty, J. (1982) Task-evoked pupillary responses, processing load, and the structure of processing resources. *Psychological Bulletin*, **91**, 276–292.

Bebbington, P. and Kuipers, L. (1994) The predictive utility of expressed emotion in schizophrenia: An aggregate analysis. *Psychological Medicine*, **24**, 707–718.

Bentall, R.P. (1990) The illusion of reality: a review and integration of psychological research on hallucinations. *Psychological Bulletin*, **107**, 82–95.

Bentall, R.P. (1994) Cognitive biases and abnormal beliefs: Towards a model of persecutory delusions. In A.S. David and J.C. Cutting (Eds.), *The Neuropsychology of Schizophrenia* (pp. 337–360). Hove: Lawrence Erlbaum.

Bentall, R.P., Kaney, S. and Dewey, M.E. (1991) Paranoia and social reasoning: An attribution theory analysis. *British Journal of Clinical Psychology*, **30**, 13–23.

Bleuler, E. (1911/1950) *Dementia Praecox or the Group of Schizophrenias*. (English Translation: J. Zinkin). New York: International Universities Press.

Bleuler, E. (1924/1976) *Textbook of Psychiatry*. (English Translation: A.A. Brill). New York: Arno Press.

Broadbent, D.E. (1958) *Perception and Communication*. London: Pergamon Press .

Cannon, T.D., Zorrilla, L.E., Shtasel, D., Gur, R.E., Gur, R.C., Marco, E.J., Moberg, P., and Price, A. (1994) Neuropsychological functioning in siblings discordant for schizophrenia and healthy volunteers. *Archives of General Psychiatry*, **51**, 651–661.

Cassens, G., Inglis, A.K., Appelbaum, P.S., and Gutheil, T.G. (1990) Neuroleptics: Effects on neuropsychological function in chronic schizophrenic patients. *Schizophrenia Bulletin*, **16**, 477–499.

Cohen, J.D., and Servan-Schreiber, D. (1993) A theory of dopamine function and its role in cognitive deficits in schizophrenia. *Schizophrenia Bulletin*, **19**, 85–104.

Cornblatt, B.A., Risch, N.J., Faris, G., Friedman, D., and Erlenmeyer-Kimling, L. (1988) The Continuous Performance Test, Identical Pairs Version (CPT-IP): I. New findings about sustained attention in normal families. *Psychiatry Research*, **26**, 223–238.

Cowan, N. (1988) Evolving conceptions of memory storage, selective attention, and their mutual constraints within the human information-processing system. *Psychological Bulletin*, **104**, 163–191.

Cutting, J., and Dunne, F. (1989) Subjective experience of schizophrenia. *Schizophrenia Bulletin*, **15**, 217–231.

Dawson, M.E., and Nuechterlein, K.H. (1984) Psychophysiological dysfunction in the developmental course of schizophrenic disorder. *Schizophrenia Bulletin*, **10**, 204–232.

Erlenmeyer-Kimling, L., and Cornblatt, B. (1987) High-risk research in schizophrenia: A summary of what has been learned. *Journal of Psychiatric Research*, **21**, 401–411.

Faraone, S.V., Seidman, L.J., Kremen, W.S., Pepple, J.R., Lyons, M.J., and Tsuang, M.T. (1995) Neuropsychological functioning among the nonpsychotic relatives of schizophrenic patients: A diagnostic efficiency analysis. *Journal of Abnormal Psychology*, **104**, 286–304.

Freedman, B., and Chapman, L.J. (1973) Early subjective experience in schizophrenic episodes. *Journal of Abnormal Psychology*, **82**, 46–54.

Frith, C.D. (1987) The positive and negative symptoms of schizophrenia reflect impairments in the perception and initiation of action. *Psychological Medicine*, **17**, 631–648.

Frith, C.D. (1992) *The Cognitive Neuropsychology of Schizophrenia*. Hove: Lawrence Erlbaum.

Garmezy, N., and Streitman, S. (1974) Children at risk: The search for the antecedents of schizophrenia. Part I. Conceptual models and research methods. *Schizophrenia Bulletin*, **1** (8), 14–90.

Goldman-Rakic, P.S. (1991) Prefrontal cortical dysfunction in schizophrenia: The relevance of working memory. In B.J. Carroll and J.E. Barrett (Eds.), *Psychopathology and the Brain* (pp. 1–23) New York: Raven Press.

Gottesman, I.I., and Shields, J. (1972) *Schizophrenia and Genetics: A Twin Study Vantage Point*. New York: Academic Press.

Gray, J.A., Feldon, J., Rawlins, J.N.P., Hemsley, D.R., and Smith, A.D. (1991) The neuropsychology of schizophrenia. *Behavioral and Brain Sciences*, **14**, 1–20.

Green M.F. (1993) Cognitive remediation in schizophrenia: Is it time yet? *American Journal of Psychiatry*, **150**, 178–187.

Green, M.F., Nuechterlein, K.H., and Breitmeyer, B. (1997) Backward masking performance in unaffected siblings of schizophrenic patients: Evidence for a vulnerability indicator. *Archives of General Psychiatry*. **54**, 465–472.

Green, M.F., Nuechterlein, K.H., and Mintz, J. (1994a) Backward masking in schizophrenia and mania: I. Specifying a mechanism. *Archives of General Psychiatry*, **51**, 939–944.

Green, M.F., Nuechterlein, K.H., and Mintz, J. (1994b) Backward masking in schizophrenia and mania: II. Specifying the visual channels. *Archives of General Psychiatry*, **51**, 945–951.

Green, M., and Walker, E. (1986) Attentional performance in positive- and negative-symptom schizophrenia. *Journal of Nervous and Mental Disease*, **174**, 208–213.

Grove, W.M., Lebow, B.S., Clementz, B.A., Cerri, A., Medus, C., and Iacono, W.G. (1991) Familial prevalence and coaggregation of schizotypy indicators: A multitrait family study. *Journal of Abnormal Psychology*, **100**, 115–121.

Hemsley, D.R. (1987) An experimental psychological model for schizophrenia. In H. Hafner, W.F. Gattaz, and W. Janzarik (Eds.), *Search for the Causes of Schizophrenia* (pp. 179–188) Berlin: Springer-Verlag.

Hemsley, D.R. (1994a) A cognitive model for schizophrenia and its possible neural basis. *Acta Psychiatrica Scandinavica*, **90** (Suppl 384), 80–86.

Hemsley, D.R. (1994b) Perceptual and cognitive abnormalities as the bases for schizophrenic symptoms. In A.S. David and J.C. Cutting (Eds.), *The Neuropsychology of Schizophrenia* (pp. 97–116) Hove: Lawrence Erlbaum.

Holzman, P.S. (1994) The role of psychological probes in genetic studies of schizophrenia. *Schizophrenia Research*, **13**, 1–9.

Iacono, W.G. (1983) Psychophysiology and genetics: A key to psychopathology research. *Psychophysiology*, **20**, 371–383.

Kahneman, D. (1973) *Attention and Effort*. Englewood Cliffs, NJ: Prentice-Hall.

Kavanagh, D.J. (1992) Recent developments in expressed emotion and schizophrenia. *British Journal of Psychiatry*, **160**, 601–620.

Kendler, K.S., Ochs, A.L., Gorman, A.M., Hewitt, J.K., Ross, D.E., and Mirsky, A.F. (1991) The structure of schizotypy: A pilot multitrait twin study. *Psychiatry Research*, **36**, 19–36.

Kraepelin, E. (1913/1919) *Dementia Praecox and Paraphrenia*. (English Translation: R.M. Barclay) Edinburgh: E. and S. Livingston. (Reprinted by Robert E. Krieger Publishing Co. Inc., Huntington, NY, 1971)

Liberman, R.P., Wallace, C.J., Blackwell, G., Eckmann, T.A., and Kuehnel, T.G. (1994) Skills training for the seriously mentally ill. In R.J. Ancill, S. Holliday, and J. Higenbotham (Eds.), *Schizophrenia: Exploring the Spectrum of Psychosis*. Chichester: Wiley.

Linzen, D.H., Dingemans, P.M., and Lenior, M.E. (1994) Cannabis abuse and the course of recent onset schizophrenic disorders. *Archives of General Psychiatry*, **51**, 273–279.

Lukoff, D., Snyder, K., Ventura, J., and Nuechterlein, K.H. (1984) Life events, familial stress, and coping in the developmental course of schizophrenia. *Schizophenia Bulletin*, **10**, 258–292.

McGhie, A., and Chapman, J. (1961) Disorders of attention and perception in early schizophrenia. *British Journal of Medical Psychology*, **34**, 103–116.

McGuffin P. (1991) Genetic models of madness. In P. McGuffin and R. Murray (Eds.), *The New Genetics of Mental Illness* (pp. 27–43). Oxford: Butterworth-Heinemann.

Maier, W. Franke, P., Hain, C., Kopp, B., and Rist, F. (1992) Neuropsychological indicators of the vulnerability to schizophrenia. *Progress in Neuro-Psychopharmacology and Biological Psychiatry*, **16**, 703–715.

Miller, S., Saccuzzo, D., and Braff, D. (1979) Information processing deficits in remitted schizophrenics. *Journal of Abnormal Psychology*, **88**, 446–449.

Nuechterlein, K.H. (1983) Signal detection in vigilance tasks and behavioral attributes among offspring of schizophrenic mothers and among hyperactive children. *Journal of Abnormal Psychology*, **92**, 4–28.

Nuechterlein, K.H. (1987) Vulnerability models for schizophrenia: State of the art. In H. Hafner, W.F. Gattaz, and W. Janzarik (Eds.), *Search for the Causes of Schizophrenia* (pp. 297–316). Heidelberg: Springer-Verlag.

Nuechterlein, K.H., Asarnow, R.F., Cantor, R., Spence, M.A., and Subotnik, K.L. (1993) The search for genetically transmitted vulnerability factors: Sibling correlations in continuous performance test, span of apprehension, and trail making test performance. Presented at the *Fourth International Congress on Schizophrenia Research*, Colorado Springs, Colorado, April 17–21, 1993.

Nuechterlein, K.H., and Dawson, M.E. (1984a) A heuristic vulnerability/stress model of schizophrenic episodes. *Schizophrenia Bulletin*, **10**, 300–312.

Nuechterlein, K.H., and Dawson, M.E. (1984b) Information processing and attentional functioning in the developmental course of schizophrenic disorders. *Schizophrenia Bulletin*, **10**, 160–203.

Nuechterlein, K.H., Dawson, M.E., Gitlin, M., Ventura, J., Goldstein, M.J., Snyder, K.S., Yee, C.M., and Mintz, J. (1992) Developmental Processes in Schizophrenic Disorders: Longitudinal studies of vulnerability and stress. *Schizophrenia Bulletin*, **18**, 387–425.

Nuechterlein, K.H., Dawson, M.E., and Green, M.F. (1994) Information-processing abnormalities as neuropsychological vulnerability indicators for schizophrenia. *Acta Psychiatrica Scandinavica*, **90** (Suppl. 384), 71–79.

Nuechterlein, K.H., Dawson, M.E., Ventura, J., Fogelson, D., Gitlin, M., Mintz, J. (1991) Testing vulnerability models: Stability of potential vulnerability indicators across clinical state. In H. Hafner and W.F. Gattaz (Eds.), *Search for the Causes of Schizophrenia*, Vol. II (pp.177–191). Berlin: Springer-Verlag.

Nuechterlein, K.H., Edell, W.S., Norris, M., and Dawson, M.E. (1986) Attentional vulnerability indicaators, thought disorder, and negative symptoms. *Schizophrenia Bulletin*, **12**, 408–426.

Nuechterlein, K.H., Parasuraman, R., and Jiang, Q. (1983) Visual sustained attention: Image degradation produces rapid sensitivity decrement over time. *Science*, **220**, 327–329.

Park, S., and Holzman, P.S. (1992) Schizophrenics show spatial working memory deficits. *Archives of General Psychiatry*, **49**, 975–982.

Rosvold, H.E., Mirsky, A., Sarason, I., Bransome, Jr., E.D., and Beck, L.H. (1956) A continuous performance test of brain damage. *Journal of Consulting Psychology*, **20**, 343–350.

Salzinger, K., Portnoy, S., and Feldman, R.S. (1978) Communicability deficit in schizophrenics resulting from a more general deficit. In S. Schwartz (Ed.), *Language and Cognition in Schizophrenia* (pp. 35–53). Hillsdale, N.J.: Lawrence Erlbaum.

Schneider, K. (1959) *Clinical Psychopathology*. New York: Grune and Stratton.

Shaner, A., Eckman, T., Roberts, L., Wilkins, J., Tucker, D., Tsuang, J., and Mintz, J. (1995) Disability income, cocaine use and repeated hospitalization among schizophrenic cocaine abusers. *New England Journal of Medicine*. **333**, 777–783

Shiffrin, R.M., and Schneider, W. (1977) Controlled and automatic human information processing: II. Perceptual learning, automatic attending, and a general theory. *Psychological Review*, **84**, 127–190.

Strauss, J.S., and Carpenter, W.T. (1981) *Schizophrenia*. New York: Plenum.

Tarrier, N., Beckett, R., Harwood, S., Baker, A., Yusupoff, L., and Ugarteburu, I. (1993) A trial of two cognitive-behavioural methods of treating drug-resistant residual psychotic symptoms in schizophrenic patients: I. Outcome. *British Journal of Psychiatry*, **162**, 524–532.

Torrey, E.F., Taylor, E.H., Bracha, H.S., Bowler, A.E., McNeil, T.F, Rawlings, R.R., Quinn, P.O., Bigelow, L.B., Rickler, K., Sjostrom, K., Higgins, E.S., and Gottesman, I.I. (1994) Prenatal origin of schizophrenia in a subgroup of discordant monozygotic twins. *Schizophrenia Bulletin*, **20**, 423–432.

Ventura, J., Nuechterlein, K.H., Lukoff, D., and Hardesty, J.P. (1989) A prospective study of stressful life events and schizophrenic relapse. *Journal of Abnormal Psychology*, **98**, 407–411.

World Health Organization (1992) *The ICD-10 Classification of Mental and Behavioral Disorders. Clinical Descriptions and Diagnostic Guidelines.* Geneva: World Health Organization.

Zubin, J., and Spring, B. (1977) Vulnerability—A new view of schizophrenia. *Journal of Abnormal Psycholgy*, **86**, 103–126.

Chapter 3

THE MEASUREMENT OF OUTCOME IN SCHIZOPHRENIA

Richard Drake, Gillian Haddock, Richard Hopkins and Shôn Lewis

The reliable and valid measurement of outcome is crucial to evaluating the effectiveness of any intervention. In schizophrenia this issue is complicated by the wide range and variability of measurable outcomes. In this chapter, we will review instruments particularly designed to evaluate functional symptomatic outcomes, with reference more briefly to global outcomes.

THE EPIDEMIOLOGY AND DIAGNOSIS OF SCHIZOPHRENIA: AN INTRODUCTION

Schizophrenia is a common disorder with lifetime risk of between 0.5 and 1 per cent. The annual incidence rate is about two new cases per 10 000 head of population per year. Men and women are both similarly at risk although men tend to have a slightly worse long term outcome. The peak age of onset of schizophrenia is in early adult life, with a median of 24 years in men and 28 years in women. Onset before 16 years and after 40 years is rare. The diagnosis of the disorder is usually characterised by the positive symptoms of delusions, hallucinations and thought disorder with criteria

Outcome and Innovation in Psychological Treatment of Schizophrenia. Edited by T. Wykes, N. Tarrier and S. Lewis.
© 1998 John Wiley & Sons Ltd

for minimum duration. Large international studies such as those run by the World Health Organization have established that the symptoms of schizophrenia occur in all cultures at approximately the same prevalence. The main difference between cultures is that in developing countries the outcome is better than in developed countries (Sartorius et al., 1986).

Although schizophrenia has been described clearly for over a century, the diagnosis of schizophrenia has attracted controversy, largely as a result of its over-use and previously low inter-rater reliability. As a result, operationalised diagnostic guidelines were developed to increase the reliability of the diagnostic classification system.

The major diagnostic criteria currently in use are those of the World Health Organization (International Classification of Diseases, tenth revision (ICD 10), (World Health Organization 1992), the *Diagnostic and Statistical Manual*, fourth edition (DSM IV) (American Psychiatric Association 1994, DSM IV) and the Research Diagnostic Criteria (RDC) (Spitzer et al., 1978). Both the ICD and DSM diagnoses are similarly structured. They consist of a list of symptoms of which at least one must be present to make the diagnosis, and a second group of which at least two must be present. The two systems differ in that ICD requires only that symptoms be present for most of one month, whereas DSM requires continuous disturbance in functioning for at least 6 months together with persistent and significant social impairment. DSM-IV has an additional category of Schizophreniform Disorder which requires the same criteria for diagnosis as schizophrenia, but which have been present for between 1 and 6 months.

The Research Diagnostic Criteria (Spitzer et al., 1978) were developed with the intention of producing patient samples which had a relatively homogeneous syndrome for research purposes, but to avoid limiting the diagnosis of schizophrenia to cases with a chronic or deteriorating course. The RDC diagnostic system encompasses a wide range of positive psychotic symptoms, and requires that these have at least a 2 week duration.

Although the reliability of these diagnostic criteria has been demonstrated in field trials, the question of the validity of different constructs of schizophrenia is harder to assess directly. Many researchers and clinicians would argue for the overall validity of current concepts of schizophrenia, based on predictive validity, response to treatment, patterns of familial aggregation and other factors (e.g. Kendell, 1988), although others are more critical (e.g. Bentall et al., 1988).

OUTCOME IN SCHIZOPHRENIA: AN OVERVIEW

The outcome of schizophrenia can be measured in many ways, and is likely to be heterogenous within each of these many dimensions. Outcome may be seen in terms of psychopathology, quality of life, social adjustment and function, or service use and overall economic costs. It can be altered, often dramatically, by a range of interventions including conventional drug treatment (see Dixon et al., 1995 for a review), social and family treatments (Lehman, 1995; and Dixon and Lehman, 1995), and psychological treatments developed more recently (for instance Haddock, Bentall and Slade, 1996).

The costs of schizophrenia to patients and the community are enormous: in0 the UK a conservative estimate of about £1.7 billion, including indirect costs, has been made in terms of 1991 prices (Davies and Drummond, 1994). The same review notes that, using a model which involved stratification of the heterogenous range of social outcomes already mentioned, the costs are very sensitive to shifts of patients from one group of dependent, impaired patients to another. In turn, this suggests that the most effective treatment of the most severely ill, if necessary using relatively expensive but efficacious treatments like clozapine, may have a dramatic effect on one measure of the costs to society as a whole. This exemplifies how much appropriate measures of outcome, sensitively applied, are critical to schizophrenia research.

RELIABILITY, VALIDITY AND RELEVANCE OF MEASURES OF OUTCOME

Reliability, validity and relevance of the measures used are key issues in the measurement of outcome, as are the reliability and validity of the constructs being examined. It is common to use a number of measures during outcome trials which may allow the testing of several hypotheses arising out of the same design. The validity and relevance of specific measures during a treatment trial may be greater, or more demonstrable, if they take into account previously demonstrated prognostic factors for schizophrenia. The most consistently demonstrated prognostic factors are summarised in Table 3.1. It is possible to use these prognostic indicators to guide the types of assessment measures which may be useful.

Assessment instruments must strike a balance between ease of use (for investigator and subject) and comprehensiveness, reliability and validity. These factors, as well as the particular features of a study, dictate the most suitable instruments in particular circumstances and have fuelled their diversification. Instruments for assessing psychopathology can be examined according to the complexity of the construct which they are intended to examine in terms of diagnoses, or subsyndromes, or dimensions of symptoms, their cognitive and behavioural correlates, or the cognitive processes hypothesised to underlie the symptoms.

INSTRUMENTS TO MEASURE THE SEVERITY OF SYMPTOMS

Intervention studies have generally been interested in examining the specific changes in severity of symptoms as a result of treatment, regardless of whether this is a social, pharmacological or a psychological treatment. As

Table 3.1   Prognostic factors in schizophrenia

Various prognostic variables predict outcome measured in different ways, including measures of severity of positive symptoms, or clinically identified relapses; service measures like rehospitalisation or time as an in-patient; or measures of social function such as occupational function, housing and marital status, and specific social function scales; or overall measures like the Global Assessment Scale (GAS). Some variables are demonstrated to affect outcome measures in all these domains ("all measures"). All prognostic factors identified have been confirmed in more than one study.

Prognostic variable	Good prognostic factors	Outcome measure most affected
Premorbid	Good adjustment (status, work, sexual), normal personality, normal IQ	All measures, especially social function
Age	Older at onset	All measures
Sex and marital status	Female, married	Relapse, readmission, social function
Initial presentation	Acute recent onset, florid positive symptoms, perplexity, affective symptoms, no blunting	Positive symptoms, relapse, time as inpatient
Family history	Absence of family history of schizophrenia, presence of family history of affective disorder	Relapse, time as inpatient
Treatment	Antipsychotics	Positive symptoms
Illness course	First episode	All measures, especially relapse and readmission
Continuing features	Absence of negative symptoms	Social function
Environment	Developing country Low expressed emotion	Relapse, GAS score
Behaviour	Not using illicit drugs or abusing alcohol	All measures
Attitude to medication	Good compliance	Relapse

a result, a number of instruments have been developed which have been designed to provide a rating of the severity of a symptom which is sensitive to change over time.

The Brief Psychiatric Rating Scale (BPRS) (Overall and Gorham, 1962)

The BPRS has been in use for over thirty years and its main advantages are its familiarity and the large amounts of normative and comparative data available. The scale was developed to provide an assessment technique for all psychiatric disorders, suited to the evaluation of patient change in drug trials. The scale items were each selected to represent a relatively independent symptom dimension. Clusters of these items, or subscales, have been identified in factor analytic studies of the scale. There are several different versions of this scale available. It is intended as a comprehensive rating scale and is not limited to schizophrenia symptoms. Symptoms are rated on a 0 to 6 scale.

The scale has its shortcomings. The guidelines for rating the original BPRS are not described in detail and the anchor points are not well specified. This means that good reliability can be hard to achieve. Various authors have achieved intraclass correlation coefficients of between 0.56 and 0.97 for various items, with median intraclass correlations and Pearson coefficients of 0.67 to 0.88 (Overall and Gorham 1962; Ventura et al., 1993). The higher levels of reliability have often been achieved by organised training programmes at different centres, frequently involving modifying the BPRS. One example is the program at UCLA, which also involves use of detailed anchor points (which have been published in Ventura et al., 1993), and maintainance of reliability by checks after initial training.

However, these levels may be hard to reproduce outside the various different programs, given the idiosyncratic nature of some of the scale items, which are sometimes only tangentially related to commonly used symptom constructs: for instance, the only item relating to hallucinations is "hallucinatory behaviour", and the item for delusions is "conceptual disorganisation". Only a small number of items are directly associated with a diagnosis of schizophrenia: four or five to positive symptoms (depending on the version used) and three items to negative symptoms. It is hard to rate delusions and to differentiate some positive and negative symptoms. In addition, the withdrawal-retardation factor (or NSS, negative symptom subscale) is composed of three items which respond differently to neuroleptics, and may not necessarily be validly combined (Kay, 1991).

The Scale for the Assessment of Positive Symptoms (SAPS) (Andreasen, 1984)

This was developed as a scale specific to schizophrenia, to assess positive symptoms, usually over the past month. It comprises a semi-structured clinical interview of the subject by a rater experienced in eliciting symptoms. Items are rated on a 0 to 5 scale and grouped into subscales of hallucinations, delusions, bizarre behaviour and disrupted speech (formal thought disorder). Six items rate hallucinations, with separate scores for severity and frequency. Delusions are rated as a composite score based on a combination of dimensions (conviction, severity, preoccupation and action on the belief).

Use of the SAPS in a number of different countries and in different languages has demonstrated that inter-rater reliability of the four categories is good, with weighted kappas for most items 0.7–1.00. Inter-rater reliability has been shown to be much reduced if raters are not provided with sufficient training or experience in the administration of the instrument (Moscarelli et al., 1987, Andreasen, 1990).

The Scale for the Assessment of Negative Symptoms (SANS) (Andreasen, 1989)

This scale is designed to rate negative symptoms mainly on the basis of behavioural observation. It is separate from, complementary to and more widely used than the SAPS. If the scale is used in conjunction with the SAPS the instruments give a fairly comprehensive rating of symptoms which is sensitive to change. The five groups of items rated in the SANS are: alogia, affective flattening (including motor items), avolition–apathy, anhedonia–asociality and attention.

Negative symptoms are more difficult to rate reliably than positive symptoms. The amount of published data on the reliability of the SANS is greater than for the SAPS (Andreasen, 1990), and it appears to be good given adequate training. Internal consistency within the five groups is high (Cronbach's alphas of between 0.67 and 0.90) and they are reasonably consistent with one another (Cronbach's alphas of 0.63–0.83). However, several studies have suggested that the attentional impairment section is less reliable and perhaps less valid than the other sections. This item correlates positively with positive symptoms and thought disorder, but it correlates less with other items on the SANS and poorly with performance on digit span tasks (Barnes, 1994).

A further problem with rating negative symptoms in schizophrenia is that they can be mimicked by depressive symptoms, which also include avolition and anhedonia, and by the side effects of some antipsychotic drugs. Nevertheless, there is evidence that negative symptoms and depressive symptoms are discriminable in schizophrenic patients (Barnes and Liddle, 1990).

Positive and Negative Syndrome Scale (PANSS; Kay et al., 1989)

This is now a widely used, comprehensive symptom rating scale in schizophrenia treatment trials. Its authors designed it to incorporate items from the BPRS, the scores of which can be derived from the longer PANSS. It is designed to permit ratings of 30 items (7 "positive" symptoms, 7 "negative" symptoms and 16 general psychopathology items) on a scale of 1 (absent) to 7 (greatest frequency, prominence and behavioural disruption). The anchor points for each item are well defined by a detailed manual. Rating is made on the basis of a mental state interview carried out by an assessor who is experienced in eliciting symptoms. The scale is designed so that the difference between scores for the positive and negative syndromes can be examined to determine which syndrome predominates and to what extent.

An attempt at validation of the positive and negative scales has been made by correlation with the SAPS and SANS. There was a high correlation between the PANSS and these scales (the Pearson correlation coefficient was 0.77 in each case) and there was a significant negative correlation between the positive and negative scales after adjustment to account for general psychopathology scores. Inter-rater reliability, internal and test–retest reliability were all good (Kay et al., 1987). The instrument aims to delineate unambiguous primary symptoms of the positive and negative syndromes of schizophrenia although the scale may be limited in that it does not provide for full direct assessment of affective symptoms.

Comprehensive Psychopathological Rating Scale (CPRS)(Asberg et al., 1978)

The CPRS is designed to measure the severity of a range of psychopathology, and comprises 40 "reported" items which are rated on the basis of interview-elicited reported symptoms and 25 which are rated following observation. Two further items, global rating and a rating of interview reliability, can also be made. Items are scored from 0 to 3, with clearly described anchor points and with possible half-point gradations, on a combination of symptom frequency and severity.

Inter-rater reliability calculated from ratings made with schizophrenic patients was greater than 0.78 for the 33 items related to schizophrenia symptoms, but lower than 0.78 for 6 items of observed behaviour (Jacobsson et al., 1978). Separate reliability data for ratings made using the affective subscale and reliability from interviews carried out in cross-cultural studies is available. Although not widely used, the CPRS has the advantage of assessing a wide range of psychotic and neurotic symptoms which can be relevant in schizophrenia.

The Psychiatric Assessment Scale (Krawiecka et al., 1977, also known as the KGV)

This short scale was originally designed for use in the assessment of change in patients familiar to the rating clinician and who were suffering a chronic psychosis (Krawiecka et al., 1977). There was no specific structured interview developed for use with the original scale as it was assumed that the clinicians who used this scale would be adequately trained to elicit symptoms. More recently, the scale has been revised to provide a detailed interview to improve reliability and assist non-clinically trained raters to elicit the necessary information needed to make a rating of the severity of symptoms (Lancashire et al., 1996; Barnes, 1994). The original scale contained eight items: four items which depended on patients' answers as a result of rater questioning and four based on behavioural observations. Items are rated from 0 to 4 and inter-rater reliability based on psychiatrist raters, as measured by the Kendall coefficient of concordance, was between 0.64 and 0.87 for reported symptoms and between 0.58 and 0.73 for observed items. Inter-rater reliability has also been investigated for mental health nurses trained to elicit symptom information and rate them using a modified version of the PAS. The results showed that mental health nurses had good inter-rater reliability using this scale following appropriate training (Lancashire et al., 1996). The instrument has been found to be sensitive to change in psychopathology (Owens and Johnstone, 1980) and has demonstrated greater reliability than the BPRS (Manchanda et al., 1986). One disadvantage is that it has limited coverage of affective symptoms.

INSTRUMENTS TO MEASURE THE SEVERITY OF SYMPTOM DIMENSIONS

A number of assessment measures have been developed which have been designed to assess the severity of specific dimensions of psychotic symptoms. These instruments have often been developed in tandem with the development in psychological treatments aimed at psychotic symptoms. Psychological treatments often target specific dimensions of symptoms independently and hence instruments which elicit and are sensitive to change in these dimensions have been needed. These instruments have generally focused on positive symptoms such as hallucinations and delusions.

The Maudsley Assessment of Delusions Schedule (MADS;Taylor et al., 1993)

The MADS takes the form of a semi-structured interview which aims to assess the nature of an individual's delusional beliefs. For example, information is elicited on the patient's conviction in the reality of their beliefs, the factors they consider to maintain the beliefs, their preoccupation, systematization and insight. These items are rated according to a series of different scales (some indicating presence or absence only, others on numerical scales). Affect associated with the beliefs and actions which are taken as a result of the patient's beliefs are also rated. Patients are also asked to comment on the reasonableness and dangerousness of those actions (Taylor et al., 1993).

The scale has been used to examine the phenomenology surrounding action on the basis of delusions (Buchanan et al., 1993), and to rate the effectiveness of cognitive-behaviour therapy on delusions (Garety et al.,

1994). It is not adapted to quick serial administration, but rather to thorough assessment of a variety of aspects of psychopathology. Inter-rater reliability coefficients for two clinical psychologists using the scale with a hospital sample of deluded patients ranged from 0.59 to 1.0, apart from the two items which involve retrospective assessment of subjects' actions (0.19 and 0.40 respectively; Wessley et al., 1993). Nevertheless, the scale's strengths are that it provides a comprehensive assessment of a wide range of the phenomenology and correlates of delusional beliefs which is not only useful in the evaluation of outcome from treatment but is also a useful clinical tool in cognitive–behaviour therapy.

Psychotic symptom rating scales (Haddock et al., submitted)

The PSYRATS (Psychotic SYmptom RATing Scales) have been developed to measure the severity of a number of dimensions of auditory hallucinations and delusions and consist of two subscales (the auditory hallucination rating scale and the delusions rating scale). Both scales comprise a semi-structured interview designed to elicit sufficient information to rate the severity of symptom dimensions on a five-point scale. The auditory hallucination rating scale is designed to rate the frequency, duration, location, loudness, associated distress (amount and intensity), negative content (amount and intensity), disruption, controllability and number of voices. The delusions rating scale is designed to rate the severity of delusional beliefs on preoccupation, duration of preoccupation, conviction, distress (amount and intensity) and associated disruption of behaviour. Inter-rater reliability has been shown to be high given a small amount of training and when raters are provided with specific guidelines in their use (with Spearman coefficients above 0.73 for all items). The scales have been used as outcome measures during a trial of cognitive-behaviour therapy and were sensitive to change in symptom dimensions over time and as a result of treatment. They can be used as a within treatment measure such as for an initial assessment interview and/or as an ongoing monitoring tool.

Beliefs about Voices questionnaire (Chadwick and Birchwood, 1995)

The Beliefs about Voices questionnaire (Chadwick and Birchwood, 1995) is a self-report questionnaire designed to elicit information relating to specific characteristics of a patient's beliefs and attitudes about their auditory hallucinations. The questionnaire is designed to categorise responses into four dimensions of voices: benevolence, malevolence, engagement and resistance. Chadwick and Birchwood (1995) showed that patients who believed their voices to be benevolent tended to engage with their voices whilst those who believed their voices to be malevolent tended to resist their voices' speech. These associations were shown to be independent of the actual content of the voices. The scale has been shown to possess high sensitivity and test–retest reliability. Although its use as an outcome tool in treatment studies has yet to be demonstrated, the questionnaire has high face validity in assessing outcome from a cognitive treatment of beliefs regarding hallucinatory experiences and could be used in conjunction with other measures. In addition, the Cognitive Assessment of Voices: Interview Schedule (Chadwick and Birchwood, unpublished) is a structured interview which is unpublished but has been used in conjunction with the above questionnaire. It is similar in item content to the MADS and is designed to elicit information to inform a cognitive formulation about a patient's auditory hallucinations. It could be used as an outcome tool although its value may be primarily as a clinical tool.

Hallucination Interview Schedule (HIS; Bentall and Haddock, 1994, unpublished)

The HIS is a structured interview schedule which assesses auditory, visual, olfactory and tactile hallucinations. In particular, phenomenological aspects of symptoms are assessed, for example regarding auditory hallucinations, duration, number of voices, frequency, location of voices, circumstances of voices, sensory characteristics of the voices, form of the voices, emotional consequences of voices, content, controllability and attributions about the voices. It is a useful clinical tool to elicit information necessary to inform a cognitive–behavioural formulation of hallucinatory experiences although its validity and reliability as an outcome tool have yet to be demonstrated.

OTHER MEASURES FOR RATING SYMPTOM DIMENSIONS

Idiosyncratic measures which have been used to measure dimensions of auditory hallucinations and delusions include the Personal Questionnaire Rapid Scaling Technique (Mulhall, 1978) and self-report diaries which are also used to report other cognitive phenomena (Haddock et al., 1996). The PQRST is designed to provide a personalised method of assessing specific aspects or dimensions of symptoms which have been identified by a therapist and patient as being important markers of change during psychotherapy. The instrument is flexible in that it allows patients to self-rate the severity of any dimension which they choose and has an in-built method of detecting inconsistency in responding. Chadwick and Lowe (1994) reported the use of PQRST to assess three delusional belief dimensions: conviction that the belief was true, preoccupation with belief, and anxiety when preoccupied with the belief. They found that the PQRST was sensitive to changes which occurred as a result of treatment. Haddock et al., (1996) also used the PQRST to monitor changes in four dimensions of auditory hallucinations: amount of time spent hallucinating, distress caused by hallucinations, disruption caused by hallucinations and the amount to which patients believed that their voices were thoughts. The technique was sensitive to changes in symptom dimensions over time.

Diaries such as those used to rate other cognitive phenomena (e.g. negative automatic thoughts; Hawton et al., 1989) have also been used widely as outcome measures in the psychological treatment of psychosis. The advantage of these types of assessments is that they provide an ongoing rating of severity of specific phenomena which will not be picked up by any other rating measure. Usually they are designed for patients to monitor their psychotic experiences and the behavioural, affective and cognitive correlates of their symptoms between therapy sessions. They are an extremely important part of any cognitive–behavioural intervention and a useful clinical tool, although their value as outcome measures is limited for group studies as their nature does not make them easily comparable across groups. In addition, their reliability and validity is not easy to measure and many psychotic patients do not wish or find it difficult to complete some types of diaries. Delespaul (1995) has reviewed a wide variety of different monitoring approaches in schizophrenia showing that it is possible to assist patients to monitor their experiences although it is necessary to be flexible in the type of tool used.

OTHER OUTCOME MEASURES

This review has attempted to provide an overview of the range of assessments which can be used to evaluate symptomatological outcome in treatment studies. There are other important outcomes which could, and often should, be assessed either in addition to those discussed above or as a subject of interest in themselves, in particular social functioning and quality of life. There are a number of instruments available to assess these factors (see Wykes, 1992 for a review). Other relevant outcomes involve carers and families, who have been shown to carry much of the burden of care for people with schizophrenia. Research suggests that they suffer from reduced social functioning and minor psychopathology. Many treatment trials have investigated the effectiveness of family interventions on patient relapse and on specific outcomes for relatives. This has resulted in a range of assessment procedures for use with relatives of schizophrenic patients (Barrowclough and Tarrier, 1992). Increasingly studies are investigating outcomes relating to service use and cost, for example the frequency and duration of in-patient hospitalization, the use of other mental health services and patients' and relatives' satisfaction with these. It may be important to measure all of these outcomes when carrying out treatment research, although the statistical power of the study will limit the number of outcomes which can be investigated with any available subject pool.

GLOBAL OUTCOME MEASURES

In NHS research and development, as well as in service monitoring, it is often attractive and appropriate to include a single, global measure of outcome. There are obviously caveats to this approach, since it is not necessarily valid to combine a number of different constructs in one item. Nonetheless, the reliability of such global assessments is surprisingly high and they are sensitive to change. The following three scales are non-specific, global ratings of outcome which are generally weighted towards impairments in social functioning.

The Global Assessment Scale (GAS) (Endicott et al., 1976).

This instrument provides a global rating of mental health rated from 1 to 100. Anchor points are provided and ratings are made on the basis of overall clinical impression rather than on the basis of a specific interview. Higher scores are indicative of better mental health. Raters assess patients' functioning over the last week against criteria specified for each 10-point interval on the scale and assign an appropriate score.

The inter-rater reliability depends on the way it is administered: a review of semi-structured interview transcripts gave the lowest inter-rater reliability coefficients, and ratings made in a group the highest (between 0.61 and 0.91; Endicott et al., 1976). The GAS correlates with other measures of severity, and reduction in scores has been associated with rehospitalization. It is a simple robust measure with some face validity, but obviously very limited and affected by many factors. The slightly modified Global Assessment of Function (GAF) Scale is included in DSM IV (American Psychiatric Association, 1994).

The Health of the Nation Outcome Scales (HoNOS) (Wing et al., 1996)

These newly derived scales are promoted by the Department of Health in the UK, and will become widely used in UK mental health services. They cover 12 domains of functioning in their twelve items. Eight involve behavioural and psychiatric disturbance, including suicidal thoughts and self-injury, aggression, cognitive problems, psychotic symptoms, affective disturbance and physical symptoms; three involve social and relationship problems, and one is related to degree of stimulation and activity. Ratings are based on non-specified assessment procedures and are designed to cover the preceding two weeks. Anchor points are fairly clearly specified and ratings are made on a five-point scale from 0 to 4, with the highest score indicating a severe clinical problem and zero indicating no clinical problem.

Clinical Global Impression scale (CGI) (Guy, 1976)

This scale can be used across the whole range of psychiatric disorder, including schizophrenia. It is the simplest of all scales designed to be used by clinicians and consists simply of a seven-point scale of severity of "mental illness" ranging from "normal, not at all ill" (attracting a score of 1) to "among the most severely ill" (attracting a score of 7). The rating are made on the basis of "clinical judgement" which is likely to effect reliability and validity. This is a scale still widely used in drug treatment research but cannot be recommended as a sole outcome measure.

CONCLUSION

Research into treatments for schizophrenia depends on reliable, valid and appropriate measurement of outcome. This review has concentrated on measures of psychopathology. The most recommended include: the widely used BPRS (Overall and Gorham 1962), though questions remain about its reliability in practice; and the more recent PANSS (Kay et al., 1989), which is more specifically designed for schizophrenia. The KGV (Krawiecka et al., 1977) has been widely investigated and is easy to use, relatively reliable and valid, but offers limited coverage of affective symptoms. Newer instruments to assess symptom dimensions have not yet been used widely. Of global outcome measures the HoNOS (Wing et al., 1996) and GAS (Endicott et al., 1976) or GAF (American Psychiatric Association 1994) are the most important.

REFERENCES

American Psychiatric Association: (1994) *Diagnostic and Statistical Manual of Mental Disorders*, Fourth Edition. Washington DC, American Psychiatric Association.

Andreasen, N.C., (1984) Scale for the Assessment of Positive Symptoms (SAPS), Department of Psychiatry, Iowa City.

Andreasen, N.C., (1989) The scale for the assessment of negative symptoms (SANS): conceptual and theoretical foundations *Brit .J. Psych.* 1989, **155** suppl 7, 49–52.

Andreasen, N.C. (1990) Methods for assessing positive and negative symptoms, in *Schizophrenia: Positive and Negative Symptoms and Syndromes. Modern Problems of Pharmacopsychiatry*, ed. N.C. Andreasen, Karger, Basel.

Asberg, M., Montgomery, S., Perris, C., Schalling, D. and Sedvall, G., The Comprehensive Psychopathological Rating Scale, *Acta Psych. Scand. Suppl.*, **277**, 5–27.

Barnes T.R.E. (1994) The assessment of negative symptoms, in *The Assessment of Psychoses. A Practical Handbook*, ed. T.R.E. Barnes, and H.E. Nelson, Chapman and Hall Medical, London.

Barnes, T.R.E. and Liddle, P.F. (1990) The evidence for the validity of negative symptoms, in *Schizophrenia: Positive and Negative Symptoms and Syndromes. Modern Problems of Pharmacopsychiatry*, ed. N.C. Andreasen, Karger, Basel.

Barrowclough, C. and Tarrier, N. (1992) *Families of Schizophrenic Patients: Cognitive-Behavioural Intervention*, Chapman and Hall, London.

Bentall, R.P. and Haddock, G. (1994) The Hallucination Interview Schedule. Unpublished scale, University of Liverpool.

Bentall, R.P., Jackson, H.F. and Pilgrim, D. (1988) Abandoning the concept of schizophrenia: Some implications of validity arguments for psychological research into psychotic phenomena, *Brit. Journ. Clin. Psychol.* **27**, 156–69.

Buchanan, A., Reed, A., Wessley, S., Garety, P., Taylor, P., Grubin, D., and Dunn, G. (1993) Acting on delusions 2: the phenomenological correlates of acting on delusions, *Brit. J. Psychol.*, **163**, 77–81.

Chadwick, P.D.J. and Birchwood, M. (1995) The omnipotence of voices II: The beliefs about voices questionnaire, *Brit. J. Psychol.*, **165**, 773–6.

Chadwick, P.D.J. and Lowe, C.F. (1994) A cognitive approach to measuring and modifying delusions, *Behaviour, Research and Therapy*, **32**, 355–67.

Davies, L.A. and Drummond, M.F. (1994) Economics and schizophrenia: the real cost, *Brit. J. Psychol.*, **165** (suppl. 25), 18–21.

Delespaul, P.A.E.G. (1995) Assessing schizophrenia in daily life–the experience sampling method. Universiteit Pers Maastricht, Maastricht.

Dixon, L.B. and Lehman, A.F. (1995) Family interventions for schizophrenia, *Schizophrenia Bull.*, **21**, (4), 631–45.

Dixon, L.B., Lehman, A.F. and Levine, J. (1995) Conventional antipsychotic medications for schizophrenia, *Schizophrenia Bull.*, **21** (4), 567–79.

Endicott, J., Spitzer, R.L., Fless, J.L. and Cohen, J. (1976) The Global Assessment Scale, *Arch. Gen. Psych.* **33**, 766–72.

Garety, P.A., Kuipers, L., Fowler, D., Chamberlain, F. and Dunn, G. (1994) Cognitive Behavioural Therapy for drug-resistant psychosis *B. J. Med. Psychol.* **67** (3), 259–71.

Guy, W., (1997) *ECDEU Assessment Manual for Psychopharmacology*, DHEW Publication No. 76, 217–22 NIMH, Rockliffe, Maryland, USA.

Haddock, G., Bentall, R.P. and Slade, P.D. (1996) Psychological treatment of auditory hallucination: focussing or distraction?. In *Cognitive-behavioural Interventions with Psychotic Disorders*, ed. G. Haddock and P.D. Slade, Routledge, London.

Haddock, G., McCarron, J. and Tarrier, N. (submitted) Scales to assess dimensions of hallucinations and delusions: the Psychotic Symptom Rating Scales (PSYRATS).

Hawton, K., Salkovskis, P.M., Kirk, J. and Clark, D.M. (1989) *Cognitive Behaviour Therapy for Psychiatric Problems: a Practical Guide*, Oxford Medical Publications, Oxford.

Jacobsson, L., Von Knorring, L., Mattsson, B., Perris, C., Edenius, B., Kettner, B., Magnusson, K. and Villemos, P. (1978) The Comprehensive Psychopathological Rating Scale—the CPRS—in patients with schizophrenia, *Acta Psychol. Scand.*, **271** 39–44.

Kay, S.R. (1991) *Positive and Negative Syndromes in Schizophrenia: Assessment and Research*, Brunner/Mazel, New York.

Kay, S., Fiszbein A. and Opler, L. (1987) The Positive and Negative Syndrome Scale (PANSS) for schizophrenia, *Schizophrenia Bull.* **13**, 261–75.

Kay, S., Opler, L. and Lindenmayer, J.-P., (1989) The Positive and Negative Syndrome Scale (PANSS): Rationale and Standardization, *Brit. J. Psychol.*, **155**, suppl. 7, 49–52.

Kendell, R.E. (1988) Long term follow-up studies: a commentary, *Schizophrenia Bull.* **14** (4), 663–7.

Krawiecka, M., Goldberg, D. and Vaughan, M. (1977) A standardised psychiatric assessment scale for rating chronic psychotic patients, *Acta Psychol. Scand.* **55**, 299–308.

Lancashire, S., Haddock, G., Tarrier, N., Baguley, I., Butterworth, C.A. and Brooker, C. (1996) The impact of training community psychiatric nurses to use psychosocial interventions with people who have sever mental health problems (submitted).

Lehman, A.F. (1995) Vocational rehabilitation in schizophrenia, *Schizophrenia Bull.* **21** (4) 645–57.

Manchanda, R., Saupe, R. and Hirsch, S.R. (1986) Comparison between the Brief Psychiatric Rating Scale and the Manchester Scale for the rating of schizophrenic symptoms, *Acta Psychol. Scand.* **74**, 563–68.

Moscarelli, M., Maffei, C., Cesana, B. et al., (1987) An international perspective on assessment of negative and positive symptoms in schizophrenia, *Am. J. Psychol.*, **144**, 1595–8.

Mulhall, D. (1978) The Personal Questionnaire Rapid Scaling Technique, *Acta Psychol Scand.*, **271**, 29–32.

Overall, J.E. and Gorham, D.R. (1962) The brief psychiatric rating scale, *Psychological Reports*, **10**, 799–812.

Owens, D.G.C. and Johnstone, E.C. (1980) The disabilities of chronic schizophrenia: their nature and the factors contributing to their development, *Brit. J. Psychol.*, **136**, 384–95.

Sartorius, N., Jablensky, A., Korten, A., Ernberg, G., Anker, M., Cooper, J.E. and Day, R. Early manifestations and first contact incidence of schizophrenia in different cultures. A preliminary report on the initial evaluation phase of the WHO Collaborative Study on Determinants of Outcome of Severe Mental Illness, *Psychol. Med.* **16**(4), 909–28.

Spitzer, R.L., Endicott, J. and Robins, E. (1978) Research Diagnostic Criteria: rationale and reliability, *Arch. Gen. Psych.*, **35**, 773–82.

Taylor, P., Garety, P., Buchanan A. et al. (1993) Measuring risk through delusions, in *Violence and Mental Disorder: Developments in Risk Assessment*, eds. J. Monahan and H. Steadman, Chicago University Press, Chicago.

Ventura, J., Green, M.F., Shaner, A. and Liberman, R.P. (1993) Training and Quality Assurance with the Brief Psychiatric Rating Scale: The Drift Busters, *Int. J. Methods in Psychiatric Research*, **3**, 221–44.

Wessley, S., Buchanan, A., Reed, A., Cutting, J., Everitt, B., Garety, P. and Taylor, P.J. (1993) Acting on Delusions I: Prevalence, *Brit. J. Psych.*, **163**, 69–76.

Wing, J.K., Curtis, R. and Beevor, A. (1996) *The Health of the Nation Outcome Scale*, Royal College of Psychiatrists, London.

World Health Organization (1992) *International Classification of Diseases*, Tenth Edition, Chapter V. Geneva.

Wykes, T. (1992) The assessment of severely disabled patients for rehabilitation. In *Schizophrenia: An Overview and Practical Handbook*, Kavanagh, D.J. (ed.) Chapman and Hall, London.

Chapter 4

COGNITIVE BEHAVIOUR THERAPY OF SCHIZOPHRENIA

David Kingdon and Douglas Turkington

STYLES AND METHODS

The application of cognitive behaviour therapy to schizophrenia is still in the early stages of development despite the first description of the use of cognitive behaviour therapy of schizophrenia over 40 years ago (Beck, 1952). Beck described in this paper a patient with paranoid schizophrenia, who began to understand his psychotic symptoms through the use of a variety of simple techniques. An examination of the stressful antecedents of the emergence of psychotic symptoms helped the patient to understand their origins. Thereafter, an appropriately paced use of reality-testing techniques was used to chip away at the edges of a systematised persecutory delusion. Behavioural homework exercises were used to back up the in-session questioning techniques. From this beginning in psychosis, Beck went on to develop effective cognitive interventions to supplement psychopharmacological approaches in depression, anxiety disorders and personality disorders. More recently, he has turned again to the treatment of delusions with cognitive behaviour therapy and illustrated how advances in cognitive psychology point to the use of particular techniques

Outcome and Innovation in Psychological Treatment of Schizophrenia. Edited by T. Wykes, N. Tarrier and S. Lewis.
© 1998 John Wiley & Sons Ltd

in treating delusional symptomatology (Alford and Beck, 1994).

In relation to drug resistant hallucinations, the efficacy of coping skills enhancement, as compared to problem solving, has been demonstrated (Tarrier et al., 1993). Haddock et al., (1993, 1996) have shown benefits for some patients in the use of focusing as compared to distraction techniques for chronic hallucinations. The outcome study by Garety et al., (1994) revealed cognitive behaviour therapy to be significantly better than the control group in terms of general symptomatology, depression, delusional conviction and distress and interference with social functioning. Chadwick and Birchwood (1994) have described schema level techniques directed at the perceived omnipotence and omniscience of voices. Patients focus on their attitudes to the content and perceived power of the voices and by changing these attitudes, change their behaviour and their use of coping skills gaining control over voice intensity and frequency.

These strategies fit in well with the empowerment of people who hear voices e.g. through the "Hearing Voices" movement as described by Romme et al. (1992). They used an examination of a patient's life history to stimulate their understanding of voice content to help patients respond to voices in a more rational way, rather than with a purely emotional response, e.g. anger, or behavioural response, e.g. withdrawal. Birchwood et al., (1989) described the crucial importance of the recognition of each patient's individual relapse profile and of training the patient to recognise the emergence of these symptoms in relation to possible trigger factors. Patients were then given a clear set of instructions as to what to do when these symptoms started to emerge. They described the efficacy of such a relapse prevention approach in schizophrenia in relation to the interception and amelioration of psychotic relapse.

A recent controlled trial of compliance therapy (Kemp et al., 1996) revealed definite improvements in compliance with neuroleptic treatment and the gains persisted for at least 6 months. Encouragingly, there was also evidence of an overall improvement in global functioning. Drury (1994) showed the importance of using individual and group cognitive techniques in hospitalised patients with schizophrenia at the earliest possible point of intervention, i.e. when the symptoms are most acute and when entrenchment has not occurred. They have pointed the way towards the possible creation of an inpatient cognitive behavioural milieu for the treatment of acute schizophrenia. This allows gentle reality-testing techniques to be consistently used before such symptoms as delusions can become entrenched and worsened by confrontational attitudes in the community. These advances in the application of specific cognitive techniques in schizophrenia have been paralleled by interest in cognitive remediation. Brenner et al., (1990) in their integrated psychological therapy, describe approaches to target the specific cognitive deficits in schizophrenia, for example, attentional deficits. A sequence of remediating programmes is used including inter-personal problem solving, verbal communication, social perception, and cognitive differentiation. An evaluation of the approach revealed definite improvements for the integrated psychological therapy group, on attention and overall psychopathology, and showed that these benefits were still present at the 18 month follow up.

In the remainder of chapter, we will describe the use of cognitive behaviour therapy with a group of patients from Sheffield and Bassetlaw, Nottinghamshire, who participated in a pilot study between 1991 and 1993 and a 5–10-year follow-up of Bassetlaw patients who were first managed using basic techniques of cognitive behaviour therapy between 1984 and 1989. The styles and methods used, the clinical themes emerging, and outcome data will be described and compared with other recent studies.

PILOT STUDY

In a pilot study of the use of cognitive behaviour therapy in schizophrenia completed in 1992, outcomes in 12 patients who received a brief, time-limited intervention were compared with those of 6 patients in a control befriending group. The acceptance criteria were that patients should be aged 16–65, have active psychotic symptoms and fulfil the research criteria of the International Classification of Diseases, 10th Edition (draft 1989 version: World Health Organization, 1989) for schizophrenia. Assessment of symptoms (using the Comprehensive Pathological Rating Scale (Asberg et al., 1978)) and length of hospitalisation was by an independent assessor. Both groups were seen by the therapist as soon as possible after the initial ratings were completed: usually within 2–4 days. Each patient received six sessions within a two-month period, and family members, where available, were to be interviewed on one or two occasions. Sessions were to be flexible in length, but with the intention of averaging 20–40 minutes per session. Three sessions took place in most instances in the first two weeks, with progressively decreasing frequency of sessions to finish 6–8 weeks after the commencement of therapy.

Treatment techniques

Treatment was based on a manual prepared prior to the trial's commencement which had been developed for training purposes (subsequently published with accompanying theoretical and case material–Kingdon and Turkington, 1994). The work of Beck in depression and anxiety was particularly influential and formed a basic foundation. This was built upon by developing a "normalising rationale" using a vulnerability-stress model (Zubin and Spring, 1977) to provide an explanation for the development of the patient's illness. This involved reviewing any relevant vulnerability factors that they had. By examining the antecedents, symptoms were traced back to the approximate time of their apparent onset. Inductive questioning and gentle exploration were used to identify any stressful circumstances or events of significance to the person themselves. Then thought patterns occurring at the time and specifically any faulty cognitions deriving from and subsequent to this period were identified.

The approach used was very flexible with an emphasis on the development and maintenance of rapport (see Fig. 4.1). The patient's clinical notes were consulted before the first session to ensure all information about symptoms and possible precipitating life events was available. This also kept to a minimum the time required for the initial assessment so that the first session, when the patient might well be quite distressed, could be used primarily for establishing rapport. A schedule was devised to facilitate recording of topics discussed and cognitive errors elicited during the sessions. Relaxation tapes were used where indicated, but were not used when it was thought that misinterpretation might occur, e.g. when patients had particular concerns about electrical equipment. This was therefore to be a comparatively brief, time-limited intervention; this study therefore contrasted with our normal practice of providing continuing cognitive behaviour therapy, albeit often in a brief attenuated form, until the patient is discharged from psychiatric care to their general practitioner, or, more usually, over an extended follow-up period.

Delusional beliefs

Attempts were made to understand delusional beliefs in collaboration with the patients by examining the ways in which significance had been attached to specific events or circumstances. Alternative explanations were then presented and debated. Relevant evidence was elicited or sought and then discussed to assist in providing credible research-based explanations for patients' individual psychopathological phenomena. With mood-syntonic delusions, e.g. elated mood with grandiosity, or paranoia with anger, the technique of "inference chaining" was mobilised. This involved tracing a delusion to its underlying irrational belief, and examining its associated implications. However, direct confrontation was carefully avoided, and tactical withdrawal used when necessary to retain rapport.

Milton et al., (1978) showed the importance of belief modification as opposed to confrontation. It is certainly clear that any form of confrontation, no matter how communicated, to the deluded schizophrenic, appears to further entrench and exacerbate delusional intensity and distress. When simple reality testing was distressing or unsuccessful, "peripheral questioning" would be used which would not directly challenge the basis of the delusion, but merely assist the patient in gathering information concerning related issues. Socratic questioning

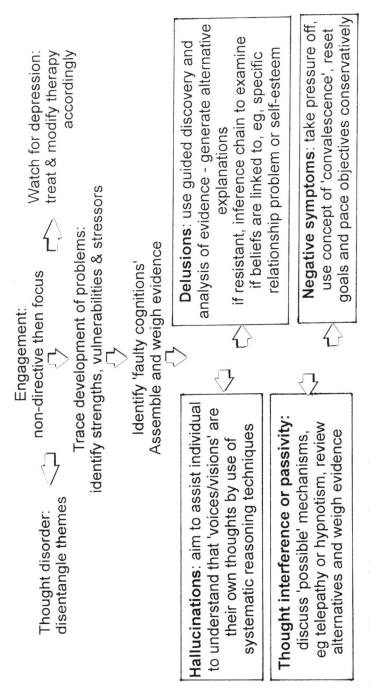

Figure 4.1   Cognitive behaviour therapy of schizophrenia : general principles.

(exploring without preconceptions) was used to gently help the patient to, for example, explore the implications of the delusion if it were to be true (Turkington et al., in press).

Emotional and behavioural reactions to the delusion often exacerbate and maintain the delusion. Such reactions involve anxiety and anger in relation to paranoid delusions, linked to social withdrawal. This means that the patient with the delusion has very little chance of testing it out in the real world. Cognitive behaviour therapy can focus on reduction in anxiety and anger and in behavioural homework so that beliefs can be tested out. (This work would normally be done with the help of the community key worker and team but this was not possible in this study where assessors and managing teams remained blind to treatment group.) Schemas linked to delusions most often relate to specialness and approval and work underneath the level of delusion at the schema level can be undertaken, allowing some gradual improvement in some patients in delusional intensity and related impact. However, it was clear that as some delusions improved, whether by using psychopharmacological treatments or cognitive behaviour therapy techniques, depression could begin to emerge. This tended to be the case when a delusion had been triggered by a major life event in which a key personal schema had been traumatised. This led to the delusion being important in preserving self-esteem. Standard cognitive behaviour therapy approaches for the treatment of depression were used and these generally allowed alternative and more secure methods of maintaining self-esteem to develop.

The comparison of delusions of control with commonly held cultural beliefs in supernatural forces, e.g. psychokinesis, allowed rational argument to be used with these by examining the scientific evidence, or lack of it, in relation to such phenomena. Simple homework assignments were set to investigate delusional beliefs and delusions of reference. Diaries or detailed recall allowed the identification of precipitating factors associated with hallucinations or delusional beliefs.

Thought-disordered speech

Harrow and Prosen (1978) examined the significance of the content of thought-disordered speech in schizophrenia. Their results demonstrated intermingling of emotionally pertinent themes in 80% but the presence of disordered logic in only 24% (7% to a severe degree). The task of the cognitive therapist when faced with a seemingly unintelligible discourse is to disentangle the most emotionally pertinent themes and to help the patient to focus on these sequentially, using thought linkage techniques and then to adopt a problem-solving, information-gathering and reality testing approach (Turkington and Kingdon, 1991). Clarification of themes was done by reviewing notes or audio or videotapes of sessions. Cognitive behaviour therapy with schizophrenic thought disorder could be hard work for both therapist and patient and sessions tended to be frequent but brief (approximately 20 minutes on average).

Voices or visions

Many patients with schizophrenic hallucinations spend large proportions of their time distressed and disturbed by these, whose origin and rationale they have not explored. Where patients found it difficult to understand the origin of their hallucinations or have delusional beliefs in relation to them, the technique of critical collaborative analysis (Kingdon and Turkington, 1994) was used in clarification: techniques of reality-testing of hallucinations can establish the uniqueness of the phenomena to the patients themselves, i.e. that the hallucinations are not audible or visible to others. A gentle questioning approach during sessions would be supported by behavioural experiments, for example, looking for the origin of the voice or vision and asking others whom they trust if they could hear the voice or see the "vision". If a voice does not occur when others are present, then making a tape recording when the voice is running and then playing it back can lead to the development of a number of possible explanations as to the origins and nature of it. A collaborative assessment was then made that the "voice" or "vision" might be coming from within, rather than from outside, their own minds. Explanations that were given for this happening included consideration of evidence that hallucinatory phenomena can be related to stressful circumstances, such as deprivation states. Patients often tend to favour parapsychological and mystical explanations, though one of the explanations that voices can be caused by the effects of stress on a vulnerable individual and that voices can be heard in the normal population when extremely stressed, can lead to some partial acceptance of the role of stress in the initiation and maintenance of the voices. The use of rational responses for voices, i.e. treating voices as classical Beckian automatic thoughts has been described (Turkington and Kingdon, 1996: Chadwick et al., 1996). This means that voices are viewed as thoughts which arise spontaneously in a person's mind which are usually negative in content or implication. Acceptance that the voice or vision is internally rather than externally generated can pave the way for improved compliance with medication and with other techniques aimed at voice reduction.

The nature of the voice content is often a mixture of obsessional and depressive themes and simply questioning the validity and belief in what the voice is saying can lead to the generation of more appropriate rational responses. These rational responses could be placed on a tape for the patient to listen to while the voices are running. Initially this sometimes led to cognitive dissonance in that voices initially flare up and this needed to be handled carefully, but thereafter if the patient could persist, they often became less intense and less frequent. It must be stressed however, that for all of these techniques to be maximally beneficial, they need to be applied in a skilled way congruent to the formulation of the patient's problems and circumstances. The approaches described seemed to be acceptable to patients and have helped many of them to start to understand the nature of their voices and to develop strategies to exert some control of voice intensity and frequency. Derogatory voices can become less troublesome and there can be marked effects on the emotional and behavioural reactions to the voices, which are usually exacerbating and maintaining factors.

Negative symptoms

Approaches to negative symptoms (Turkington and Kingdon, 1996) initially focused on drug resistant positive symptoms, as described above. This allowed secondary negative symptoms (Andreasen, 1989) to gradually improve. Gentle activity scheduling with mastery and pleasure recording, could then start to assist with lowered drive and poor self-care. (Again, this work, as with so many of the other techniques described, would normally benefit from input from the community key worker). Recognition and treatment of co-existing depression and neuroleptic related side effects, could make an impact on some cases of suspected blunting and alogia but also the development of a relaxed relationship with the therapist often uncovered reserves of humour and responsiveness in the patient hitherto submerged. Hogg (1996) describes the importance of also linking to social skills training.

Fears of mental degeneration, violence or madness itself, were "decatastrophised" with patients, families and their professional carers. The patient confronted by a "mystifying psychotic world" develops catastrophic cognitions due to the cultural context in which these symptoms occur. Anxiety stimulated by anxiogenic cognitions about "being locked up", untreatability and progressive deterioration, actively exacerbate some psychotic symptoms, for example, hallucinations (Slade, 1973). Depressogenic cognitions of hopelessness and despair lead not only to deterioration in mood, but often to suicidal ideation. Birchwood et al., (1993) reviewed incidence figures showing 20% of patients to be depressed during the acute episode and up to 65% in those with chronic illness. This mixture of anxious and depressive cognitions in a setting of psychotic deterioration and nihilistic beliefs is one in which compliance with neuroleptic and other treatments is almost uniformly poor. 75% of those with first episode schizophrenia show poor compliance (Kissling, 1992) and up to 50% of patients discharged from hospital fail to take even 75% of the medication prescribed (Buchanan, 1992). The cognitive behaviour therapy techniques were therefore also used to enhance compliance with neuroleptic medication to synergistically treat acute symptomatology and prevent relapse.

Befriending group

The control group were provided with regular therapist contact, in addition to the normal management provided by their treatment team. The intention was to control for time and for non-specific components of therapist contact. So that assessors, families, and the treatment team would remain blind to the randomisation, both controls and their families were interviewed by the author for a similar period and at similar intervals of time to the cognitive behaviour therapy group. The control interviews consisted for the most part of non-directive discussion around neutral topics, such as the patient's interests and domestic matters. However, a specifically medical explanation was prepared for use where patients, particularly those with pre-existing paranoid ideas, and families found difficulty in accepting a doctor who avoided discussing medical matters with them. For this purpose, a standard description and explanation of schizophrenia was drawn up; this was circulated to senior psychiatric colleagues for validation, and was then used in discussions with patients, where appropriate. If questions about leave arrangements, medication, etc. were raised, the patient was referred to the appropriate treatment team. Occasionally, where this was appropriate to maintain rapport, messages were passed to the team by the interviewer.

Results of pilot study

Comparison of changes in global Comprehensive Psychopathology Rating Scale scores significantly favoured the cognitive behaviour therapy group. Overall CPRS scores reduced in both groups but there was no significant difference between them. Hospital stay over the six-month period from the commencement of therapy was less in the cognitive behaviour therapy group (mean: 4.8:10.2 weeks) but this did not reach significant levels. These results were sufficiently promising for a larger study to be established in patients who have persistent positive symptoms, and this study is proceeding.

FOLLOW-UP STUDY

In 1991, we published the results of a follow-up of 64 patients collected and treated over a period of five years who ranged from long-stay hospital patients to those experiencing a first episode managed using cognitive behaviour therapy (Kingdon and Turkington, 1991). They have now been followed prospectively over at least a further five years. The styles of therapy used with four themes, which have been identified, are outlined, and outcome for the whole group and for those managed throughout using cognitive behaviour therapy are described. The themes described are compared with recent research into syndromes of schizophrenia.

These patients were a broadly representative sample from an area of average morbidity. They consisted of patients divided between two consultants who took up posts in Bassetlaw, North Nottinghamshire (population 102 000) in 1984 and subsequent referrals thereafter. There is no evidence of any systematic bias affecting this sample; few patients were referred outside or into the district during the period studied. The service had previously been provided from a large mental hospital sited 35 miles away from Bassetlaw. It was replaced by a network of facilities (Groves, 1990) including an admission ward on a District General Hospital site, day hospital and accommodation for people with severe mental illness ranging from intensively nursed houses to support in their own homes (Kingdon et al., 1991). A multidisciplinary mental health team works with local authority and voluntary agencies, etc, in providing support and treatment. The team were trained informally and with some formal sessions in the appropriate use of cognitive behaviour therapy with their caseload.

All patients were traced through hospital and GP records at both five and ten years; a small number had moved outside the district but most were in it or nearby, i.e. there had not been a substantial drift to urban centres or elsewhere. Information about their current situation was obtained if they were in contact with services. When they were not, their situation at the most recent contact with health services is detailed; all were currently registered with general practitioners and had seen them or other health workers within one year of the follow-up. Two were current acute inpatients, three were residents in the district's hospital hostels which provide rehabilitation and continuing care and six were in some form of supported accommodation. Three had died; there had been no verdicts of suicide, but one died of orphenadrine toxicity after being out for an evening drinking with friends. He had a history of abusing drugs, including procyclidine, and it was thought that he had been abusing the orphenadrine. The other two died of heart failure and a malignant melanoma. None were currently in prison or homeless; one patient had been convicted of indecent assault and spent time in a local locked ward and one was convicted of theft and motor vehicle offences and may have spent a short period in prison for these offences.

CLINICAL THEMES

Examination of the casenotes and data suggested that four groups with similar characteristics—clinical themes—emerged within the sample. The groups differed in a number of characteristics and had been managed according to these characteristics. These groups are described for their heuristic value but, as yet, are speculative and represent only a clinical impression. Discussion about them at a series of workshops with mental health workers has confirmed that they are themes which are recognisable in a wide variety of clinical settings. The terms used to describe them are obsessional psychosis, drug-related psychosis, anxiety psychosis and sensitivity disorder.

Obsessional psychosis

A small number of patients appeared to be suffering from symptoms which represented misattribution of thoughts, such as hallucinations, because the nature of those thoughts was experienced as profoundly distasteful or distressing and consequently they seemed to be rejected as their own thoughts; "I could not possibly think something as obscene or aggressive as that...". This seems closely related to a definition of obsession; which are ideas, thoughts or images which are involuntarily produced (as are hallucinations), occurring recurrently and persistently and experienced as being senseless and repugnant (as are the type of hallucinations occurring in this group) but unlike obsessions, patients do not recognise hallucinations as products of their own minds. The nature of the hallucinations involved is that they have abusive, violent or sexual content and are in the second person, e.g. "you are a child molester", or they command the person to do unpleasant things, e.g. "kill yourself" or "kill that child". They are repetitive and distressing, and fluctuating insight is present. Sometimes they are associated with trauma, e.g. sexual abuse; the voice of the perpetrator may be heard and resisted because of the associated distress. On other occasions, major depression may have precipitated hallucinations, or suicidal and depressive thoughts, which have become persistent either because of the traumatic effect that the thoughts themselves had or simply that the patient resists suicidal ideas, e.g. where their religion precludes such actions, which become insistent and hallucinatory in quality. The hallucinations are sensed as alien but seem essentially to be a misunderstanding of "automatic thoughts".

Management followed similar lines to that described above. It has been directed at reattributing hallucinations from external phenomena to lead to acceptance by the patient that they are misidentified thoughts and so internally generated (Fig. 4.2). Some simple reality testing may be necessary to establish with the person that their "voices" are their own thoughts. First they are asked if others can hear their voices, which they usually perceive as spoken clearly if not loudly. Usually they are aware that this is not the case and so explanations as to why this might be the case are explored. Patients in this group may have their own explanation for this but usually, when it is discussed, they also find it puzzling. If they have explanations, these are explored and the evidence for and against their explanation weighed. Following this, an alternative explanation is developed. This requires discussion of the nature and possible content of "automatic thoughts", i.e. that the thoughts entering individuals minds can be bizarre,

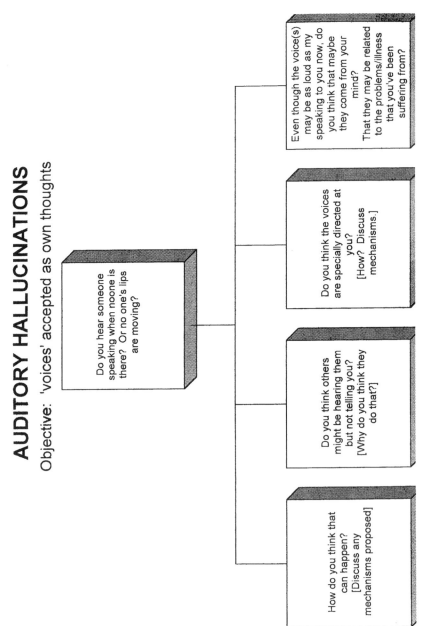

Figure 4.2 Exploration of auditory hallucinations.

sexual and violent, may be worsened by mental health problems, but that usually such thoughts are simply disregarded. Because they have such thoughts, this does not mean that they are evil or perverted. The illness that they have is recognised as causing hallucinations as are a variety of stressful circumstances and examples of these are described (Kingdon and Turkington, 1994). Undermining the "omnipotence of the voices" (Chadwick and Birchwood, 1994) can markedly reduce the distress experienced and subsequently, in combination with medication, the frequency of the hallucinations themselves. It may be asserted that because a thought comes into a person's mind this does not mean that an action must ensue, i.e. because they think "kill yourself" they do not have to act upon it. The evidence that they have not acted on such thoughts, as is the case with this group (see below under drug-related psychosis), can be cited to substantiate this. Response to medication seems variable (although in one case, clomipramine proved dramatically effective). Modified "exposure" techniques whereby the content is gently explored or "focusing" (Bentall, Haddock and Slade, 1994), may have a role.

Drug-related psychosis

A number of patients in the study had used hallucinogenics, especially amphetamines, LSD, and "ecstasy", prior to initial presentation. Their first admission was usually in the context of a drug-induced psychosis when there was clear evidence of drug abuse on urine sampling. Frequently the drug abuse continued in the early months, if not years of their illness, but nevertheless a diagnosis had been made of schizophrenia in the confirmed absence of such abuse. However, the psychotic symptoms were usually direct reproductions of those occurring when they had been using drugs. These symptoms were often paranoid in nature, sometimes directly related to fear about the consequences of taking illicit substances, e.g. "the Columbian mafia are after me", "my food or drinks are being spiked with drugs", "people who use drugs are reading my thoughts through the television". Diagnosis was frequently difficult and delayed. It was complicated by evidence of personality disorder—rebellion against parents and authority figures seemed common. Families were frequently disrupted and relationships fraught with levels of critical expressed emotion often high. Onset occurred at the time of peak onset of schizophrenia, i.e. mid-teens to early twenties. Opiates did not seem to have been used commonly by the group, however cannabis frequently had been. Excessive use of cannabis may have contributed to onset of symptoms or been a factor in relapse but in general terms it seemed to be used as a non-specific relaxant, similar to alcohol, and it was the use of more potent hallucinogenics which precipitated the initial presentation.

Initial stages of management were difficult. Compliance with treatment—

medication, admission to hospital and other psychosocial management—was generally poor, in the early stages at least. Early diagnosis would seem to be important and erring on the side of caution necessary, if only to ensure that families had support and were provided with accessible services when crises arose. The involvement of a carer needed to be proactive and patient. Modifying high expressed emotion directed towards the patient and formal carers, and also by the patient towards their parents and formal carers, was a focus. Compliance management needed to be flexible with full information being given. Collaborative negotiation of medication and other strategies meant that compromises were often necessary, e.g. "I'd like you to take this amount of medication but if you don't want to, maybe build it up slowly and see what works for you ...". A formulation would be developed which took into account the drug experiences which were usually accepted as having been noxious and then a course of management agreed, and then reassessed as progress or lack of it occurred. Hallucinations and paranoid symptoms were often presented as intrusive memories of the drug experience and directly related back to them to restrict delusional elaboration.

Anxiety psychosis

Some patients presented with acute onset which seemed to be stress-related, e.g. work pressure. A prodromal period of increasing anxiety and perplexity was succeeded often quite abruptly by delusional crystallisation. A delusional perception or conclusion arising from specific thoughts "explained" what was happening to them and this produced relief and conviction in the delusional idea. Onset was at varying ages and not just in the peak period around the late teens and twenties. Frequently the patient was relatively isolated, either through geography—family and friends were living distant from them or they simply had few personal contacts, e.g. through death of close relatives—or personally, they might be living with family but not communicate with them, the fears and concerns that they had.

Early response tended to be good, when discussion began near the commencement of the illness. It was more difficult when beliefs were more entrenched through being held for longer periods of time. Secondary factors complicated recovery also, i.e. the effects of stigmatisation which could reinforce paranoid beliefs and enhance the reduction in self-esteem which made the acceptance of error and depression more likely. Further episodes could develop in response to stress but these were often short-lived.

Management of anxiety psychosis involved tracing the antecedents of the initial episode even when this had been many years before. The process of developing a clear picture of the precipitating factors occurring allowed the construction of a rationale which explained the disorder to the patient in a way which provided an alternative to the delusional explanation that they had developed and which seemed so convincing and such a relief to them initially. An explanation of a vulnerability–stress model of schizophrenia was used in support of this. In a subgroup of patients with delusions for which tracing antecedents did not work, inference chaining sometimes proved useful. This was particularly the situation with some patients with grandiose delusions. The technique involved asking the patient what it meant, or what would be the consequences for them, if their belief were accepted by others. The response varied but could then be followed through further to identify ways in which the delusions might be compensating for something they felt was lacking in their life, e.g. respect, and then trying to specify as precisely as possible the nature of that lack, e.g. respect from whom? Then alternative ways of achieving that end, e.g. being respected by family members, could be discussed, effectively bypassing the delusional system which tended to reduce its interference in their lives.

When they occurred, hallucinations were reality-tested and coping strategies introduced. Thought disorder could seriously disrupt therapy but by focusing on themes sequentially and detecting which were currently causing greatest concern, it was possible to develop meaningful communication. Metaphor was used at times and simply imprecise, if not erroneous, terminology could interfere with discussion such that when a term was used in a way that the therapist could not understand, the person was interrupted to clarify meaning.

Sensitivity disorder

Finally, and possibly at the other end of the spectrum from anxiety psychosis, was a group of patients who seemed extremely sensitive to relatively minor stressors, e.g. starting work, breaking up with a girlfriend or going to university. Patients presented with gradual onset in their teens or early twenties although there might be an acute illness leading to contact with services. They tended to be relatively shy and socially inexperienced. Expressed emotion amongst parents tended to involve overprotection or criticism which tended not to be particularly overt. Positive symptoms arose intermittently and ideas or delusions of reference, thought broadcasting and paranoid ideation seemed relatively frequent but most prominent were negative symptoms.

Management of sensitivity disorder involved setting realistic goals for the patient and carer to reduce perceptions of stress in the first instance. Realistic activity scheduling, which meant accepting the degree of disability and then slowly aiming to modify it, was introduced. When patients spent time up at night and sleeping in the day, this was explored to see whether this was a protective strategy against over-stimulation. Social skills and assertiveness were developed in an informal way. Delusions of reference were managed using diaries to record specific incidents when the patient thought they were being referred to on TV or radio. Where diary keeping was difficult, specific recall was used to isolate precise comments heard and alternatives discussed. Paranoid ideas were explored and beliefs tested out. Thought interference was discussed as telepathy, experimental evidence which disputes the possibility of transmission of complex thoughts evaluated and alternative explanations provided.

CLINICAL SUBGROUPS

Review of the frequency of the groups in the 64 patients produced the following tentative results: obsessional psychosis—1–2%; drug-related psychosis—7%; anxiety psychosis—50–55%; sensitivity disorder—40–45%. (The low frequency of obsessional psychosis contrasted with later clinical experience and it may be that this sample has underestimated its frequency.)

Research to differentiate schizophrenia into themes and subgroups has tended to concentrate on symptom groupings. Other factors have not usually been included but may be relevant, as proposed here, e.g. sociodemographic factors (e.g. age and sex), mode of onset (gradual or abrupt) or type of precipitant, i.e. major life event, minor life stress or use of hallucinogenics. Traditional classification of schizophrenia was into hebephrenia, paranoid, catatonic and undifferentiated groups although Liddle and Barnes (1990) have proposed "reality distortion", "disorganisation" and "psychomotor poverty" on the basis of symptom clusters. One new approach by Harvey et al. (1996) proposed four behavioural syndromes of schizophrenia. These four behavioural syndromes are: "thought disturbance", "social withdrawal", "depressed behaviour" and "antisocial behaviour". A review of correlations between symptoms and these factors suggest that there may be a correspondence between them and the classification proposed here. that is between thought disturbance and anxiety "anxiety psychosis", "social withdrawal" and "sensitivity disorder", "depressed behaviour" and "obsessional psychosis" and "antisocial behaviour" and "drug- related psychosis". But this needs further investigation to see whether superficial similarities are substantiated.

PATTERNS OF ILLNESS

The outcome of the 64 patients is illustrated in Fig. 4.3 and that of the 15 with first episode between 1984 and 1989 who were managed in that

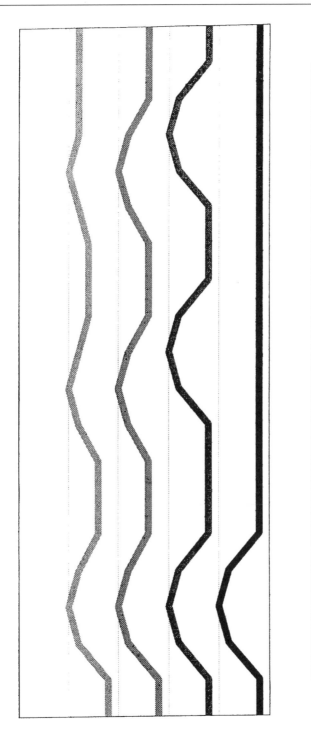

■ Course 1 (16%) ■ Course 2 (42%) ■ Course 3 (26%) ■ Course 4 (16%)

Figure 4.3 Five-year course of illness classified as in Watt et al. (1983) in 64 CBT treated patients.

episode (and subsequent episodes when they were still resident in the district) using cognitive behaviour therapy, in Fig. 4.4. The patterns illustrated (taken from Watt et al., 1983) depict four courses of illness:

1. single episode with return to premorbid functioning
2. more than one episode with return to premorbid functioning
3. one or more episode but without full return to level of premorbid functioning
4. repeated episodes without full return to level of premorbid functioning after first episode and with further deterioration after subsequent ones.

Direct comparison with other samples is fraught with problems: Johnstone et al., (1991) traced 532 patients over a 3–15 year period: 81 were untraceable and 69 had died: 40 naturally; 4 uncertain: 24 (4.3% of the total) unnatural: 7 suicide; 15 open; 2 no inquest. Prudo and Blum (1987) report a five year follow-up of 100 patients from the London Centre of the International Pilot Study of Schizophrenia, aged 16–44 years old, and excluding "chronic patients". Outcome for the 88 patients traced: 6 had died of whom 5 were suicides. Course 1. 19%—no further episode; no residual symptoms; Course 2. 30%—further episodes; time in episode less than 1 year; Course 3. 10%—1–2.5 years in episode; Course 4. 41%—more than 2.5 years (including deceased). Watt et al., (1983) in Aylesbury followed up 121 patients including 48 first admissions. Outcome in 107 patients traced was 8 died (number of suicides not given) Course 1. (as described by Shepherd) 16% and 23% (1st admission group); Course 2. 32% and 35%; Course 3. 9% and 8%; Course 4. 43% and 33%. Whilst comparisons are difficult, the group described above as a whole seem to have made at least acceptable progress. The first episode group have now had at least a 5 year follow up and are continuing to do well. A randomised controlled study of CT in early schizophrenia (the "SOCRATES" study funded by the Medical Research Council and the NHS) is now proceeding.

DISCUSSION

Evaluation of cognitive behaviour therapy in schizophrenia is still in its early phases but positive results are emerging from controlled studies. The long-term outcome looks promising especially when patients are managed from first episode. The clinical themes described here are speculative but may be useful in management and training. We intend to use data from studies currently proceeding to assess the validity, or otherwise, of these themes and will revise or refine them further. They may assist us to differentiate "schizophrenia" into groups, provide us with terms which are more acceptable and less stigmatising for patients, and most of all cost-effective techniques to use for distressing and disabling symptoms.

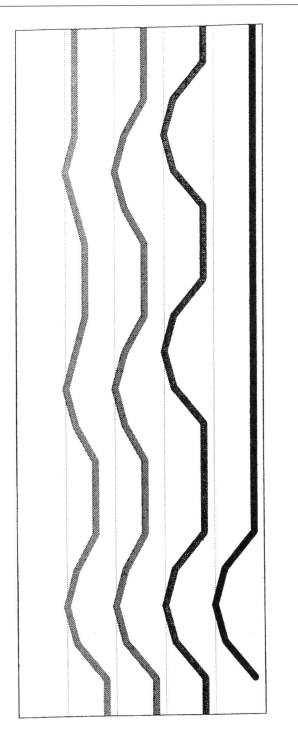

Figure 4.4 Five-year course of illness 15 CBT treated first-episode patients.

ACKNOWLEDGEMENTS

Acknowledgements are due to Carolyn John, Paul Rowlands, and Michael Hopegill who assisted with the pilot study.

REFERENCES

Alford, B.A. and Beck, A.T. (1994) Cognitive therapy of delusional beliefs. *Behaviour Research and Therapy* **32**(3), 369–380.

Andreasen, N.C. (1989) Neural mechanisms of negative symptoms. *British Journal of Psychiatry*, **155** (Supp. 7), 93–98.

Asberg, M., Montgomery, S.A., Perris, C., Schalling, D. and Sedvall, G. (1978) The comprehensive psychopathological psychological rating scale. *Acta Psychiatrica Scandinavica Suppl.* **271**, 5–27.

Beck, A.T. (1952) Successful out-patient psychotherapy of a chronic schizophrenic with a delusion based on borrowed guilt. *Psychiatry* **15**, 305–312

Bentall, R, Haddock, G and Slade, P. (1994) Cognitive behavior therapy for persistent auditory hallucinations. *Behavior Therapy,* **25**, 51–66.

Birchwood, M., Smith, J., MacMillan F., et al., (1989) Predicting relapse in schizophrenia: the development and implementation of an early signs monitoring system using patients and families as observers. *Psychological Medicine,* **19**, 649–656.

Birchwood, M., Mason R., Macmillan, F. and Healy, J. (1993) Depression demoralisation and control over psychotic illness: A comparison of depressed and non-depressed patients with a chronic psychosis. *Psychological Medicine,* **23**, 387–395.

Brenner, H.D., Hodel, B. and Roper, V. (1990) Integrated cognitive and behavioural interventions in the treatment of schizophrenia. *Psychological Rehabilitation Journal,* **13**(3), 41–43.

Buchanan, A. (1992) A two year prospective study of treatment compliance in patients with schizophrenia. *Psychological Medicine,* **22**, 787–797.

Chadwick, D and Birchwood, M. (1994) The omnipotence of voices. A cognitive approach to auditory hallucinations. *British Journal of Psychiatry,* **164**, 190–201.

Drury, V. (1994) Recovery from acute psychosis. In Birchwood, M. and Tarrier, N., Eds., *Psychological Management of Schizophrenia*. Chichester: Wiley.

Fowler, D., Garety, P.A. and Kuipers, L. (1995) *Cognitive Behaviour Therapy for People with Psychosis: a Clinical Handbook*. Chichester: Wiley.

Garety, P.A., Kuipers, L., Fowler, D., Chamberlain, F. and Dunn, G. (1994) Cognitive behaviour therapy for drug resistant psychosis. *British Journal of Medical Psychology,* **67**, 259–271.

Groves, T. (1990) After the asylums: the local picture. *British Medical Journal,* **300**, 1128–1130.

Haddock, G., Bentall, R.P. and Slade, P.D. (1993) Psychological treatment of auditory hallucinations: Two case studies. *Behavioural and Cognitive Psychotherapy,* **21**, 335–346.

Haddock, G., Bentall, R.P. and Slade, P.D. (1996) Psychological treatment of auditory hallucinations: Focusing or distraction? In Haddock, G. and Slade, P.D. Eds. *Cognitive Behavioural Interventions with Psychotic Disorders*. London, Routledge.

Harrow, M. and Prosen, M. (1978) Intermingling and disordered logic as influences on schizophrenic thought disorders. *Archives of General Psychiatry,* **35**, 1213–1218.

Harvey, C.A., Curson, D.A., Pantelis, C., Taylor, J. and Barnes, T.R.E. (1996) Four behavioural syndromes of schizophrenia. *British Journal of Psychiatry*, **168**, 562–570.

Hogg, L. (1996) Psychological treatments for negative symptoms. In *Cognitive Behavioural Interventions with Psychotic Disorders*. In Haddock, G. and Slade, P.D., Eds, London, Routledge.

Johnstone, E. et al., (1991) Disabilities and circumstances of schizophrenic patients— a follow-up study. *British Journal of Psychiatry*, **159** (suppl 13), 38–39.

Kemp, R. Hayward, P., Applewhaite G., Everitt, B. and David, A. (1996) Compliance therapy in psychotic patients: randomised controlled trial. *British Medical Journal*, **312**, 345–349.

Kingdon, D.G. and Turkington, D. (1991) Preliminary report: the use of cognitive behavioural techniques with a normalizing rationale in schizophrenia. *Journal of Nervous and Mental Diseases*, **179**, 207–211.

Kingdon, D.G. and Turkington, D. (1994) *Cognitive-Behavioral Therapy of Schizophrenia*. New York: Guilford Press and London: Lawrence Erlbaum.

Kingdon, D.G., Turkington, D., Malcolm, K., et al., (1991) Replacing the mental hospital: community provision for a district's chronically psychiatrically disabled in domestic environments. *British Journal of Psychiatry*, **158**, 113–116.

Kissling, W. (1992) Ideal and reality of neuroleptic relapse prevention. *British Journal of Psychiatry*, **161** (Suppl. 18), 133–139.

Liddle, P. and Barnes, T.R.E. (1990) Syndromes of chronic schizophrenia. *British Journal of Psychiatry*, **157**, 558–561.

Milton, F., Patwa, V.K. and Hafner, R.J. (1978) Confrontation vs belief modification in persistently deluded patients. *British Journal of Psychology*, **51**, 127–130

Prudo, R. and Blum, H.M. (1987) Five year outcome and prognosis in schizophrenia: A report from the London Field Research Centre of the International Pilot Study of Schizophrenia. *British Journal of Psychiatry* **150**, 345–354.

Romme, M.A.J., Honig, A., Noordhoorn, E.O. and Escher, A.D.M.A.C. (1992) Coping with hearing voices, an emancipatory approach. *British Journal of Psychiatry* **160**, 99–103.

Slade, P.D. (1973) The psychological investigation and treatment of auditory hallucinations: a second case report. *British Journal of Medical Psychology*, **46**, 293–296.

Tarrier, N., Beckett, N., Harwood, S., Baker, A., Yusupoff, L. and Ugarteburu, I. (1993) A trial of two cognitive–behavioural methods of treating drug–resistant residual symptoms in schizophrenia patients: I. Outcome. *British Journal of Psychiatry*, **162**, 524–532.

Turkington, D. and Kingdon, D.G. (1991) Ordering thoughts in thought disorder. *British Journal of Psychiatry*, **159**, 160–161.

Turkington, D. and Kingdon, D.G. (1996) Using a normalising rationale in the treatment of schizophrenic patients. In Haddock, G. and Slade, P.D. Eds *Cognitive Behavioural Interventions with Psychotic Disorders*. London: Routledge.

Turkington, D., John, C.H., Siddle, R., Ward, D. and Birmingham, L. (in press) Cognitive therapy in the treatment of drug-resistant delusional disorder. *Clinical Psychology and Psychotherapy*.

Watt, D.C., Katz, K. and Shepherd, M. (1983) The natural history of schizophrenia: a five year prospective follow-up of a representative sample of schizophrenics by means of a standardized clinical and social assessment. *Psychological Medicine*, **13**, 663–70.

World Health Organization. (1989) *International Classification of Diseases 10th Edition* (draft 1989 version) Geneva: WHO.

Chapter 5

DEPRESSION AND SUICIDAL THINKING IN PSYCHOSIS: A COGNITIVE APPROACH

Max Birchwood and Zaffer Iqbal

INTRODUCTION

The disparity between psychotic illness and depression has, until recently, remained a fundamental distinction in the psychiatric and psychological understanding and treatment of these mental disorders. This divide can be charted through the evolution of the research and comprehension of the mechanisms behind the onset and recovery models of either disorder. The "medical model" resulted in the utilisation of neuroleptic treatments to combat and regulate schizophrenic pathology, widely acknowledged as a means of controlling the disorder in many patients (Davis and Casper, 1977; Bennie, 1985). Psychological models of depression are well developed and propose that dysfunctional thinking and perception raise the individual's vulnerability to depression. Hence the use of cognitive therapy (Beck, 1967; Beck, Hollon and Young, 1985) which is reported to be twice as effective in preventing relapse in depressives than antidepressant use alone (Williams, 1989).

Outcome and Innovation in Psychological Treatment of Schizophrenia. Edited by T. Wykes, N. Tarrier and S. Lewis.
© 1998 John Wiley & Sons Ltd

The development of assessment instruments have allowed clinicians to evaluate the potential overlap between psychosis and depression (Leff, 1990). Hence, the prevalence of depression in psychosis received acknowledgement and incorporation into diagnostic regimens, primarily as schizo-affective disorder (DSM-III) and more recently as "post schizophrenic depression" (ICD-10). Depression is now regarded as an integral part of the course of psychotic illness (Siris, 1991) and a possible precursor to suicide if associated with hopelessness (Drake and Cotton, 1986).

DEPRESSION IN PSYCHOSIS

Prevalence of comorbidity

The prevalence of depression in psychosis ranges from 22% to 75% depending upon the criteria used (Koreen, Siris, Chakos, Alvir, Mayerhoff and Lieberman, 1993). Johnson (1981) reports 53% of schizophrenics maintained on neuroleptic medication at follow-up experienced a depressive episode. Siris (1991, 1995) outlines over 30 studies investigating depression in schizophrenia and reports varying incidence rates, from as little as 7% and to a maximum of 65%, although the most frequently recorded figure is 25% (see Table 5.1). This diversity is most commonly attributed to the numerous diagnostic criteria available to assess symptoms and the variations in patient environment.

Depression as intrinsic to psychosis

The term "intrinsic" suggests that the depression is an essential aspect of the syndrome of positive symptoms of schizophrenia. As such, depressive symptoms should be discernible at one or more stages during the course of an acute psychotic episode. Powerful evidence is available from the literature in support of the intrinsic depression theory. It is argued that a relationship between positive symptoms and depression is upheld by studies where depression has been observed prior to (Hirsch and Jolley, 1989), during (Knight and Hirsch, 1981) and following (i.e. "postpsychotic depression"; McGlashan and Carpenter, 1976) the onset of acute psychosis.

Leff (1990) argues that the hierarchical schema of symptoms developed by Foulds and Bedford (1975) implies that as part of the psychosis, an individual should also display "symptoms of affective psychoses", e.g. grandiose delusions, "symptoms of neurotic disorder", e.g. phobic anxiety, and "non-specific psychological symptoms", e.g. irritability (see Figure 5.1). Thus, a schizophrenic patient at level 4 should also display "symptoms of affective psychoses", "symptoms of neurotic disorder" and "non-specific psychological symptoms", i.e. levels 3, 2 and 1 respectively. Conversely,

Table 5.1 Studies reporting incidence of secondary depression in cases of schizophrenia (after Siris, 1995)

Study (n)	Psychosis definition	Definition of postpsychotic interval	Depression definition	Percentage depressed
Roy (1981) (n = 100)	DSM III for schizophrenia	4–10 years	Treatment with ECT or antidepressants	39
Van Putten (1978) (n = 94)	Newly admitted patients with Feigner criteria for schizophrenia	Length of acute hospital stay	Increase in BPRS depression scale	38
Leff et al. (1988) (n = 31)	Newly admitted patients with PSE/CATEGO definition of schizophrenia	Until discharged or until six months	Depressed mood as assessed by PSE	45
Birchwood et al. (1993) (n = 49)	CATEGO class "s" for schizophrenia	Randomly selected from outpatient depot for treatment clinic	Score of at least 15 on BDI	29
Harrow et al. (1994) (n = 54)	Research Diagnostic Criteria (RDC) for schizophrenia	Prevalence during 1 year preceding follow-up interview	Presence of a full depressive syndrome by RDC	37

Green, Nuechterlein, Ventura and Mintz (1990) investigated the relationship between psychotic symptoms and depression at two-weekly periods over the course of one year. Although the resultant data indicates that depressive pathology occurs prior to the onset of positive symptoms, no significant temporal relationship existed for the onset of depression over the span of the psychotic episode. The findings suggest that recovery from acute psychosis is not the sole factor determining the onset of depression. Finally, Johnson (1981) argues that depression emergent following psychosis may be a distinct entity from that surrounding the acute stage of the illness. This is particularly relevant as depressive symptoms do emerge in long-term maintained patients without prevailing acute psychosis.

Depression as a dysphoric response to neuroleptics

Various suggestions have been made as to the role of neuroleptic medication in the development of depression in psychosis. A drug-induced syndrome of akinesia has been described, as a "behavioural state of diminished spontaneity characterised by few gestures, unspontaneous

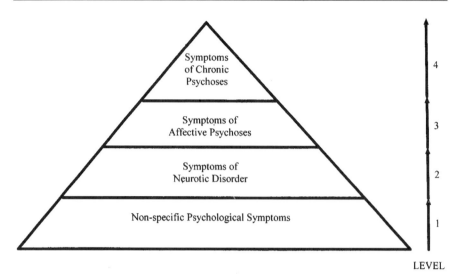

Figure 5.1   The hierarchical schema of symptoms (Foulds and Bedford, 1975)

speech, apathy and difficulty with initiating usual activities" (Rifkin, Quitkin and Klein, 1975), which has a high association with depressive type symptoms. Van Putten and May (1978) suggested that "akinetic" depression may provide a means of distinguishing depression following psychosis from other affective disorders, and reported that antiparkinsonian medication improved the depression. Other side-effects such as anhedonia, where the individual is unable to feel pleasure, akathisia and motor symptoms might also lead to the development of depressive symptoms. However, a ten-year follow-up study by Berrios and Bulbena (1987) refutes the claim that neuroleptic drugs are a causal factor in the onset of depression in psychosis, suggesting that more likely factors were excessive relapse, extent of auditory hallucinations and duration of illness.

Siris (1995) suggests that as neuroleptics block dopamine receptors and dopamine is associated with feelings of pleasure, it is arguable that an anhedonia-type state results. There is acknowledgement that in individual cases, such a "pharmacogenic" depression may develop. However, theories suggesting that depression is a response to neuroleptics are, in most cases, fundamentally flawed. Leff (1990) amongst others, provides results where subjects' depressive symptoms decreased as acute psychotic pathology was combated by the administration of neuroleptic drugs. Furthermore, analyses which differentiate patients on the basis of whether they are/are not depressed do not, in the main, find that neuroleptic therapy is a discriminating variable (Hirsch and Jolley, 1989). Patients receiving neuroleptic treatment are not found to be more depressed than those not receiving such drugs (Berrios and Bulbena, 1987).

Depression as a case of "mistaken identity"

It has been argued that depression in psychosis is an erroneous concept which only arises as the many diagnostic systems employed fail to provide a clear picture of the different disorders. As such, the past lack of consensus for diagnosing schizophrenia (Pope, 1983), the failure to eliminate cases of schizo-affective disorder and the use of heterogeneous populations are some of the factors which may lead to the different explanations. Munro (1987) highlights the diagnostic problem by outlining three "grey areas" where errors occur in the differentiation between affective disorders and schizophrenia: "mistaken identity", as affective and psychotic symptoms can be observed in both disorders; "interbreeds" as some patients have a long-standing mixture of psychotic and affective disorders; and "distinct syndromes" which resemble schizophrenia or affective disorder, e.g. delusional disorder and brief reactive psychosis. Although this argument may provide an answer to the different stated incident rates for depression in psychosis, it is unlikely that diagnostic uncertainty is the whole explanation.

The diagnostic difficulties associated with deciphering depressive symptoms in psychosis from other extraneous variables also extend to the negative symptoms of schizophrenia. (Barnes, Curson, Liddle and Patel, 1989). Recent work suggests that the experienced clinician should have little difficulty in separating the two. Newcomer, Faustman, Yeh and Csernansky (1990) report that depression and negative psycho-pathology can be successfully distinguished through the use of appropriate instruments such as the subscales of the Brief Psychiatric Rating Scale (Overall and Gorham, 1962). Siris (1995) suggests that the clinical feature of "blue mood" is the most likely aspect to allow the diagnostic separation of negative symptoms and depression, as it is generally present in the latter. Finally, Haskins, Shutty and Kellogg (1995) report the development of a reliable tool for the assessment of spontaneous prosody, prosodic repetition and comprehension, and recognition of facial affect, which can aid the clinician's assessment of negative affect, as opposed to depressed mood.

Depression as a reaction to psychosis

Although our understanding of unipolar depression has benefited greatly from the application of cognitive and psycho-social frameworks (Beck, Rush, Shaw and Emery, 1979; Brown and Harris, 1989), such an approach has not been adopted for the study of depression in psychosis. It has been argued that depression following a psychotic illness may be a reaction to the changes associated with the psychosis itself. Individuals experience a radical change in their personal lifestyles and commonly express feelings of alienation and loss of self-esteem. Roy, Thompson and Kennedy (1983) suggest that patients with negative symptoms are at greater risk as these can cause difficulties for the patient in commencing his or her lifestyle, and may also lead to further undesirable life events. Barnes et al., (1989) observed that subjective experiences of deficits in chronic schizophrenia, in areas such as thinking, feeling and perception, were associated with vulnerability to depression. The development of a depressive illness following an acute psychotic phase can be regarded as a sign of "acceptance" of the psychosis, and has been regarded anecdotally as a favourable prognostic sign (Roth, 1970). Comparisons of schizophrenic subjects who had and had not developed depression suggest that the experience of psychosis is a major factor in the onset of depression (Chintalapudi, Kulhara and Avasthi, 1993). Depressed subjects were found to have had a significantly longer duration of the acute psychotic phase, better premorbid adjustment, i.e. good social and sexual adjustment prior to the onset of psychosis, and an excess of stressful life events. Similarly, results from Birchwood, Mason, MacMillan and Healy (1993) show that depression following acute psychosis may be viewed as a psychological response (demoralisation) to an apparently uncontrollable life event (the psychosis) and all its attendant disabilities.

In summary, the nosological confusion surrounding depression in psychosis has hindered its explanation. The intrinsic depression theory does not account for chronic or recurring depression where the commencement of a psychotic episode has not occurred. Depression has not been shown to occur through the use of neuroleptic medication although side-effects such as akinesia and akathisia may contribute. True negative symptoms should be discernible to the careful assessor as distinctly different from depressive pathology. The application of wider research from unipolar depression, specifically cognitive and psycho-social schools of thinking, may allow for a clearer understanding of depression in psychosis. Early work does suggest that the individual perceives his or her psychosis as a traumatic life event which carries many potential disabilities.

SUICIDE IN PSYCHOSIS

Prevalence

Suicide is regarded as one of the most important problems in the mental health field at the present time. Parasuicidal risk in psychosis averages 20–30% (Birchwood and Preston, 1991; Roy, 1986). Completed suicide occurs in approximately 10% of cases of schizophrenia (Department of Health, 1992). The extent of the problem is such that 3800 schizophrenia sufferers committed suicide in the USA in one year alone (Jones, Stein, Stanley, Guido, Winchell and Stanley, 1994). The prevalence of suicidal thinking in one long-term follow-up study was 40% (MacGlashan, 1984).

For these and other reasons, the Health of the Nation initiative (Department of Health, 1992) sets a national target to reduce the rate of all suicides by at least one third by the year 2000.

PREDICTING SUICIDE

The difficulty of risk assessment is acknowledged by clinicians and researchers alike (Jenkins, Griffiths and Wylie, 1994). In schizophrenia, as in unipolar depression, suicide attempts, age and gender are indicators of future suicide. For example, a study by Westermeyer, Harrow and Marengo (1991) followed up over 550 patients, with either psychotic or nonpsychotic disorders, over a period of approximately 4 years. The sample was relatively young (mean age = 23 years) and slightly more than half of the subjects were first-admission patients. The results clearly indicated a significantly higher proportion of subjects with psychotic illness committed suicide than nonpsychotics, and that the risk was higher for early stage, young male schizophrenic patients. Other factors which increased suicidal risk further when coupled with these variables were high intelligence and never having married. The researchers suggest that psychotic patients who are severely unhappy with their lives due to the chronic nature of their illness and inability to cope with its debilitating effects, will develop feelings of hopelessness and a vulnerability to suicidal behaviour.

The predictive efficacy of these variables is not however high. For example, the most promising precursor is normally considered to be parasuicide, but the relationship between parasuicide and suicide in schizophrenia is not straightforward, and there is no consensus between the studies (Allebeck, Varla, Kristjansson and Wistedt, 1987; Drake, Gates, Cotton and Whittaker, 1985). One problem is that the prevalence of suicide is so high among people with schizophrenia who share other risk factors (youth, male gender, etc.). Nevertheless the ability to predict who in the long term will kill themselves using known risk factors such as history of deliberate self-harm, age, gender, parasuicide, high education level, etc. is little better than chance (Pokorny, 1983).

PRECURSORS OF SUICIDE

Recent research has isolated three factors which may provide a better understanding of the dynamics between psychotic illness and suicide: depression, hopelessness and suicidal ideation. Jones et al., (1994) investigated whether depression and positive or negative symptoms of schizophrenia differentiated patients with and without a history of suicide. Their findings indicated that depression during the acute phase of the illness was a significant factor in distinguishing between the suicidal and non-suicidal histories of subjects, although negative symptoms were not a distinguishing factor. Depression during the most recent admission prior to suicide was reported by Addington and Addington (1992) and their sample was followed up over the course of the following 12 months. However, the work of Drake and Cotton (1986) concluded that it was depressed mood and the psychological aspects of depression (unresponsiveness, guilt, hopelessness) and not the vegetative symptoms which were important; for example depression in the absence of hopelessness was not predictive of later suicide.

The importance of hopelessness is entirely consistent with the theme of factors known to distinguish suicide non-attempters from attempters and completers (Drake et al., 1985), which include fear of mental disintegration in the context of high personal expectations (as indexed by high IQ, educational achievement and poor current work functioning). Depressed mood peaks during acute psychosis (Leff, 1988) and in the immediate postpsychotic phase (Siris, Morgan and Fagerstrom, 1987), which probably accounts for the high risk of suicide during this period (Goldacre, Seagrott and Hawton, 1993; King, 1994). Even among outpatient suicides reported by Drake et al., (1985), 70% had killed themselves within 6 months of discharge.

We conclude that depression, hopelessness and suicidal ideation during and immediately following an episode of acute psychosis are necessary but not sufficient conditions for suicide, and this demonstrates that suicide often occurs in the context of a distressed mental state. The presence of these *psychological* vulnerabilities, we believe, supports a cognitive framework for depression and suicide in schizophrenia. Our recent collaborative study of 110 schizophrenic patients followed up for twelve months subsequent to an acute episode of psychosis suggests a sound rationale for pursuing this stratagem (see Table 5.2, which shows percentage prevalence for depression, hopelessness and suicidal thinking). The need for treatment is further underlined by a 20% increase in depression scores at 4, 8 or 12 months compared to the point of discharge from hospital (recovery). The targeting

Table 5.2 Twelve month prevalence of depression, hopelessness and suicidal thinking (from Birchwood, Chadwick and Trower, 1997)

Assessment points	*At least moderately depressed	At least moderately and moderately hopeless	At least moderately depressed or suicidal thinking/ plans
Recovery, 4, 8, 12 months	68.3%	36.6%	44.9%

*Using the Calgary Depression Scale (for schizophrenia)—Addington, Addington and Maticka-Tyndale, 1993.

of these aforementioned precursors would be essential. To develop an effective intervention we also need a theoretical model of depression and suicide to understand the role of these risk variables. Here we argue that patients' appraisals of the meaning of their psychosis and its symptoms provides such a backdrop. We consider below the appraisal of symptoms, illness and their implications for self-evaluation.

COGNITIVE APPRAISAL OF SELF, SYMPTOMS AND ILLNESS

Appraisal of symptoms: the case of auditory hallucinations

Depression has been linked to the presence of auditory hallucinations (Berrios and Bulbena, 1987; Barnes et al., 1989) and we have found some two-thirds of our sample of patients exhibited residual voices alongside at least moderate levels of depression (Birchwood and Chadwick, 1997). The depressive pathology observed in this group, although linked to the presence of auditory hallucinations, can be clearly defined in terms of key beliefs held by the individual about the power and purpose or intent of their voices (Chadwick and Birchwood, 1994; 1995), as opposed to voice topography or content. As with Milgram's (1974) famous experiment which highlighted the power of the experimenter and the compliance of subjects in administering what they believed to be lethal electrical shocks to other subjects, results of these studies confirmed a similar foundation for auditory hallucinations. Subjects in these studies reported that voices were imbued with power and authority; *malevolent* or persecutory voices were resisted and aroused feelings of hostility, fear, anger and depression. Conversely, *benevolent* voices were regarded as reassuring and even amusing in some cases.

A recent study (Birchwood and Chadwick, 1997) investigated whether these key beliefs about voices' power and purpose or intent would be associated with depression. Sixty-two participants, who had at least two years of history of auditory hallucinations, were assessed concerning their appraisal of voices' meaning and power, and the evidence for these beliefs and their affective and behavioural responses using the Cognitive Assessment of Voices Schedule (CAV; Birchwood and Chadwick, 1997) and Beliefs about Voices Questionnaire (BAVQ; Chadwick and Birchwood, 1995). Results showed that voices were regarded as "very powerful" in 89.3% of instances of malevolent voices and in 82.4% of benevolent voices. Beliefs about power and purpose/intent appear therefore to be orthogonal.

No significant differences were found between malevolent and benevolent voices in terms of the frequency, loudness or clarity of voices, nor "powerful" or benign voices (see Table 5.3). The form of the auditory hallucinations was assigned into three categories: commands and/or advice and/or comments; running commentary; and insults or threats. Again no significant differences emerged between the overall form of the voice and the beliefs of malevolence, benevolence or power (*see Table 5.3*).

In order to investigate the links between voice content and patients' beliefs, blind raters were given voice content information alongside responses from the CAS. These responses refer to data in which subjects are asked whether a particular belief has been expressed by the voice (e.g. the identity of the voice) and what evidence they can give for the belief, and include patient's beliefs about meaning and compliance. The raters judged the extent to which each belief followed directly from voice content. For example, a belief about the identity of the voice could be supported by a variety of different levels of evidence, and hence result in different ratings:

The voice was "x"   Rating: "belief follows directly"
It's what "y" would say   Rating: "belief requires an inference"
No reason, but I think it's "z"   Rating: "no relationship"

The results (see table 5.4) of the analysis revealed that beliefs followed directly from voice content in 24% of cases, were inferential in 45% of cases,

Table 5.3   Beliefs and topography/form of voices (mean (S.D.))

	Malevolent	Benevolent	Benign	Powerful	Not powerful
Topography					
Frequency	1.9 (1.2)	25.5 (1.5)	2.5 (0.9)	2.1 (1.3)	2.7 (0.9)
Volume	2.4 (1.2)	3.1 (1.1)	3.2 (0.9)	2.7 (1.2)	2.9 (1.2)
Clarity	1.7 (1.1)	1.6 (0.9)	1.8 (1.5)	1.6 (0.9)	2.1 (1.6)
Affect	1.3 (0.7)	3.3 (1.1)	2.3 (0.8)		
Content					
Commands/ advice/ comments	81%	83%	70%	70%	82%
Derogatory	9.5%	8.3%	0%	20%	9.1%
Commentary/ advice	9.5%	0%	30%	10%	6.1%

Table 5.4   Relationship between voice content and beliefs

Relationship with voice content	Beliefs			
	Identity %	Meaning %	Compliance %	All beliefs %
Follows directly	15.8	30.8	35.5	24.0
Requires an inference	68.4	28.2	38.7	45.1
No relationship	15.8	41.0	25.8	27.5

and showed no relationship in 27.5%, in clear support of the cognitive model.

Subjects reporting malevolent voices were more likely to be depressed (Beck Depression Inventory score > 15) than those with benevolent voices (68% vs. 35%). Subjects reporting very "powerful" voices were twice as likely to be depressed as their counterparts (see table 5.5), even when voice topography, content and psychotic symptoms were taken into account.

The major contribution of this research is that it has clearly defined that *beliefs* about voices and not voice topography or content hold the key to understanding the high level of depression in many people with auditory hallucinations. We believe that the sense of entrapment in the context of a threatening and powerful entity leads to feelings of powerlessness and hence depression. The implication of these findings is that challenging the power and authority of voices using cognitive therapy will reduce this sense of entrapment which we predict will ease depression (Chadwick, Birchwood and Trower, 1996).

Ethnosemantic beliefs about psychotic illness

The psychological literature on identity and coping with long-term mental illness regards the patient as an active agent searching for meaning and control over his/her illness and experiences. Theories centre upon the patient's reaction to the diagnosis. Rejection of the construct "mental illness" is construed in a similar way in most theoretical perspectives: these are variously "denial" (Shepherd, 1984); "sealing over" or playing down the impact of illness leading to rejection of help and labels (McGlashan, Levy and Carpenter, 1975); or label rejection derived from labelling theory (Scheff, 1975). Acceptance on the other hand is viewed somewhat differently in different perspectives. The labelling model sees it as a more passive form of conforming to the stereotype of incompetence and poor self control. Shepherd (1984) sees the individual as exaggerating his/her

Table 5.5 Depression and voice beliefs

	Malevolent	Benevolent	Neither	Significance*	
				Overall	M vs. rest
BDI mean (S.D.)	23.6 (11.7)	15.7 (11.3)	16.1 (11.0)	< 0.05	< 0.01
Mood	14..5 (8.0)	9.1 (6.6)	10.1 (8.0)	< 0.05	< 0.02
Vegetative	3.1 (2.3)	2.6 (2.0)	1.6 (1.8)	< 0.06	< 0.05
Denigration	3.8 (3.3)	3.1 (2.9)	3.1 (2.8)	N.S.	N.S.
% Depressed	68%	35%	47%		

*Based on one-way ANOVA and planned polynomial comparisons.

problems within the sick role as a defensive manoeuvre to preserve dignity ("I am unable to face up to the demands of life because my illness is so severe"). McGlashan, Levy and Carpenter (1975), however, see this as one outcome in an "integrating" process in which the patient accepts the responsibility for illness, searches for meaning and attempts to integrate it into previous experience. The possibility that some patients can accept their illness and feel a sense of mastery over it is implicit in this approach and is viewed by some as the most appropriate "psychotherapeutic" model (Warner, Taylor, Powers and Hyman, 1989) akin to "informed control" or "empowerment" (Birchwood, 1991). Patients' needs for, and attempts to, self-regulate their illness, have been described in detail by Brier and Strauss (1983) and Strauss (1989), and have been documented in patients' attempts to self manage their symptoms (Falloon and Talbot, 1981) or their early signs of relapse (Birchwood et al., 1992). In terms of the impact on disability, an internal locus of control in the context of acceptance of illness (the "psychotherapeutic" model) rather than denial of illness seems to be associated with a more favourable outcome (Soskis and Bowers, 1969; McGlashan and Carpenter, 1981; Warner, Taylor, Powers and Hyman, 1989).

Estroff (1989), Strauss (1989) and Taylor and Perkins (1991) have stressed the importance of identity and self-image as part of the process of adjusting to long-term illness, which might clearly bear upon the development of depression. Strauss (1989) and Estroff (1989) argue that in addition to the fact of illness and its controllability, there are in the West a number of social and scientific images or beliefs about mental illness, schizophrenia in particular, which present a challenge to the individual's premorbid self-image: that the person *is* the disorder (as implied by psychoanalytical theory) as opposed to a person *with* a disorder; that the illness is a social judgement hence stigmatising; that the mentally ill should be socially segregated or contained; and that mental illness and capacity for independence are incompatible. It would seem possible that the absorption of these beliefs by the psychotic patient may contribute to the development of depression.

The hypothesis that depression in schizophrenic patients can be understood in terms of their beliefs about the controllability of psychosis and the internalisation of pernicious cultural stereotypes was explored (Birchwood et al., 1993). Eighty-five randomly selected outpatients with a diagnosis of schizophrenia or bipolar disorder participated in the study, of whom 34% were depressed. The Personal Beliefs about Illness Questionnaire (PBIQ) was specifically developed for the study and assessed the internalisation of five ethnosemantic constructs: *self as illness* measures the extent to which subjects' believe that the origins of their illness lie in their personality or psyche; *control over illness* assesses the level of control subjects' perceive over their illness; *stigma* evaluates whether subjects' believe their illness is a social judgement upon them; *social containment* assesses beliefs in social segregation and control of the mentally ill, and *expectations* measures subjects' views on the degree to which their illness affects their capacity for independence.

Comparisons between the depressed and non-depressed subjects revealed that the depressed group internalised these ethnosemantic beliefs as negative self-evaluations and viewed themselves as powerless to control their illness. The results support the notion that depression is associated with the perceived controllability and acceptance of the stereotypes associated with mental illness. We believe these results support Warner et al's (1989) "psychotherapeutic model", which suggests that therapy should encourage blame-free acceptance and mastery of illness through cultivating means of controlling illness, for example learning to anticipate and control early signs of relapse (Birchwood, 1995) and voices (Chadwick and Birchwood, 1994).

Loss, humiliation and entrapment as appraisals of psychotic illness

Research into the role of life events in triggering the onset of unipolar depression in a sample of community-based female subjects (Brown, Harris and Hepworth, 1995) provides a framework which helps to understand how patients might appraise the emergence of a psychotic illness and its social implications. Although lowering of self-esteem has been linked to depression (Beck et al., 1979), theories based upon "social mentalities" suggest that the implications for power and rank of certain life experiences involving loss are of significance in the emergence of depressive symptoms (Gilbert, 1992). Depression in such instances is believed to result in: the lowering of self-esteem as a result of acceptance of a subordinate role ("loss"); events which threaten the individual's position or status ("humiliation"), and the perception of containment in a punishing cycle of events which results in the perceived inability to reaffirm an identity or sense of belonging ("entrapment"). Brown, Harris and Hepworth (1995) concluded that such experiences, which triggered feelings of humiliation and entrapment were more important in provoking depression than the perception of loss alone. These concepts have clear application to the way patients construct their psychotic illness.

As suggested by Birchwood et al., (1993) the experience of psychosis can as a result of the stigma attached to such disorders result in feelings of humiliation. The experience and expectation of recurring symptoms in relapsing psychotics and/or the presence of residual voices may lead to feelings of entrapment and defeat. In order to test this hypothesis a cohort of patients described in Birchwood et al., (1993) were followed up 2.5 years later in order to determine the stability of these appraisals and whether *changes* in depression over this period were linked to changes in appraisal of illness (Rooke and Birchwood, in submission). A high level of stability of BDI scores over this long time period was observed. Stability (see Table 5.6) was apparent in the appraisals of entrapment, loss of social role and attribution of causality (self vs. illness), but not for perceived loss of social status and humiliation.

Once again, replicating earlier findings, comparisons between depressed and non-depressed patients revealed that depressed subjects perceived themselves as more entrapped in their illness and also to have lost more in terms of their social role. Also, depressed subjects experienced more compulsory admissions, a greater drop in employment and a higher level of delusional pathology. A discriminant function analysis where the depressed/non-depressed groups were compared including the variables of entrapment, loss of social role and the internal attribution of causality. In order to capture longitudinal information, each variable was added at the inclusion period as well as at follow-up (see Table 5.7). Seven variables were selected and belief in entrapment at both follow-up and inclusion were the main contributors. The other selected variables were hallucinations, compulsory admission, insight, drop in employment and loss of social role.

As there was some intra-individual change in BDI scores, a regression equation was constructed to determine whether this could be predicted by changes in the appraisal of psychosis over this time period. The results (see Table 5.8) indicate that depression at follow-up could be predicted using

Table 5.6 Stability and change in key appraisals

	Inclusion		Follow-up (30 months)			
Appraisals	Mean	SD	Man	SD	p	Correlation
Control over illness (entrapment)	9.3	2.2	8.6	3.0	N.S.	0.422*
Social containment (humiliating need to be socially marginalised	4.5	1.1	4.0	1.4	< 0.05	0.30
Expectations (loss of autonomy/social role	6.9	2.1	6.8	2.4	N.S.	0.67*
Stigma (humiliating devaluation of self)	6.5	1.8	6.3	2.1	N.S.	0.30
Attribution: self vs. illness	8.7	2.1	7.7	2.4	N.S.	0.55*

*$p < 0.01$.

Table 5.7 Variables selected in the discriminant function analysis (depressed vs non-depressed at follow-up)

Variable	Wilk's lambda	Rao's V	Change in Rao's V
Entrapment (follow-up)	0.74	15.6	15.6*
Hallucinations	0.58	33.1	4.3[†]
Entrapment (inclusion)	0.55	37.5	4.5[†]
Compulsory admissions	0.51	42.8	5.3[†]
Insight (PSE 9)	0.48	47.8	4.9[†]
Drop in employment	0.47	49.7	3.6[†]
Loss of autonomy/social role	0.45	53.7	3.9[†]

*$p < 0.001$.
[†]$p < 0.05$.

Table 5.8 Regression equation predicting BDI score at follow-up

Variable	Standardised Beta-weight	T	p
BDI (inclusion)	0.45	3.65	< 0.001
PBIQ: Entrapment (change score)	0.39	3.70	< 0.001
PBIQ: Entrapment (at inclusion)	0.39	3.70	< 0.001

information about depression at inclusion together with information about *changes* in the appraisal of entrapment over this time.

We suggest that it is the events that punctuate a long-term difficulty such as psychosis, (for example, compulsory admissions, persistent voices, loss of job), that may be appraised as signifying loss and entrapment and confirm the absence of a way forward in respect of core roles, relationships and autonomy. Such events are likely to be ego involving since autonomy and success in roles and relationships (Oatley and Bolton, 1985) are endemic in western culture. Also such events can confirm a disbelief in the individual's ability to reaffirm a sense of identity and belonging (Price, Sloman, Gardner, Gilbert and Rohde, 1994), and encourage engulfment and internalisation of the schizophrenic identity as a defensive manoeuvre (Birchwood et al., 1993).

CONCLUSIONS

We have argued that the person with psychosis appraises their psychosis and the events that punctuate it (voices, compulsory admission, social marginalisation) as signifying the loss of a valued role or goal, and at the same time as entrapping the individual, who thus fails to assert an identity and sense of belonging. A theoretical model of depression and suicide, which may link depression and hopelessness on the one hand and suicide on the other, is presented by Gilbert (1992) and suggests that the depressed and suicidal person perceives him/herself humiliated by shattering life events and entrapped. Brown, Harris and Hepworth's (1995) suggestion is that humiliation and entrapment were of greater importance in provoking depression than experiences of loss or danger alone. A similar approach, backed by substantial empirical support, is postulated by Baumeister (1990) who proposes an "escape theory" of suicide. Here the individual is argued to hold unrealistically high expectations and following the experience of bad outcomes, builds internal attributions for these outcomes so making self-awareness painful. Hence the individual ends up deriving a self-evaluation which is inadequate, incompetent, unattractive or guilty (hence procreating negative affect). Baumeister suggests that the person tries to prevent self-awareness and emotion by escaping into a disinhibited and irrational state of mind called "cognitive deconstruction". Suicide finally emerges as an escalation of the person's wish to escape from life's problems and their implications for the self. We believe that psychosis prevents the individual from asserting a positive identity and allows the individual only to confront these painful aspects of self from which there is often only one form of escape—suicide.

We believe cognitive therapy is ideally suited to focus on these appraisals and thus allow the individual to assert an identity. The key to such an intervention would be the identification and challenging of the main appraisals held regarding self and psychosis (Chadwick, Birchwood and Trower, 1996); self and symptoms (e.g. beliefs about the power and malevolence of voices can be challenged; Chadwick and Birchwood, 1994); and negative global self-evaluations together with goal setting in valued interpersonal and achievement domains, and the solidarity of a group setting can be used to bolster self-regard through the challenging of negative social stereotypes as developed by Drury, Birchwood, Cochrane and MacMillan (1996) in their study of cognitive therapy in acute psychosis. A controlled trial of cognitive therapy for depression, hopelessness and implications for the self is currently in hand in conjunction with Dr. Peter Trower and Professor Paul Gilbert. We hope that this most intractable of problems may yet yield to psychological therapy.

REFERENCES

Addington, D. and Addington, J. (1992). Attempted suicide and depression in schizophrenia. *Acta Psychiatrica Scandanavica*, **85**, 288–291.

Addington, D., Addington, J. and Maticka-Tyndale, E. (1993). Assessing depression in schizophrenia: the Calgary depression scale. *British Journal of Psychiatry*, **163** (supplement 22), 39–44.

Allebeck, P., Varla, A., Kristjansson, E. and Wistedt, B. (1987). Risk factors for suicide among patients with schizophrenia. *Acta Psychiatrica Scandanavica*, **76**, 414–419.

Barnes, T. R. E., Curson, D. A., Liddle, P. F. and Patel, M. (1989). The nature and prevalence of depression in chronic schizophrenic in-patients. *British Journal of Psychiatry*, **154**, 486–491.

Baumeister, R. F. (1990). Suicide as escape from self. *Psychological Review*, **97**, 90–113.

Beck, A. T. (1967). *Depression: Clinical, experimental and theoretical aspects*. New York: Harper and Row.

Beck, A. T., Hollon, S. D. and Young, J. E. (1985). Treatment of depression with cognitive therapy and amitriptyline. *Archives of General Psychiatry*, **42**, 142–148.

Beck, A. T., Rush, A. J., Shaw, B. F. and Emery, G. (1979). *Cognitive Therapy of Depression*. New York: Guilford Press.

Bennie, E. H. (1985). Rapid stabilisation with a depot neuroleptic in acute schizophrenia: A new role for fluphenazine decanoate. In A. A. Schiff, M. Roth and H. L. Freeman (Eds), *Schizophrenia: New Pharmacological and Clinical Developments*. London: Royal Society of Medicine.

Berrios, G. E. and Bulbena, A. (1987). Post psychotic depression: the Fulbourn cohort. *Acta Psychiatrica Scandanavica*, **76**, 89–93.

Birchwood, M. (1991). A new paradigm for psychotherapy for individuals with schizophrenia: the individual-illness interaction. *Bulletin of the Royal College of Psychiatrists*, **15**, 38–39.

Birchwood, M. (1995). Early intervention in psychotic relapse: cognitive approaches to detection and management. *Behaviour Change*, **12**, 2–19.

Birchwood, M. and Chadwick, P. D. (1997). The omnipotence of voices III: Testing the validity of the cognitive model. *Psychological Medicine*, **27**, 1345–1353.

Birchwood, M., MacMillan, F. and Smith, J. (1992). Early intervention. In M. Birchwood and M. Tarrier (Eds), *Innovation in the Psychological Management of Schizophrenia*. Chichester: John Wiley & Sons.

Birchwood, M., Mason, R., MacMillan, F. and Healy, J. (1993). Depression, demoralisation and control over psychotic illness: A comparison of depressed and non-depressed patients with a chronic psychosis. *Psychological Medicine*, **23**, 387–395.

Birchwood, M. and Preston, M. (1991). Schizophrenia. In W. Dryden and R. Rentoul (Eds), *Adult Clinical Problems*. London: Routledge.

Brier, A. and Strauss, J. S. (1983). Self control in psychotic disorders. *American Journal of Psychiatry*, **40**, 1141–1145.

Brown, G. W. and Harris, T. O. (1989). *Life Events and Illness*. New York: Guilford Press.

Brown, G. W., Harris, T. O. and Hepworth, C. (1995). Loss humiliation and entrapment among women developing depression: a patient and non-patient comparison. *Psychological Medicine*, **25**, 7–21.

Chadwick, P. D. and Birchwood, M. (1994). Challenging the omnipotence of voices: A cognitive approach to auditory hallucinations. *British Journal of Psychiatry*, **164**, 190–201.

Chadwick, P. D. and Birchwood, M. (1995). The omnipotence of voices II: The Beliefs about Voices Questionnaire. *British Journal of Psychiatry*, **166**, 773–776.

Chadwick, P. D., Birchwood, M. and Trower, P. (1996). *Cognitive Therapy for Delusions, Voices and Paranoia*. Chichester: John Wiley & Sons.

Chintalapudi, M., Kulhara, P. and Avasthi, A. (1993). Post-psychotic depression in schizophrenia. *European Archives of Psychiatry and Clinical Neuroscience*, **243**, 103–108.

Davis, J. M. and Casper, R. (1977). Antipsychotic Drugs: Clinical Pharmacology and therapeutic use. *Drugs*, **14**, 260–282.

Department of Health. (1992). *The Health of the Nation*. London: HMSO.

Drake, T. and Cotton, T. (1986). Suicide among schizophrenics: A comparison of attempted and completed suicides. *British Journal of Psychiatry*, **149**, 784–787.

Drake, R., Gates, C., Cotton, P. and Whittaker, A. (1985). Suicide amongst schizophrenics: Who is at risk? *Journal of Nervous and Mental Disease*, **172**, 613–617.

Drury, V., Birchwood, M., Cochrane, R. and MacMillan, F. (1996). Cognitive therapy and recovery from acute psychosis: a controlled trial. *British Journal of Psychiatry*, **169**, 593–601.

Estroff, S. E. (1989). Self-identity and subjective experiences of schizophrenia: in search of the subject. *Schizophrenia Bulletin*, **15**, 189–196.

Falloon, I.R.H. and Talbor, R.E. (1981). Persistent auditory hallucinations: coping mechanisms and implications for management. *Psychological Medicine*, **11**, 329–339.

Foulds, G. A. and Bedford, A. (1975). Hierarchy of classes of personal illness. *Psychological Medicine*, **5**, 181–192.

Gilbert, P. (1992). *Depression: the Evolution of Powerlessness*. Hove: Lawrence Erlbraum Associates.

Goldacre, M., Seagrott, V. and Hawton, K. (1993). Suicide after discharge from psychiatric inpatient care. *Lancet*, **342**, 283–286.

Green, M. F., Nuechterlein, K. H., Ventura, J. and Mintz, J. (1990). The temporal relationship between depressive and psychotic symptoms in recent-onset schizophrenia. *American Journal of Psychiatry*, **147**, 179–182.

Harrow, M., Yonan, C. A., Sands, J. R. and Marengo, J. (1994). Depression in schizophrenia: Are neuroleptics, akinesia or anhedonia involved? *Schizophrenia Bulletin*, **20**, 327–338.

Haskins, B., Shutty, M. S. and Kellogg, E. (1995). Affect processing in chronically psychotic patients: development of a reliable assessment tool. *Schizophrenia Research*, **15**, 291–297.

Hirsch, S. R. and Jolley, A. G. (1989). The dysphoric syndrome in schizophrenia and its implications for relapse. *British Journal of Psychiatry*, Supplement 5, 46–50.

Jenkins, R., Griffiths, S. and Wylie, I. (1994). *The prevention of suicide*. London: HMSO.

Johnson, D. A. W. (1981). Studies of depressive symptoms in schizophrenia: The prevalence of depression and its possible causes. *British Journal of Psychiatry*, **139**, 89– 101.

Jones, J. S., Stein, D. J., Stanley, B., Guido, J. R., Winchell, R. and Stanley, M. (1994). Negative and depressive symptoms in suicidal schizophrenics. *Acta Psychiatrica Scandanavica*, **89**, 81–88.

King, E. (1994). Suicide in the mentally ill: an epidemiological sample and implications for clinicians. *British Journal of Psychiatry*, **165**, 658–663.

Knight, A. and Hirsch, S. R. (1981). Revealed depression and drug treatment of schizophrenia. *Archives of General Psychiatry*, **40**, 893–896.

Koreen, A. R., Siris, G. S., Chakos, M., Alvir, J., Mayerhoff, D. and Lieberman, J. (1993). Depression in first-episode schizophrenia. *American Journal of Psychiatry*, **150**, 1643– 1648.

Leff, J. (1988). The clinical course of depressive symptoms in schizophrenia. *Schizophrenia Research*, **1**, 25–30.

Leff, J., Tress, K. and Edwards, B. (1990). Depressive symptoms in the course of schizophrenia. In L. E. DeLisi (Ed), *Depression in Schizophrenia*. Washington (USA): American Psychiatric Press.

MacGlashan, T. (1984). What has become of the psychotherapy of schizophrenia? *Acta Psychiatrica Scandanavica*, **90**, supplement 384(5), 147–152.

McGlashan, T. H. and Carpenter, W. T. (1976). An investigation of the postpsychotic depressive syndrome. *American Journal of Psychiatry*, **133**, 14–19.

McGlashan, T. H. and Carpenter, W. T. (1981). Does attitude towards psychosis relate to outcome? *American Journal of Psychiatry*, **138**, 797–801.

McGlashan, T. H., Levy, S. T. and Carpenter, W. T. (1975). Integration and sealing over: clinically distinct recovery styles from schizophrenia. *Archives of General Psychiatry*, **32**, 1269–1272.

Milgram, S. (1974). *Obedience to authority*. New York: Harper and Row.

Munro, A. (1987). Neither lions nor tigers: Disorders which lie between schizophrenia and affective disorders. *Canadian Journal of Psychiatry*, **32**, 296–297.

Newcomer, J. W., Faustman, W. O., Yeh, W. and Csernansky, J. G. (1990). Distinguishing depression and negative symptoms in unmedicated patients with schizophrenia. *Psychiatry Research*, **31**, 243–250.

Oatley, K. and Bolton, W. (1985). A social theory of depression in reaction to life events. *Psychological Review*, **92**, 372–388.

Overall, J.E. and Gorham, D.R. (1962). The Brief Psychiatric Rating Scale. *Psychological Reports*, **10**, 799–812.

Pokorny, A. (1993). Predictors of suicide in psychiatric patients. *Archives of General Psychiatry*, **40**, 249–253.

Pope, H. G. (1983). Distinguishing bipolar disorder from schizophrenia in clinical practice: guidelines and case reports. *Hospital and Community Psychiatry*, **34**, 322–328.

Price, J., Sloman, L., Gardner, R., Gilbert, P. and Rohde, P. (1994). The social competition hypothesis of depression. *British Journal of Psychiatry*, **164**, 309–315.

Rifkin, A., Quitkin, F. and Klein, D. F. (1975). Akinesia: A poorly recognised drug induced extrapyramidal behavioural disorder. *Archives of General Psychiatry*, **32**, 672– 674.

Rooke, O. and Birchwood, M. (in submission). Loss humiliation and entrapment as appraisals of schizophrenic illness: a prospective study of depressed and non-depressed patients.

Roth, S. (1970). The seemingly ubiquitous depression following acute schizophrenic episodes: A neglected area of clinical discussion. *American Journal of Psychiatry*, **127**, 51–58.

Roy, A. (1986). Suicide in schizophrenia. In A. Roy (Ed.), *Suicide*. Baltimore: Williams and Wilkins.

Roy, A., Thompson, R. and Kennedy, S. (1983). Depression in chronic schizophrenia. *British Journal of Psychiatry*, **142**, 465–470.

Scheff, T. J. (1975). Schizophrenia as ideology. In T. J. Scheff (Ed.), *Labeling Madness*. Englewood Cliffs (NJ): Prentice Hall.

Shepherd, G. (1984). *Institutional care and rehabilitation*. London: Longman.

Siris, S. G. (1991). Diagnosis of secondary depression in schizophrenia: Implications for DSM-IV. *Schizophrenia Bulletin*, **17**, 75–98.

Siris, S. G. (1995). Schizophrenia. In S. R. Hirsch and D. R. Weinberger (Eds), *Schizophrenia*. Oxford: Blackwell Science.

Siris, S. G., Morgan, V. and Fagerstrom, R. (1987). Adjunctive imipramine in the treatment of postpsychotic depression. *Archives of General Psychiatry*, **44**, 533–539.

Soskis, D. A. and Bowers, M. B. (1969). The schizophrenia experience: a follow-up study of attitude and posthospital adjustment. *Journal of Nervous and Mental Disease*, **149**, 443–449.

Strauss, J. S. (1989). Subjective experiences of schizophrenia: towards a new dynamic II. *Schizophrenia Bulletin*, **15**, 179–188.

Taylor, K. E. and Perkins, R. E. (1991). Identity and coping with mental illness in long-stay rehabilitation. *British Journal of Clinical Psychology*, **30**, 73–85.

Van Putten, T. and May, P. (1978). "Akinetic depression" in schizophrenia. *Archives of General Psychiatry*, **35**, 1101–1107.

Warner, R. W., Taylor, D., Powers, M. and Hyman, J. (1989). Acceptance of the mental illness label by psychotic patients: effects on functioning. *American Journal of Orthopsychiatry*, **59**, 398–409.

Westermeyer, J. F., Harrow, M. and Marengo, J. T. (1991). Risk for suicide in schizophrenia and other psychotic and non-psychotic disorders. *Journal of Nervous and Mental Disease*, **179**, 259–266.

Williams, J. M. G. (1989). Cognitive treatment of depression. In K. R. Herbst and E. S. Paykel (Eds), *Depression: An Integrative Approach*. Oxford: Heinemann Professional Publishing.

Chapter 6

THE EVALUATION OF COGNITIVE BEHAVIOURAL THERAPY FOR PSYCHOSIS

Philippa Garety, Graham Dunn, David Fowler and Elizabeth Kuipers

INTRODUCTION

There have been relatively few studies to date which have systematically evaluated cognitive behavioural therapy for people with psychosis; of the group of investigations which has been conducted, single case studies form the greater part. A recent book (Fowler, Garety and Kuipers, 1995) reviews this literature; the authors conclude that while there are promising indications of the potential of the approach, firm evidence of efficacy based on the results of a number of controlled trials has not yet been demonstrated. Specific questions about the relative effectiveness of different components of therapy, the characteristics of patients who benefit, the optimum length of therapy and the maintenance of therapeutic gains, also all remain to be thoroughly investigated. Of further theoretical and therapeutic interest are questions about the mechanisms of therapeutic change. For example, if delusions are treated successfully, is that because the beliefs a person holds are changed, or because the way a person reasons

Outcome and Innovation in Psychological Treatment of Schizophrenia. Edited by T. Wykes, N. Tarrier and S. Lewis.
© 1998 John Wiley & Sons Ltd

is altered or because attentional or attributional biases, possibly mediated by affective disturbance, are corrected? For such questions, larger random controlled trials are needed, and a number of these are currently under way.

It is timely, then, to consider the methodology appropriate to the evaluation of cognitive behavioural therapy for people with psychosis, in terms of measures, design and analysis. In this chapter we will address these issues, with particular reference to the treatment of delusions and hallucinations, drawing on our recent pilot study (Garety, Kuipers, Fowler, Dunn and Chamberlain, 1994) to illustrate the discussion.

MEASUREMENT

What should be assessed?

Clearly the choice of assessments for the evaluation of therapeutic outcome depends on the goals of therapy. Shapiro (1996) points out that the construct validity of an outcome study is threatened if the outcome measures are not sufficiently specific to the problem under treatment, or not relevant to the goals of treatment. In the studies which have been recently reported of cognitive behavioural therapy, a variety of therapy targets have been reported. Three examples illustrate this.

Firstly, Tarrier and his colleagues, in their random controlled trial of coping strategy enhancement and problem solving, focused on reducing the number and severity of a range of psychotic symptoms and on improving mood and social functioning (Tarrier, Beckett, Harwood, Baker, Yusupoff and Ugarteburu, 1993). Chadwick and Lowe (1990), in contrast, aimed primarily to reduce delusional conviction in their series of six single cases. However, they also had a number of secondary goals, concerned with reducing preoccupation and distress directly attributed to the delusions and general improvements in mood. Haddock, Bentall, and Slade (1996) applied cognitive behavioural techniques to the management of auditory hallucinations, aiming to reduce their "severity" including, as measures of this, voice frequency, distress, beliefs about the voices and disruption to activities.

Different treatments may, therefore, have different targets with the result that there may be little overlap in assessments between studies. Nonetheless, in the studies just described there was more overlap in treatment goals than in the measures employed. Froyd, Lambert and Froyd (1996), in a review of psychotherapy outcome measurement, comment on the very wide diversity of measures used in outcome studies with a consequent impossibility of developing an integrated picture of outcome research results. They argue that researchers should attempt to agree some "best" measures. This call is echoed by Shapiro (1996) who comments that meta-analysis is a useful method for overcoming some of the difficulties created by insufficient statistical power of individual studies; he suggests that researchers should anticipate the inclusion of their studies in a meta-analysis and seek to use closely comparable outcome measures. At this early stage of outcome research for cognitive behavioural therapy for psychosis perhaps an explicit attempt to agree key measures is feasible.

Changes in the conceptualisation of hallucinations and delusions

The conceptualisation of psychotic symptoms may also crucially influence the nature of the measures used for evaluation. Over the 1980s there has been a gradual development in the understanding of the key positive psychotic symptoms, delusions and hallucinations. Before the 1980s these symptoms were generally characterised as clearly abnormal, discrete entities, which could be assessed as present or absent and were uni-dimensional, the dimension of interest often called "severity". Affect was seen as irrelevant. They were also typically assessed by an observer rather than by self-report.

One influential assessment device in Britain, the Present State Examination (PSE; Wing, Cooper and Sartorius, 1974), broadly reflected this approach. Delusions, for example, were treated as present, absent or partial, based on an informal assessment of conviction, the sole dimension of interest. The assessment was interview-based and all judgements were made by the interviewer. A notable additional feature of the PSE was that delusions were not considered in isolation, but assessed with other symptoms; different types of delusions (in terms of a content categorisation) were also identified.

A number of studies over the eighties led to a re-evaluation of this traditional conceptualisation of delusions and hallucinations. The application of cognitive psychology led to the recognition that delusions as beliefs and hallucinations as perceptual experiences could be seen as sharing features of some beliefs and experiences reported in the general population. (For a full discussion of these ideas, see Slade and Bentall (1988) on hallucinations and Garety and Hemsley (1994) on delusions.) This recognition of continuities between psychotic and nonpsychotic experiences has had a number of implications.

Multi-dimensional approaches

Firstly, it has become apparent that beliefs and perceptual experiences are best viewed as dimensional—more or less firmly believed or more or less frequently experienced—and multi-dimensional; for delusions, conviction, preoccupation, distress and action have emerged as key dimensions (Garety and Hemsley, 1987; Brett-Jones, Garety and Hemsley, 1987), while hallucinations can be characterised in terms of a variety of variables, for example, frequency, distress, interference and hostility (Haddock, Bentall and Slade, 1996). Personal questionnaires (Garety, 1985) have been found to provide a flexible and reliable self-report method for the multi-dimensional assessment of these symptoms. An interesting recent study examined the variability of dimensions of delusions over time in response to cognitive behavioural therapy (Sharp, Fear, Williams, Healy, Lowe, Yeardon and Holden, 1996). Using both personal questionnaires and a new multi-dimensional assessment device (the Maudsley Assessment of Delusions (MADS), Wessely, Buchanan, Reed, Everitt, Garety, Cutting and Taylor, 1993), these researchers confirmed that the dimensions of preoccupation and acting on the belief systematically varied independently of conviction.

Analysis of beliefs and thinking processes

Cognitive models of symptoms have also emphasised a closer analysis of beliefs and thinking processes. Delusions, traditionally thought of as fixed and unresponsive to evidence, have been shown to respond (variably) to experience and evidence and to be associated with a variety of biases in reasoning and attributional style (see Garety and Hemsley, 1994, for a review). This work has had implications for therapy, but also is relevant to the understanding of therapy process. For example, Sharp et al., (1996), using the MADS, noted that belief maintenance factors (which include the active search for evidence to maintain or refute the belief and noticing of events or experiences which confirm the belief) were consistently associated with conviction during therapy and that those people who showed a positive response to therapy showed changes in these factors. The beliefs people hold about their auditory hallucinations have also been demonstrated to be associated with the distress experienced (Chadwick and Birchwood, 1994). These researchers have argued that a target of therapy for voices should be the attributions made about them and have provided a new questionnaire to assess these (the Beliefs about Voices Questionnaire, Chadwick and Birchwood, 1995).

Affect and self-esteem

Whereas previously, psychotic symptoms themselves and the people who hold them were viewed as characterised by lack of affect, the eighties also witnessed the recognition of the potential role of affect and self-esteem as centrally involved in the formation and maintenance of symptoms and, more generally, the importance of depression and anxiety in the person with psychosis (Bentall, Kinderman and Kaney, 1994; Birchwood, Mason, McMillan and Healy, 1993). The assessment of general mood states (depression and anxiety) and self-esteem is needed, both because these are legitimate targets of therapy and also because they may elucidate change processes in therapy.

Delusions and hallucinations have also been found to be frequently distressing, the nature of the distress varying, occurring sometimes as anxiety and sometimes as depression (see, for example, Garety and Hemsley, 1987). Sharp et al., (1996) have argued cogently for rating idiosyncratic affective dimensions of delusions, using self-generated mood labels, rather than using standard mood ratings, since there is a wide range in the precise features of affective responses.

Content

Finally, the content of delusions and hallucinations were, in the traditional view, largely irrelevant to an understanding of these symptoms, although it did play a role in categorisation. Recently, however, there has been a growing interest in developing theories of delusions which are content-specific, such as Bentall and colleagues' work on persecutory delusions; and a similar concern to relate the content of hallucinations to understanding their origin (e.g. Chadwick and Birchwood, 1994) and to explore content in treatment (e.g. Fowler, Garety and Kuipers, 1995; Kingdon and Turkington, 1994). There has, however, been no work as yet in developing reliable new content assessments for delusions or hallucinations.

To summarise, a number of important changes in the conceptualisation of the key positive psychotic symptoms of hallucinations and delusions have taken place over the past decade and a half. These changes are summarised in Table 6.1.

These shifts represent a recognition that delusions and hallucinations are not best viewed as meaningless symptoms but rather as complex beliefs and experiences which the person actively constructs in a dynamic interplay between the personality, past experience, affect and current events. Both assessment and therapy therefore require a matching sensitivity and complexity, fully taking account of the person's subjective experience.

Table 6.1 Changes in conceptualisation of delusions and hallucinations

Traditional	Revised
Dichotomous	Dimensional
Uni-dimensional	Multi-dimensional
Fixed	Potentially responsive to events
Irrational	Reasoning biases may be present
Affect irrelevant to theory and therapy	Affect relevant
Content irrelevant to theory and therapy	Content relevant

Conclusions

The choice of measures in outcome research must be influenced by a number of factors. These include the specificity and relevance of the measures to the treatment goals, the degree to which other researchers are using the same measures and their adequacy in terms of the conceptualisation of the phenomenon being measured; this latter point is especially relevant to delusions and hallucinations, since our view of them has developed considerably in recent years.

METHODOLOGICAL ISSUES WITH CONTROLLED TRIALS

In addition to the selection of the measures, outcome research is confronted with a number of difficulties in design and method. In a recent chapter, Shapiro (1996) addresses these difficulties cogently and interested readers are recommended to read this for a review of the methodological problems common to all psychotherapies. However, some problems seem to be particularly acute in the treatment of people with psychosis. The evaluation of cognitive behaviour therapy for psychosis is now occurring in a number of centres in the United Kingdom where randomised controlled trials are under way. The only such trial already published is that of Tarrier et al., (1993), while Haddock, Bentall and Slade (1996) have reported preliminary results of their study. Our group has completed a pilot study (Garety et al., 1994), which we will describe below, as an illustration of some of the points raised here. We are currently conducting a larger randomised controlled trial. Our experience has raised a number of methodological issues, which include sample attrition, missing data, methods of statistical analysis and issues of clinical significance.

Sample attrition and missing data

Existing studies point to high rates of sample attrition from first referral to completion of treatment or follow-up. Even once therapy has commenced, participant drop-out can be high and missing data points arising from participants' failure to attend for appointments (for various reasons) are common. Thus, Haddock, Bentall and Slade (1996) report that of 63 referred for therapy, 33 patients were allocated to a treatment or control condition and six patients dropped out of treatment. Haphazardly missing data during the treatment phase are not reported, although a further 7 patients were not available at follow-up.

To minimise the difficulties of sample attrition, a clinical trial needs to be designed to be as simple and as easy to administer as possible. There should not be any administrative or design complications to give participants (many of whom may be paranoid) any additional reasons to drop out of the study. The therapeutic approach within treatment sessions has to ensure that continued participation is encouraged, and made a priority. While this can be a problem for participants in the "active" arm of the trial, it is likely to be even more of a problem for the control arm, once participants realise what is (or is not) on offer. (As Shapiro (1996) notes, in most psychotherapy outcome studies, the participants (patients and therapists alike) are well aware of what treatment is being provided—participant "blindness" is not a viable proposition, and may influence not only retention rates but also expectancies. It is also of note that evaluators are seldom able to remain "blind" to treatment condition; patients' accounts of their experiences will, Shapiro notes, almost inevitably give away the nature of the treatment they have had.)

It cannot be stressed too much that every effort should be made to avoid missing data, particularly arising from participant drop-out. However, some drop-out is inevitable. If the drop-out or refusal to participate occurs prior to randomisation, then this will not bias the results. Technically, these participants never entered the trial. Note that informed consent should be given *prior* to randomisation in conventional trials. Once random allocation has taken place, the participants are in the trial and as much relevant data as possible should be obtained from them. All randomly allocated participants should be accounted for in the analysis of the data, even if they never entered the treatment phase of the trial. It is very likely, for example, that some patients will refuse to participate once they know that they are not being offered their preferred treatment. For this reason, the "control treatment" should be seen as potentially useful by the participants. Once the treatment phase has started, there are still likely to be differential drop-out rates in the different arms of the trial, depending on how useful the participants perceive their treatment to be.

If participants drop out of therapy, it is important to try to obtain outcome data on them (however crude) and to discover the reasons for drop-out. Wherever possible, data from all participants (including those providing only very limited amounts of data) should be included in the analysis and presentation of results. This is because in an outcome trial of the type we are considering, the assessment is not of the effectiveness of specific ingredients of treatment but rather of a comparison of one form of treatment with another. If it is not possible to include every patient in the analysis, then the investigators should assess the likely biases in the results arising from this. For example, investigators could assume the worst possible outcome in the drop-outs in the "active" arm of the trial, and the best possible ones in the controls, and then reassess the results to see how robust they are to drop-out. More advanced methods of coping with drop-out are discussed by Little (1995).

Data presentation and analysis

Methods of presenting data (including graphs) and statistical analysis should be able to cope with missing data as discussed above. Summary statistics, for example, should not be naively calculated for each time point, based only on the data available at that particular time. In our trials, not only do the symptoms being treated (delusions and/or hallucinations) differ from one patient to another (as assessed by personal questionnaire, for example) but so does the approach to the treatment of these problems. Each patient will have a characteristic starting point and also a rate of improvement (or, in some cases, deterioration) during and after the treatment phase of the trial. Both of these characteristics can be regarded as random variables in the statistical analysis. The mean and standard deviation (or variance) of these random variables can then be used to describe the typical response to treatment in the two groups and the variability in the two groups. This is the basis of modern so-called random-effects models for the analysis of longitudinal data (see, for example, Diggle, Liang and Zeger, 1994; or Hand and Crowder, 1996). Suitable computer programs for this type of analysis are BMDP 5V and SAS PROC MIXED. Software for multi-level modelling (Goldstein, 1995) is also particularly useful. Note that these types of model explicitly allow for individual differences in the form of random effects. Clinicians who claim that statistical methods are inappropriate for the evaluation of psychotherapies because they are limited to analysing means, and do not account for individual patient differences, are simply revealing their ignorance of statistics and of recent developments in statistical methodology. In a sense, the random effects model can be thought of as a method of meta-analysis to combine a series of single case studies, but always bearing in mind that the single cases have been part of a controlled experiment incorporating random allocation to the competing arms of the trial.

Clinical and statistical significance

In the foregoing discussion, we have described methods of statistical analysis suitable for the type of data set typical of a clinical trial, with its variable amounts of missing data and individual patient characteristics and treatment. It is a truism, but noteworthy, nonetheless, that statistical significance is not the same as clinical significance. As Shapiro (1996) notes, from a practitioner's perspective, statistical power may be counter-productive if it enables researchers to report statistically reliable results based on trivially small differences between groups assigned to alternative treatments. Procedures to ascertain the clinical significance of change have been developed: for example, clinically significant improvement may be thought to have occurred if a person's score on a clinically relevant measure improves more than could have been expected on the basis of measurement error alone, and reaches a level after treatment that would be more characteristic of the general population than of people requiring treatment

(Shapiro, 1996). However, it is difficult to see why the use of a measurement error is a measure of clinical significance—the change could still be trivial. A better approach would be to assess the change relative to the day-to-day variability of the person's scores in the absence of an intervention, such as given by baseline data over an extended period. Furthermore, achieving a reduction of scores to general population levels, is clearly an unsuitable criterion for the treatment of people with psychosis: they are unlikely to reach the level of functioning to be found in the general population and yet they may still make changes of practical and subjective importance. Hansen and Lambert (1996), in a review of methods of assessing clinical significance, note this latter criticism and suggest the use of multiple reference groups, representing low to high levels of disturbance.

In our pilot study, we did not attempt to assess the clinical significance of change. However, we are now attempting to define criteria for clinically significant change, based on estimates of the variability in the scores over time of our control group, who did not receive cognitive behavioural therapy. Using the five scores for each control participant on each key measure, we will then be able to calculate the variability in scores for the reference population. Cut-offs for clinically significant change can then be defined. When inspecting individual cases, the stability of the change should also be considered. The application of a clear criterion of clinically significant change will be helpful in addressing a number of questions about outcome, including how many participants show improvement and on which measures, the identification of treatment non-responders and the timing of clinically significant change on different measures.

A PILOT STUDY EVALUATION OF COGNITIVE BEHAVIOURAL THERAPY FOR PSYCHOSIS

In this section, we report briefly on our pilot study (Garety et al., 1994). This study was designed to discover whether we could engage clients with psychosis with our therapeutic approach (Fowler, Garety and Kuipers, 1995); to "road-test" our assessments; and to find out if the results of therapy would justify proceeding to a larger randomised controlled trial; as noted above, this larger trial is now in progress. We also were conscious of some of the methodological hazards discussed above and, while seeking to minimise sample attrition, we employed measures and statistical methods which aimed to take account of some of the difficulties.

Goals of therapy and assessment measures

In our approach, the goals of therapy may address any or all of three major goals: (a) to reduce the subjective distress and interference with a person's life which arises from the experience of psychotic symptoms, particularly delusions and hallucinations; (b) to increase the understanding of psychotic disorders and to foster motivation to engage in self-regulatory or coping behaviours; and (c) to reduce depression, low self esteem and hopelessness. This approach therefore requires a wide range of assessments to cover all possible targets of therapy. It also calls for a multi-dimensional approach to delusions and hallucinations, addressing not only conviction and frequency, but also measures of subjective distress and interference, such as acting on delusions. Insight and the participants' appraisals of their problems should be assessed, as well as mood, self-esteem and social functioning. Finally, in order to take account of the full range of symptoms that may be present and subject to change over therapy, broad symptom measures are needed.

Timing of assessments

In therapy trials, some measures may be given only before and after treatment and at follow-up, while others may be administered more often, during the course of therapy. In this study, we chose to administer a number of assessments at monthly intervals, in order to track the development of change and to further our understanding of therapy process; the other measures, given pre- and post-therapy, were used simply to assess efficacy. Clearly, a follow-up assessment is also desirable to establish whether any therapy benefits are maintained over time; in the pilot study reported here, completed within a strict one-year time limit, this was not possible.

Measures

Full details of the assessments are given in Garety et al., (1994) and Kuipers, Garety and Fowler (1996). Here the key assessments will be listed.

Before and after the intervention

• Present State Examination (PSE, Wing, Cooper and Sartorius, 1974)— employed to elicit current symptoms and to derive a CATEGO classification
• Maudsley Assessment of Delusions Schedule (MADS, Wessely et al., 1993)—a multi-dimensional assessment of delusions, with eight dimensions
• Insight scale (David, 1990)
• Rosenberg Self-esteem Scale (Rosenberg, 1965)
• Appraisal of Problems Measure (Garety et al., 1994)—an idiosyncratically constructed self-report measure of the appraisal of the distress and interference arising from patient's "most important" problems

- Life Skills Profile (Rosen, Hadzi Pavlovic and Parker, 1989)—a social functioning measure completed by a relative or key worker.

Before and after the intervention and at monthly intervals

- Personal Questionnaires assessing three key dimensions of hallucinations or delusions identified by the PSE. Conviction, preoccupation and distress were measured for each delusion (Brett-Jones, Garety and Hemsley, 1987)
- Brief Psychiatric Rating Scale (Overall and Gorham, 1962)
- Beck Depression Inventory (Beck, Ward, Mendelson, Mock and Erbaugh, 1961)
- Social Avoidance and Distress Scale (Watson and Friend, 1969)—a measure of social anxiety
- Hustig and Hafner Hallucinations Assessment (Hustig and Hafner, 1990)—a multi-dimensional assessment of hallucinations.

These measures proved acceptable to all but 1 of 21 participants; this person could not attend and concentrate sufficiently at the initial assessment phase and was therefore excluded.

Statistical analysis

The measures which were only administered pre- and post-therapy were analysed by constructing change scores in participants where both measures were available and then comparing the groups with t tests. Clearly, in the light of the earlier discussion, this method suffers acutely from the problems of sample attrition and missing data. By reduced numbers, it loses statistical power, but it may also be subject to non-random biases. Therefore, our main outcome assessments were based on a different treatment of the repeated measures.

The analysis of the repeated measures (taken up to six times, with a variable amount of missing data) was carried out using the variance components software REML (Scottish Agricultural Statistical Services, Edinburgh) and the general mixed model program 5V in BMDP. The estimates of the mean values of patients' symptom scores were derived using REML in a way that copes with many of the potential sources of missing data. BMDP 5V was used to re-analyse selected results to check the robustness of the findings to various model assumptions. On the whole, the models were simpler than the full random effects models described in the methodology section above, since the amount of data in this pilot study was insufficient to warrant the extra effort. The fitted models are referred to as regression models in Hand and Crowder (1996), their key difference from the random effects model being the assumption of a common rate of improvement in participants in each arm of the trial.

This over-simplification will be relaxed in the analysis of our current trial.

Outcome

The results of the study will be briefly reported here. Interested readers are referred to Garety et al., (1994) for full details.

Participants

Brief details of the participants are given in Tables 6.2 and 6.3. They were predominantly male, carried a diagnosis of schizophrenia and had lengthy psychiatric histories. At initial assessment, all participants in the therapy group were currently deluded and proportionately fewer were suffering from auditory hallucinations than in the waiting list control group. Pre-treatment scores on the Brief Psychiatric Rating Scale indicate moderate levels of symptomatology and the groups scored as mildly to moderately depressed. All participants were prescribed neuroleptic medication

Table 6.2 Participants' demographic data

Variable	Therapy group ($N = 13$)		Controls ($N = 7$)	
	Mean	Range	Mean	Range
Age (years)	39.6	21–70	37.6	26–53
Duration of illness (years)	16.5	6–30	10.9	5–20
Number of admissions	2.9	1–5	2.0	1–3
Predicted IQ (NART)	108	94–125	112	98–125
Gender	Male	($N = 12$)	Male	($N = 6$)
	Female	($N = 1$)	Female	($N = 1$)

Table 6.3 Participants' clinical data at initial assessment

Variable	Therapy group ($N = 13$)	Control group ($N = 7$)
Clinical diagnosis:	Schizophrenia 12 Schizo-affective 1	Schizophrenia 7
PSE: one or more current delusions	13	5
PSE: one or more current hallucinations	5	5
PSE: Altered perception	2	3
	Mean (SD)	Mean (SD)
Brief Psychiatric Rating Scale	34.4 (5.6)	29.9 (6.9)
Beck Depression Inventory	18.0 (11.5)	15.9 (10.2)

throughout the trial. There were no significant differences between the groups on any of the demographic or pre-treatment clinical measures.

Therapy

Our approach to therapy has been described in detail in Fowler, Garety and Kuipers (1995). The therapy employs a cognitive behavioural approach to reduce distress associated with psychotic symptoms, to develop coping and self-management strategies and to improve mood and self-esteem. The focus is on an individualised case formulation and a collaborative relationship based upon a detailed assessment which draws on cognitive theories of psychosis.

Therapy was offered at weekly and fortnightly intervals over six months. Clients received an average of sixteen sessions (range 11–22). Thirteen clients commenced therapy, but one dropped out after three sessions after a change in medication and a major relapse. A second person, despite continuing in therapy, became suspicious of the researcher doing the assessments and so could not be reassessed. Therapy was carried out by three of the authors (PAG, EK and DF), clinical psychologists experienced with working with psychotic clients.

Results

A summary of the results is presented here. There is a striking reduction in the level of conviction with which delusions were held, as assessed by

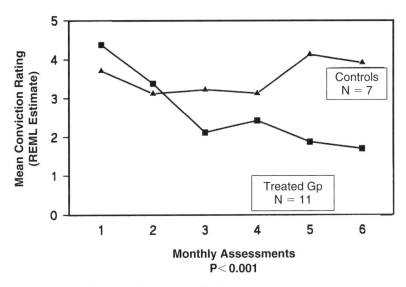

Figure 6.1   Fall in delusional conviction during treatment

personal questionnaires (p <0.01; see Figure 6.1). This variable was assessed repeatedly and was therefore analysed using REML estimates.

There were also significant changes, on pre–post assessment, in action associated with delusions assessed by the MADS ($p<0.05$) and changes in delusional preoccupation on the MADS just failed to reach significance ($p=0.07$) (Table 6.4). The Appraisal of Problems Measure showed a significant reduction in self-reported distress ($p<0.05$) and interference from problems ($p<0.05$) (also Table 6.4).

General symptomatology, as assessed by the Brief Psychiatric Rating Scale (REML estimates), showed a significant reduction in the treated group, ($p<0.01$; see Table 6.5) as did depression measured by the Beck Depression Inventory ($p<0.05$; see Table 6.6).

A number of measures did not show significant improvements in the treated group. These included distress associated with the delusions, whether assessed by personal questionnaire or the MADS, insight, social anxiety, self-esteem and social functioning.

Discussion

While some of the assessments were conducted only pre- and post-therapy, as noted, we selected certain measures for monthly assessments. In addition to allowing for more sophisticated statistical treatment, this allows inspection of the rate and timing of change in key variables. While delusional conviction showed reductions from the first month of therapy, it

Table 6.4 Summary of measures taken only before and after therapy

Variable	N	Therapy group change score		N	Control group change score		t	d.f.	p
		Mean	SD		Mean	SD			
MADS									
Preoccupation	11	0.82	0.9	7	0.1	0.4	1.9	16	0.07
Total Action	11	1.5	1.3	7	−0.1	1.5	2.4	16	0.03
Total Distress	11	1.5	2.5	7	0.7	1.4	0.7	16	0.50
Appraisal of Problems Questionnaire									
Distress	11	0.8	1.2	7	−0.6	1.0	2.6	16	0.02
Interference	11	0.8	0.9	7	−0.1	0.9	2.3	16	0.04
Life Skills Profile	11	2.4	0.9	6	−0.3	7.5	0.5	15	0.62
Insight Scale	11	2.8	11.8	7	2.1	1.9	0.5	16	0.65
Rosenberg Self-esteem Questionnaire	11	−0.6	5.7	7	−2.4	11.2	0.4	16	0.66

is of interest that the depression scores decreased later (after the second month) and also showed a rise at the post-therapy assessment. This was consistent with the therapists' experience of focusing on the affective

Table 6.5 Before and after measures on the Brief Psychiatric Rating Scale

Monthly assessment	Therapy group					Control group			
	Mean	SD	N	REML est		Mean	SD	N	REML est
Before therapy									
1	34.4	5.6	12	34.4		29.9	6.9	7	29.8
During therapy									
2	32.5	7.1	9	30.9		31.7	7.0	7	31.7
3	30.3	6.4	9	30.8		31.4	7.2	7	31.4
4	29.5	6.0	10	29.2		31.6	10.0	5	30.6
5	28.4	5.1	10	28.1		32.4	9.8	5	31.4
After therapy									
6	30.2	10.4	8	28.5		36.7	11.0	3	31.9

$p < .01$.
Note. REML estimates: allow for bias due to drop-outs or missing values.

Table 6.6 Before and after measures on Beck Depression Inventory

Monthly assessment	Therapy group					Control group			
	Mean	SD	N	REML est		Mean	SD	N	REML est
Before therapy									
1	18.0	11.5	13	18.0		15.9	10.2	7	15.9
During therapy									
2	19.6	9.8	9	18.9		17.1	14.8	7	17.1
3	15.2	10.8	9	18.9		19.1	13.3	7	19.1
4	12.0	11.9	10	13.5		17.4	13.3	5	16.0
5	10.8	10.3	10	11.8		19.8	16.5	5	18.4
After therapy									
6	15.7	13.0	9	15.5		27.0	15.6	3	20.5

$p < .05$
Note. REML estimates: allow for bias due to drop-outs or missing values.

aspects later and noting that, with some patients, further work remained to be done at the end of six months. The monthly assessments added weight to the impression that therapy might usefully be extended for a longer period with a view to more effective work on depression. The wide ranging assessments also demonstrated that anxiety, self-esteem and social functioning had not improved significantly, so that greater attention was needed on these aspects in our future study.

Finally, the multi-dimensional approach to the assessment of delusions was informative. While conviction and action showed clear changes on our measures and preoccupation an encouraging trend, the distress associated with the delusion did not decrease. Despite this, general self-reported distress and depression showed reductions. Why was this so? One possibility is that where a delusional belief was distressing, because, for example, it involved extreme threat, the person who comes to believe it less may feel less generally distressed and preoccupied but may continue to rate that particular belief as distressing. This will warrant further exploration.

CONCLUSIONS

The evaluation of cognitive behavioural therapy for psychosis is an exciting but complex task. The preliminary findings of the small number of published studies are promising. However, a variety of challenges is presented to investigators. These include the difficulties of engaging clients in treatment and for assessment; the possibility of high drop-out; the measurement of symptoms which vary over time; the need for multi-dimensional assessment approaches; and the importance of detecting small and specific changes in what may be an enduring illness. Nevertheless, it is possible to conduct well-designed research trials to evaluate outcome, using suitable measures and statistical techniques which take account of missing data. The growing recognition of the value of attending to clinical significance and of the potential benefits of using comparable measures across studies should assist the development of outcome research for psychological interventions for psychosis. With improved methodology and more studies, we can hope to answer increasingly specific questions about treatment effectiveness, and, in turn, aim to develop new and more refined treatments.

REFERENCES

Beck, A.T., Ward, C.H., Mendelson, M., Mock, T. and Erbaugh, J. (1961) An inventory for measuring depression. *Archives of General Psychiatry* **4**: 561–71.
Bentall, R.P., Kinderman, P. and Kaney, S. (1994) Self, attributional processes and abnormal beliefs: towards a model of persecutory delusions. *Behaviour Research and Therapy* **32**: 331–41.

Birchwood, M., Mason, R., McMillan, F. and Healy. J. (1993) Depression, demoralization and control over illness: a comparison of depressed and non–depressed patients with chronic psychosis. *Psychological Medicine* **23**: 387–95.

Brett-Jones, J., Garety, P.A. and Hemsley, D. (1987) Measuring delusional experiences: a method and its application. *British Journal of Clinical Psychology* **26**: 257–65.

Chadwick, P. and Birchwood, M. (1994) The omnipotence of voices: a cognitive approach to auditory hallucinations. *British Journal of Psychiatry* **164**: 190–201.

Chadwick, P, and Birchwood, M. (1995) The omnipotence of voices II: The beliefs about voices questionnaire. *British Journal of Psychiatry* **165**: 773–6.

David, A. (1990) Insight and psychosis *British Journal of Psychiatry* **156**: 225–32.

Chadwick, P. and Lowe, F. (1990) The measurement and modification of delusional beliefs. *Journal of Consulting and Clinical Psychology* **58**: 225–32 .

Diggle, P.J., Liang, K.-Y. and Zeger, S.L. (1994) *Analysis of Longitudinal Data* Oxford: Oxford University Press.

Fowler, D., Garety, P.A. and Kuipers, L. (1995) *Cognitive Behaviour Therapy for People with Psychosis* Chichester: John Wiley.

Froyd, J.E., Lambert, M.J. and Froyd, J.D. (1996) A review of practices of psychotherapy outcome measurement. *Journal of Mental Health* **5**: 17–24.

Garety, P.A. (1985) Delusions: Problems in definition and measurement. *British Journal of Medical Psychology* **58**, 25–34.

Garety, P.A. and Hemsley, D.R. (1987) Characteristics of delusional experience. *European Archives of Psychiatry and Neurological Sciences* **236**: 294–8.

Garety, P.A., Hemsley, D.R. (1994) *Delusions : Investigations into the Psychology of Delusional Reasoning* Maudsley Monographs, Oxford : Oxford University Press.

Garety, P.A., Kuipers, L., Fowler, D., Dunn, G. and Chamberlain, F. (1994) Cognitive Behaviour Therapy for Drug Resistant Psychosis. *British Journal of Medical Psychology* **67**: 259—271.

Goldstein, H. (1995) *Multilevel Statistical Models* (2nd Edition) London: Edward Arnold.

Haddock, G, Bentall, R.P., and Slade, P.D. (1996) Psychological Treatment of Auditory Hallucinations: Focusing or distraction? Chapter 3 in G. Haddock and P.D. Slade (eds) *Cognitive Behavioural Interventions with Psychotic Disorders* London: Routledge.

Hand, J.D. and Crowder, M. (1996) *Practical Longitudinal Data Analysis* London: Chapman & Hall.

Hansen, N.B. and Lambert, M.J. (1996) Clinical significance: an overview of methods. *Journal of Mental Health* **5**: 17–24.

Hustig, H.H., and Hafner, R.J. (1990) Persistent auditory hallucinations and their relationship to delusions and mood. *Journal of Nervous and Mental Disease* **178**: 264–7.

Kingdon, D.G. and Turkington, D. (1994) *Cognitive Behavioural Therapy of Schizophrenia* Hove: Lawrence Erlbaum.

Kuipers, L., Garety, P.A., Fowler, D. (1996) An outcome study of cognitive behavioural treatment for psychosis. Chapter 7 in G. Haddock and P. Slade (Eds) *Cognitive Behavioural Interventions with Psychotic Disorders* London: Routledge.

Little, R.J.A. (1995) Modeling the drop-out mechanism in repeated-measures studies. *Journal of the American Statistical Association* **90**: 1112–1121.

Overall, J. and Gorham, D. (1962) The Brief Psychiatric Rating Scale. *Psychological Reports* **10**: 799–812.

Rosen, A., Hadzi Pavlovic, D. and Parker, G (1989) The Life Skills Profile: a measure of assessing function and disability in schizophrenia. *Schizophrenia Bulletin* **15**: 325–37.

Rosenberg, M. (1965) *Society and Adolescent Self-Image* Princeton, NJ: Princeton University Press.

Shapiro, D.A. (1996) Outcome Research Chapter 10 in G. Parry and F.N. Watts (eds) *Behavioural and Mental Health Research* 2nd Edition Hove: Erlbaum.

Sharp, H.M., Fear, C.F., Williams, J.M.G., Healy, D., Lowe, C.F., Yeardon, H. and Holden, R. (1996). Delusional Phenomenology—Dimensions of Change. *Behaviour Research and Therapy* **34**: 123–142.

Slade, P.D and Bentall, R.P. (1988) S*ensory Deception: Towards a Scientific Analysis of Hallucinations* London: Croom Helm.

Tarrier, N., Beckett, R., Harwood, S., Baker, A., Yusupoff, L. and Ugarteburu, I. (1993) A trial of two cognitive-behavioural methods of treating drug-resistant residual psychotic symptoms in schizophrenic patients: 1 Outcome. *British Journal of Psychiatry* **162**: 524–32.

Watson, D. and Friend, R. (1969) The measurement of social evaluative anxiety. *Journal of Consulting and Clinical Psychology* **33**: 448–57.

Wessely, S., Buchanan, A., Reed, A., Everitt, B., Garety, P., Cutting, J. and Taylor, P.J. (1993) Acting on Delusions I : Prevalence. *British Journal of Psychiatry* **163**, 69—76.

Wing, J.K., Cooper, J.E. and Sartorius, N. (1974) *The Measurement and Classification of Psychiatric Symptoms* Cambridge: Cambridge University Press.

Chapter 7

PSYCHOLOGICAL PROCESSES AND DELUSIONAL BELIEFS: IMPLICATIONS FOR THE TREATMENT OF PARANOID STATES

Richard Bentall and Peter Kinderman

INTRODUCTION

In this chapter we will review research into psychological processes involved in the formation and maintenance of delusions, and consider the implications of these findings for the cognitive–behavioural treatment of psychosis. Most of what we will say will specifically concern persecutory delusions, as these have been the focus of our research efforts. However, many of the findings we will review also have implications for other kinds of delusional systems.

It is fair to say that the psychology of delusions has only recently become the focus of intensive research; when Oltmanns and Maher published an edited book on this topic in 1988, the contributors were able to review very little in the way of empirical data and, as a consequence, many of the contributions were highly speculative. In the eight years since that book's appearance, however, a substantial body of research into delusions has started to appear in the psychiatric and psychological literature.

Outcome and Innovation in Psychological Treatment of Schizophrenia. Edited by T. Wykes, N. Tarrier and S. Lewis.

Delusions as meaningful phenomena

One reason why delusions have been neglected by psychological researchers until quite recently concerns certain prejudices that have existed about the relationship between delusions and normal beliefs and attitudes. In a highly influential account, Jaspers (1913/1963) argued that the abnormal beliefs of psychiatric patients are generally held with extraordinary conviction, have bizarre or impossible content, and are impervious to counter-argument or the impact of experience. However, he further suggested that true delusions differ from normal beliefs because they are "ununderstandable", which is to say that they are unamenable to empathy and cannot be understood by reference to the patient's background and experience (see Walker, 1991 for a detailed discussion of Jasper's position). This account, which implies an unbridgeable chasm between normal beliefs and the beliefs of severely ill psychiatric patients, has recently been echoed by Berrios (1991) who has asserted that delusions are, "Empty speech acts, whose informational content refers to neither world or self. They are not the symbolic expression of anything."

Attractive though Jasper's account may seem to researchers who wish to advocate an exclusively biological model of psychosis, it is difficult to square with empirical evidence which points to a continuum or continua running from normal beliefs and attitudes to delusional beliefs. In an influential paper, Strauss (1969) argued that it is possible to identify abnormal beliefs which have some but not all of the hallmarks of full-blown delusions. Subsequent investigators have shown that the beliefs of both normal individuals and psychiatric patients can be classified on dimensions such as conviction, extension, bizarreness, disorganization, preoccupation and distressfulness which may be to some extent orthogonal to each other (Garety and Hemsley, 1987; Harrow, Rattenbury, and Stoll, 1988; Kendler, Glazer, and Morgenstern, 1983). A further indication that delusional beliefs are not entirely separate from normal beliefs is their content. If delusions were "empty speech acts' as asserted by Berrios, they should concern a wide range of unconnected themes. In fact, the most common delusions observed in psychiatric patients (for example beliefs of persecution or grandiosity) reflect important existential issues (Musalek, Berner, and Katschnig, 1989) or concerns about the individual's position in the social universe (Bentall, 1994).

Could delusions reflect perceptual abnormalities?

Perhaps because of the absence of systematic empirical research available at the time, Oltmanns and Maher's (1988) book was dominated by Maher's (1974, 1988, 1992) account of delusion-formation. According to Maher, delusions are invariably the product of rational inferences about anomalous experiences. On closer examination, this account consists of two logically unrelated elements: first Maher proposes the positive hypothesis that delusions are always a reaction to some kind of unusual perception and, second, he proposes the negative hypothesis that delusions are *never* the product of abnormal (nonperceptual) cognitive processes.

Evidence from research indicates that Maher's positive hypothesis is valid in some but not all cases. Early studies showing a statistical association between slow onset deafness (which, it might be thought, would lead some people to wonder why others are whispering in their presence) and paranoid ideation (Cooper, Garside, and Kay, 1976; Kay, Cooper, Garside, and Roth, 1976) have not been supported by later investigations (Moore, 1981; Watt, 1985). However, considerable evidence has accumulated indicating that delusional misidentifications (for example, the Capgras delusion, in which the individual believes that a loved one has been replaced by a doppelganger, impostor, or robot of some sort) are often the product of neuropsychological abnormalities which prevent the individual from properly recognizing faces (Ellis and de Pauw, 1994; Ellis and Young, 1990; Young, 1994). In a detailed examination of interviews conducted with a large group of young "schizotypal" individuals, Chapman and Chapman (1988) found that every possible relationship between anomalous perceptions and delusions was represented in their data. In some cases apparently delusional ideas indeed seemed to be rational interpretations of unusual experiences but, in others, delusions seemed to occur in the absence of anomalous perceptions and, in still others, anomalous perceptions did not evoke delusional interpretations.

Maher's second hypothesis that delusions are never the products of (nonperceptual) cognitive abnormalities is vulnerable to the demonstration of a single instance to the contrary. Maher (1974) cited some rather old studies of syllogistic reasoning (a precisely defined format of logical exploration such as "A equals B, B equals C, therefore A equals C") with broadly defined "schizophrenic" patients to support his claim that deluded patients reason in a normal fashion. However, the relevance of this kind of reasoning to real life situations is unclear and, in any case, not all patients diagnosed as schizophrenic suffer from delusions. In the following sections of this chapter, we will review evidence that cognitive abnormalities are implicated in delusions, mainly from studies which have been reported since the publication of Oltmanns and Maher's (1988) book. We will also consider the implications of this evidence for the cognitive–behavioural treatment of psychosis.

THE ROLE OF COGNITIVE PROCESSES IN DELUSIONS

Most of the research which has so far been conducted into the role of psychological abnormalities in psychosis has focused on cognitive deficits—gross difficulties in processing information as measured by tests of attention and memory (Bentall, 1992). For example, it has been found that patients with a diagnosis of schizophrenia are handicapped when processing information from the iconic store (Green and Nuechterlein, 1994), perform poorly on tests of attention (Green, 1992), and also perform poorly on a variety of other tests which measure their ability to use the past regularities of experience to regulate cognitive processing (Hemsley, 1993). These kinds of findings have led some authors to propose influential stress-vulnerability models of schizophrenia, which suggest that psychotic breakdown reflects the failure of cognitively vulnerable individuals to cope with particularly stressful episodes in their lives (Nuechterlein and Dawson, 1984; Neuchterlein, Dawson, Ventura, Fogelson, Gitlin, and Mintz, 1991; Zubin and Spring, 1977). According to such models, cognitive vulnerability factors are a product of neurobiological deficits which are presumed to play a causal role in psychosis. If stresses which overload the vulnerable cognitive system can be avoided the individual should be able to lead a relatively symptom-free existence. There is no doubt this kind of account has been highly successful in inspiring psychosocially orientated clinicians (for example, those who have focused on the "expressed emotion" of family members) who have developed interventions that reduce environmental stressors and hence the probability of psychotic relapse (Leff and Vaughn, 1980; Tarrier, 1990).

Probabilistic reasoning deficits

Despite the considerable achievements of the stress-vulnerability and other deficit models of psychosis, most models of this sort are nonspecific, and do not attempt to explain the development of particular symptoms such as delusions and hallucinations. Nonetheless, some authors have tried to construct models which implicate cognitive deficits specifically in the causation and maintenance of delusions. For example, Hemsley and Garety (1986) have argued that delusions might be caused by an inability to correctly utilize probabilistic information when reasoning about hypotheses. Consistent with this account, a number of investigators have found that deluded patients perform poorly when asked to evaluate hypotheses in the light of successively presented probabilistic information (Dudley, John, Young, and Over, 1997; Garety, Hemsley, and Wessely, 1991; Huq, Garety, and Hemsley, 1988; John and Dodgson, 1994; Young and Bentall, 1995). This difficulty seems to reflect the deluded patient's inability to integrate information perceived over a period of time—when asked how they would test particular hypotheses deluded patients appear to reason normally (Bentall and Young, 1996).

It is easy to see that a difficulty in assessing the plausibility of hypotheses might make the individual so afflicted vulnerable to accepting ideas that seem nonsensical to others. However, it seems unlikely that this account will be sufficient to explain the phenomenology of delusional states. The fact that these symptoms tend to concern particular themes—for example, persecution and grandiosity—suggests that they must at least in part reflect cognitive *biases*—the preferential processing of information of particular content (Bentall, 1994). Indeed, the probabilistic reasoning of deluded patients appears to be most abnormal when they are reasoning about social or self-referent information (Dudley, John, Young and Over, in press; Young and Bentall, 1997).

Selective information processing biases

In an attempt to construct a behavioural model of paranoia, Ullmann and Krasner (1969) suggested that the patient's abnormal attention to threat-related stimuli might serve to maintain a delusional belief. However, the role of selective attention in delusions has not been addressed empirically until quite recently.

Several studies have employed the emotional Stroop paradigm, which is a variant of a test originally developed by Stroop (1935). In this test, subjects are shown words printed in a number of different ink colours and are asked to name the colours but not the words themselves. This requirement creates response competition between the natural tendency to read the words and the requirement to name the colours, and this competition is greatest when the words are emotionally salient and preferentially attended to. As a consequence, psychiatric patients tend to be slower when colour-naming words which relate particularly to their type of psychopathology, an effect which has been demonstrated for disorders such as depression (using depression-related words, Williams and Broadbent, 1986), anxiety (using anxiety-related words, Mathews and MacLeod, 1985) and anorexia nervosa (using food-related words, Channon, Hemsley, and de Silva, 1988).

Bentall and Kaney (1989) asked patients suffering from persecutory delusions (henceforth "paranoid" patients) and depressed and normal controls to colour-name threat-related, depression-related and neutral words. The paranoid patients showed abnormally slowed colour-naming for the threat-related words, a finding which was replicated by Fear, Sharp, and Healy (1996). In a similar study which will be described in more detail below, Kinderman (1994) asked paranoid, depressed and normal subjects to colour-name positive and negative trait words as well as neutral words, and found that both clinical groups but especially the paranoid patients were slow to name the trait words, particularly if the words were negative. In a recent single case study with a patient suffering from the Cotard delusion (the belief that she was dead), slowed colour-naming for death-related words was observed when the patient was delusional but not when her symptoms had remitted (Leafhead, Young, and Szulecka, 1996). Taken together, these findings suggest that abnormal attention to particular kinds of information is involved in delusions, but that this kind of information-processing bias may only be present in patients when they are floridly symptomatic.

Abnormal attention to threat-related information should be associated with other kinds of cognitive biases, for example the preferential recall of such information. Kaney, Wolfenden, Dewey, and Bentall (1992) asked paranoid, depressed and normal subjects to recall stories which either did or did not contain propositions about threats. Although the paranoid patients recalled less information than the control subjects, they recalled more information that was specifically threat-related. In a subsequent study, Bentall, Kaney, and Bowen-Jones (1995) gave deluded and control subjects a free-recall task in which they were presented with a mixed list of threat-related, depression-related and neutral words. Whereas the depressed controls showed a specific recall bias for depression-related words, replicating a previous finding by McDowell (1984), the deluded patients showed a recall bias towards both threat-related and depression-related words.

A further prediction can be made on the basis of the emotional Stroop and memory findings. Deluded patients should give high estimates of the frequency of negative life events because estimates of frequency tend to be influenced by the availability of relevant information in memory (Kahneman, Slovic, and Tversky, 1982). To test this hypothesis, Kaney, Bowen-Jones, Dewey, and Bentall (1997) asked paranoid patients, depressed and normal controls to estimate the frequency with which they and typical others had experienced specific negative, neutral and positive interactions with others in the past, and also the frequency with which they and others might expect to experience such events in the future. In this study, the paranoid subjects were divided into those who also experienced depression and those who did not. No differences were observed for estimates of the frequency of past or future events. However, the depressed subjects and the paranoid subjects (whether or not they were depressed) gave high estimates of the frequency of negative events in comparison with the normal controls.

Attributional abnormalities

Equally consistent findings indicative of the role of cognitive biases in paranoid delusions have emerged from studies of patients "attributions' or causal explanations for positive and negative events. Causal attributions or explanations play an important role in ordinary human life: Zullow, Oettingen, Peterson, and Seligman (1988) have estimated that a statement containing the word "because" or implying a "because" can be found in approximately every hundred words of recorded speech. It is fairly obvious that many of the beliefs of deluded patients amount to abnormal attributions, which is to say that they seem to be abnormal attempts to explain events in the individual's life.

Until recently, most efforts to explore the relationship between causal attributions and psychopathology had been made in the context of depression research, and it will be helpful to briefly review this research before proceeding to examine the relationship between attributions and delusions. Abramson, Seligman, and Teasdale (1978) argued that depressed patients tend to make abnormally internal (self-blaming), stable and global explanations for negative events. Partly to test this hypothesis, Peterson, Semmel, Von Baeyer, Abramson, Metalsky, and Seligman (1982) developed the Attributional Style Questionnaire (ASQ), which requires people to think of probable causes for hypothetical positive and negative events affecting themselves, and then to rate their own causal statements on three bipolar scales of internality (whether the cause implicates the self or other people or circumstances), stability (whether the cause will be present in the future) and globalness (whether the cause will influence a wide range of events in the individual's life, or only particular events). Ratings are made on seven-point scales, for example from "totally due to me" (7 on the internality–externality scale) to "totally due to other people or circumstances" (1 on the internality–externality scale). Therefore, one might expect a response to an item "You go out on a date and it goes badly" such as "because I am a boring and unintelligent person" to be rated as internal, stable and relatively global. This would contrast with a response such as "because it was a Friday we were both tired after a week at work" which might be to be rated as external, unstable and relatively specific.

Although research into the "attributional style" of depressed patients has generally found the association between attributions and symptomatology predicted by Abramson and her colleagues (Brewin, 1985; Sweeny, Anderson, and Bailey, 1986), subsequent revisions of the model have focused more on the stability and globalness of attributions than on internality judgements (Abramson, Metalsky, and Alloy, 1989). Moreover, a number of authors have pointed out that the pessimistic attributional style attributed to depressed patients is probably related to low self-esteem rather than depression (Tennen and Herzenberger, 1987; Tennen, Herzenberger, and Nelson, 1987) and that the causal status of attributions in depressive symptomatology has yet to be established (Robins and Hayes, 1995).

In contrast to research on depression, research on delusions has focused specifically on internality judgements. In an initial study using the ASQ, Kaney and Bentall (1989) found that paranoid patients in comparison with both normal and depressed controls tended to make abnormally internal attributions for positive events and abnormally external attributions for negative events (see Figure 7.1). This finding was substantially replicated

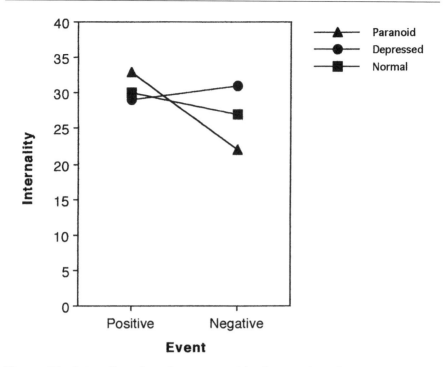

Figure 7.1 Internality data from paranoid, depressed and normal subjects, collected using the Attributional Style Questionnaire (from Kaney and Bentall, 1989).

by Candido and Romney (1990) and also by Fear et al., (1996). Fear and his colleagues also tested a small group of nonparanoid deluded patients (mainly patients suffering from grandiose delusions) and obtained similar results. Comparable findings have also been obtained using a different approach. Kaney and Bentall (1992) asked both paranoid patients and controls to play computer games which were "rigged" so that subjects either won or lost. After each game subjects completed a short questionnaire in which they were asked to estimate the degree to which they had control over the outcome. Replicating a previous finding by Alloy and Abramson (1979), the depressed subjects were "sadder but wiser"; that is, they believed they had little control in either condition. The normal subjects demonstrated a robust "self-serving bias", claiming more control over the win than the lose condition. This bias was significantly more evident in the paranoid group.

Taken together, these findings demonstrate a consistent relationship between paranoid (and perhaps other) delusions and attributional style. However, two caveats are warranted when interpreting these findings. First, the difficulty in demonstrating a causal relationship between the pessimistic attributional style and depression should caution us against leaping to the assumption that attributional processes are causal in delusions. Second, it is possible to question Abramson et al.,'s (1978) admittedly influential characterization of the internality dimension. White (1991), in particular, has noted that respondents in attributional surveys often find it difficult to answer internality questions. Moreover, a number of authors have pointed out that the internality subscales of the ASQ show very poor internal reliability (Reivich, 1995; Tennen and Herzenberger, 1985).

In fact, the internality dimension of the ASQ, by asking respondents to chose between causes that implicate the self and those which implicate "other people or circumstances", appears to confound two types of external attributions—those which implicate bad luck or situational factors and those which implicate the actions of others. That paranoid patients typically blame negative events on the intentions of others is evident from the definition of the disorder. Moreover, Kaney and Bentall (1989), in addition to asking patients to complete the ASQ also asked their subjects to complete a multidimensional locus of control scale designed by Levenson (1974). Although this scale did not discriminate between patient's attributions for positive and negative events, it did provide separate scores indicative of individuals' tendency to attribute events to internal causes, chance factors or powerful others. Not surprisingly, paranoid patients scored highly on the powerful others subscale.

In order to rectify the ASQ's failure to distinguish between external–personal and external–situational causes, Kinderman and Bentall (1996a) designed a new questionnaire called the Internal, Personal and Situational Attributions Questionnaire (IPSAQ). This questionnaire provides two separate scores: an internalizing bias score which measures the individual's tendency to attribute positive rather than negative events to the self, and a personalizing bias score, which reflects the proportion of external attributions for negative events which implicate other persons rather than situational factors. It should be recognized that this questionnaire (as with many measures of causal attributions) is restricted in scope. Beliefs concerning causal attributions are complex. The ASQ investigates internality, stability and globalness. Other analyses have focused on such factors as the degree to which individuals believe they have control over the situation. The IPSAQ is solely concerned with the distinction between three loci of causal attribution: internal; external–personal and external–situational. Clearly, other, complementary aspects of causal attribution are worthy of investigation.

Kinderman and Bentall (1996a) found that the reliability of the IPSAQ is much superior to that of the ASQ, and that personalizing bias scores in normal subjects correlate significantly with scores on a questionnaire measure of paranoid ideation. In a subsequent study, it was observed that both paranoid and normal subjects in comparison with depressed patients showed a robust externalizing bias but that the paranoid patients also showed a highly abnormal personalizing bias (Kinderman and Bentall, 1997a). This personalizing bias seemed to reflect the deluded patients' general inability to make external–situational attributions for either positive or negative events.

A COGNITIVE MODEL OF PARANOID DELUSIONS

The findings reviewed in the previous section suggest that paranoid delusions (and perhaps other types of delusions) have a functional significance. The most obvious explanation for patients' need to attribute negative events to external causes is that this prevents such causes from being attributed to the self. On this view, patients' delusional attributions are a dysfunctional mechanism for the maintenance of a positive perception of the self. This account is similar to earlier psychoanalytic accounts of paranoia, which suggested that delusions have a defensive function (Colby, Faught, and Parkinson, 1979; Winters and Neale, 1983; Zigler and Glick, 1988), but is framed in such a way that it is open to empirical investigation.

One implication of this account is that it might be useful to examine the relationship between attributional processes and self-representations in both deluded patients and normal subjects. It has long been recognized that each of us develops quite complex understandings of the self (Mead, 1934), and modern cognitive psychologists have argued that these self-representations have multiple aspects (Higgins, 1987; Markus and Wurf, 1987). For example, Higgins (1987) has argued that we have representations of our *actual-selves* (our perception of ourselves as we actually are), our *ideal-selves* (how we would like to be) and *ought-selves* (how we feel we ought to be). Until recently, studies of the self-concept in psychotic patients have mostly used unidimensional measures. These studies have found that psychotic patients, in general, show low self-esteem (Ibelle, 1961; Kaplan, 1975; Rogers, 1958; Silverstone, 1991; Wylie, 1979) but that paranoid patients are an exception and tend to report high levels of self-esteem (Havner and Izard, 1962). Other studies have indicated that psychotic patients have poorly elaborated (Robey, Cohen, and Gara, 1989) and contradictory (Gruba and Johnson, 1974) self-concepts.

In an attempt to make sense of these findings, and in order to understand the respective roles of the self and attributional processes in paranoid delusions, we have proposed a model (shown in Figure 7.2) based on Higgins' (1987) Self-Discrepancy Theory (SDT) . SDT concerns the effects of discrepancies between different self-representations. According to SDT, discrepancies may exist between different domains of the self (the actual-self, ideal-self and ought-self). However, SDT also proposes that we have different viewpoints on the self, and that discrepancies may exist between

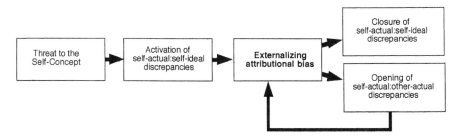

Figure 7.2   Model linking showing the relationship between self-discrepancies and attributional processes in paranoid patients (from Bentall, Kinderman and Kaney, 1994).

these viewpoints. For example, we may have views about how our parents think we actually are, how they would like us to be and how they think we ought to be, and these representations may or may not be concordant with our own actual, ideal and ought self-representations.

Until recently, research on self-discrepancies has focused on discrepancies between the domains as considered from the viewpoint of the self. Clinically depressed and dysthymic non-clinical subjects report discrepancies between the actual-self and the ideal-self, whereas socially phobic or clinically anxious patients report discrepancies between the actual-self and the ought-self (Scott and O'Hara, 1993; Strauman, 1989; Strauman and Higgins, 1988). Moreover, manipulations of these self-discrepancies in normal subjects have been shown to lead to predictable changes in mood (Strauman and Higgins, 1987), autobiographical memory (Strauman, 1992) and even physiological functioning (Strauman and Higgins, 1987; Strauman, Lemieux, and Coe, 1993).

In our original SDT model (which did not distinguish between the two kinds of external attributions—external-personal and external-situational—described earlier) we pointed to evidence (already reviewed in the section on selective information processing biases above) that paranoid patients are particularly attentive to the kinds of threatening stimuli that are likely to activate underlying or implicit negative representations of the actual-self (Bentall, Kinderman, and Kaney, 1994). These events also, therefore, threaten to trigger discrepancies between the patients' actual self-representations and their ideal and ought self-representations. In the case of paranoid individuals, externalizing causal attributions are evoked in such situations ("I am not responsible for the bad things that are happening to me, other people are"). These attributions result in a reduction of the discrepancies between the actual-self and the ideal and ought self-representations ("I am as good as I would like to be") but inevitably trigger discrepancies between self-perceptions and representations of others' views of the self ("Other people must hate me"). We have subjected this model to empirical tests which have involved assessments of both implicit and explicit self-representations, further studies of attributional processes, and studies of the predicted dynamic relationships between attributions and self-representations in normal subjects.

Self-representations in paranoid patients

We have examined the explicit self-discrepancies of patients with delusions of persecution (Kinderman and Bentall, 1996b), using measures derived from Higgin's (1987) work. In this study, we elicited subjects' actual-self, ideal-self and ought-self representations, and also their representations of how their parents viewed them (parents were chosen because they were the only "others' which all subjects were able to report about). Consistent with our model, paranoid patients alone displayed a high degree of consistency between actual self-representations and ideal and ought self-representations, but marked discrepancies between self-perceptions and the believed perceptions of parents about the self. Paranoid patients also believed that their parents had more negative views of them than did non-patient participants or depressed controls.

The hypothesis that deluded patients have an implicit, but explicitly denied, negative self-concept has been more difficult to test but has been supported by a number of studies. Kinderman (1994) directly assessed the explicit self-concept of deluded patients prior to administering the emotional Stroop task described earlier (see section on selective information processing biases). When asked to endorse negative and positive trait words according to whether they were felt to accurately describe the self, paranoid patients, like normals, endorsed many more positive than negative items. However, in contrast to the normals, the deluded patients and depressed controls both demonstrated substantial interference when colour-naming positive and especially negative trait words, indicating that such words were particularly salient for them.

Fear, et al., (1996) reported that deluded patients showed high scores on the Dysfunctional Attitude Scale (DAS; Weissman and Beck, 1978), which measures beliefs or attitudes which delineate excessively rigid and perfectionistic criteria for evaluating personal performance and self-worth. Such attitudes, it might be thought, would leave the individual vulnerable to the activation of self-discrepancies, and therefore high scores are consistent with our model. In a similar study, Bentall and Kaney (1996) also asked deluded and control subjects to complete the DAS but, in order to control for the effect of depression which is often reported by paranoid patients and which is known to be associated with high DAS scores, the paranoid group in this study was divided into comorbidly depressed and nondepressed subgroups. Both subgroups showed high DAS scores comparable with those observed by Fear and his colleagues.

Relationship between self-representations and attributions

The research so far discussed has demonstrated that patients suffering from paranoid and perhaps other types of delusions make abnormal attributions, and also that they perform abnormally on explicit and implicit measures of self-representation. However, none of the studies so far outlined have systematically investigated the impact of attributions on self-representations and vice versa. In order to address this issue, we carried out two experiments with normal subjects (Kinderman and Bentall, submitted). In the first, subjects completed a self-discrepancies questionnaire before and after completing a measure of causal attribution. Internal attributions for negative events were associated with increases in discrepancies between self-actual and self-ideal representations. However, in this first study we failed to differentiate between external–personal and external–situational attributions and simply predicted that external attributions would be associated with increases in discrepancies between self-actual representations and other-actual representations (that is, with an increased conviction that others would have a negative attitude towards the self). This prediction was not supported: external attributions were, rather, associated with reductions in both self-actual:self-ideal discrepancies and self-actual:other-actual discrepancies. However, *post hoc*, analyses revealed a significant difference between the effects of personal and situational external attributions. Not surprisingly, external–personal attributions of the sort made by paranoid patients were associated with the increase in self-actual:other-actual discrepancies as predicted by our SDT model of paranoia. On the other hand, external–situational attributions led to a reduction in self-actual:other-actual discrepancies. This finding, which was replicated in a second experiment using the Internal Personal and Situational Attributions Questionnaire, confirms the importance of distinguishing between the two kinds of external attributions, and also makes sense from a common sense perspective. Blaming oneself (depressed patients' natural response to adverse events) understandably leads to a more negative view of the self. The paranoid's tendency to blame others just as understandably leads to the belief that others have hostile intent towards the self. Ordinary people, on the other hand, are expert excuse makers and readily construct situational accounts ("I'm late because of the traffic was terrible") which implicate neither self or others.

An interesting finding from these experiments was that the relationship between attributions and self-representations appeared to be reciprocal. The kind of attributions that subjects made predicted changes in self-representations between time 1 (the first time the subjects completed the self-discrepancies questionnaire) and time 2 (the second time they completed the questionnaire). However, self-discrepancies at time 1 also predicted attributions—the greater the number of self-discrepancies reported by subjects the more internal their attributions were for negative events.

The foregoing observations raise the question of what would happen if attributions could be elicited from paranoid patients in such a way that the activation of self-discrepancies could be avoided. Information pertaining to this issue was obtained in a study in which we reported a further analysis of our initial ASQ data from paranoid patients (Kinderman, Kaney, Morley, and Bentall, 1992). It will be recalled that the ASQ requires subjects to generate causal statements about hypothetical negative events prior to self-rating these statements on scales of internality, globalness and stability. Most researchers have simply used the convenient numerical ratings when reporting ASQ findings. However, when we further examined our ASQ data we found that judges who independently rated subjects' causal statements typically agreed with the normal and depressed subjects' internality ratings. However, deluded patients self-rated as external many causal statements that were rated by the independent judges as internal. One possible explanation for this is that paranoids are much more cautious about attributing negative events to the self when explicitly asked a "who or what is to blame?" question (which would be likely to activate self-discrepancies) than when generating causal statements. Unfortunately, Fear et al., (1996) were unable to replicate this finding and so it must be treated with caution.

In another attempt to address this question, Lyon, Kaney, and Bentall (1994) employed a non-obvious measure of attributional style developed by Winters and Neale (1985), presented to subjects as a test of memory. Both deluded and depressed patients responded similarly on this measure by making *internal* attributions for negative events. However, on a traditional attributional style measure the deluded patients made external attributions for negative events as previously found by Kaney and Bentall (1989) and Candido and Romney (1990). Scores on the traditional attributional measure presumably reflected the paranoid patients' explicit attempts to maintain a positive view of the self whereas their responses on the non-obvious measure presumably reflected their implicit negative self-representations.

AETIOLOGICAL SPECULATIONS

We began this review by considering the distinction between cognitive deficits and cognitive biases, arguing that delusions could not be entirely explained by reference to deficits alone. In the subsequent discussion of the role of cognitive biases in delusions we have emphasized the role of attributional processes and self-representations. However, important questions remain unresolved. In particular, the model outlined is essentially descriptive—although it describes cognitive abnormalities which seem to be involved in persecutory delusions, it does not indicate how these cognitive abnormalities arise. If we can explain the origins of paranoid patients' cognitive abnormalities we can move from description to aetiology. The aetiologies of psychopathological phenomena are, of course, notoriously difficult to investigate, and the comments that follow are necessarily highly speculative.

Where does the externalizing bias come from: The effects of early environment?

We have already observed that depression researchers have experienced great difficulty when trying to show that a pessimistic attributional style precedes the onset of depression, and therefore constitutes a vulnerability factor rather than a state-marker of depressed mood. Typically, depression researchers have pursued this issue by studying either normal people who have a high probability of experiencing negative life events (for example, students facing examinations) or patients who are recovering from depression (see Robins and Hayes, 1995, for a review of this literature). The assumption behind these research strategies has been that attributional abnormalities, if they are causal in depression, should be measurable prior to episodes of illness and should persist after recovery has been completed. This assumption should not be accepted uncritically. If, as we have observed, there is a reciprocal relationship between attributions and self-representations, relatively small abnormalities in both of these cognitive domains would be magnified by a series of negative experiences. Indeed, it seems reasonable to think of persecutory delusions as the final product of an iterative sequence of events in which external–personal attributions are repeatedly evoked by threatening events with ever-increasing strength. Psychologists who have developed mathematical systems models of these kinds of iterative processes have shown that very small initial changes can, over a period time, produce dramatic, even qualitative changes in psychological state (van Geert, 1994).

These observations do not absolve us of the need to account for the origins of the deluded patient's cognitive style, however. Evidence suggestive that a bias towards making external attributions may precede the onset of florid psychosis was observed in the Israeli High-Risk Study of children of schizophrenic patients, in which it was found that an external locus of control in adolescence was predictive of poor mental health in adulthood (Frenkel, Kugelmass, Nathan, and Ingraham, 1995). Two further strands of evidence point to the possibility that the paranoid patient's early environment may play a role in the development of this kind of attributional vulnerability. First, depression researchers have observed significant correlations between parental attributional style and the attributional style of children (Seligman, Peterson, Kaslow, Tanenbaum,

Alloy, and Abramson, 1984) and that the causal attributions typical of depressed patients occur in the children of depressed parents (Hoffart and Torgesen, 1991). These findings indicate that cognitive styles can be transmitted between generations and that these styles involve both self-perception and attributional biases. Second, the observation that parental criticism may precipitate relapse in psychiatric patients (Brown, Birley, and Wing, 1972; Leff and Vaughn, 1980; Rund, 1994) suggests the possibility that prolonged exposure to a highly critical environment would provide the conditions necessary for the iterative magnification of attributional abnormalities. Although the aetiological significance of parental expressed emotion has yet to be adequately evaluated there is at least some evidence that familial emotional climate is related to the subsequent onset of psychotic disorders in vulnerable individuals (Valone, Norton, Goldstein, and Doane, 1983).

Where does the personalizing bias come from: The effects of cognitive deficits?

The aetiological speculations that we have so far considered concern the paranoid patient's externalizing bias. However, we have seen that paranoid patients exhibit not only an externalizing bias, but also a specific tendency to make external–personal rather than external–situational attributions when confronted with negative events. This tendency is puzzling, given that the external-situational attributions made by normal people appear to be psychologically benign. While paranoid patients' tendency to make external attributions for negative events can readily be understood in motivational terms, it is less obvious that the personalizing bias can be explained in this way. Perhaps the paranoid patient's generation of attributions which specifically implicate the intentions of others reflects a difficulty in understanding situational factors.

One process that might mediate between the kind of gross cognitive deficits discussed earlier in this chapter (for example, deficits in attention and hypothesis-testing) and abnormal attributional biases is the ability to understand and conceptualize the mental processes of other people. This ability—somewhat misleadingly known as having a Theory of Mind (ToM) because it involves individuals speculating about the mental states of others—is considered to play an important role in ordinary social interactions, and the developmental consequences of deficits in this ability have been extensively investigated. A number of investigators have argued that ToM deficits play a possible causal role in autism and Asberger's syndrome (Baron-Cohen, 1995; Frith, 1989; Happé and Frith, 1994; Leslie, 1991). For example, autistic children, in comparison with appropriate controls, tend to suggest that others would look for hidden objects in places where they (the children) know them to be, despite observing that the others cannot have this knowledge (Baron-Cohen, Leslie, and Frith, 1985).

Frith (1992) has argued that difficulties in representing the mental states of others may also play a role in schizophrenia symptoms, particularly paranoia. Consistent with this suggestion, Corcoran, Frith, and Mercer (1995) observed that patients diagnosed as suffering from schizophrenia performed poorly on a task requiring participants to draw inferences from indirect but clear hints. Similarly, Frith and Corcoran (1996) found that schizophrenia patients presented with simple stories accompanied by cartoons performed poorly when answering questions which required them to infer the mental state of one of the characters. Detailed analyses of the data from these studies indicated that paranoid patients and a group of patients with positive and negative behavioural signs performed particularly poorly on the ToM questions.

As Frith (1994) has observed, it is obvious that psychotic patients with ToM deficits will encounter difficulty when they attempt to understand the intentions of significant others. However, an account of paranoia constructed exclusively in terms of ToM deficits fails to make it obvious why such patients invariably believe that others are of malevolent intent (paranoid patients might otherwise simply report that they cannot understand what others think, or might attribute inaccurate but nonmalevolent intentions to others.) This attribution of malevolence becomes more understandable when ToM deficits are considered in the context of the attributional abnormalities already discussed in the earlier sections of this chapter. Most people, when confronted with a friend or acquaintance who appears to behave unreasonably towards them (for example, a friend who ignores them) make excuses for the other party. For example, we may conclude that our friend is stressed, is feeling ill, or has had a particularly bad day. These kinds of situational attributions for negative social interactions require us to take the other person's perspective. If we are unable to do this, and if we are unwilling to blame ourselves for the negative event, we are left with the conclusion that the friend deliberately set out to hurt us—an external–personal attribution.

To test this hypothesis we have recently carried out a study with normal subjects, in which we have examined the relationship between social reasoning as measured by an attribution task, and performance on a ToM task (Kinderman, Dunbar, and Bentall, in press). Undergraduate subjects completed a ToM task and also completed the Internal, Personal and Situational Attributions Questionnaire (IPSAQ). As we predicted, those individuals who were poor at inferring the mental states of others made causal attributions that were significantly different from those individuals relatively skilled at this kind of social cognition. Specifically, individuals who made relatively many errors on questions measuring ToM ability attributed significantly more negative events to persons as opposed to situational factors.

It is possible that ToM deficits help to explain the episodic nature of paranoid ideation. In our study of the relationship between ToM deficits and attributional processes, we observed that our subjects found ToM tasks much more difficult than control questions which were formally of comparable complexity. Understanding other people's mental states, it seems, requires considerable mental effort. Such effortful processes are likely to be undermined by the kinds of gross cognitive deficits that psychotic patients experience during acute phases of their illness. As vulnerability researchers have noted, such gross cognitive deficits, in turn, probably reflect biological dysfunctions of the central nervous system (Nuechterlein and Dawson, 1984; Nuechterlein et al., 1991).

We must repeat that the forgoing discussion of aetiological factors has been highly speculative. Much more research is required before the conjectures we have made about the role of environmental and biological factors in paranoid cognition can be accepted as "proven". However, at present there seems to be at least some evidence that points to possible causal pathways—both environmental and biological—which may play a role in the development of paranoid delusions. These causal pathways are summarized in Figure 7.3.

FROM THEORY TO THERAPY

In this chapter, we have described a programme of research that has linked paranoid delusions to attentional processes, attributions, self-representations and, finally, to the capacity to understand the mental states of others. Although attributional abnormalities play the central role in this account, we have argued that these should not be seen in isolation and must be understood in the context of the other kinds of cognitive abnormalities we have considered. We will conclude by briefly discussing the implications that our model has for the cognitive–behavioural treatment of deluded patients.

If delusions reflect abnormal attributions in the way that we have suggested, changing patients' attributions should result in a reduction in paranoid symptomatology. However, the self-protective function of the deluded patient's attributional style presents something of a dilemma for the cognitive–behaviour therapist. There is a danger that directly confronting patients with evidence that is inconsistent with their delusions will lead to an exacerbation of symptomatology or, more likely, outright resistance by the patient.

One approach to this problem would be to devise methods of questioning patients' beliefs that are not too threatening. A number of cognitive–behavioural strategies which have shown considerable promise appear to work in this way. For example, Watts, Powell, and Austin (1973) devised an approach they called "belief modification", in which patients are

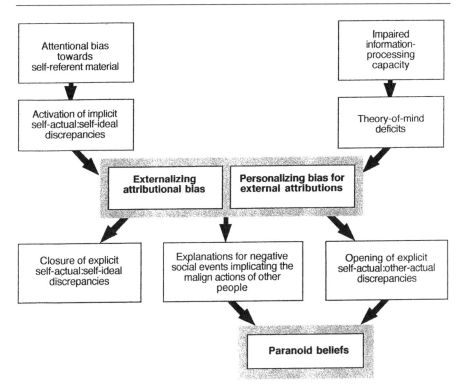

Figure 7.3 Hypothetical aetiological pathways implicated in paranoid delusions.

first challenged about peripheral aspects of their delusional system, before later being confronted about their core beliefs. More recently, Chadwick and Lowe (1990) have advocated strategies which lead patients to construct their own tests of their delusional hypotheses. There is little doubt that these approaches are effective with some patients. Several small-scale CBT trials which have utilized these as well as other cognitive–behavioural techniques with psychotic patients have reported successful outcomes (Garety, Kuipers, Fowler, Chamberlain, and Dunn, 1994; Kingdon and Turkington, 1991; Tarrier, Beckett, Harwood, Baker, Yusupoff, and Ugarteburu, 1993) and a number of larger scale trials are now approaching completion.

A further cognitive–behavioural strategy, which we have derived directly from the account of delusions we have offered in this chapter, makes use of the three-locus typology of internality judgements. It will be recalled that judgements of internality can be classified as internal, external–situational and external–personal. Internal attributions for negative events tend to make self-ideal discrepancies accessible, may lead to depression, and therefore should not be encouraged by the therapist. External–personal attributions lead to paranoia whereas external–situational attributions appear to be psychologically benign. It follows that therapists should be able to challenge paranoid patients' personalizing attributional style by encouraging them to make external–situational attributions. This might be done, for example, by asking patients to think of difficult episodes in their life and to consider the causes of those episodes. In the event of patients generating either internal or external–personal causes, therapists might encourage patients to think about situational factors which may have played a role.

We have recently reported a case-study of this kind of cognitive-behaviour therapy with a paranoid patient (Kinderman and Bentall, 1997b). Systematic measurement of paranoid anxiety and attributional processes over time allowed an examination of the relationship between these variables within a single individual. As predicted, the patient, when paranoid, exhibited an external–personalizing attributional style, blaming other individuals for negative events. Following therapy specifically targeted at altering the pattern of attributions generated by the patient, his level of expressed paranoia, as assessed by a number of measures, fell

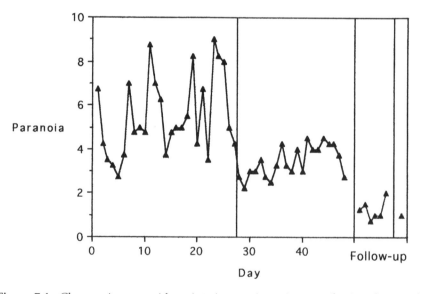

Figure 7.4 Changes in paranoid anxiety in a patient given attribution therapy for paranoid delusions (from Kinderman and Bentall, 1997b). Daily recordings were made of paranoid ideation on a 10 cm visual analogue scale labelled ranging from "Not at all worried about any conspiracy" to "Extremely worried about a conspiracy". Data are presented in two phases of treatment, with phase 1 being before and phase 2 after instructions to develop alternative situational explanations for ambigious events. Follow-up records occurred on days 82 to 87 (the 12th week after commencement of treatment) and on day 147.

dramatically (see Figure 7.4). The patient's attributional style, as measured by the IPSAQ, also changed in the expected direction during the course of therapy.

The findings from this case study require replication. Moreover, it must be emphasized that the strategy we have outlined is one amongst many which have recently been developed for the treatment of psychotic patients. However, the case study illustrates one of the strengths of the cognitive–behavioural approach to treatment—that research into psychopathology and research into interventions inform and influence each other. It is likely that further research into the cognitive and aetiological processes involved in delusions and other types of psychotic experiences will lead to further innovations in treatment.

REFERENCES

Abramson, L.Y., Metalsky, G.I. and Alloy, L.B. (1989) Hopelessness depression: A theory-based subtype of depression. *Psychological Review*, **96**, 358–372.

Abramson, L.Y., Seligman, M.E.P. and Teasdale, J.D. (1978) Learned helplessness in humans: Critique and reformulation. *Journal of Abnormal Psychology*, **78**, 40–74.

Alloy, L.B. and Abramson, L.Y. (1979) Judgements of contingency in depressed and non-depressed students: Sadder but wiser? *Journal of Experimental Psychology: General*, **108**, 441–485.

Baron-Cohen, S. (1995) *Mindblindness: An essay on autism and theory of mind.* Cambridge, Mass.: MIT Press.

Baron-Cohen, S., Leslie, A.M. and Frith, U. (1985) Does the autistic child have a "theory of mind"? *Cognition*, **21**, 37–46.

Bentall, R.P. (1992) Psychological deficits and biases in psychiatric disorders. *Current Opinion in Psychiatry*, **5**, 825–830.

Bentall, R.P. (1994) Cognitive biases and abnormal beliefs: Towards a model of persecutory delusions. In A.S. David and J.Cutting (Eds.), *The Neuropsychology of Schizophrenia* (pp. 337–360) London: Lawrence Erlbaum.

Bentall, R.P. and Kaney, S. (1989) Content-specific information processing and persecutory delusions: An investigation using the emotional Stroop test. *British Journal of Medical Psychology*, **62**, 355–364.

Bentall, R.P. and Kaney, S. (1996) Abnormalities of self-representation and persecutory delusions. *Psychological Medicine*, **26**, 1231–1237.

Bentall, R.P., Kaney, S. and Bowen-Jones, K. (1995) Persecutory delusions and recall of threat-related, depression-related and neutral words. *Cognitive Therapy and Research*, **19**, 331–343.

Bentall, R.P., Kinderman, P. and Kaney, S. (1994) The self, attributional processes and abnormal beliefs: Towards a model of persecutory delusions. *Behaviour Research and Therapy*, **32**, 331–341.

Bentall, R.P. and Young, H.F. (1996) Sensible-hypothesis-testing in deluded, depressed and normal subjects. *British Journal of Psychiatry*, **168**, 372–375.

Berrios, G. (1991) Delusions as "wrong beliefs": A conceptual history. *British Journal of Psychiatry*, **159** (Supplement 14), 6–13.

Brewin, C.R. (1985) Depression and causal attributions: What is their relation? *Psychological Bulletin*, **98**, 297–309.

Brown, G.W., Birley, J.L.T. and Wing, J.K. (1972) Influence of family life on the course of schizophrenia disorders: Replication. *British Journal of Psychiatry*, **121**, 241–258.

Candido, C.L. and Romney, D.M. (1990) Attributional style in paranoid vs depressed patients. *British Journal of Medical Psychology*, **63**, 355–363.

Chadwick, P. and Lowe, C.F. (1990) The measurement and modification of delusional beliefs. *Journal of Consulting and Clinical Psychology*, **58**, 225–232.

Channon, S., Hemsley, D.R. and de Silva, P. (1988) Selective processing of food words in anorexia nervosa. *British Journal of Clinical Psychology*, **27**, 259–260.

Chapman, L.J. and Chapman, J.P. (1988) The genesis of delusions. In T.F. Oltmanns and B.A. Maher (Eds.), *Delusional beliefs* (pp. 167–183) New York: John Wiley.

Colby, K.M., Faught, W.S. and Parkinson, R.C. (1979) Cognitive therapy of paranoid conditions: Heuristic suggestions based on a computer simulation. *Cognitive Therapy and Research*, **3**, 55–60.

Cooper, A.F., Garside, R.F. and Kay, D.W. (1976) A comparison of deaf and non-deaf patients with paranoid and affective psychoses. *British Journal of Psychiatry*, **129**, 532– 538.

Corcoran, R., Frith, C.D. and Mercer, G. (1995) Schizophrenia, symptomatology and social inference: Investigating "theory of mind" in people with schizophrenia. *Schizophrenia Research*, **17**, 5–13.

Dudley, R.E.J., John, C.H., Young, A.W. and Over, D.E. (1997) Normal and abnormal reasoning in people with delusions. *British Journal of Clinical Psychology*, **36**, 243–258.

Dudley, R.E.J., John, C.H., Young, A.W. and Over, D.E. (in press) The effect of self-referent material on the reasoning of people with delusions. *British Journal of Clinical Psychology*.

Ellis, H.D. and de Pauw, K.W. (1994) The cognitive neuropsychiatric origins of the Capgras delusion. In A.S. David and J.C. Cutting (Eds.), *The Neuropsychology of Schizophrenia* (pp. 317–335) Hove: Erlbaum.

Ellis, H.D. and Young, A.W. (1990) Accounting for delusional misidentifications. *British Journal of Psychiatry*, **157**, 239–248.

Fear, C.F., Sharp, H. and Healy, D. (1996) Cognitive processes in delusional disorder. *British Journal of Psychiatry*, **168**, 61–67.

Frenkel, E., Kugelmass, S., Nathan, M. and Ingraham, L.J. (1995) Locus of control and mental health in adolescence and adulthood. *Schizophrenia Bulletin*, **21**, 219–226.

Frith, U. (1989) *Autism: Explaining the Enigma*. Oxford: Blackwell.

Frith, C.D. (1992) *The Cognitive Neuropsychology of Schizophrenia*. Hillsdale, NJ: Lawrence Erlbaum.

Frith, C. (1994) Theory of mind in schizophrenia. In A.S. David and J.C. Cutting (Eds.), *The Neuropsychology of Schizophrenia* Hove: Erlbaum.

Frith, C. and Corcoran, R. (1996) Exploring "theory of mind" in people with schizophrenia. *Psychological Medicine*, **26**, 521–530.

Garety, P.A. and Hemsley, D.R. (1987) The characteristics of delusional experience. *European Archives of Psychiatry and Neurological Sciences*, **236**, 294–298.

Garety, P.A., Hemsley, D.R. and Wessely, S. (1991) Reasoning in deluded schizophrenic and paranoid patients. *Journal of Nervous and Mental Disease*, **179**(4), 194–201.

Garety, P.A., Kuipers, L., Fowler, D., Chamberlain, F. and Dunn, G. (1994) Cognitive behavioural therapy for drug-resistant psychosis. *British Journal of Medical Psychology*, **67**, 259–271.

Green, M.F. (1992) Information processing in schizophrenia. In D.J. Kavanagh (Ed.), *Schizophrenia: An overview and practical handbook* (pp. 45–58) London: Chapman and Hall.

Green, M.F. and Neuchterlein, K.H. (1994) Mechanism of backward masking in schizophrenia. In A.S. David and J.C. Cutting (Eds.), *The Neuropsychology of Schizophrenia*. Hove: Erlbaum.

Gruba, F.P. and Johnson, J.E. (1974) Contradictions within the self-concepts of schizophrenics. *Journal of Clinical Psychology*, **30**, 253–254.

Happé, F. and Frith, U. (1994) Theory of mind in autism. In E. Schopler and G.B. Mesibov (Eds.), *Learning and Cognition in Autism*. New York: Plenum Press.

Harrow, M., Rattenbury, F. and Stoll, F. (1988) Schizophrenic delusions: An analysis of their persistence, of related premorbid ideas and three major dimensions. In T.F. Oltmanns and B.A. Maher (Eds.), *Delusional Beliefs* (pp. 184–211) New York: John Wiley.

Havner, P.H. and Izard, C.E. (1962) Unrealistic self-enhancement in paranoid schizophrenics. *Journal of Consulting Psychology*, **26**, 65–68.

Hemsley, D.R. (1993) A simple (or simplistic?) cognitive model for schizophrenia. *Behaviour Research and Therapy*, **7**, 633–645.

Hemsley, D.R. and Garety, P.A. (1986) The formation and maintenance of delusions: A Bayesian analysis. *British Journal of Psychiatry*, **149**, 51–56.

Higgins, E.T. (1987) Self-discrepancy: A theory relating self and affect. *Psychological Review*, **94**, 319–340.

Hoffart, A. and Torgesen, S. (1991) Causal attributions in first degree relatives of depressed and agoraphobic inpatients. *Comprehensive Psychiatry*, **32**, 458–464.

Huq, S.F., Garety, P.A. and Hemsley, D.R. (1988) Probabilistic judgements in deluded and nondeluded subjects. *Quarterly Journal of Experimental Psychology*, **40A**, 801–812.

Ibelle, B.P. (1961) Discrepancies between self-concepts and ideal self-concepts in paranoid schizophrenics and normals. *Dissertation Abstracts*, **21**, 2004–2005.

Jaspers, K. (1913/1963) *General Psychopathology* (Hoenig, J., Hamilton, M.W., Trans.) Manchester: Manchester University Press.

John, C.H. and Dodgson, G. (1994) Inductive reasoning in delusional thought. *Journal of Mental Health*, **3**, 31–49.

Kahneman, D., Slovic, P. and Tversky, A. (1982) *Judgement under Uncertainty: Heuristics and biases*. Cambridge: Cambridge University Press.

Kaney, S. and Bentall, R.P. (1989) Persecutory delusions and attributional style. *British Journal of Medical Psychology*, **62**, 191–198.

Kaney, S. and Bentall, R.P. (1992) Persecutory delusions and the self-serving bias. *Journal of Nervous and Mental Disease*, **180**, 773–780.

Kaney, S., Bowen-Jones, K. and Bentall, R.P. (1997) Frequency and consensus judgements of paranoid, paranoid-depressed and depressed psychiatric patients: Subjective estimates for positive, negative and neutral events. *British Journal of Clinical Psychology*, **36**, 349–364.

Kaney, S., Wolfenden, M., Dewey, M.E. and Bentall, R.P. (1992) Persecutory delusions and the recall of threatening and non-threatening propositions. *British Journal of Clinical Psychology*, **31**, 85–87.

Kaplan, H.B. (1975) *Self-attitudes and Deviant Behaviour*. Pacific Pallisades: Goodyear.

Kay, D.W., Cooper, A.F., Garside, R.F. and Roth, M. (1976) The differentiation of paranoid from affective psychoses by patients' premorbid characteristics. *British Journal of Psychiatry*, **129**, 207–215.

Kendler, K.S., Glazer, W. and Morgenstern, H. (1983) Dimensions of delusional experience. *American Journal of Psychiatry*, **140**, 466–469.

Kinderman, P. (1994) Attentional bias, persecutory delusions and the self concept. *British Journal of Medical Psychology*, **67**, 53–66.

Kinderman, P. and Bentall, R.P. (1996a) The development of a novel measure of causal attributions: The Internal Personal and Situational Attributions

Questionnaire. *Personality and Individual Differences*, **20**, 261–264.

Kinderman, P. and Bentall, R.P. (1996b) Self-discrepancies and persecutory delusions: Evidence for a defensive model of paranoid ideation. *Journal of Abnormal Psychology*, **105**, 106–114.

Kinderman, P. and Bentall, R.P. (1997a) Causal attributions in paranoia: Internal, personal and situational attributions for negative events. *Journal of Abnormal Psychology*.

Kinderman, P. and Bentall, R.P. (1997b) Attributional therapy for paranoid delusions: A case study. *Behavioural and Cognitive Psychotherapy*, **25**, 269–280.

Kinderman, P. and Bentall, R.P. (submitted) The self and explanatory style: The impact of internality judgements on the accessibility of self-discrepancies.

Kinderman, P., Dunbar, R.I.M. and Bentall, R.P. (in press) Theory-of-mind deficits and causal attributions, *British Journal of Psychology*.

Kinderman, P., Kaney, S., Morley, S. and Bentall, R.P. (1992) Paranoia and the defensive attributional style: Deluded and depressed patients' attributions about their own attributions. *British Journal of Medical Psychology*, **65**, 371–383.

Kingdon, D.G. and Turkington, D. (1991) Preliminary report: The use of cognitive behaviour therapy and a normalizing rationale in schizophrenia. *Journal of Nervous and Mental Disease*, **179**, 207–211.

Leafhead, K.M., Young, A.W. and Szulecka, T.K. (1996) Delusions demand attention. *Cognitive Neuropsychiatry*, **14**, 5–16.

Leff, J.P. and Vaughn, C. (1980) The interaction of life-events and relatives' expressed emotion in schizophrenia and depressive neurosis. *British Journal of Psychiatry*, **136**, 146–153.

Leslie, A.M. (1991) The theory of mind impairment in autism: Evidence for a modular mechanism of development? In A. Whiten (Ed.), *Natural Theories of Mind* Oxford: Blackwell.

Levenson, H. (1974) Activism and powerful others: Distinctions within the concept of internal-external control. *Journal of Personality Assessment*, **38**, 377–383.

Lyon, H.M., Kaney, S. and Bentall, R.P. (1994) The defensive function of persecutory delusions: Evidence from attribution tasks. *British Journal of Psychiatry*, **164**, 637–646.

McDowell, J. (1984) Recall of pleasant and unpleasant words in depressed subjects. *Journal of Abnormal Psychology*, **93**, 401–407.

Maher, B.A. (1974) Delusional thinking and perceptual disorder. *Journal of Individual Psychology*, **30**, 98–113.

Maher, B.A. (1988) Anomalous experience and delusional thinking: The logic of explanations. In T.F. Oltmanns and B.A. Maher (Eds.), *Delusional Beliefs*. New York: Wiley.

Maher, B.A. (1992) Models and methods for the study of reasoning in delusions. *Revue Europeenne de Psychologie Applique*, **42**, 97–102.

Markus, H. and Wurf, E. (1987) The dynamic self-concept: A social psychological perspective. *Annual Review of Psychology*, **38**, 299–337.

Mathews, A.M. and MacLeod, C. (1985) Selective processing of threat cues in anxiety states. *Behaviour Research and Therapy*, **23**, 563–569.

Mead, G.H. (1934) *Mind, self and society from the standpoint of a social behaviorist.* Chicago: University of Chicago Press.

Moore, N.C. (1981) Is paranoid illness associated with sensory defects in the elderly? *Journal of Psychosomatic Research*, **25**, 69–74.

Musalek, M., Berner, P. and Katschnig, H. (1989) Delusional theme, sex and age. *Psychopathology*, **22**, 260–267.

Nuechterlein, K.H. and Dawson, M.E. (1984) A heuristic vulnerability-stress model of schizophrenic episodes. *Schizophrenia Bulletin*, **10**, 300–312.

Nuechterlein, K.H., Dawson, M.E., Ventura, J., Fogelson, D., Gitlin, M. and Mintz, J. (1991) Testing vulnerability models: Stability of potential vulnerability indicators across clinical state. In H. Hafner and W.W. Gattaz (Eds.), *Search for the Causes of Schizophrenia* Heidelberg: Springer.

Oltmanns, T.F. and Maher, B.A. (Eds.) (1988) *Delusional beliefs*. New York: John Wiley.

Peterson, C., Semmel, A., Von Baeyer, C., Abramson, L., Metalsky, G.I. and Seligman, M.E.P. (1982) The Attributional Style Questionnaire. *Cognitive Therapy and Research*, **3**, 287–300.

Reivich, K. (1995) The measurement of explanatory style. In G.M. Buchanan and M.E.P. Seligman (Eds.), *Explanatory style* (pp. 21–48) Hillsdale, New Jersey: Lawrence Erlbaum.

Robey, K.L., Cohen, B.D. and Gara, M.A. (1989) Self-structure in schizophrenia. *Journal of Abnormal Psychology*, **98**, 436–442.

Robins, C.J. and Hayes, A.H. (1995) The role of causal attributions in the prediction of depression. In G.M. Buchanan and M.E.P. Seligman (Eds.), *Explanatory Style* (pp. 71–98) Hillsdale, New Jersey: Lawrence Erlbaum.

Rogers, A.H. (1958) The self-concept in paranoid schizophrenia. *Journal of Clinical Psychology*, **14**, 365–366.

Rund, B.R. (1994) The relationship between psychosocial and cognitive functioning in schizophrenic patients and expressed emotion and communication deviance in their parents. *Acta Psychiatrica Scandinavica*, **90**, 133–140.

Scott, L. and O'Hara, M.W. (1993) Self-discrepancies in clinically anxious and depressed university students. *Journal of Abnormal Psychology*, **102**, 282–287.

Seligman, M.E., Peterson, C., Kaslow, N.J., Tanenbaum, R.L., Alloy, L.B. and Abramson, L.B. (1984) Attributional style and depressive symptoms among children. *Journal of Abnormal Psychology*, **93**, 235–238.

Silverstone, P.H. (1991) Low self-esteem in different psychiatric conditions. *British Journal of Clinical Psychology.*, **30**, 185–188.

Strauman, T.J. (1989) Self-discrepancies in clinical depression and social phobia: Cognitive structures that underlie emotional disorders? *Journal of Abnormal Psychology*, **98**, 14–22.

Strauman, T.J. (1992) Self-guides, autobiographical memory, and anxiety and dysphoria: Toward a cognitive model of vulnerability to emotional distress. *Journal of Abnormal Psychology*, **101**, 87–95.

Strauman, T.J. and Higgins, E.T. (1987) Automatic activation of self-discrepancies and emotional syndromes: When cognitive structures influence affect. *Journal of Abnormal Psychology*, **98**, 14–22.

Strauman, T.J. and Higgins, E.T. (1988) Self-discrepancies as predictors of vulnerability to distinct syndromes of chronic emotional distress. *Journal of Personality*, **56**, 685–707.

Strauman, T.J., Lemieux, A.M. and Coe, C.L. (1993) Self-discrepancy and natural killer cell activity: Immunological consequences of negative self-evaluation. *Journal of Personality and Social Psychology*, **64**, 1042–1052.

Strauss, J.S. (1969) Hallucinations and delusions as points on continua function: Rating scale evidence. *Archives of General Psychiatry*, **21**, 581–586.

Stroop, J.R. (1935) Studies of interference in serial verbal reactions. *Journal of Experimental Psychology*, **18**, 643–662.

Sweeny, P. anderson, K. and Bailey, S. (1986) Attributional style and depression : A meta-analytic review. *Journal of Personality and Social Psychology*, **50**, 774–791.

Tarrier, N. (1990) The family management of schizophrenia. In R.P. Bentall (Ed.), *Reconstructing Schizophrenia* (pp. 254–282) London: Routledge.

Tarrier, N., Beckett, R., Harwood, S., Baker, A., Yusupoff, L. and Ugarteburu, I.

(1993) A trial of two cognitive-behavioural methods of treating drug-resistant residual psychotic symptoms in schizophrenic patients I: Outcome. *British Journal of Psychiatry*, **162**, 524–532.

Tennen, H. and Herzenberger, S. (1985) Attributional Style Questionnaire. In S.J. Keyser and R. C. Sweetland (Eds.), *Test Critiques*. Westport: Test Corporation of American.

Tennen, H. and Herzenberger, S. (1987) Depression, self-esteem and the absence of self-protective attributional biases. *Journal of Personality and Social Psychology*, **52**, 72– 80.

Tennen, H., Herzenberger, S. and Nelson, H.F. (1987) Depressive attributional style: The role of self-esteem. *Journal of Personality*, **55**, 631–660.

Ullmann, L.P. and Krasner, L. (1969) *A psychological approach to abnormal behaviour.* Englewood Cliffs: Prentice-Hall.

Valone, K., Norton, J.P., Goldstein, M.J. and Doane, J.A. (1983) Parental expressed emotion and affective style in an adolescent sample at risk of schizophrenia spectrum disorders. *Journal of Abnormal Psychology*, **92**, 279–285.

van Geert, P. (1994) *Dynamic systems of developments: Change between complexity and chaos.* New York: Harvester Wheatsheaf.

Walker, C. (1991) Delusions: What did Jaspers really say? *British Journal of Psychiatry*, **159** (Supplement 14), 94–103.

Watt, J.A. (1985) The relationship of paranoid states to schizophrenia. *American Journal of Psychiatry*, **142**, 1456–1458.

Watts, F.N., Powell, E.G. and Austin, S.V. (1973) The modification of abnormal beliefs. *British Journal of Medical Psychology*, **46**, 359–363.

Weissman, A.N. and Beck, A.T. (1978) Development and validation of the Dysfunctional Attitude Scale. Paper presented at the *Annual Meeting of the Association for the Advancement of Behavior Therapy*, Chicago.

White, P.A. (1991) Ambiguity in the internal/external distinction in causal attribution. *Journal of Experimental Social Psychology*, **27**, 259–270.

Williams, J.M.G. and Broadbent, K. (1986) Distraction by emotional stimuli: Use of a Stroop task with suicide attempters. *British Journal of Clinical Psychology*, **25**, 101– 110.

Winters, K.C. and Neale, J.M. (1983) Delusions and delusional thinking: A review of the literature. *Clinical Psychology Review*, **3**, 227–253.

Winters, K.C. and Neale, J.M. (1985) Mania and low self-esteem. *Journal of Abnormal Psychology*, **94**, 282–290.

Wylie, R.C. (1979) *The Self-concept. Revised edition.* Lincoln: University of Nebraska Press.

Young, A.W. (1994) Recognition and reality. In E.M.R. Critchley (Ed.), *The neurological boundaries of reality* (pp. 83–100) London: Farrand Press.

Young, H.F. and Bentall, R.P. (1995) Hypothesis testing in patients with persecutory delusions: Comparison with depressed and normal subjects. *British Journal of Clinical Psychology*, **34**, 353–369.

Young, H.F. and Bentall, R.P. (in press) Probabilistic reasoning in deluded, depressed and normal subjects: Effects of task difficulty and meaningful vs nonmeaningful material. *Psychological Medicine*.

Zigler, E. and Glick, M. (1988) Is paranoid schizophrenia really camouflaged depression? *American Psychologist*, **43**, 284–290.

Zubin, J. and Spring, B. (1977) Vulnerability: A new view of schizophrenia. *Journal of Abnormal Psychology*, **86**, 103–126.

Zullow, H.M., Oettingen, G., Peterson, C. and Seligman, M.E.P. (1988) Pessimistic explanatory style in the historical record: CAVEing LBJ, Presidential candidates, and East versus West Berlin. *American Psychologist*, **43**, 673–682.

Chapter 8

THE EFFECTS OF A REMEDIATIONAL APPROACH TO COGNITIVE THERAPY FOR SCHIZOPHRENIA

William Spaulding, Dorie Reed, Daniel Storzbach, Mary Sullivan, Martin Weiler and Charles Richardson

The idea of directly treating the cognitive and neuropsychological impairments of schizophrenia originated in experimental psychopathology laboratories, when researchers noticed that sometimes changes in the intensity or configuration of the stimuli in their experiments altered the performance impairments of their schizophrenic subjects (Cromwell, 1975; Cromwell and Spaulding, 1978; Spaulding, Storms, Goodrich, and Sullivan, 1986). There were early reports that seemingly immutable cognitive characteristics actually change in the course of recovery from psychiatric disorders (Kaplan, 1974). These came about the same time as early findings that cognitive behavioral treatment interventions may improve schizophrenic patients' cognitive and behavioral functioning (Meichenbaum, 1969; Meichenbaum and Cameron, 1973). More recently, well-controlled experiments have accumulated evidence that at least some schizophrenic subjects' performance on certain cognitively demanding

Outcome and Innovation in Psychological Treatment of Schizophrenia. Edited by T. Wykes, N. Tarrier and S. Lewis.
© 1998 John Wiley & Sons Ltd

tasks can improve, at least under laboratory conditions (Bellak, Mueser, Morrison, Tierney, and Podell, 1989; Benedict, Harris, Markow, McCormick, Nuechterlein, and Asarnow, 1994; Green, Satz, Ganzell, and Vaclav, 1992; Kern and Green, 1994; Vollema, Geurtsen, and van Voorst, 1995).

Experimental psychopathology did become quite successful in advancing an understanding of the etiology of schizophrenia. A paradigmatic example of achievements in this domain can be found in the contribution by Nuechterlein in this volume (Chapter 2). Also, neuropsychology has become more involved with schizophrenia (Asarnow, Nuechterlein, and Marder, 1983; Goldstein, 1991; Gray, Feldon, Rawlins, Hemsley, and Smith, 1991; Gur, Gur, and Saykin, 1990; Heaton, Vogt, Hoehn, Lewis, Crowley, and Stallings, 1979; Levin, Yurgelun-Todd, and Craft, 1989; Lewis, Nelson, and Eggertsen, 1979; Magaro and Chamrad, 1983; Robbins, 1990; Silverstein and Arzt, 1985; Sweeney, Haas, and Li, 1992; Weinberger and Berman, 1988), and there is much convergence between neuropsychological and psychopathological paradigms. Application of these advances to the treatment realm has come more slowly, but today it is clearly evident in the work of Robert Olbrich and Hans Brenner and their respective colleagues (see chapter 13), the Nebraska group, and several others.

The key idea in this approach is that specific cognitive functions impaired in schizophrenia can be changed, and that this leads to improved personal and social functioning. Performance changes come about through practice or rehearsal of specific cognitive abilities. The main techniques therefore are to isolate impaired processes, optimize the conditions under which they operate, and strengthen them through exercise, perhaps as one would isolate and exercise weak muscle groups in physical therapy. Laboratory measures of cognitive functioning are key components in this process.

The term "cognitive remediation" is often used to describe this approach, but this is not necessarily to imply that the mechanism of the treatment effect involves some sort of repair of cognitive processes. If fact, the mechanisms by which changes in performance occur, if they do occur, are poorly understood. Over the years, a number of hypothetical mechanisms have been suggested or discussed, to varying degress of specificity. They can be grouped for heuristic purposes into four types:

1. *Prosthetic mechanisms*, in which new skills are established to replace or compensate for impaired abilities.
2. *Remediational mechanisms*, in which the impaired processes undergo actual repair.
3. *Reorganizational mechanisms*, related to remediation, but treatment is thought of as facilitation of naturally occuring neurophysiological and/or neurocognitive recovery processes.

4. *Educational/attributional mechanisms*, which focus on the content rather than the process of cognition, and like prosthetic mechanisms, do not necessarily involve changing impairments.

So far, experimental studies have concentrated on establishing that cognitive impairments in schizophrenia can indeed change, with systematic analysis of mechanisms deferred (Corrigan and Storzbach, 1993). There's still much scepticism that the cognitive impairments of schizophrenia *can* change, either spontaneously over the course of the disorder, or in response to treatment (Bellack, 1992). Pharmacotherapy appears to be quite limited in improving cognition beyond that associated with stabilization from an acute psychosis (Goldberg, Greenberg, Griffin, Gold, Kleinman, Pickar, Schulz and Weinberger, 1993; Meltzer, Lee, and Ranjan, 1994; Weinberger, Aloia, Goldberg, and Berman, 1994). It's also well known that traditional psychotherapy is usually ineffective for schizophrenia, and this sometimes is inappropriately generalized as an expectation about other psychological approaches. There's an urgent need to establish an empirical database which shows that cognitive approaches have potential efficacy in the clinical armamentarium.

OUTCOME METHODOLOGY AND COGNITIVE REMEDIATION

Outcome studies of cognitive remediation are distributed along a continuum of experimental design characteristics (see Spaulding, 1992). The poles of this continuum are defined at one end by laboratory studies of task performance changes, and at the other end by clinical outcome studies of integrated treatment regimens. Laboratory studies of task performance changes are usually designed to isolate specific interventions' effects on highly specific performance measures (e.g. Green et al., 1992). These studies help establish that schizophrenic performance can improve under certain conditions, and they provide clues about the mechanisms of treatment effects, but they reveal little about potential clinical benefits of those changes. Integrated treatment outcome studies usually combine cognitive remediation with various other pharmacological and psychosocial treatments to evaluate their overall effect (e.g. Brenner et al., 1992, and Chapter 13 of this volume). These studies typically show broader, more clinically relevant treatment effects, but the design does not permit a confident conclusion that cognitive remediation contributes a unique or additive component to overall outcome.

In the mid-range of the design continuum are studies of relatively specific interventions, conducted in a clinical environment, which evaluate effects on both laboratory measures of cognitive performance and clinical measures of personal and social functioning (e.g. Benedict et al.,1994).

These studies corroborate the effects of specific treatments on specific cognitive measures, but they also show a limited degree of generalization of these effects to clinically important aspects of functioning. Little can be concluded about how much the cognitive interventions could contribute when included in a fully integrated multimodal regimen of treatment and rehabilitation.

Thus, the outcome database on cognitive remediation is somewhat ambiguous at this point. It is clear that at least some cognitive impairments can be improved with specific interventions. However, if the specific interventions are not integrated into a more comprehensive treatment and rehabilitation regimen, there is little evidence that they produce clinically meaningful changes. When the specific interventions are integrated in a more comprehensive regimen, it is unclear whether overall outcome is incrementally enhanced by the cognitive parts of the regimen, or whether cognitive remediation provides nothing different from other psychosocial modalities. This is the issue addressed in the experimental study described in the rest of this chapter.

THE NEBRASKA IPT STUDY PROJECT

For the past several years, the Nebraska research group has been conducting a highly controlled clinical outcome trial specifically designed to determine the unique contributions of cognitive remediation to comprehensive psychiatric rehabilitation for chronic schizophrenia. The treatment modality chosen for study is an American version of Integrated Psychological Therapy (IPT), a modality developed by Hans Brenner and his colleagues at the University of Bern (Brenner, Hodel, Roder and Corrigan, 1992). IPT is a fairly comprehensive group-format modality, similar in design and format to the more familiar social skills training programs that enjoy increasingly widespread use. IPT is divided into five subprograms, the first three of which focus on cognitive abilities and impairments. The final two subprograms are virtually identical to social skills training.

IPT was chosen for study for several reasons. It is procedurally quite replicable, with published manuals now available in both German and English (Brenner, Roder, Hodel, Kienzle, Reed and Liberman, 1994). There have been several partially controlled outcome trials which suggest that it is generally effective in enhancing the personal and social functioning of patients with chronic schizophrenia. It is modular, so that its more explicitly cognitive-remediational subprograms can be separately studied. Despite its modular nature, IPT is easily integrated into a more comprehensive treatment and rehabilitation regimen. It is highly accessible, requiring a manageable amount of specialized therapist skill beyond those skills required for social skills training in a severely impaired population (although it is important to note that the latter skills are considerable). The explicitly cognitive subprograms of IPT include a spectrum of specific techniques, addressing a spectrum of cognitive impairments found in schizophrenic patients. Most importantly, the Nebraska group has enjoyed the generous support and enthusiastic collaboration of Hans Brenner and his colleagues, ensuring a high fidelity replication of the original modality.

Experimental design

To evaluate the hypothesis that the IPT cognitive subprograms contribute incrementally and uniquely to overall outcome, the design of an outcome trial requires a control and an experimental condition. The experimental condition is IPT. The control condition chosen for study is "supportive group therapy," a generic modality commonly used to maintain or enhance personal and social functioning among chronic schizophrenic patients. A *Supportive Therapy Manual* was developed specifically for this project, by combining the nonspecific aspects of the ITP manual (i.e. those which describe the general context of the treatment, the optimal demeanor of the therapist, logistical considerations, etc.) with procedures adopted from accounts of group therapy work with chronic psychiatric patients. The supportive modality was designed to match IPT with respect to group size, length and frequency of sessions. The IPT therapist in the project was a clinical psychologist with extensive background in social skills training for chronic schizophrenic patients, and in the cognitive psychopathology and neuropsychology of schizophrenia. The supportive therapists were social workers with extensive experience in group therapy for chronic schizophrenic patients, but no background in cognitive psychopathology or neuropsychology.

An additional design requirement is for a standard regimen, a collection of pharmacological and psychosocial treatments available to all subjects, regardless of design condition (Spaulding, 1992). The standard regimen is a comprehensive psychiatric rehabilitation program, the Community Transition Program (CTP). The CTP is a 40-bed inpatient unit located in the Lincoln Regional Center, a public psychiatric hospital. Its mission in the mental health system is to return the most severely disabled patients in the system to less restrictive community-based programs. It is a referral unit which accepts transfers from private and public psychiatric services throughout the state of Nebraska. Patients are referred to the CTP because they have failed to respond to conventional treatment and cannot safely be served in less restrictive settings. Those admitted to the CTP have chronic schizophrenia or another disorder in the schizophrenia spectrum, severe cognitive and behavioral deficits even when optimally medicated and neurophysiologically stabilized, and a history of grossly inadequate personal and social functioning.

The CTP provides a comprehensive regimen of pharmacotherapy, social and living skills training, behavior modification, patient education and training in self-management of their disorder, occupational therapy, family education and consultation, and social services. The amount of formal treatment, training and other structured activity for an individual patient ranges from 10 to 40 hours per week, depending on the capacity of the patient. In an evaluation of CTP outcome during seven years prior to the beginning of the IPT project, patients had shown a 75% reduction in hospital use during two years after CTP treatment, compared to the two years before.

Outcome measures

The measure of primary importance in this study is the Assessment of Interpersonal Problem-Solving (AIPS; Donahoe, unpublished). The AIPS is a social skill performance task. Several video-taped social interaction vignettes are played for the subject. After each vignette the subject is asked a number of questions about what went on in the vignette, whether there was a problem or conflict, the nature of the problem, and related circumstances. The subject is asked to describe an appropriate solution or behavioral strategy for the problem, and finally, to actually role-play the solution with the examiner. The entire task is videotaped, and later scored by trained observers who rate a number of aspects of the subject's task performance. The observational ratings are then compiled as several scale scores. The AIPS and similar measures have played important roles in evaluating the effectiveness of social skills training and related treatments for patients with chronic schizophrenia (Bowen, Wallace, Glynn, Nuechterlein, Lutzger, and Kuehnel, 1994; Donahoe, Carter, Bloem, Hirsch and et al., 1990; Sullivan, Marder, Liberman, Donohoe and et al., 1990; see also Bellack and Morrison, 1987; Bellack, Morrison, and Mueser, 1989; D'Zurilla and Maydeu-Olivares, 1995.

As a measure of outcome for cognitive treatment, the AIPS is optimally situated on a continuum that ranges from highly specific laboratory measures to highly summative clinical and ecological measures. On the one hand, the AIPS provides a fairly detailed and specific picture of behavioral functioning, and it can be used in the time frame over which cognitive treatment effects are expected to occur. This makes it a good candidate for detecting treatment effects and for stimulating hypotheses about mechanisms. On the other hand, the AIPS measures behavior in the domain of social skills, which are known to be relevant to personal and social functioning and to overall rehabilitation outcome. Therefore, positive changes on the AIPS are suggestive of clinically meaningful benefits.

The Nebraska study project also includes a number of laboratory measures of cognition, clinical measures of psychiatric status and measures of personal and social functioning in natural environments. The laboratory measures are included to provide clues about effect mechanisms, but in view of the equivocal evidence that changes in specific cognitive functions in isolation produce meaningful clinical change, the laboratory data must be interpreted with caution. The clinical and ecological measures are included to fully characterize the subject sample, and to provide some intial estimates of the potential value of cognitive treatment. However, the study design was optimized for the primary purpose of detecting a treatment effect, not for determining the potential benefits or cost-effectiveness of cognitive treatment. Drawing such conclusions from the outcome measures, including the AIPS, would be inappropriate and premature. Also, the clinical and ecological measures require a longer time frame, and are collected as follow-up data one year after treatment. Analyses of the follow-up data have only just begun. The data reported here are limited to the initial six-month period of treatment.

Assessment and treatment procedures

The outcome trial proceeded as 6 months of intensive treatment followed by one year of continued rehabilitation. Before beginning the intensive treatment, patients were determined to be neurophysiologically and behaviorally stable, with a status post acute psychosis sufficiently impaired to require an intensive level of care and rehabilitation. A cohort of 8–12 patients was selected at the beginning of each 6-month cycle. Each subject was randomly assigned to either the experimental or control condition, and began receiving either cognitive or supportive therapy. The standard regimen was provided to all subjects from the time they were admitted to the CTP, through the intensive treatment period, until discharge. Most patients were discharged from the CTP 6–12 months after the end of the intensive treatment period. Follow-up assessment of these patients was conducted in their aftercare settings.

The study included eight successive cohorts over a 4-year period, yielding a final sample size of 91 patients, 49 in the cognitive treatment condition and 42 in the supportive therapy condition. The difference between the conditions was due to chance differences in cohort sizes accumulated over the 4 years. There was less than 5% attrition over the entire project (not surprisingly, as the subjects at first were institutionalized and later were in a highly supervised community setting, and none had the inclination or resources to leave the area). There were no differences between the cognitive and supportive treatment groups at the beginning of the intensive treatment period on any of the demographic, clinical or laboratory measures, except for an isolated difference on the Anxiety–Depression factor of the BPRS. With more than 30 group contrasts, this is well within the number of differences expected by chance.

During the week before the beginning of each intensive treatment period, each cohort member received a comprehensive assessment, including the AIPS, a diagnostic evaluation, and a battery of interview-based and laboratory measures of behavior and cognitive functioning. This assessment was repeated at the end of the 6-month period.

Midway through the intensive treatment period each cohort member began a 3-month course of conventional social skills training, medication management training and leisure skills training, using standard materials and procedures disseminated by the UCLA Center for Rehabilitation of Schizophrenia, in widespread use in the USA. This course of skill training was a substitute for the social skill components of IPT. Thus, all patients received the equivalent of the social skill parts of IPT, while only the patients in the cognitive treatment condition received the cognitive parts of IPT. Unlike IPT, the cognitive (or supportive) treatment continued for the entire 6-month period, overlapping during the second half with the social skills training.

All clinical and research personnel involved in the study were blind to group assignment, except for the cognitive and supportive therapists and the principal investigator. The two modalities were conducted at the same times in two adjacent rooms located on a different floor from the CTP. Routine clinical documentation did not reveal which of the modalities a patient actually attended. All indications were that the blind was sustained throughout the study.

Results

There was a significant improvement in all four independent subscales of the AIPS for all study subjects during the 6-month intensive study period (for the Fs of all ANOVA repeated measure main effects, $p < 0.001$). This is not suprising for a rehabilitation program built around social skills training. In addition, the group means for all four subscales show a differential improvement for the subjects who received cognitive therapy. For two of the subscales, "Articulation" and "Content," the F of the ANOVA group-by-repeated measure interaction term reaches statistical significance (for Articulation, $F=$, $p < 0.052$; for Content, $F=$, $p < 0.034$). This is strong support for the hypothesis that IPT had a unique and specific beneficial effect on acquisition of social skill in the course of rehabilitation.

Several of the interview-based clinical measures showed statistically significant improvements for both treatment groups. These included the Disorganization, Paranoia and Hallucination/delusion factors of the Brief Psychiatric Rating Scale (BPRS; Lukoff, Liberman and Nuechterlein, 1986), the General Psychopathology and Positive Symptoms subscales of the Positive and Negative Syndrome Scale (PANSS; Kay, Fizbein and Opter 1987), and the Scale for the Assessment of Thought, Language and Communication (TLC; Andreasen, 1986). The BPRS disorganization factor also showed a differential change in the expected direction, with cognitive therapy subjects showing more gains than supportive therapy subjects (ANOVA interaction $F = 5.0$, $p < 0.028$). It is not surprising that a social-learning-based rehabilitation program would produce improvements in behaviors associated with acute schizophrenia, such as positive symptoms and disorganization. Similar effects have been observed in outcome studies of cognitive and cognitive–behavioral treatment (Alford and Correia, 1994). Presumably, this represents the cumulative effect of better self-regulation and more appropriate social behavior. The differential effect of IPT on BPRS Disorganization suggests that cognitive treatment enhances the broader effects of skill training and other rehabilitation modalities on bizarre and distractable behavior as observed in an interview situation. However, little more can be inferred with confidence from this finding.

Laboratory measures of preattentional visual feature processing, the COGLAB backward masking and span of apprehension tasks (Spaulding, Garbin and Crinean, 1989), showed statistically significant improvement for all subjects, while the COBLAB reaction time and continuous performance tasks did not. The COGLAB span of apprehension task shows a significant group by repeated measure interaction effect ($F = 4.07$; $p < 0.047$), reflecting greater improvement in the cognitive therapy group. The principle cognitive demand of this task is to rapidly accomodate to a multi-element stimulus array after a block of single-element array trials. Thus, the change does not so much reflect stimulus feature processing *per se* as optimal readiness to perform the multi-element task condition. This is consistent with recent evidence that visual feature processing impairments in schizophrenia are the result of deficient executive processes which exercise "top-down" regulation of more molecular and automatic feature analytic processes.

All the measures of memory and executive-level cognitive processes (Trails B, Tactile Performance Test, COGLAB Card Sorting, Denman memory scales, Rey learning tasks; see Goldstein, 1991) showed significant improvements for all subjects. This alone is a significant finding, as no previous study has shown that any treatment intervention has produced changes in this domain, including the older and newer antipsychotic drugs. There was no "no treatment" control in this study to eliminate the possibility of practice effects, but the 6-month lapse between assessments and the utter lack of change in previous studies allow a fairly confident inference that the complete rehabilitation regimen in this study produced improvements in higher-level cognitive functions. There is no evidence of a differential effect of cognitive therapy on memory and executive-level performance.

To summarize the results of the Nebraska IPT outcome study so far, the data suggest that psychiatric rehabilitation produces improvements across several domains, including cognitive, behavioral and social functioning.

The overall effects of rehabilitation on cognitive functioning are nonspecific treatment effects. In addition, cognitive therapy contributes uniquely to the overall effects, at least in the domain of social skills acquisition. There is some tentative evidence that the cognitive therapy effect involves improved cognitive readiness for processing complex stimulus arrays, reduced distractibility and less disruption by bizarre behavior.

INDIVIDUAL DIFFERENCES AND TREATMENT MECHANISMS

Remediational approaches to cognitive therapy appear to have potential for clinical efficacy in rehabilitation. The next step in research is to shift experimental design priorities, from rigorous detection of unique treatment effects to quantitative appraisal of the importance of these effects. This will require consideration of a number of complex issues which address questions not of whether there are treatment effects, but how, when, for whom, and in conjuction with what other rehabilitation modalities.

A major limiting factor in the Nebraska study was the limited attention given to individual differences among the subjects. Even within a treatment-refractory schizophenia-spectrum population, there is considerable variance in neurophysiological, cognitive and behavioral functioning. These differences contribute to differences in the overall outcome of rehabilitation (Wykes and Dunn, 1992; Wykes, Sturt, and Katz, 1990), and the outcome of cognitive treatment is probably no exception. Even casual observation of IPT groups suggests that at any given time the therapy procedures are meaningful to only a subset of the patients. Different patients seem to engage optimally with different parts of IPT. Patients' receptivity probably changes over the course of their disorder as well. For a therapeutic approach like this to be maximally effective, a great deal of individual tailoring will probably be necessary.

A better understanding of the mechanisms of the treatment effects, and how they interact with the impairments of schizophrenia, should provide important clues about how to best apply cognitive remediation. The Nebraska group has begun development of a theoretical model which integrates what is known about the course of schizophenia with its cognitive and behavioral characteristics, in ways that may provide a framework for understanding the mechanisms of treatment effects, as well as a rational approach to clinical decision making. The heart of the model is a 3-factor view of schizophrenic cognition. To treat any patient optimally, that patient's status with regard to the three factors must be determined. Factor 1 reflects static, pervasively distributed impairments, prognostically significant but probably not accessible by psychosocial interventions. Factor 2 reflects episode-linked impairments, primarily in the domain of memory and executive processing, and responsive to pharmacology and other treatments which resolve the acute episode. Factor 3 reflects the longer-term organizational integrity of higher-level cognitive processes, especially in working memory and executive processing. These processes are thought to become dysfunctional in the wake of psychotic episodes, yet may not spontaneously reorganize after neurophysiological stabilization. Cognitive remediational approaches may facilitate reorganization of Factor 3 processes, producing in turn a better response to various psychosocial rehabilitation modalities.

What might be the neurophysiological substrate of Factor 3 dysfunction? A mechanistic model based on Hullian learning theory has been described by Broen and Storms (1966), in which the learned hierarchical organization of associations between stimuli and responses temporarily collapses. A more contemporary metaphor is suggested by the familiar event of a "computer crash". When a computer system "crashes" the system is not necessarily structurally damaged. However, the informational contents of core memory, including the *operating system*, which manages most of the computer's internal and external operations, may be obliterated or "corrupted." With problems in the operating system, the computer suffers an "executive dysfunction" (the appeal of this metaphor is enhanced by the Nebraska study finding of strong nonspecific psychosocial treatment effects on executive-level cognition). Diagnosis and reassembly of a computer's operating system can take considerable time, and there are particular sequences by which the reassembly must proceed.

Recent theoretical developments suggest possible neurophysiological mechanisms for a "brain crash" and subsequent recovery of key executive operations. Theorizing converges on the limbic basal ganglia, subcortical nuclei suspected of having various roles in the etiology of schizophrenia (Csernansky, Murphy and Faustman, 1991; Gray, 1995; Swerdlow and Koob, 1987; Pantelis and Nelson, 1994; Walker, 1994). Single unit recording in primates suggests involvement of basal ganglia neurons in the processing of task-relevant contextual information and the organization of behavior, including complex response-reinforcer associations, self-initiated movement, and delayed response tasks usually associated with frontal cortical function (Schultz, Apicella, Romo and Scarnati, 1995). Convergent evidence from studies of human biobehavioral disorders has implicated the basal ganglia in impairments of executive-level functions such as problem-solving and cognitive flexibility (Gabrielli, 1995; Pantelis and Nelson, 1994).

Dopamine, the principal neurotransmitter of the basal ganglia, appears to function as a reinforcement signal that guides the learning of diverse behavioral responses (see reviews by Schultz, Romo et al., 1995; Wickens and Kotter, 1995). Intracaudate injection of dopamine agonists enhances behavioral learning (Packard and White, 1991) . Based on this evidence, it has been hypothesized that dopaminergic afferents participate in adjustment of synaptic function of cortical inputs to striatal spiny neurons during reinforcement learning (Wickens and Kotter, 1995) . Corticostriatal synapses could be strengthened by concurrent presynaptic, postsynaptic, and dopaminergic activity. As dopamine reinforcement enhances synaptic function, striatal activity is biased in favor of reinforced responses.

Houk and Wise (Houk, 1995; Houk and Wise, 1993) have integrated these findings in a model of cerebral information-processing that suggests a possible source of Factor 3 impairment in schizophrenia. In their model, basal ganglia neurons integrate convergent signals from multiple cortical regions. In learning situations, those neurons' dopaminergic input provides a "training signal" that enhances synaptic function of cortical activity patterns which are crucial to performing the task being learned. The functional enhancement of those activity patterns then endures as "learned" components of task performance. Also, striatal output disinhibits specific thalamocortical loops, resulting in sustained activation of prefrontal neural assemblies that support working memory used in the planning, selection, and control of task-relevant responses (Goldman-Rakic, 1987). Thus, these processes establish and maintain routines for invoking the basic neurocognitive operations necessary for optimal performance of particular tasks, much as a computer operating system selects programs and devices needed to execute particular commands.

In this model, dopamine dysregulation during a psychotic episode could inappropriately "reinforce" irrelevant neural activity patterns. This would increase the probability of inefficient, disorganized or inappropriate selection of basic neurocognitive responses, such as concept formation, memory storage and retrieval, or problem-solving. The disruption would endure beyond the period of actual dopamine dysregulation, because inappropriate responses had been enhanced through inappropriate dopaminergic reinforcement. A period of intensive differential reinforcement of relevant activity patterns may be necessary to re-establish efficient and appropriate selection of basic neurocognitive responses. This suggests the general rehabilitation strategy of providing corrective learning experiences, and may account for the nonspecific effects of psychiatric rehabilitation on executive-level functioning. Cognitive remediation strategies may further enhance this "re-learning" process through specific and explicit reinforcement of the most basic cognitive operations required for routine executive functioning.

CONCLUSION

Treatment and rehabilitation of schizophrenia has made significant gains over the past two decades, due to advances in both psychopharmacological and psychosocial approaches to treatment. Cognitive remediation promises to be another useful addition to the rehabilitation armamentarium, provided enough can be learned about its impact on individual patients to allow strategic, cost-effective application. To achieve the necessary level of clinical efficiency, it will be necessary to develop our understanding of the neurophysiological and neurocognitive mechanisms of cognitive impairment in schizophrenia, and apply this understanding to assessment of individual differences among patients.

REFERENCES

Alford, B., and Correia, C. (1994). Cognitive therapy of schizohrenia: Theory and empirical status. *Behavior Therapy*, **25**, 17–33.

Andreasen, N. (1986). Scale for the assessment of thought, language and commuication (TLC). *Schizophrenia Bulletin*, **12**, 473–482.

Asarnow, R.F., Nuechterlein, K.H. and Marder, S.R. (1983). Span of apprehension performance, neuropsychological functioning, and indices of psychosis-proneness. *Journal of Nervous and Mental Disease*, **171**, 662.

Bellack, A.S. (1992). Cognitive rehabilitation for schizophrenia: Is it possible? Is it necessary? *Schizophrenia Bulletin*, **18**(1), 43–50.

Bellack, A.S. and Morrison, R.L. (1987). The nature of social skill in schizophrenia. Paper presented at Annual Meeting of the American Psychiatric Association, Chicago.

Bellack, A.S., Morrison, R.L. and Mueser, K.T. (1989). Social problem solving in schizophrenia. *Schizophrenia Bulletin*, **15**(1), 101–116.

Bellak, A., Mueser, K., Morrison, R., Tierney, A. and Podell, K. (1989). Remediation of cognitive deficits in schizophrenia: Training on the Wisconsin Card Sorting Test. *American Journal of Psychiatry*, **147**, 1650–1655.

Benedict, R., Harris, A., Markow, T., McCormick, J., Nuechterlein, K. and Asarnow, R. (1994). Effects of attention training on information processing in schizophrenia. *Schizophrenia Bulletin*, **20**, 537–546.

Bowen, L., Wallace, C., Glynn, S., Nuechterlein, K., Lutzger, J. and Kuehnel, T. (1994). Schizophrenics' cognitive functioning and performance in interpersonal interactions and skills training procedures. *Journal of Psychiatry Research*, **28**(3), 289–301.

Brenner, H.D., Hodel, B., Roder, V. and Corrigan, P. (1992). Treatment of cognitive dysfunctions and behavioral deficits in schizophrenia. *Schizophrenia Bulletin*, **18**(1), 21–26.

Brenner, H., Roder, V., Hodel, B., Kienzle, N., Reed, D. and Liberman, R. (1994). *Integrated Psychological Therapy for Schizophrenic Patients*. Toronto: Hogrefe and Huber.

Broen, W. and Storms, L. (1966). Lawful disorganization: The process underlying a schizophrenic syndrome. *Psychological Review*, **73**, 265–279.

Corrigan, P. and Storzbach, D. (1993). The ecological validity of cognitive rehabilitation for schizophrenia. *Journal of Cognitive Rehabilitation*, **11**, 14–21.

Cromwell, R.L. (1975). Assessment of schizophrenia. *Annual Review of Psychology*, **26**, 593–619.

Cromwell, R.L. and Spaulding, W. (1978). How schizophrenics handle information. In W.E. Fann, I. Karacan, A.D. Pokorny, and R.L. Williams (Eds.), *The Phenomenology and Treatment of Schizophrenia* (pp. 127–162). New York: Spectrum.

Csernansky, J.G., Murphy, G.M. and Faustman, W.O. (1991). Limbic/mesolimbic connections and the pathogenesis of schizophrenia. *Society of Biological Psychiatry*, **30**, 383–400.

Donahoe, C., Carter, M., Bloem, W., Hirsch, G. and et al., (1990). Assessment of interpersonal problem solving skills. *Psychiatry*, **53**(4), 329–339.

Donahoe, C.P. (unpublished). Assessment instrument for problem-solving skills. Available from the author at Audi Murphy Veterans Administration Medical Center, San Antonio, Texas.

D'Zurilla, T. and Maydeu-Olivares, A. (1995). Conceptual and methodological issues in social problem-solving assessment. *Behavior Therapy*, **26**(3), 409–432.

Gabrielli, J. (1995). Contribution of the basal ganglia to skill learning and working memory in humans. In J.C. Houk, J.L. Davis, and D.G. Beiser (Eds.), Models of information processing in the basal ganglia (pp. 277–294). Cambridge, MA: The MIT Press.

Goldberg, T., Greenberg, R., Griffin, S., Gold, J., Kleinman, J., Pickar, D., Schulz, S. and Weinberger, D. (1993). The effects of clozapine on psychiatric symptoms in patients with schizophrenia. *British Journal of Psychiatry*, **162**, 43–48.

Goldman-Rakic, P.S. (1987). Circuitry of the prefrontal cortex and the regulation of behavior by representational knowledge, Handbook of physiology. The nervous system. Higher functions of the brain (vol. V, pp. 373–417). Bethesda, Maryland: American Physiological Society.

Goldstein, G. (1991). Comprehensive neuropsychological test batteries and research in schizophrenia. In S.R. Steinhauer, J.H. Gruzelier, and J. Zubin (Eds.), *Handbook of Schizophrenia, vol. 5: Neuropsychology, psychopathology and information processing* (pp. 525–551). Amsterdam: Elsevier Science.

Gray, J.A. (1995). A model of the limbic system and basal ganglia: Applications to anxiety and schizophrenia. In M.S. Gazzaniga (Ed.), *The Cognitive Neurosciences* (pp. 1165–1176). Cambridge, Mass.: The MIT Press.

Gray, J.A., Feldon, J., Rawlins, J.N.P., Hemsley, D.R. and Smith, A.D. (1991). The neuropsychology of schizophrenia. *Behavioral and Brain Sciences*, **14**, 1–84.

Green, M., Satz, P., Ganzell, S. and Vaclav, J. (1992). The WCST and schizophrenia: Remediation of a stubborn deficit. *American Journal of Psychiatry*, **149**.

Gur, R.E., Gur, R.C. and Saykin, A.J. (1990). Neurobehavioral studies in schizophrenia: Implications for regional brain dysfunction. *Schizophrenia Bulletin*, **16**, 445–452.

Heaton, R.K., Vogt, A.T., Hoehn, M.M., Lewis, J.A., Crowley, T.J. and Stallings, M.A. (1979). Neuropsychological impairment with schizophrenia vs. acute and chronic cerebral lesions. *Journal of Clinical Psychology*, **35**, 46–53.

Houk, J.C. (1995). Information processing in modular circuits linking basal ganglia and cerebral cortex. In J.C. Houk, J.L. Davis, and D.G. Beiser (Eds.), *Models of Information Processing in the Basal Ganglia* (pp. 3–9). Cambridge, MA: The MIT Press.

Houk, J.C. and Wise, S.P. (1993). Outline for a theory of motor behavior: Involving cooperative actions of the cerebellum, basal ganglia, and cerebral cortex. In P. Rudomin, M.A. Arbib, and F. Cervantes-Perez (Eds.), *From Neural Networks to Artificial Intelligence*, (pp. 452–470). Heidelberg: Springer-Verlag.

Kaplan, R. (1974) *The cross-over phenomenon: Three studies of the effect of training and information on process schizophrenic reaction time*. Unpublished doctoral dissertation, University of Waterloo, Ontario, Canada.

Kay, S., Fizbein, A. and Opler, L. (1987). The positive and negative syndrome scale (PANSS) for schizophrenia. *Schizophrenia Bulletin*, **13**, 261–276.

Kern, R.S. and Green, M.F. (1994). Cognitive prerequisites of skill acquisition in schizophrenia: Bridging micro- and macro-levels of processing. In W. Spaulding (Eds.), *Cognitive Technology in Psychiatric Rehabilitation*. Lincoln, NE: University of Nebraska Press.

Levin, S., Yurgelun-Todd, D. and Craft, S. (1989). Contributions of clinical neuropsychology to the study of schizophrenia. *Journal of Abnormal Psychology*, **98**, 341–356.

Lewis, R.F., Nelson, R.W. and Eggertsen, C. (1979). Neuropsychological test performances of paranoid schizophrenic and brain-damaged patients. *Journal of Clinical Psychology*, **35**, 54–59.

Lukoff, D., Liberman, R. and Nuechterlein, K. (1986). Symptom monitoring in the rehabilitation of schizophrenic patients. *Schizophrenia Bulletin*, **12**(4), 578–603.

Magaro, P.A. and Chamrad, D.L. (1983). Information processing and lateralization in schizophrenia. *Biological Psychiatry*, **18**, 29–44.

Meichenbaum, D. (1969). The effects of instructions and reinforcement on thinking and language behavior of schizophrenics. *Behavior Research and Therapy*, **7**, 101–114.

Meichenbaum, D.M. and Cameron, R. (1973). Training schizophrenics to talk to themselves: A means of developing attentional controls. *Behavior Therapy*, **4**, 515–534.

Meltzer, H., Lee, M. and Ranjan, R. (1994). Recent advances in the pharmacotherapy of schizophrenia. *Acta Psychiatrica Scandinavica*, **90** (384) (Supplementum), 95–101.

Packard, M.G. and White, N.M. (1991). Dissociation of hippocampus and caudate nucleus memory systems by posttraining intracerbral injection dopamine agonists. Behavioral Neuroscience, **105**(2), 295–306.

Pantelis, C. and Nelson, H.E. (1994). Cognitive functioning and symptomatology in schizophrenia: The role of frontal-subcortical systems. In A.S. David and J.C. Cutting (Eds.), *The Neuropsychology of Schizophrenia*. Hove, U.K.: Lawrence Erlbaum Associates.

Robbins, T.W. (1990). The case for frontostriatal dysfunction in schizophrenia. *Schizophrenia Bulletin*, **16**, 391–402.

Schultz, W., Apicella, P., Romo, R. and Scarnati, E. (1995). Context-dependent activity in primate striatum reflecting past and future behavioral events. In J.C. Houk, J.L. Davis, and D.G. Beiser (Eds.), *Models of Information Processing in the Basal Ganglia* (pp. 11–27). Cambridge, MA: The MIT Press.

Schultz, W., Romo, R., Ljungberg, T., Mirenowicz, J., Hollerman, J.R. and Dickinson, A. (1995). Reward-related signals carried by dopamine neurons. In J.C. Houk, J.L. Davis, and D.G. Beiser (Eds.), *Models of Information Processing in the Basal Ganglia* (pp. 233–248). Cambridge, MA: The MIT Press.

Silverstein, M.L. and Arzt, A.T. (1985). Neuropsychological dysfunction in schizophrenia: Relation to associative thought disorder. *Journal of Nervous and Mental Disease*, **173**, 341–346.

Spaulding, W. (1992). Some methodological prerequisites for outcome studies of cognitive treatment of schizophrenia. *Schizophenia Bulletin*, **18**, 39–42.

Spaulding, W., Garbin, C. and Crinean, W. (1989). The logical and psychometric prerequisites for cognitive therapy for schizophrenia. In H. Brenner and W. Boker (Eds.), *The Role of Mediating Processes in Understanding and Treating Schizophrenia*. Zurich: Huber.

Spaulding, W.D., Storms, L., Goodrich, V. and Sullivan, M. (1986). Applications of experimental psychopathology in psychiatric rehabiitation. *Schizophrenia Bulletin*, **12**(4), 560–577.

Sullivan, G., Marder, S., Liberman, R., Donohoe, P. and et al., (1990). Social skills and relapse history in outpatient schizophrenics. *Psychiatry*, **53**(4), 340–345.

Sweeney, J.A., Haas, G.L. and Li, S. (1992). Neuropsychological and eye movement abnormalities in first-episode and chronic schizophrenia. *Schizophrenia Bulletin*, **18**, 283–293.

Swerdlow, N.R. and Koob, G.F. (1987). Dopamine, schizophrenia, mania, and depression: Toward a unified hypothesis of cortico-striato-pallidothalamic function. *Behavioral and Brain Science*, **10**, 197–245.

Vollema, M., Geurtsen, G. and van Voorst, A. (1995). Durable improvements in Wisconsin Card Sorting Test performance in schizophrenic patients. *Schizophrenia Research*, **16**(3), 209–215.

Walker, E. (1994). Developmentally moderated expressions of the neuropathology underlying schizophrenia. *Schizophrenia Bulletin*, **20**(3), 453–480.

Weinberger, D., Aloia, M., Gldberg, T. and Berman, K. (1994). The frontal lobes and schizophrenia. *Journal of Neuropsychiatry*, **6**, 419–427.

Weinberger, D.R. and Berman, K.F. (1988). Speculation on the meaning of cerebral metabolic hypofrontality in schizophrenia. *Schizophrenia Bulletin*, **14**, 157–168.

Wickens, J. and Kotter, R. (1995). Cellular models of reinforcement. In J.C. Houk, J.L. Davis, and D.G. Beiser (Eds.), *Models of Information Processing in the Basal Ganglia* (pp. 187–214). Cambridge, MA: The MIT Press.

Wykes, R. and Dunn, G. (1992). Cognitive deficit and the prediciton of rehabilitation success in a chronic psychiatric group. *Psychological Medicine*, **22**, 389–398.

Wykes, T., Sturt, E. and Katz, R. (1990). The prediction of rehabilitative success after three years: The use of social, symptom and cognitive variables. *British Journal of Psychiatry*, **157**, 865–870.

Chapter 9

COERCION, ADHERENCE OR COLLABORATION? INFLUENCES ON COMPLIANCE WITH MEDICATION

Michael McPhillips and Tom Sensky

Maintenance medication following recovery from an acute episode of schizophrenia reduces the risk of relapse in the ensuing year by 60-70% (Johnson, 1993). A meta-analysis of studies of antipsychotic withdrawal has revealed relapse rates over an average of 10 months of 16% for patients staying on medication and 53% for those withdrawing (Gilbert et al., 1995). This advantage in reducing relapse rates persists for up to five years and beyond, following recovery from an episode (Kane, 1987). Although some patients fail to respond adequately to medication, the great majority could avoid further relapse and rehospitalization by adhering to maintenance medication in the full prescribed dose.

In routine *clinical* practice, only a proportion of patients suitable for maintenance medication actually take it, resulting in a relapse rate of approximately 45%, up to three times greater than research studies would predict (Kissling, 1994). Patients who volunteer to participate in research studies may be more likely than others to comply with treatment (Kane and

Outcome and Innovation in Psychological Treatment of Schizophrenia. Edited by T. Wykes,
N. Tarrier and S. Lewis.

Borenstein, 1985), and being part of a research study tends in any case to have overall benefits for those patients participating.

The latter part of this chapter will summarize some interventions aiming to improve compliance. However, effective development of appropriate interventions focused on improving compliance requires understanding of factors which may influence compliance. Factors will be considered which may determine *overall* compliance, although in practice, these influences are more subtle and selective. In particular, determinants of compliance are likely to differ substantially in acute episodes of schizophrenia and during maintenance prophylactic treatment.

The account below focuses on factors relevant to compliance in schizophrenia. Clinicians may regard those with schizophrenia as particularly prone to poor compliance, for example because of the possible impact of the disorder on insight. However, there are striking similarities between non-compliance rates reported in schizophrenia and in other chronic illnesses (Table 9.1).

COMPLIANCE AND ITS ASSESSMENT

Compliance may be defined as *patient acceptance of recommended health behaviours* (Wright, 1993). When applied to taking prescribed medications as recommended, compliance can be measured by self-report, by the reports of others (such as carers or family), by pill counts when the patient attends clinics, or by measuring drug levels in the patient's blood. Researchers have also in some instances relied on references to poor compliance in the patients' records. None of these methods of assessment is entirely satisfactory (Wright, 1993). Where researchers have included more than one assessment method, some have reported good correlations between different compliance measures (e.g. Brown et al., 1987), while others have found very poor agreement (e.g. Boczkowski et al., 1985). This is particularly problematic where researchers have tested complex models

Table 9.1 Prevalence rates (%) of non-compliance with medications in chronic illnesses

Tuberculosis	37
Leprosy	32
Diabetes/heart failure	42
Epilepsy	37
Diabetes/arthritis	32
Schizophrenia	33

Data for schizophrenia from Kane (1986) and for other illnesses from Wright (1993).

using only self-reported compliance (e.g. Chan, 1984; Kelly et al., 1987). Such models, in common with more recently developed scales measuring attitudes to medication (see below), can at best test patients' *intentions* or *attitudes*. These do not equate with *behaviour*, as some of the studies described below demonstrate.

Although research in compliance has most commonly focused on taking prescribed medications, there are clearly other ways in which patients might not follow clinicians' recommendations. These include taking non-prescribed drugs, missing appointments, and defaulting altogether from follow-up. It is commonly assumed that these forms of non-compliance are all interlinked. Clinical observation lends support to this assumption, but research evidence is lacking. The discussion below will concentrate mainly on compliance with prescribed medications, because this has been the focus of most research.

CAUSES OF NON-COMPLIANCE

Factors which may be important determinants of compliance in schizophrenia are summarized in Table 9.2.

Factors related to the illness

During acute psychotic episodes, non-compliance is associated with severity of symptoms, notably increased psychotic disturbance and lack of insight (Marder et al., 1983; Hoge et al., 1990). Patients who comply well show more depressive symptoms than non-compliers (Hoge et al., 1990). In this context, it may be relevant that when patients relapse despite continuing to take medication, their presentations on admission tend to be characterized by affective disturbance, while those who relapse after a period off medication tend to have more psychotic symptoms (McEvoy et al., 1984; Bartko et al., 1988). This suggests the possibility of initial

Table 9.2 Potential causes of non-compliance with maintenance medication in schizophrenia

Factors in the patient	Comorbid drug abuse, cultural beliefs, attitudes to illness and treatment
Factors related to the illness	Specific delusions about medication or the medical team, cognitive impairments, negative symptoms
Factors in the environment	Untoward influence from family or spouse, peer pressure
Factors related to the medication	Adverse effects, especially extrapyramidal
Factors in the medical team	Ambivalent attitude to medication, negative attitudes to patient, disorder or prognosis

withdrawal from medications eventually giving rise to circumstances which further exacerbate non-compliance.

Following discharge from inpatient care, compliance is not associated with symptomatology or illness severity (Bartko et al., 1988; Van Putten et al., 1976). Van Putten and co-workers have suggested that the psychotic symptoms of some recidivist medication refusers may be comforting or ego-syntonic. However, others have failed to demonstrate this as a significant contributor to non-compliance (Buchanan, 1992).

Cognitive impairments are frequently found in schizophrenia. Psychometry reveals deficits in information processing. It is possible that impaired ability to assess the risks and consequences of relapse might predispose some patients to poor compliance. Through negative symptoms, other patients may become passively noncompliant by failing, through poor motivation and apathy, to attend to receive medication. Neither phenomenon has been systematically studied.

Factors in the environment

Compliance is aided by support from family or friends, and by being employed (Renton, 1963, Young et al., 1986). However, some of these may be associations, not causes. The same factors that put the individual at a social disadvantage may cause poor compliance.

Research is lacking on the role of the health system itself in facilitating compliance although it is acknowledged that these factors are important (Dencker and Dencker, 1995). Increased geographical distance to the clinic, waiting times, and prescription costs would be expected to contribute to compliance problems. These factors are readily amenable to change.

Factors related to the medication

The probability of compliance is inversely proportional to the number of drugs prescribed and the frequency with which they are to be taken (Porter, 1969). Some studies have failed to demonstrate this (e.g. Buchanan, 1996), but this may be because of other confounding influences on compliance. For example, day hospital attendance or assertive follow-up are likely to reduce the problems with compliance due to complex medication regimes. Once-daily regimens have been shown to aid compliance (Blackwell, 1973). As many as 60% of patients have difficulty in understanding simple packaging instructions (Boyd et al., 1974). Calendar packets and dosset boxes are helpful in this circumstance (Linkewich et al., 1974). Use of depot antipsychotic medication does not necessarily reduce non-compliance (Buchanan, 1996), with extended follow-up revealing non-compliance rates of over 40% (Curson et al., 1985).

Adverse effects have been consistently reported to be associated with noncompliance (Young et al., 1986).

Extrapyramidal side effects
There are substantial methodological problems in conducting research in this area (Hummer and Fleischhacker, 1996). Weiden et al., (1986) have suggested that early experience of acute dystonias may sensitise the patient and produce later non-compliance, but others have failed to substantiate this (Fleischacker et al., 1994). Akathisia, a common and particularly unpleasant symptom frequently missed by professionals, has been found by some researchers to predict future non-compliance (Van Putten et al., 1976, Weiden et al., 1986). Akinesia may also be important in this respect (Buchanan, 1996).

Subjective experience of antipsychotic medication
Van Putten (1974) reported a subjective sensation of dysphoria occurring in some patients within 24 hours of taking oral neuroleptics. It is unclear whether this symptom is actually a mild form of akathisia. Awad and Hogan (1994) found that "dysphoric" responders showed more extrapyramidal symptoms and less clinical improvement. An initial dysphoric response to medication predicted short-term non-compliance (Hogan et al., 1983). Sedation, depression and dysphoria are reported complications of neuroleptics but may occur for independent reasons. Recently, the term *neuroleptic-induced deficit syndrome* (NIDS) has been coined to draw attention to these symptoms occurring as side effects of antipsychotics (Lewander, 1994). However, this putative syndrome lacks operational criteria and is difficult to distinguish from the related phenomena of negative symptoms, depression and extrapyramidal side effects.

Other side effects
The effect of other neuroleptic side effects on compliance has not been systematically measured. Sexual dysfunction, including loss of libido, erectile impotence, retrograde ejaculation and anorgasmia affects up to 80% of patients (Falloon et al., 1978) but is rarely asked about. Weight gain may cause some patients to stop taking medication.

Substance misuse

Comorbid substance misuse in schizophrenia has been considered a major correlate of non- compliance (Bebbington, 1995). However, this is strongly concentrated in young males, whereas non-compliance shows little propensity to cluster in any demographic group (see below). Pristach and Smith (1990) reported that a majority of inpatients with schizophrenia were non-compliant with medication before admission and that most of these patients reported being non-compliant when drinking alcohol. Patients may fear an interaction between medication and alcohol, sometimes because of medical advice. Schneier and Siris (1987) suggested that patients with schizophrenia may titrate their medication and drugs of abuse against their positive and negative symptoms. It remains uncertain whether compliance problems cause, result from, or merely coexist with substance misuse.

Factors related to the medical team

Many authors have proffered sensible advice such as adopting an attitude of acceptance, improving patient education and fostering collaboration over medication and other aspects of treatment between the patient and the team (Katz and Solomon, 1958; Falloon, 1984; Wright, 1993; Eisenthal et al., 1979). Goldberg et al., (1977) and others have reported that more frequent outpatient supervision is associated with improved compliance with medication. Weiden et al., (1986) cautioned that doctors may experience patients with schizophrenia as incurable and may also fail to sympathize with the reasons their patients offer for refusing to take medication.

The beliefs and attitudes of the medical team might be expected to influence patients' compliance, since the team has an essential role in educating the patient about the illness, its management and prognosis. Irwin et al., (1971) reported that, where the doctor considered medication an essential component of management of schizophrenia, compliance with medication was better than in cases where the doctor was ambivalent. In an audit of 213 German psychiatrists, Kissling (1994) reported that 30% of his respondents suggested no relapse prevention for first-episode patients and only 10% recommended treatment for more than one year. Respondents varied widely in their estimates of prevalence rates of relapse and of tardive dyskinesia. Significantly, reported reluctance to recommend medication for relapse prevention correlated with the extent to which the risk of relapse was underestimated and that of tardive dyskinesia overestimated. While it is not possible to generalize from this study to practice in other countries, it seems likely that a significant proportion of non-compliance with maintenance medication may be attributable to inadequate understanding of the balance between benefits and risks of maintenance medication by those professionals who offer advice to people with schizophrenia. An added factor is the potential lack of coherence in information available to the patient and family from different professional sources (Soskis, 1978).

The patient's general practitioner is often directly involved in prescribing medications, and is thus in a strong position to monitor and influence compliance. However, there appears to be very little research bearing on this aspect of the management of compliance in schizophrenia.

Factors in the patient

Sociodemographic factors
These have generally failed to predict compliance. Non-compliance with

psychiatric medication is a global behaviour affecting people of both sexes and all ages and social classes approximately equally (Buchanan, 1992).

Psychological factors
A consistent finding is that nothing predicts future behaviour so well as previous behaviour. Previous failures in compliance are a strong predictor of future non-compliance (Buchanan, 1996). Rates of refusal increase in proportion with number of previous hospitalizations and episodes of refusal. However, in recent years attention has focused on longstanding attitudes or beliefs the patient may hold about medication and illness, within the framework of the Health Belief Model (HBM) (Becker and Mamain, 1975) or the self-regulatory model (Leventhal et al., 1992). A substantial body of research has accumulated examining these attitudes as predictors of compliance. Implicit in this research is the assumption that the patient is a rational consumer, continually evaluating his illness and treatment before deciding whether or not to make use of it. This hypothesis accords the patient an active part in deciding his treatment. It also offers the possibility of persuading the patient to alter his decision once the reasons for it have been clarified.

Kelly et al., (1987), reviewing the usefulness of this model in examining medication compliance, cite several studies examining single elements of the HBM in psychiatric populations. For example, patients are less likely to comply with medication when they do not believe they are ill (Marder et al., 1983). Relatively few studies have examined the elements of the HBM simultaneously. Connelly et al., (1982), using operationalized definitions, found that HBM components together accounted for 7% of the variance in overall adherence scores. Kelly et al., (1987) found that susceptibility, barriers and cues to action were significantly associated with compliance. Each component explained 10–12% of the variance in compliance. Perceived severity and benefits were predictors of recent medication errors but not of long-term compliance. They concluded that the HBM components account for around 20% of the variance in compliance among psychiatric outpatients. In contrast, Pan and Tantam (1989) reported that irregular attenders did not differ in their health beliefs from age and sex-matched regular attenders, and suggested that the influence of health beliefs may wane over time. Additions to the HBM have been proposed, including factors such as the quality of the doctor–patient relationship, the complexity of treatment and the personality of the patient (Christensen, 1978). These factors may act as modifiers of the decision-making process described above. Past experience of medication might be another potent modifier. Insufficient attention has been paid to the idea of non-compliance as a learned behaviour. Early experience of distressing medication side effects may reduce subsequent compliance (see above).

A variety of scales aim to measure aspects of the patient's subjective experience. Soskis and Bowers (1969) developed an attitude scale which correlated with compliance in their hands, but not in other studies (Buchanan, 1996). Weiden et al., (1994) have based their Rating of Medical Influences (ROMI) scale on the Health Belief Model, and established its reliability in a population of people with schizophrenia. Sellwood and Tarrier (W.Sellwood, personal communication, 1995) are developing another measure, the Attitudes to Medication (ATM), also based on the Health Belief Model. Naber et al., (1994) reported a 38-item assessment based on Likert scale ratings completed by the patient. In a sample of patients in clinical remission, ratings on this measure predicted non-compliance with maintenance medication over the next six months. This study also illustrates some of the complex problems in research into patients' subjective experiences. It is difficult to devise scales which reliably separate subjective dysphoria from clinically relevant depression, drug-induced akinesia and akathisia, and negative symptoms and other illness factors. Study designs featuring a period of assessment on and off neuroleptic medication would avoid these pitfalls but might not be ethically justifiable.

Factors relevant to carers or family

The Health Belief Model can be applied equally well to carers and others who are important in the patient's life. Such individuals can be extremely important in influencing the patient's own attitudes. Family expressed emotion can have a substantial effect on relapse rates (Leff and Vaughn, 1985). Expressed emotion in turn may be determined by the attitudes and causal attributions of family members (Brewin et al., 1991, Harrison and Dadds, 1992). A recent meta-analysis has reported that interventions for high expressed emotion, though not always successful in reducing expressed emotion, show significant benefits on compliance with medications (Mari and Streiner, 1996).

MANAGEMENT OF NON-COMPLIANCE

Strategies can be classified based on the extent to which collaboration is sought with patients and carers. At one extreme are methods imposed on the patient, such as use of compulsory admission or other legal measures. At the other, the patient is fully involved in developing individualized collaborative strategies, using cognitive–behavioural techniques or motivational interviewing. Between these extremes are methods which offer a general rather than an individual focus, such as some forms of psychoeducation, or attention to the type and frequency of antipsychotic drugs administered. While these interventions cannot be all be considered strictly *psychological*, psychological interventions must be assessed in the wider context of compliance strategies as a whole.

Legal and other methods to improve compliance

During inpatient admission, patients' compliance can be carefully monitored and optimized, particularly where taking medication is a requirement of compulsory admission. However, problems are more likely on discharge from inpatient care. Few countries or states have legal provisions which oblige the patient to accept his or her care plan, including medications, following discharge into the community. Where such provisions exist, their effects have seldom been systematically evaluated. In England and Wales, provisions for supervised discharge into the community have been introduced too recently to allow evaluation of their effects. However, for patients legally detained in hospital on treatment orders, some psychiatrists interpreted the 1983 Mental Health Act as allowing patients to be discharged from hospital on "extended leave" while still on the legal order. In 1985, this practice was tested in the Courts and determined to be illegal. However, data on patients managed in this way prior to 1985 demonstrated that, with the psychiatric team having recourse to possible legal measures (notably compulsory readmission), the compliance of patients was significantly improved with both medications and outpatient appointments (Sensky et al., 1991). Moreover, patients whose "extended leave" was ended in 1985 when the practice was judged illegal showed significantly worse compliance subsequently than others who were taken off "extended leave" on clinical grounds.

Similar improvements in compliance might be expected under other equivalent circumstances, for example when patients' receipt of their social security benefits is contingent on attending their outpatient appointments.

Interventions involving the medical regime

Simplifying the regime and providing written instructions are obvious first steps in the management of compliance problems. Where appropriate, the use of calendar packs or dosset boxes may improve compliance where forgetfulness or poor communication is the cause of the problem. Alternatively, relatives or community carers may be recruited to help to supervise medication.

Where individuals tend to be forgetful or disorganized, depot preparations of antipsychotic medications may be appropriate. They are also helpful in "covert" non-compliance, that is, where there is evidence of poor compliance despite the patient's expressed willingness to take medications. As the risk of relapse after discontinuing medication remains elevated for many months, the advantages of depot medication are not apparent unless patients are followed for longer than one year (Kane, 1983). In the only double-blind study which has achieved this, 42% of patients on oral fluphenazine relapsed in the second year compared with 8% of the patients on depot (Hogarty et al., 1979). Shorter studies have shown much smaller differences (e.g. Buchanan, 1996).

Psychoeducation

Purely educational measures to improve compliance are based on the assumptions that patients lack knowledge about their condition and its treatment, and that attempts to educate them hitherto have been inadequate. Evidence supporting these assumptions is equivocal. Chan (1984) reported that knowledge about medications increased compliance. Clary et al., (1992) found that on discharge from inpatient psychiatric care, the majority of patients have incomplete knowledge of the names of medications and the schedule for taking them. However, compared with matched controls with physical illnesses, people with psychiatric disorders were found to be better informed about side effects and risks of their medications, although less knowledgeable about the names and purpose of medications (Soskis, 1978). Nearly all the medical patients felt that they took medication out of choice, but only 56% of schizophrenic inpatients felt the same. Only 6% of their sample suffered from schizophrenia. However, it seems that while knowledge of medication among people with schizophrenia may be deficient, it is no worse than among medical inpatients or other psychiatric inpatients. Many psychoeducational packages go beyond only imparting information, to include helping patients and families to develop strategies to cope with stresses and solve problems more effectively (Goldstein, 1995). In practice, some such packages are impossible to distinguish from cognitive–behavioural interventions (see below).

Education of patients

Inpatient education has been shown to increase knowledge as measured by questionnaire and to briefly increase outpatient compliance with medication (Seltzer et al., 1980; Goldman and Quinn, 1988, Lowe et al., 1995). Recently, MacPherson and colleagues (1996) reported a controlled trial demonstrating improved knowledge, but no change in beliefs about compliance, among outpatients with schizophrenia one month after a three-session educational intervention. It is advantageous to present educational material in verbal and written form (Munetz and Roth, 1985). However, initial gains in knowledge may not be maintained (Streiker et al., 1986). It has been suggested that fear-based education might be counterproductive (Blackwell, 1976), although Brown et al., (1987) reported that education about specific side effects, including tardive dyskinesia, did not affect compliance. A subgroup of patients with movement disorders and/or negative symptoms have tended to fare worse than others in educational interventions (MacPherson et al., 1996).

Education of carers
Psychoeducation packages should be considered for family members, who can exert considerable influence on compliance (Falloon, 1984). There is some evidence that psychoeducation can reduce problems with compliance, improve attitudes to care services and reduce inpatient readmission rates (Kelly and Scott, 1990). However, interpretation of the results of this study is complicated by the fact that one third of patients initially recruited failed to enter the trial and a further 27% failed to complete the study. A more comprehensive family intervention not only improved compliance but reduced the amount of medication required (Falloon et al., 1985).

Behavioural and cognitive interventions

Falloon et al., (1982) developed a behavioural family management package, based on a view of compliance as complex learned behaviour modified by environmental contingencies (Falloon, 1984). This package was used in a randomized trial of behavioural family therapy and psychoeducation. Better compliance was obtained in a group randomized to systematic education and behavioural family therapy than in a those given supportive therapy (Falloon et al., 1982). Boczkowski et al., (1985) compared a behavioural-tailoring (BT) programme with psychoeducation (PE) and controls using 12 outpatients with schizophrenia in each group and a three month follow-up period. Compliance scores derived from pill-count were greatest for the BT group. The PE group did not differ from controls on pill-count scores although their knowledge of medication improved more than the other two groups. Eckman et al., (1990) developed a Medication Management Module, featuring a manual, a patient's workbook and a demonstration video coupled with psychoeducational and behavioural interventions. The compliance measures were observer ratings by physicians and carers on a four-point scale. One hundred and sixty patients were followed up for three months. There were significant gains in all areas measured, suggesting that patients can be taught skills which they retain and use, with resulting improvements in compliance. However, this study included no control group for placebo effects. Further, in the absence of reliable measures of compliance, it is difficult to interpret the results.

A major difficulty with this study, and a number of the others cited, is its short duration. Any clinically relevant assessment of compliance with maintenance medication in schizophrenia requires a follow-up period of at least two years. There is other evidence that brief family interventions, although potentially beneficial in the short-term, fail to have enduring benefits (Tarrier et al., 1988). It has also been argued that, whatever the benefits of psychological interventions in the short-term, some people with schizophrenia will, if followed up for longer periods, "revert" to higher relapse rates unless interventions are continued (Hogarty et al., 1991).

The successful applications of cognitive–behavioural techniques in schizophrenia have given rise to numerous treatment manuals. Given the likely relevance to compliance of patients' beliefs and attitudes, cognitive–behavioural interventions might be expected to be helpful, and their potential importance has been acknowledged (Perris and Skagerlind, 1994; Day and Bentall, 1996). In view of the importance of compliance to prognosis, it is surprising that, with some exceptions (for example Kingdon and Turkington, 1994; Nelson, 1997), available treatment manuals offer little specific guidance on optimizing compliance.

One cognitive approach is to work with the patient to develop a "normalizing rationale" for his/her disorder, based on a stress-vulnerability model (Kingdon and Turkington, 1991). Symptoms which respond most favourably to conventional anti-psychotic medications are construed as variants of normality to which everyone is vulnerable under particular stressful circumstances. Medication can be considered as one method of reducing such vulnerability as part of a comprehensive analysis of costs and benefits in developing an appropriate management plan with the patient. In this approach, managing medications and other aspects of compliance form an integral part of the therapy. Recently, encouraging results have been reported using an alternative approach, focusing more specifically on compliance and based on motivational interviewing (Kemp et al., 1996). In a comparison of compliance therapy and a non-specific counselling control intervention for inpatients admitted with acute psychotic disorders, improvements in compliance (rated by staff blind to the intervention which each patient received) were sustained after six months.

CONCLUSIONS

In other chronic illnesses which require the patient to follow a regular medical regime, such as diabetes, the term *compliance* has been replaced with *adherence*. Compliance has come to signify passive acceptance by the patient of professional advice and help, whereas adherence implies an active role for the patient, reaching his/her own decisions about how to manage the disorder. Adherence should whenever possible be based on a continuing collaboration between the patient, his/her carers and the professionals involved (Dencker and Liberman, 1995 ; Bebbington, 1995).

In schizophrenia, it is not possible to abandon completely the notion of compliance, although it is essential in any care plan to encourage the patient's active participation as far as possible. The scope for doing this, some might argue, is limited by the special circumstances of schizophrenia, notably the loss of insight which may be part of the disorder. However, the concept of impaired insight remains unclear, as does its precise relevance to adherence. People who suffer from diseases not apparently characterized by poor insight show similar levels of non-compliance to those in schizophrenia, and clinicians are very familiar with patients who, despite vehemently denying any disorder, are willing to remain in hospital and to accept treatment.

An integrated psychological approach to compliance requires a model of compliance with medication as a continuum of behaviour between total refusal and total acceptance. Further, compliance varies markedly over time and is modified by a multitude of internal and external factors. In the early phase of a psychotic breakdown, the patient may be inaccessible for a variety of reasons and coercion may be necessary. The clinical team should remain aware that the harm done to the therapeutic relationship at this time may be expressed as non-compliance with medication following recovery. Strenuous efforts should be made as early as possible to optimize medication and to build rapport with the patient and with family and carers. As recovery proceeds, coercion should give way to self-motivated adherence. A combination of education, practical advice and vigilant attention to side effects by the clinical team may result in a collaborative effort between patient and doctor to achieve the maximum functioning with the minimum morbidity.

Research methodology to study compliance is fraught with difficulty. Apart from the need for longer term follow up already noted, plus the difficulty in designed appropriate control interventions, two problems predominate. First, it is very difficult to reliably measure compliance directly. Second, those who comply poorly with their treatment are also the least likely to volunteer for research projects, and much research to date has therefore excluded the very subjects who constitute the targets for its findings. Nevertheless, research as well as empirical evidence has highlighted numerous interventions which might be beneficial in improving compliance with care plans, including medications, in schizophrenia. Relatively few research interventions have been targeted exclusively at improving compliance among those who comply poorly, but it is clear that more broadly focused psychological treatments for patients as well as carers can have a substantial impact on compliance. There has been little research on the impact on patients' compliance of knowledge, attitudes and working methods of members of the multiprofessional team. This is particularly surprising given the pivotal role of the mental health team in the care of the patient and family. Even those interventions which show promise have been tested almost exclusively in research settings, or by specialist teams, alongside and in addition to the standard care package. Much work is still required to integrate these interventions into routine clinical care.

REFERENCES

Awad, A.G. and Hogan, T.P. (1994) Subjective response to neuroleptics and the quality of life: implications for treatment outcome. *Acta Psychiatrica Scandinavica* **89** (suppl 380), 27–32.

Bartko, G., Herczeg, I. and Zandor, G. (1988) Clinical symptomatology and drug compliance in schizophrenic patients. *Acta Psychiatrica Scandinavica* **77**, 74–76.

Bebbington, P.E. (1995) The content and context of compliance. *International Journal of Clinical Psychopharmacology* **9** (Suppl 5), 41–50.

Becker, M.H. and Mamain, L.A., (1975) Sociobehavioral determinants of compliance with health and medical care recommendations. *Medical Care* **XIII**, 10–24.

Blackwell, B.(1973) Rational use in drug therapy. Chapter 13 in *Rational Psychopharmacology and the Right to Treatment*, (Ed. Ayd, F.J.) Baltimore: Ayd Medical Communication.

Blackwell, B. (1976) Treatment adherence. *British Journal of Psychiatry*, **129**, 513–531.

Boczkowski, J.A., Zeichner, A. and De Santo, N. (1985) Neuroleptic compliance among chronic schizophrenic outpatients: an intervention outcome report. *Journal of Consulting and Clinical Psychology* **53**, 666–671.

Boyd, J.R., Covington, T.R., Stanaszek, W.F. and Coussons, R.T. (1974) Drug Defaulting. II. Analysis of non-compliance patterns. *American Journal of Hospital Pharmacy* **31**, 485–491.

Brewin, C.R., MacCarthy, B., Duda, K. and Vaughn, C.E. (1991). Attribution and expressed emotion in the relatives of patients with schizophrenia. *Journal of Abnormal Psychology* **100**, 546–554.

Brown, C.S., Wright, R.G. and Christensen, D.B. (1987) Association between type of medication instruction and patients' knowledge, side effects and compliance. *Hospital and Community Psychiatry* **38**, 55–60.

Buchanan, A. (1992) A two-year prospective study of treatment compliance in patients with schizophrenia. *Psychological Medicine* **22**, 787–797.

Buchanan, A. (1996) *Compliance with Treatment in Schizophrenia*. Hove, Sussex: Psychology Press.

Chan, D.W. (1984) Medication compliance in a Chinese psychiatric outpatient setting. *British Journal of Medical Psychology* **57**, 81–89.

Christensen, D.B. (1978) Drug-taking compliance: A review and synthesis. *Health Services Researc* **13**, 171–187.

Clary, C., Dever, A. and Schweizer, E. (1992) Psychiatric inpatients' knowledge of medication at hospital discharge. *Hospital and Community Psychiatry* **43**, 140–144.

Connelly, C.E., Davenport, Y.B. and Nurnberger, J.I. (1982) Adherence to treatment regimen in a lithium carbonate clinic. *Archives of General Psychiatry* **39**, 585.

Curson, D.A., Barnes, T.R.E., Bamber, R.W., Platt, S.D., Hirsch, S.R. and Duffy, J.C.(1985) *British Journal of Psychiatry* **146**, 469–474.

Day, J.C. and Bentall, R.P. (1996) Neuroleptic medication and the psychosocial treatment of psychotic symptoms: some neglected issues in *Cognitive-behavioural Interventions with Psychotic Disorders* (Eds G. Haddock and P.D. Slade), London: Routledge.

Dencker, S.J. and Dencker, K. (1995) The need for quality assurance for a better compliance and increased quality of life in chronic schizophrenic patients. *International Clinical Psychopharmacology*, 9 (suppl. 5), 35–40.

Dencker, S.J. and Liberman, R.P. (1995) From compliance to collaboration in the treatment of schizophrenia. *International Clinical Psychopharmacology* **9** (Suppl 5), 75–78.

Eckman, T.A., Liberman, R.P., Phipps, C.C. and Blair, K.E. (1990) Teaching medication management skills to schizophrenic patients. *Journal of Clinical Psychopharmacology* **10**, 33– 38.

Eisenthal, S., Emery, R., Lazare, A. and Udin, H. (1979) Adherence and the negotiated approach to patienthood. *Archives of General Psychiatry* **36**, 393–398.

Falloon, I.R.H. (1984) Developing and maintaining adherence to long-term drug taking regimens. *Schizophrenia Bulletin* **10**, 412–417.

Falloon, I., Watt, D.C. and Shepherd, M. (1978) A comparative controlled trial of pimozide and fluphenazine decanoate in the continuation treatment of schizophrenia. *Psychological Medicine* **8**, 59–70.

Falloon, I.R.H., Boyd, J.L., McGill, C.W., Razani, J., Moss, H.B. and Gilderman, A.M. (1982) Family management in the prevention of exacerbations of schizophrenia. *New England Journal of Medicine* **306**, 1437–1440.

Falloon, I.R., Boyd, J.L., McGill, C.W., Williamson, M., Razani, J., Moss, H.B., Gilderman, A.M. and Simpson, G.M. (1985) Family management in the prevention of morbidity of schizophrenia: clinical outcome of a two-year longitudinal study. *Archives of General Psychiatry* **42**, 887–896.

Fleishhacker, W.W., Meise, U., Gunther, V. and Kurz, M. (1994) Compliance with antipsychotic drug treatment: influence of side effects. *Acta Psychiatrica Scandinavica* **89** (suppl 382), 11–15.

Gilbert, P.L., Harris, J., McAdams, L.A. and Jeste, D.V. (1995) Neuroleptic withdrawal in schizophrenic patients: a review of the literature. *Archives of General Psychiatry* **52**, 173–188.

Goldberg, S.C., Schooler, N.R., Hogarty, G.E. and Roper, M. (1977) Prediction of relapse in schizophrenic out-patients treated by drug and sociotherapy. *Archives of General Psychiatry* **34**, 171–184.

Goldman, C.R., Quinn, F.L. (1988) Effects of a patient education programme in the treatment of schizophrenia. *Hospital and Community Psychiatry* **39**, 282–286.

Goldstein, M.J. (1995) Psychoeducation and relapse prevention. *International Clinical Psychopharmacology* **9** (Suppl 5), 59–69.

Harrison, C.A. and Dadds, M.R. (1992) Attributions of symptomatology: an exploration of family factors associated with expressed emotion. *Australian and New Zealand Journal of Psychiatry* **26**, 408–416.

Hogan, T.P., Awad, A.G. and Eastwood, M.R. (1983) A self-report scale predictive of drug compliance in schizophrenics: reliability and discriminative ability. *Psychological Medicine* **13**, 177–183.

Hogarty, G.E., Schooler, N.R., Ulrich, R.F., Mussare, F., Herron, E. and Ferro, P. (1979) Fluphenazine and social therapy in the aftercare of schizophrenic patients. Relapse analyses of a two-year controlled study of fluphenazine decanoate and fluphenazine hydrochloride. *Archives of General Psychiatry* **36**, 1283–1294.

Hogarty, G.E., Anderson, C.M. and Reiss, D.J., Kornblith, S.J., Greenwald, D.P.,Ulrich, R.F., Carter, M. and the EPICS Research Group (1991) Family psychoeducation, social skills training and maintenance chemotherapy in the aftercare of schizophrenia. II. Two year effects of a controlled study on relapse and adjustment. *Archives of General Psychiatry* **48**, 340–347.

Hoge, S.K, Appelbaum, P.S., Lawlor, T., Beck, J.C, Litman, R., Greer, A., Gutheil, T. and Kaplan, E. (1990) A prospective, multicentre study of patients' refusal of medication. *Archives of General Psychiatry* **47**, 949–956.

Humneer, M. and Fleischhacken, W.W. (1996) Compliance and outcome in patients treated with antipsychotics. *CNS Drugs* **5** (Suppl. 1), 13–30.

Irwin, D.S., Witzel, W.D. and Morgan, D.W. (1971) Phenothiazine intake and staff attitudes. *American Journal of Psychiatry* **127**, 1631–1635.

Johnson, D.A.W. (1993) Depot neuroleptics. In *Antipsychotic Drugs and their Side-effects*. (Ed. Barnes, T.R.F.). London: Academic Press, pp. 205–212.

Kane, J.M. (1983) Problems of compliance in the outpatient treatment of schizophrenia. *Journal of Clinical Psychiatry* **44**, 3–6.

Kane, J.M. (1986) Prevention and treatment of neuroleptic noncompliance. *Psychiatric Annals,* **16**, 576–579.

Kane, J.M. (1987) Treatment of schizophrenia. *Schizophrenia Bulletin* **13**,133–156.

Kane, J.M. and Borenstein, M. (1985) Compliance in the long-term treatment of schizophrenia. *Psychopharmacological Bulletin* **21**, 23–27.

Katz, J. and Solomon, R.Z. (1958) The patient and his experiences in an out-patient clinic. *Archives of Neurology and Psychiatry* **80**, 86–92.

Kelly, G.R. and Scott, J.E. (1990) Medication compliance and health education among outpatients with chronic mental disorders. *Medical Care* **28**, 1181–1197.

Kelly, G.R., Mamon, J.A. and Scott, J.E. (1987) Utility of the Health Belief Model in examining medication compliance among psychiatric outpatients. *Social Science and Medicine* **25**, 1205– 1211.

Kemp, R., Hayward, P., Applewhaite, G., Everitt, B. and David, A. (1996) Compliance therapy in psychotic patients: randomized controlled trial. *British Medical Journal* **312**, 345–349.

Kingdon, D.G. and Turkington, D. (1991) The use of cognitive behaviour therapy with a normalizing rationale in schizophrenia. Preliminary report. *Journal of Nervous and Mental Disease* **179**, 207–211.

Kingdon, D. and Turkington, D. (1994) *Cognitive-behavioural Therapy of Schizophrenia.* Hove, Sussex: Lawrence Erlbaum.

Kissling, W. (1994) Compliance, quality assurance and standards for relapse prevention in schizophrenia. *Acta Psychiatrica Scandinavica* **89** (suppl 382), 16–24.

Leff, J. and Vaughn, C. (1985) *Expressed Emotion in Families.* New York: Guilford Press.

Leventhal, H., Diefenbach, M. and Leventhal, E.A. (1992) Illness cognition: using common sense to understand treatment adherence and affect cognition interactions. *Cognitive Therapy and Research* **16**, 143–163.

Lewander, T. (1994) Neuroleptics and neuroleptic-induced deficit syndrome. *Acta Psychiatrica Scandinavica* **89** (suppl. 382), 8–13.

Linkewich, J.A., Catalano, R.B. and Flack, H.L. (1974) The effect of packaging and instruction on out-patient compliance with medication regimens. *Drug Intelligence in Clinical Pharmacy* **8**, 10–15.

Lowe, C.J., Raynor, D.K., Courtney, E.A., Purvis, J. and Teale, C. (1995) Effects of self medication programme on knowledge of drugs and compliance with treatment in elderly patients. *British Medical Journal* **310**, 1229–1231.

McEvoy, J.P., Allison, C., Howe, B.A. and Hogarty, G.E. (1984) Differences in the nature of relapse and subsequent in-patient course between medication-compliant and non-compliant schizophrenic patients. *Journal of Nervous and Mental Disease* **172**, 413–416.

MacPherson, R., Jerrom, B. and Hughes, A. (1996) A controlled study of education about treatment in schizophrenia. *British Journal of Psychiatry* **168**, 709–717.

Marder, S.R., Mebane, A., Chien, C.P., Winslade, W.J., Swann. E. and Van Putten, T. (1983) A Comparison of patients who refuse and consent to neuroleptic treatment. *American Journal of Psychiatry* **140**, 470–472.

Mari, J.J. and Streiner, D. (1996) The effects of family intervention for those with schizophrenia. *Cochrane Database of Systematic Reviews* **3**.

Munetz, M.R. and Roth, L.H. (1985) Informing patients about tardive dyskinesia. *Archives of General Psychiatry* **42**, 866–871.

Naber, D., Walther, A., Kircher, T, Hayek, D. and Holzbach, R. (1994) Subjective effects of neuroleptics predict compliance. In *Prediction of Neuroleptic Treatment Outcome in Schizophrenia: Concepts and Methods.* (Eds Gaebel, W., Awad, R.), Heidelberg: Springer, 85–98.

Nelson, H.E. (1997) *Cognitive Behavioural Therapy with Schizophrenia: a Treatment Manual.* Cheltenham: Stanley Thornes (in press).

Pan, P.C. and Tantam, D. (1989) Clinical characteristics, health beliefs and compliance with maintenance treatment: a comparison between regular and irregular attenders at a depot clinic. *Acta Psychiatrica Scandinavica* **79**, 564–570.

Perris, C. and Skagerlind, L. (1994). Cognitive therapy with schizophrenic patients. *Acta Psychiatrica Scandinavica* **89** (Suppl. 382), 65–70.

Porter, A.M.W. (1969) Drug defaulting in a general practice. *British Medical Journal*, **i**, 218– 222.

Pristach, C.A. and Smith, C.M. (1990) Medication compliance and substance abuse among schizophrenic patients. *Hospital and Community Psychiatry* **41**, 1345–1348.

Renton, C.A., Affleck, J.W., Carstairs, G.M. and Forrest, A.D. (1963) A follow-up of schizophrenic patients in Edinburgh. *Acta Psychiatrica Scandinavica* **39**, 548–600.

Schneier, F.R. and Siris, S.G. (1987) A review of psychoactive substance misuse in schizophrenia: patterns of drug choice. *Journal of Nervous and Mental Diseases* **175**, 641–652.

Sensky, T., Hughes, T. and Hirsch, S. (1991) Compulsory psychiatric treatment in the community: I. A controlled study of treatment with extended leave under the Mental Health Act: special characteristics of patients and impact of treatment. *British Journal of Psychiatry* **158**, 792–799.

Soskis, D.A. (1978) Schizophrenic and medical in-patients as informed drug consumers. *Archives of General Psychiatry* **35**, 645–649.

Soskis, D.A. and Bowers, M.B. (1969). The schizophrenic experience. *Journal of Nervous and Mental Diseases* **149**, 443–449.

Tarrier, N., Barrowclough, C., Vaughn, C., Bamrah, J.S., Porceddu, K., Watts, S. and Freeman, H. (1988) The community management of schizophrenia: a controlled trial of a behavioural intervention with families to reduce relapse. *British Journal of Psychiatry* **153**, 532–542.

Van Putten, T. (1974) Why do schizophrenic patients refuse to take their drugs? *Archives of General Psychiatry* **31**, 67–72.

Van Putten, T., Crumpton, E. and Yale, C. (1976) Drug refusal in schizophrenia and the wish to be crazy. *Archives of General Psychiatry* **31**, 1443–1445.

Weiden, P.J., Shaw, E. and Mann, J.J. (1986) Causes of neuroleptic noncompliance. *Psychiatric Annals* **16**, 571–575.

Weiden, P., Rapkin, B., Mott, T.Zygmunt, A., Goldman, D., Hortvitz-Lennon, M. and Frances, A. (1994) Rating of Medication Influences (ROMI) Scale in Schizophrenia. *Schizophrenia Bulletin* **20**, 297–307.

Wright, E.C. (1993) Non-compliance – or how many aunts has Matilda? *The Lancet* **342**, 909–913.

Young, J.L., Zonana, H.V. and Shepler, L. (1986) Medication non-compliance in schizophrenia: codification and update. *Bulletin of the American Academy of Psychiatric Law* **14**, 105–122.

Chapter 10

BIOBEHAVIORAL THERAPY: INTERACTIONS BETWEEN PHARMACOTHERAPY AND BEHAVIOR THERAPY IN SCHIZOPHRENIA

Robert Liberman, Stephen Marder, B.D. Marshall, Jr., Jim Mintz and Timothy Kuehnel

As the first author of this chapter, I looked back over the 30 years of my work in schizophrenia and saw the dawn of behavior therapy for psychotic disorders starting in the 1950s and 1960s in the work of Skinner and his students—Azrin, Ayllon, and Lindsley. I also saw the disaffected eclipse of psychodynamic psychotherapy, which 30 years ago, was completing a decades-long stint as the "only hope" for curing schizophrenia. Antipsychotic medications had arrived and were "flexing their muscles", as

Portions of this chapter were adapted or reproduced with permission of The American Psychiatric Association from articles published in the *AJP*.

Outcome and Innovation in Psychological Treatment of Schizophrenia. Edited by T. Wykes, N. Tarrier and S. Lewis.

psychiatry was finally entering its scientific period through the door of controlled, clinical trials of drugs like chlorpromazine, thioridazine, and trifluoperazine. Soon to follow were the empirical validations of the token economy and other applications of behavioral learning principles to schizophrenia (Liberman et al., 1973; Paul and Lentz, 1977; Liberman and Mueser, 1989).

But behavior therapy never fulfilled its promise in the treatment of schizophrenia (Moss, 1994; Boudewyns, 1986; Bellack and Mueser, 1993) and most practitioners—whether they be psychologists, social workers, nurses, or psychiatrists—now believe that the only answers to the cause and treatment of schizophrenia lie in the biological realm through optimal pharmacotherapy. This belief system has been recently buoyed by the arrival of a new generation of antipsychotic drugs that appear more effective with fewer side effects than the conventional antipsychotics (Marder and Meibach, 1994).

However, over this 30 year period, I have not given up the effort to help persons with schizophrenia using behavioral techniques. Perhaps this eternal optimism, coming from a middle-aged, grizzled warrior of institutional wars, derives from my never having encountered a person with schizophrenia whose quality of life I have not been able to help improve, at least to some extent, using *biobehavioral techniques*. Having participated in the development of the community mental health movement (Liberman et al., 1976) and the field of psychiatric rehabilitation (Liberman, 1992), I am fully aware of the inadequacies and limitations of our current "state of the art" in treating schizophrenia—both biologically and behaviorally. For this reason, we must be encouraged to witness a new generation of psychological methods for schizophrenia, described in this text, that holds promise for improving the impairments, disabilities, and handicaps of persons with schizophrenia. At the same time, to avoid later disappointments and derogation of the effects of cognitive behavior therapy with schizophrenia, it is essential that psychological treatments be applied to individuals who have well-diagnosed schizophrenia, a criticism already leveled at the first crop of studies in this genre (Bouchard et al., 1996). The first blush of successful case studies must also be extended to the arena of randomized, controlled research, where double blind assessments and standardization of antipsychotic medications are rigorously employed.

Before describing two "state of the art" studies of *biobehavioral therapy for schizophrenia* from our UCLA Research Center for Severe Mental Illnesses, an important point needs to be made: namely, there is no such thing as "psychological therapy for schizophrenia! Psychological and social therapies are always accompanied by pharmacological treatment and to ignore the latter is to obscure the contributions of the former. In other words, "psychological therapy" is a misnomer, a fantasy, born of those blinded to the essential role of antipsychotic medication in what is almost always a joint *biobehavioral* or *biopsychosocial intervention.*

Paying "lip service" to the importance of drug therapy in schizophrenia by stating that all subjects were "stabilized on medication prior to beginning their psychological treatment belies the following realities:

1. Different medications, different doses, and different combinations of medications yield different degrees and duration of stabilization; furthermore, different side-effect profiles can importantly influence learning (such as benztropine, or Cogentin, an anticholinergic agent often used to treat side effects, which has potent effects on impairing memory).

2. Prescribing psychiatrists who are not intrinsically on the research team studying a new psychological therapy may often change the type and dose of medication *ad lib* without considering the phase of the protocol that the subject is in nor the control vs. experimental group assignments.

3. A new generation of more effective antipsychotic agents are being introduced, some of which will powerfully affect the cognitive functions being described in the psychological therapies found in the other chapters of this book. For example, risperidone appears to improve and even normalize verbal working memory in schizophrenic individuals who had been refractory to other, more conventional medications (Green et al., 1997; McGurk and Green, 1997).

In this chapter, we shall describe two studies that were designed to tease out the joint pharmacological and behavioral effects of treatment of schizophrenia. Both studies were carried out within our UCLA Research Center for Severe Mental Illnesses. One study took place at the Camarillo-UCLA Clinical Research Unit at the Camarillo State Hospital where the inpatient population was primarily treatment-refractory, with many years of continuous illness, disability, and hospitalization; the other study took place at the Psychopharmacology Unit of the West Los Angeles VA Medical Center where outpatients were studied who had a history of responding to conventional antipsychotic drugs but where noncompliance leads to a rapidly "revolving door" of admission–discharge–readmission.

A careful reading of this chapter will illustrate the importance of identifying the differences between schizophrenic populations, treatment settings, clinicians, pharmacological regimens, and types of behavior therapy used. These variables often make interpreting the results of published accounts of psychological therapies difficult: They should be clearly articulated in all studies that seek publication where both pharmacological and psychological or behavioral treatments are being used.

OPTIMAL DRUG AND BEHAVIOR THERAPY FOR TREATMENT REFRACTORY SCHIZOPHRENIC PATIENTS

Despite the advent of clozapine, many thousands of patients with schizophrenia remain refractory to pharmacotherapy and customary forms of psychosocial treatment. Estimates of treatment refractoriness approximate 25% of persons with schizophrenia, a problem of public mental health magnitude, given the residence of these individuals in state hospitals, community facilities, prisons, and on the streets. Since many of these patients receive high doses of neuroleptics for extended time periods with adverse effects (Brenner et al., 1990; Liberman et al., 1994) and because virtually nothing is known about the utility of high-dose neuroleptics in the refractory schizophrenic patient, we conducted a systematic trial of decremental dose-reduction of haloperidol in 13 institutionalized schizophrenic patients. Once the optimal dose was identified, each patient participated in an intensive and individualized behavior therapy program.

The hypotheses of this pilot, exploratory study were as follows:

1. The benefit–risk ratio of therapeutic to side effects of haloperidol (HPL) would improve with lowering of the HPL dose as it reached the same therapeutic window in the plasma that has previously been documented for acute, treatment-responsive schizophrenic patients (Van Putten et al., 1990).
2. Subsequent to reaching the optimal dose, patients would show further improvements in negative symptoms, social communication, instrumental role functioning, self-care skills and intolerable, deviant behaviors when exposed to personalized behavior therapy.

METHODS

Subjects and setting

Ten male and 3 female patients ranging in age between 20-42 (mean = 32), who met DSM-IIIR criteria for schizophrenia and were receiving at least 50 mg per day of haloperidol or its equivalent, were entered into the study at different times over an 18 month period. Treatment refractoriness (Brenner et al., 1990) was defined as psychotic symptoms rated as "moderately severe" or worse on the BPRS persisting for at least two years despite prolonged trials of treatment with various neuroleptics; at least 14 months of continuous treatment at Camarillo State Hospital (mean = 57 months) without prospect of release; two or more trials of neuroleptics at dose levels of 1000 mg/day chlorpromazine equivalents; and functional behavioral deficits and deviances that were incompatible with community adaptation. Ten of thirteen patients had a history of assaultiveness.

The study was conducted on the 11 bed, Camarillo-UCLA Clinical

Research Unit where nursing staff were trained in systematic behavioral observations and interventions. The ward environment was standardized by operationalized, planned and scheduled biobehavioral treatments that included training in activities in daily living, training in social and independent living skills, recreation therapy, time-out from reinforcement for aggression or property destruction, and a token economy (Glynn et al., 1994).

Procedures

All patients were maintained at their referral levels of high daily, oral doses of neuroleptic drugs for at least two months, during which time those not on HPL were converted to an equipotent dose of HPL. All other medications were stopped except anti-Parkinson drugs; lorazepam or sodium amytal were used on an as-needed basis for behavioral dyscontrol.

HPL dose was reduced every five weeks according to a fixed schedule: 65, 50, 35, 20, 15, 5, and 0 mg/day. Dosage was reduced as long as the patient was rated as "unchanged" or "improved" by a staff consensual rating on the Clinical Global Impression Scale (CGI) (Guy, 1976). If the patient was rated "slightly worse", the dosage was held steady for another five weeks; if there was no subsequent deterioration, the dosage was further reduced. If a patient was rated "much worse" or "very much worse" on the CGI, dosage reduction was stopped, and the patient was returned to the previous higher effective dosage and kept at that dosage. Each dosage level was tested for a minimum of five weeks; one week to attain a new steady state plus four weeks for evaluation of clinical outcome at this level.

With blood drawn in the morning, 10–12 hours after the last dose, plasma HPL assays were done by a very sensitive high-performance liquid chromatographic (HPLC) method (Midha et al., 1988) that has limits of quantitation of less than 50 pg/ml HPL or reduced HPL.

At entry into the study, each patient had three target problem behaviors specified, and quantified on the Idiosyncratic Target Symptom Scale (May, 1968), that were viewed as the principal obstacles to discharge readiness. Problems included polydipsia, screaming and agitation, assaultiveness, incontinence, incoherence, and mumbling, inaudible speech. After at least five weeks at the optimal dose (with maintenance of this dose throughout the rest of the study), patients received individualized behavior analysis and therapy for their target problems. Therapeutic interventions included required relaxation, overcorrection, shaping and fading of prompts and reinforcement, discrete trials conversation skills training, and self-control procedures. The phase of individualized behavior therapy ensued for up to one year and typically more than one intervention was used before optimal improvement of the target problems was noted.

Assessment measures

Psychopathology, functional behavior, and side-effect ratings were conducted at entry into the study and on the fifth week of each dosage level, as well as during the final week of the behavior therapy phase, using the following instruments: the Brief Psychiatric Rating Scale (BPRS), Activities of Daily Living Checklist, Mobility–Affect–Cooperation–Communication Scale (Ellsworth, 1957), Idiosyncratic Target Symptom Scale, CGI, Social Interaction Scale, violations of unit rules as reflected by token fines, Columbia Unified Parkinson's Disease Rating Scale (Fahn and Elton, 1987), Barnes Akathisia Scale (Barnes, 1989) and the Assessment of Involuntary Movement Scale (AIMS).

For the purposes of data analysis, study periods were delimited as follows: the *dosage* baseline was the last rating period prior to the start of dosage reduction; and *optimal dose* was the average of all rating periods that occurred after the lowest effective dose was determined, but before the start of intensive behavior therapy. For the analyses of changes associated with intensive behavior therapy, the pre-treatment ratings were taken from the last rating period during the optimal dose phase prior to the start of the behavior therapy, and posttreatment scores were based on the five week rating period during which the behavior therapy had its maximal impact on behaviors targeted for change. Two subjects left against medical advice prior to participating in the behavior therapy phase.

RESULTS

The 13 patients tolerated a mean reduction of 63 % (median = 70%) from a mean of HPL of 63.1 mg/day (SD + 12.5, range 50–80 mg/day) to 23.1 mg/day (SD +16.3, range 0–65 mg/day). The dosage reduction was paralleled by a comparable drop in HPL plasma levels. At the higher dose of HPL, patients had proportionately higher levels of reduced HPL, which is thought to be associated with poor response to this drug. At the clinically optimal dose of HPL, plasma levels of HPL were similar to plasma levels in acutely psychotic and drug-responsive schizophrenic patients for all but one of the patients (Van Putten et al., 1992).

On the average, the 13 patients improved on the BPRS total score (mean change -5.6, SD $+8.71$ $t = 2.31$, df $= 12$, $p = 0.04$) and the BPRS anxious-depression cluster (mean change -1.3, SD $+2.0$, t $= 2.43$, d.f. $= 12$ p $= 0.03$), with a trend toward improvement on the BPRS thought disturbance cluster (mean change -1.9, SD $+3.5$, $t = 2.0$, d.f. $= 12$, $p = 0.07$). On the CGI index, three patients were rated as worse, four were the same, and six were improved. At the optimal dose, the benefit/risk ratio of symptoms/side effects improved substantially since all patients experienced fewer side effects in akathisia (total Barnes score 2.1 vs. 1.2, $t = -1.99$, d.f. = 10, $p = 0.04$), one-tailed) and less EPS (total Columbia score 13.2 vs. 5.8, $t = 2.64$, d.f. = 10, $p = 0.01$, one-tailed). All statistical tests were two-tailed except for those evaluating side effects, in line with prior predictions of change.

No statistically significant changes were noted on the AIMS (tardive dyskinesia), which was expected since the substantial reduction in HPL dose would be associated with uncovering of the dopamine receptors in the basal ganglia which produce tardive dyskinesia. There were no significant improvements noted in the functional behavioral measures concurrent with dosage reduction to the optimal dose, including assault and property destruction. When reaching their lowest dose (mean 7.5 mg/day), 10 of 13 of the patients showed global worsening on the CGI, which triggered their titration upward to the next higher dose that was found to be optimal. During the period at lowest dose, seven of the patients required 1–2 doses of adjunctive, prn lorazepam for behavioral control. One patient was remarkably improved at a dose of 0 mg, but this individual eventually relapsed into a florid psychosis after 20 weeks on placebo. Except for this patient, the other 9 who either improved or remained clinically the same sustained the clinical status on their optimal dose for a minimum of one year of follow-up.

At the end of the behavior therapy phase, three patients showed further marked improvement on the CGI beyond their clinical status at the optimal dose phase, with two reaching successful discharge from hospital. As hypothesized, the negative symptom, withdrawal–retardation cluster improved, but nonsignificantly, during the behavior therapy phase. Twenty-six functional and behavioral measures were examined that were hypothesized to improve with behavior therapy. Only one improved significantly by univariate t-test for correlated means, that being a reduction in patient's refusals to perform activities of daily living—such as showering and making their beds ($t = 2.43$, d.f. = 10, $p = 0.036$). This single result could clearly have been due to chance.

However, we did observe consistent results across these correlated measures of behavioral functioning, with 23 of the 26 measures showing a mean improvement during the behavior therapy phase. The first principal component in these measures accounted for 46% of the variance, and appeared to represent overall improvement. Eighteen of the measures had loadings on this component of 0.50 or greater and the signs of the loadings were all consistent in direction, with measures of positive qualities loading positively, and those representing negative characteristics loading negatively. An overall improvement index, or measure of the first principal component, was computed by standardizing each measure, and then summing change scores (appropriately reflected as indicated by the loading on the first component) across the standardized items. Improvement on this overall index of daily, functional behaviors was significant ($t = 2.84$, d.f. = 10, $p = 0.017$).

DISCUSSION

This study shows that it was possible to gradually reduce the dose of neuroleptic in 11 of 13 very chronic, treatment-refractory schizophrenic patients who were thought by their treatment staff to all require high-dose neuroleptic therapy. As a result of the dosage reduction to the optimal level, the patients on average were symptomatically and behaviorally improved, were less dysphoric, and definitely experienced fewer side effects; thus, their benefit/risk ratios markedly improved without jeopardy of increased aggression or behavioral dyscontrol.

The use of an individualized dosage decrement protocol such as was done in this study, titrating the dose against measurable psychopathology, side effects and disturbing behaviors, may provide an antidote to the "ratchet" effect of non-rational "creeping dosage" escalation of neuroleptic drugs in response to short-term behavioral events in patients who are limited responders to neuroleptics at best. Thus, we recommend that clinicians utilize empirically guided treatment with the BPRS or target symptom scales assisting in the adjustment or titration of medication dose.

Interestingly, the two patients who could not tolerate substantial dosage reduction were also the only two subjects characterized by substantially aberrant performance on the degraded stimulus, Continuous Performance Test and the Span of Apprehension Test (Green et al., 1993). This suggests a relationship between markedly impaired central nervous system information processing and a higher threshold for therapeutic effects from neuroleptics. If these two patients were removed from the analysis, the mean dosage reduction tolerated by the other 11 was 88 percent.

Treatment-specific effects were noted, with HPL-dose reduction producing improvements in positive symptoms, depression, anxiety, and side effects while the addition of intensive behavior therapy yielded improvements in functional behavior and negative symptoms. The findings partially replicate studies that reported improvements in psychopathology with reduction of neuroleptic medication in schizophrenic outpatients (Leblanc et al., 1989) and inpatients (Faraone et al., 1989) and with cognitive-behavior therapy in neuroleptic-resistant schizophrenic patients (Paul and Lentz, 1977; Tarrier et al., 1993; Glynn and Mueser, 1992). While the causal relationship of dosage reduction to clinical improvement requires testing in a random assignment of patients to dose reduction vs. continuation of former dose, it appears that many institutionalized, treatment-refractory schizophrenic patients can benefit from a systematic and monitored dosage reduction in league with intensive and personalized behavior therapy.

We will now shift from neuroleptic resistant, institutionalized schizophrenic patients to treatment-responsive outpatients who experience frequent relapses and rehospitalizations. With outpatients, the intensive techniques of individualized behavior therapy are not feasible and the behavioral therapy of choice has been social skills training.

BEHAVIORAL SKILLS TRAINING VS. SUPPORTIVE GROUP PSYCHOTHERAPY FOR OUTPATIENTS WITH SCHIZOPHRENIA: TWO-YEAR OUTCOME

Among the most promising psychosocial approaches for schizophrenia has been the use of social skills training (SST) (Wallace and Liberman, 1985). The interest in this treatment results from the observation that impairments in social functioning are largely responsible for the poor quality of life and social isolation of individuals with schizophrenia (Bellack and Mueser, 1993; Bellack et al., 1984; Liberman et al., 1985.) Methods for SST have largely been based upon learning principles. As a result, SST uses structured educational methods with social reinforcement, modeling, and role playing.

There are several good arguments for combining a skills training psychosocial treatment with a low-dosage, antipsychotic medication strategy. On the one hand, the combination of skills learned and support provided by the psychosocial intervention may buffer or reduce stress and enhance coping skills, reducing relapse risk and the need for higher doses of medication. Another argument is that the extrapyramidal side effects of antipsychotic medications, particularly akinesia and akathisia, interfere with patient participation in psychosocial treatments (Van Putten and Marder, 1987.) Thus, reduced doses of antipsychotic medication could facilitate rehabilitation through reductions in secondary negative symptoms and side effects, such as drowsiness, lack of motivation, anhedonia, lack of responsiveness to social or other reinforcement, and poor concentration.

This study was carried out in the context of a larger investigation that also focused on strategies for treating patients with reduced doses of maintenance antipsychotic medication. We have previously described the advantages and limitations of a strategy that included combining a low dose of fluphenazine decanoate (5–10 mg every 14 days) with supplemental oral fluphenazine hydrochloride when patients demonstrated early evidence of impending relapse (Marder et al., 1994). In that study patients who received oral supplementation were more likely to remain stable during the second year following randomization. We have also previously described the efficacy of skills training in this study for the acquisition and durability of medication and self-management skills (Eckman et al., 1992.) This report describes the effects of SST and supportive group therapy (SGT) on the risk of psychotic relapse and social adjustment for patients who participated in this trial.

METHODS

The subjects were 80 male outpatients undergoing treatment at the West Los Angeles VA Medical Center. All fulfilled DSM III-R criteria for schizophrenia based upon a review of medical records and symptom profiles which were documented using the Present State Examination. Each subject had at least two documented episodes of acute schizophrenic illness or at least two years of continuing psychotic symptoms. The average patient was close to 40 years old, and had been ill for more than 10 years. Most were unmarried and non-white.

Stabilization

Prior to study entry, each patient was stabilized on a low dose of fluphenazine decanoate (5–10 mg every 14 days). The dose was set at 5 mg unless there was a history that a higher dose was needed to prevent psychotic exacerbations. Patients who could not be stabilized for two or more months on 10 mg or less of fluphenazine decanoate (FD) given every two weeks were dropped from the study during the stabilization period.

Psychosocial conditions

After completing the prestudy stabilization, patients were randomly assigned to receive either behavioral skills training (SST) or supportive group therapy (SGT). Each treatment was administered twice weekly for 90 minutes each visit for the first six months, then weekly for 90 minutes for up to a total of two years if subjects remained engaged in the protocol. The entry of new study subjects was timed so that patients could begin the study in cohorts of approximately 10 patients with five assigned to each condition.

Behavioral skills training (SST)

Subjects participated in a series of skills training modules (Liberman et al., 1989) that were administered in a group setting. Subjects participated in modules on Medication Self-Management and Symptom Self-Management during the first six months of the trial. As the names denote, these modules comprise skill areas with educational objectives for recognizing symptoms and side effects, self-administration and monitoring of medication, negotiating medication issues with doctors and other providers, avoiding street drugs and alcohol, and identifying warning signs of relapse. A social problem solving module was completed during the second six months. This module was designed to enhance the ability to recognize social barriers to attaining life goals in the community and to generate, select, and implement appropriate solutions to these barriers. Finally, a successful living skills module was completed by subjects who continued into the final year of the study. This module enabled subjects to identify and pursue individualized and personal goals using the basic model of social skills training (Hierholzer and Liberman, 1989).

The SST procedures were designed to compensate for the symptom and cognitive deficits that are associated with schizophrenia. Cognitive restructuring principles, repeated behavioral rehearsal, video modeling, and abundant positive social reinforcement were used by the group leader to overcome the intrusions of symptoms, distractibility, and lack of motivation that some patients demonstrated.

Each of the modules had a similar structure. They began with an "introduction to self-management" (highlighting the rationale for the training, and the goals and benefits of the training, enhancing motivation to participate); moved to a "training segment" (in which the substantive knowledge and skills were trained); next moved to phases that taught problem-solving skills in the areas of "resource management" and "overcoming outcome problems"; and finally terminated in "in vivo exercises" and "homework assignments" where patients practiced the acquired skills in their natural environments. The training was continued for each patient until criteria for mastery of the knowledge and skills were reached.

The SST modules were administered by one or two therapists per session. The therapists included a Ph.D. psychologist, an occupational therapist, a masters level psychologist, a registered nurse, and a social science technician.

Supportive group psychotherapy (SGT)

To provide a rigorous test of the value of the specific skill-building elements in the behavioral skills training, a comparison psychosocial therapy was delivered to a control cohort that provided a comparable intensity of treatment and was considered the standard psychotherapeutic approach for chronic schizophrenics. The comparison treatment was supportive group psychotherapy (SGT) which was guided by goals for reality adaptation. This approach has been shown to be effective for outpatients with schizophrenia in controlled studies (Malm, 1982; May, 1984) and has received consensual support in reviews of psychosocial treatments (May, 1976; Rutan and Cohen 1989; Liberman, 1994).

The SGT therapist was a Ph.D. level psychologist with experience in working with persons having schizophrenia. Group size (4–8 members per cohort) and frequency (90 minutes twice weekly) were comparable to the SST condition. In SGT the therapist encouraged patients to set personal goals and harnessed group dynamics, such as cohesion, to assist patients in exploring problems and obstacles that were associated with meeting these goals. In addition, the therapist encouraged the group members to work together to learn new methods of coping with everyday life stressors, problems and situations, using open-ended questions, reflection, empathy, warmth, and gentle encouragement.

Information about mental illness and its treatment was provided by the therapist in a supportive atmosphere and discussion of the information by the group was encouraged. However, the therapist, who was trained in expressive and supportive therapy principles, assiduously avoided using structured behavioral or skills training techniques, such as modeling, homework assignments, and *in vivo* practice. As an independent indicator of the "attractiveness" of SGT and the satisfaction of patients with its value, there were no differences between the attendance and attrition in the two psychosocial conditions.

Drug treatment conditions

The drug treatment conditions were described in detail in a prior publication (Marder et al., 1994). Patients were evaluated weekly with the Idiosyncratic Prodromal Scale (IPS), an instrument which continued the symptoms that were reported to occur most reliably before relapses for each individual patient. For each item a scale (with 100 points) was developed with anchor points which described the range in severity for that symptom, and the threshold for meeting prodromal criteria. At each clinic visit, the severity of these symptoms was rated and the total compared with their baseline severity during the pre-study period of stabilization. When increases in severity met individualized criteria, patients were considered to be in a prodrome.

About half (n = 36) of the patients did experience a prodrome at some point during the study. When subjects experienced a prodrome, they were randomly assigned either to receive oral fluphenazine (5 mg) or a placebo, administered twice daily under double-blind conditions. Patients receiving either oral fluphenazine or placebo were then followed until they either became stable, or worsened to the point of fulfilling criteria for a "psychotic exacerbation" or relapse. During exacerbations, open label, oral medication was provided, usually consisting of fluphenazine, 5 mg twice daily. When patients stabilized they were returned to their original fixed dose of fluphenazine decanoate. If they again fulfilled criteria for a prodrome at a later time, they were treated under the same double-blind condition as they were for the first prodrome.

All of the recruited patients participated in the clinical trial of SST versus SGT, but only half of them met criteria for a prodrome during the study and participated in the drug supplementation trial. Analyses of the combined benefits of supplemental medication and skills training were only done with that subsample.

Outcome measures

Severity of psychotic and other symptoms was assessed "blindly" at monthly clinic visits by a trained clinical assessor using the Brief Psychiatric Rating Scale (BPRS). Since the patients were well stabilized at study entry, average symptom severity over the two-year study period showed little change from baseline. For this reason, the principal measure of symptom outcome was psychotic exacerbation. The exacerbation criterion was a worsening of 4 points or more on the sum of the BPRS cluster scores for Thought Disturbance and Hostile-Suspiciousness, or an increase of 3 or more on either cluster.

Psychosocial outcome was measured at baseline and every six months for the two year duration of the study using the patient version of the Social Adjustment Scale II (Schooler, 1979). The rater was a clinician who was not blind to the psychosocial treatment condition. This scale assesses social functioning using a semistructured interview. The validity of this instrument in outpatients with schizophrenia has been previously demonstrated (Glazer et al., 1980). Subjects were rated on subscales which evaluated work role (including student role), household role, parental role, extended family role, conjugal and nonconjugal sexual role, romantic involvement, social and leisure activities, and personal well-being.

Data analyses

The basic data analytic model for the SAS II cluster scores and total was the general mixed model ANOVA with repeated measures. The design included two between subject treatment factors, psychosocial treatment and drug, crossed to form a 2 (SST, SGT) $\times$ 3 (drug, placebo, never assigned) factorial design. About half of the subjects were never assigned to a supplemental drug condition because they never had an identified prodrome. The other half were randomized either to drug or placebo after the first prodrome. Repeated measures were obtained at four follow-up points (every six months over two years), and linear effects of time were also included in the statistical model as a within-subject factor. Each SAS II cluster was analyzed separately. Follow-up tests included simple effects analyses of psychosocial treatment differences within each drug condition, within the same framework. These planned contrasts used pooled error terms and pooled error d.f. Baseline level was included as a covariate in each analysis.

In addition to using drug condition as a fixed design factor, crossed with psychosocial treatment, it was also included as a time-varying covariate.

The reason was that, at the time of the first testing, a substantial number of subjects who subsequently entered the drug supplementation study, had not yet been assigned. Treating such subjects as equivalent to those who were never assigned to drug was incorrect, because subjects who ultimately entered the drug supplementation study were much less stable clinically. The inclusion of time-varying covariates in the models permitted evaluation of the "intent to treat" category, but also allowed for variation associated with whether or not subjects were actually receiving supplementation at the time of testing. Estimated values were thus adjusted for changes in actual drug treatment status and for linear trends within treatment groups over time (estimated at the mean time to follow-up, which was just over one year or roughly 59 weeks). Analysis of exacerbation risk was done with proportional hazards regression models, using the fixed treatment factors and time-varying drug treatment covariates as described (SAS Proc PHREG).

RESULTS

Effects of psychosocial condition on social adjustment

In our analysis of the effects of the psychosocial and drug treatment condition on cluster totals for the SAS II, we found significant main effects favoring SST over SGT on two of the six cluster totals examined. These were personal well-being (treatment main effect, $F = 6.95$, d.f. $= 1.95$, $p = 0.010$), and the total SAS II (treatment main effect $F = 6.05$, d.f. $= 1.94$, $p = 0.016$). In both cases, outcomes were better with SST. Neither main effects of time nor interactions of time with psychosocial effects were significant in any SAS area (p-levels ranged from 0.19 to 0.90, median $= 0.57$).

The interaction of psychosocial treatment and drug treatment condition was also significant in three areas. The clusters involved were personal well-being, social-interpersonal (treatment x drug interaction $F = 3.96$, d.f. $= 1.95$, $p = 0.022$), External Family (treatment $\times$ drug interaction $F = 3.S8$, d.f. $= 2.94$, $p = 0.032$). We therefore compared the psychosocial treatments separately within each drug treatment stratum. A fairly consistent trend was seen for the advantage of SST over SGT to be greatest in the context of combined treatment with active drug supplementation. The SST–SGT difference was greatest in the active drug supplementation condition for all SAS II clusters except work. In fact, among patients assigned to active drug supplementation, significant differences favoring SST were found in the social-interpersonal ($t = 2.16$, d.f. $= 95$, $p = 0.034$, effect size $= 0.89$), personal well-being ($t = 2.92$, d.f. $= 93$, $p = 0.004$, effect size $= 1.30$) and total SAS II areas ($t = 3.2$, d.f. $= 94$, $p = 0.002$, effect size $= 1.22$). In contrast, no added benefit was observed with SST in any SAS II scale area among patients assigned to placebo supplementation.

Prediction of psychosocial treatment effects

We also used general linear mixed model analyses to study interaction between clinical and demographic variables and the psychosocial treatments. We first focused on the possibility that symptom severity at baseline was related to social outcome, but did not find any interactions with treatment condition for baseline BPRS cluster scores for thought disturbance, paranoid hostility, retardation, or depression with the total SAS score (MANOVA, $F > 1$, d.f. 5.74, $p = 0.71$).

The relationships of demographic variables with social adjustment were then examined. Interactions of psychosocial treatment modality and age, ethnicity (dichotomized as white versus minority), education level, illness duration, or marital status (dichotomized as ever married versus never) were all nonsignificant. However, the interaction of the psychosocial treatment condition and age of onset (dichotomized at the median of 24 years) was highly significant ($F = 10.59$, d.f. $= 1.89$, $p = 0.0016$; Bonferroni-adjusted $p = 0.01$). Significant benefits of SST were only seen among those subjects with a younger age of onset ($n = 27$, $F = 13.83$, d.f. $= 1.24$, $p = 0.001$). Patients with a younger age of onset who received SST had the best overall social outcomes, as measured by the SAS II Total, differing significantly from all three of the other groups (all $p < 0.01$ by pairwise contrast).

Effects of psychosocial condition on rates of exacerbation

The factorial proportional hazards regression model revealed no appreciable difference between the full cohorts of patients treated with SST or SGT in the risk of psychotic exacerbation. For example, of patients who received SST, 46% survived without exacerbations at the end of the first year while in the SGT condition, 42.6% survived after the first year.

On an exploratory basis, we used stepwise proportional hazard regression (SAS Proc PHREG) with time-varying covariates to examine the specific differential risk associated with each combination of psychosocial and drug treatment, both before entering the drug supplement study as well as afterward. Among the subjects who were randomized to placebo supplementation, exacerbation risk was significantly higher among patients in the SGT-control psychosocial condition. Prior to drug randomization, there were no significant differences between SST and SGT ($X^2 = 0.52$, d.f. $= 1$, $p = 0.47$) in terms of exacerbations, and after supplementation began, there was still no difference between psychosocial conditions for those assigned to active drug ($X^2 = 0.22$, d.f. $= 1$, $p = 0.64$). However, among patients assigned to placebo supplementation, risk of exacerbation was significantly higher for those in the SGT control psychosocial condition ($X^2 = 5.14$, d.f. $= 1$, $p = 0.02$). The difference between the groups was most dramatic in the period immediately after randomization to drug condition. Eight weeks after randomization, for example, survival rates were 90% in the SST group, and 40% in the SGT group; by twelve weeks, the difference was 90% versus 27%. After twelve weeks, survival rates began to converge, and over the whole two-year follow-up period, all but four patients in the placebo supplementation group eventually exacerbated.

DISCUSSION

We found that a program of behaviorally oriented social skills training can result in improvements in important areas of social adjustment. This result was affected by the concurrent drug treatments, being most pronounced among those patients who had been assigned to active drug supplementation. There were no differences between psychosocial modalities in terms of social adjustment outcomes for patients who were assigned to the placebo group.

We also found that an early age of onset had important effects on social adjustment outcomes. The difference between SST and SGT was much larger among patients with a relatively early onset of schizophrenia. Among those with later age of onset (i.e., after the median 24 years), social outcomes with SST and SGT appeared equal. One might speculate that patients with later age of onset had more time prior to the first schizophrenic break to develop mature social and interpersonal skills, while those with early onsets were more deficient in those areas and thus more responsive to focused behavioral skill training. Consistent with this, the patients with earlier onsets in this sample had poorer SAS scores in every cluster area at baseline.

SST, in comparison to SGT, was associated with a reduced risk of psychotic exacerbation for patients who were randomly assigned to placebo supplementation. Among patients who were assigned to active drug supplementation, and among those never assigned to supplementation at all, the two psychosocial treatments did not differ with regard to exacerbation rates. Both of those groups were less vulnerable to exacerbation than the placebo patients, the former because of the protection afforded by active supplementation, and the latter because they were more stable and less prone to exacerbation in general. The "control–control" group was expected to be a highest risk, and in fact exacerbation rates were signficantly higher in that combined treatment condition than in any other. These findings suggested that SST confers a protective effect against relapse that may be similar to and substitutive with antipsychotic medication.

Our results regarding the benefits of SST for social outcomes are consistent with most of the prior literature. With regard to reducing exacerbation risk, several investigators have found that social skills training, alone or combined with family pscyhoeducation, was associated with reduced relapse rates when compared with controls over a one–two-year time period (Tarrier et al., 1993; Falloon et al., 1985; Hogarty et al., 1986; Hogarty et al., 1991). Two recent meta-analyses of SST in schizophrenia have found that, while the benefits of SST are stronger for improvements in social skills functioning, significant effects were also identified for symptom improvement, acceleration of discharge from hospital, and reduced relapse rates (Benton and Schroeder, 1990; Corrigan, 1991). Our own finding of the value of SST on relapse prevention applied only to the subgroup of patients who were unstable enough to enter the drug supplementation study, and then received only placebo. Thus, SST may reduce exacerbation risk most in high-risk individuals whose medication management is sub-optimal. In customary clinical settings where patients' compliance with medication is often less than optimal, SST may be of considerable value in delaying or preventing relapse.

In the current study, the effects of SST were most substantial on subscales measuring social and leisure functioning and personal well-being, areas that are commonly perceived as being the most refractory to treatment. These findings—together with the previous studies of skills training—provide additional support for the effectiveness of skills training methods for improving the social adjustment of patients with schizophrenia (Bellack et al., 1984; Liberman et al., 1986; Mueser et al., 1995). In contrast, patients who received a relatively intensive program of supportive group psychotherapy demonstrated very little change in their social adjustment.

Our study—together with the work of others—suggests that in schizophrenia, pharmacological and psychosocial treatments can be targeted at specific manifestations of the disorder. Optimizing a patient's pharmacotherapy can play an important role in minimizing the risk of psychotic relapse. Social skills training may confer some protection against relapse also, at least among relatively unstable patients whose medication regime is not optimal. Furthermore, in the context of adequate drug maintenance, SST appears to play an important role in treating the deficits in social skills that are an important component of the disorder. The art of treating chronic schizophrenia rests in the design of long-term treatment strategies that combine biological and psychosocial treatments that are tailored to the deficits of the individual patients.

Finally, it was observed that the combined strategy of providing active drug supplementation at the time incipient worsening of psychotic symptoms is first observed, and consistent skills training throughout the follow-up period, resulted in the best social outcomes.

Clinicians might raise the question of whether it is possible to teach skills effectively across the range of residual positive and negative symptoms. In this regard, this report supplements a previous publication in which we studied whether patients who participated in SST were able to acquire the skills that were taught in the modules. Using standardized role play tests, we found that patients who received SST demonstrated statistically significant improvements in skills that were included in the medication and symptom management modules (Eckman et al., 1992). Moreover, patients maintained their skills in an assessment that took place one year later. It was also notable that even patients with high levels of both positive and negative symptoms were able to acquire skills. This suggested that behavioral skills training may be effective for a large proportion of severely disabled patients with schizophrenia.

SUMMARY

These two studies have shown the value and limitations of behavior therapy in the treatment of schizophrenia. Treatment of symptoms and psychopathology, as well as prevention or delay of relapse, are still predominantly a matter for pharmacotherapy. Especially with the new generation of atypical antipsychotic drugs, we can expect a broader array of patients with previously refractory symptoms to respond to antipsychotic drug therapy. The protective effects of maintenance antipsychotic drugs against relapse also are much greater than can be documented with a psychological treatment, such as social skills training.

On the other hand, when the targets of treatment are psychosocial functioning, the treatment of choice is behavior therapy. Both intensive and focused behavioral treatment of self-care skills and deviant behaviors for long-term, hospitalized, inpatients and social skills training for the social and community functioning of outpatients appear to be prepotent over medication. For a truly comprehensive treatment effect, *biobehavioral therapy* that combines behavioral and biological components must be utilized.

The future promise of new psychological treatments for schizophrenia will be realized only if: (1) subject populations are clearly and reliably evaluated using structured and replicable methods of symptom solicitation, ratings and diagnosis; (2) concomitant pharmacotherapy is well specified and controlled; and (3) hypotheses are drawn from a conceptual framework that connects treatments with their specified and expected outcome dimensions.

ACKNOWLEDGMENTS

These studies were supported in part by NIMH Clinical Research Center Grant MH30911, by a Merit Review Grant from the Department of Veterans Affairs Medical Research Service, Grant Number R01-MH41573 from the National Institute of Mental Health, and a research grant from the California Department of Mental Health. The research projects were approved by the Human Subjects Protection Committee of UCLA, the State of California Health and Welfare Agency, and the West Los Angeles VA

Medical Center. All subjects signed informed consents prior to participating in these studies.

Reprint requests to Robert Paul Liberman, M.D., Community and Rehabilitative Psychiatry Section (116AR), West Los Angeles VA Medical Center, 11301 Wilshire Boulevard, Los Angeles, CA 90073.

This chapter contains reports that were adapted from previously published articles in The American Journal of Psychiatry and are reprinted here, in part, with permission of that journal and The American Psychiatric Association.

REFERENCES

Baldessarini, R.J., Cohen, B.M. and Teicher, M.H. (1988) Significance of neuroleptic dose and plasma level in the pharmacological treatment of psychosis. *Arch Gen Psychiatry*, **45**, 79–91.

Barnes, T. (1989) A rating scale for drug-induced akathisia. *Brit J Psychiatry*, **154**, 672–676.

Bellack, A.S. and Mueser, K. (1993) Psychosocial treatment for schizophrenia. *Schiz Bulletin*, **19**, 317–336.

Bellack, A.S., Turner, S.M., Hersen, M. and Luber, R.F. (1984) An examination of the efficacy of social skills training for chronic schizophrenia patients. *Hosp Community Psychiatry*, **35**, 1023–1028.

Benton, M.K. and Schroeder, H.E. (1990) Social skills training with schizophrenics, a meta-analytic evaluation. *J Consulting Clinical Psychology*, **58**, 741–747.

Bouchard, S., Vallieres, A., Roy, M.A. and Maziade, M. (1996) Cognitive restructuring in the treatment of psychotic symptoms in schizophrenia. *Behavior Therapy*, **27**, 257–278.

Boudewyns, P.A., Fry, T.J. and Nightingale, E.J. (1986) Token economy programs in VA Medical Centers. Where are they today? *The Behavior Therapist*, **6**, 126–127.

Brenner, H.D., Dencker, S.J., Goldstein, M.J., Hubbard, J.W., Keegan, D.L., Kruger, G., Kulhanek, F., Liberman, R.P., Malm, U. and Midha, K.K. (1990) Defining treatment refractoriness in schizophrenia. *Schiz Bulletin*, **16**, 551–561.

Corrigan, P.W. (1991) Social skills training in adult psychiatric populations, a meta-analysis. *J Behavior Therapy Experimental Psychiatry*, **22**, 203–210.

Eckman, T.A., Wirshing, W.C., Marder, S.R., Liberman, R.P., Johnston-Cronk, K., Zimmerman, K. and Mintz, J. (1992) Technology for training schizophrenics in illness self-management, A controlled trial. *Amer J Psychiatry*, **149**, 1549–1555.

Ellsworth, R.B. (1957) *The MACC Behavioral Adjustment Scale*. Santa Monica CA, Western Psychological Service.

Fahn, S. and Elton, R.L. (1987) Unified Parkinson's Disease Rating Scale. In *Recent Developments in Parkinsons's Disease*, Vol II, edited by Fahn, S., Marsden, C.D., Goldstein, M., Caine, C.D., Florham Park, N.J.: Macmillan.

Faraone, S.V., Green, A.I., Brown, W., Yin, P. and Tsuang, M.T. (1989) Neuroleptic dose reduction in persistently psychotic patients. *Hosp Comm Psychiatry*, **40**, 1193–1195.

Glazer, W.M., Aaronson, H.S., Prusoff, B.A. and William, D.H. (1980) Assessment of social adjustment in chronic ambulatory schizophrenics. *J Nervous and Mental Disease*, **168**, 493–497.

Glynn, S.M. and Mueser, K.T. (1992) Social learning programs. In *Handbook of Psychiatric Rehabilitation*, edited by Liberman, R.P. New York: Macmillan.

Glynn, S., Liberman, R.P., Kuehnel, T.G., Bowen, L. and Marshall, B.D. (1994) Behavior therapy on the Camarillo-UCLA Clinical Research Unit, in *Behavior Therapy in Psychiatric Settings*, edited by Corrigan, P.W., Liberman, R.P. New York: Springer.

Green, M.F., Marshall, B.D., Wirshing, W.C., Ames, D., Marder, S.R., McGurk, S., Kern, R.S. and Mintz, J. (1997) Does risperidone improve verbal working memory in treatment-resistant schizophrenia? *Am J Psychiatry*, **154**, 799-804.

Green, M.F., Mintz, J., Bowen, L., Marshall, B.D., Kuehnel, T.G., Hayden, J.L. and Liberman, R.P. (1993) Prediction of response to haloperidol reduction by the span of apprehension measures for treatment refractory schizophrenic patients. *Am J Psychiatry*, **150**, 1415–1416.

Guy, W. (Ed.). (1976) *ECDEU Assessment Manual for Psychopharmacology*, revised. DHEW Publication No (ADM)76–338. Rockville, MD:NIMH.

Hogarty, G.E., Anderson, C.M., Reiss, D.J., Kornblith, S.J., Greenwald, D.P, Jabna, C.D. and Medonia, K.J. (1986) Family psychoeducation, social skills training, and maintenance chemotherapy in the after-care treatment of schizophrenia, I. One year effects of a controlled study on relapse and expressed emotion. *Arch Gen Psychiatry*, **43**, 663–642.

Hogarty, G.E., Anderson, C.M., Reiss, D.J., Kornblith, S.J., Greenwald, D.P, Ulrich, R.F. and Carter, M. (1991) Family psychoeducation, social skill training, and maintenance chemotherapy in the after-care treatment of schizophrenia, II. Two-year effects of a controlled study on relapse and adjustment. *Arch Gen Psychiatry*, **48**, 340–347.

Kuehnel, T.G., Liberman, R.P., Marshall, B.D., Bowen, L. (1992) Behavior therapy for treatment-refractory, institutionalized schizophrenics. In *Effective Psychiatric Rehabilitation, New Directions for Mental Health Services*, No. 53, edited by Liberman, R.P. San Francisco: Jossey-Bass.

Leblanc, G., Cormier, H.J., Gagne, M.A. and Vaillancourt, S. (1989) Effects of neuroleptic reduction in schizophrenic outpatients receiving high doses. Paper presented at the 142nd Annual Meeting of the American Psychiatric Association, San Francisco, California, May 6–12).

Liberman, R.P. (1992) *Handbook of Psychiatric Rehabilitation*. New York: Allyn and Bacon.

Liberman, R.P. (1994) Psychosocial treatments for schizophrenia. *Psychiatry*, **57**, 104–114.

Liberman, R.P., King, L.W. and DeRisi, W.J. (1976) Behavior therapy in community mental health. In *Handbook of Behavior Therapy and Modification*, edited by Zeitenberg, H. Englewood Cliffs, NJ: Prentice Hall.

Liberman, R.P., Massel, H.K., Mosk, M.D., Wong, S.E. (1985) Social skills training for chronic mental patients. *Hosp Community Psychiatry*, **36**, 396–403.

Liberman, R.P., DeRisi, W.J. and Mueser, K.T. (1989) *Social Skills Training for Psychiatric Patients*. New York: Pergamon Press.

Liberman, R.P., Van Putten, T., Marshall, B.D., Mintz, J., Bowen, L., Kuehnel, T.G., Aravagiri, M. and Marder, S.R. (1994) Drug and behavior therapy for treatment refractory schizophrenia. *Amer J Psychiatry*, **151**, 756–759.

McEvoy, J.P., Hogarty, G.E. and Steingard, S. (1991) Optimal dose of neuroleptic in acute schizophrenia, A controlled study of the neuroleptic threshold and higher haloperidol dose. *Arch Gen Psychiatry*, **148**, 739–745.

McGurk, S. and Green, M.F. (1997) Risperidone's effect on spatial and verbal working memory. Submitted for publication, *Biological Psychiatry*.

Malm, U. (1982) The influence of group therapy on schizophrenia. *Acta Psychiatrica Scandanavica*, Suppl. 297, 1–65.

Marder, S.R. and Meibach, R.C. (1994) Risperidone in the treatment of schizophrenia. *Amer J Psychiatry*, **151**, 825–835.

Marder, S.R., Asarnow, R.F. and Van Putten, T. (1988) Information processing and maintenance dose requirements in schizophrenia. *Psychopharm Bulletin*, **24**, 247–250.

Marder, S.R., Wirshing, W.C., Van Putten, T., Mintz, J., McKenzie, J., Johnson-Cronk, K., Lebell, M. and Liberman, R.P. (1994) Fluphenazine versus placebo supplementation for prodromal signs of relapse in schizophrenia. *Arch Gen Psychiatry*, **41**, 280–287.

May, P.R.A. (1968) *Treatment of Schizophrenia*. New York, Science House.

May, P.R.A. (1976) Psychotherapy and pharmacotherapy of schizophrenia. In *Successful Psychotherapy*, edited by J.L. Claghorn. New York: Brunner/Mazel.

May, P.R.A. (1984) A step forward in research in psychotherapy of schizophrenia. *Schizophrenia Bulletin*, **10**, 604–607.

Midha, K.K., Cooper, J.K., Hawes, E.M., Hubbard, J.W., Korchinski, E.D. and McKay, G. (1988) An ultrasensitive method for the measurement of haloperidol and reduced haloperidol in plasma by high-pressure liquid chromatography with coulometric detection. *Ther Drug Monitoring*, **10**, 177–183.

Moss, G.R. Selling behavioral technology in the health care marketplace. In *Behavior Therapy in Psychiatric Hospitals*, edited by Corrigan, P.W., Liberman, R.P. New York, Springer (1994) pp. 221–248.

Paul, G.L., Lentz, R. (1977) *Psychosocial Treatment of Chronic Mental Patients*. Cambridge: Harvard University Press.

Rutan, J.S. and Cohen, A. (1989) Group Psychotherapy. In *Outpatient Psychiatry, Diagnosis and Treatment*, edited by Lazare, A. Baltimore, Williams and Wilkins, pp. 645–654.

Schooler, N., Hogarty, G. and Weissman, M. (1979) Social Adjustment Scale II (SAS II). In *Materials for City Mental Health Program Evaluators*, edited by Hargreaves, W.A., Attkisson, C.C. and Sorenson, J.E. (Publ. No. 79–328.) Washington, DC, U.S. Department of Health and Human Services.

Tarrier, N., Beckett, R., Harwood, S., Baker, A., Yusupoff, L. and Ugarteburu, I. A trial of two cognitive–behavoural methods of treating drug-resistant residual psychotic symptoms in schizophrenic patients. *Brit J Psychiatry*, 1993) 262, 524–532.

Van Putten, T. and Marder, S.R. (1987) Behavioral toxicity of antipsychotic drugs. *J Clin Psychiatry*, **48**, 13–19, supp.

Van Putten, T., Marder, S.R. and Mintz, J. (1990) A controlled dose comparison of haloperidol in newly admitted schizophrenic patients. *Arch Gen Psychiatry*, **47**, 754–758.

Van Putten, T., Marder, S.R., Mintz, J. and Poland, R.E. (1992) Haloperidol plasma levels and clinical response. A therapeutic window relationship. *Amer J Psychiatry*, **149**, 500–505.

Wallace, C.J. and Liberman, R.P. (1985) Social skills training for patients with schizophrenia, A controlled clinical trial. *Psychiatry Research*, **15**, 239.

Wing, J.K., Cooper, J.E. and Sartorius, N. (1974) *The Measurement and Classification of Psychiatric Symptoms*, London: Cambridge University Press.

Chapter 11

WORKING WITH CARERS: INTERVENTIONS FOR RELATIVE AND STAFF CARERS OF THOSE WHO HAVE PSYCHOSIS

Elizabeth Kuipers

INTRODUCTION

My main aim in this chapter is to attempt to integrate the empirical evidence now available on the impact of caring for a severely mentally ill relative, the quality of the resulting relationship between carer and client, and how this can then be used to predict outcome and inform interventions. Such research has clear implications for service provision, and this will be discussed.

I would like to start with some quotations from the Camberwell Family Interview (CFI), to illustrate the issues that come up when carers are asked to talk about their relationship with someone who has severe mental illness (SMI), and the range of ratings that can be made during such interviews. These comments underline both the impact of care on relationships, the range of responses that occur, and the similarities that are apparent

Outcome and Innovation in Psychological Treatment of Schizophrenia. Edited by T. Wykes, N. Tarrier and S. Lewis.
© 1998 John Wiley & Sons Ltd

between relative and staff carers, despite their ostensibly different roles. All staff were key workers to these clients; i.e. responsible for coordinating their care in the community.

> I wished I could make him a baby again... I wished I could make him smaller and smaller so I could wrap him and just carry him everywhere I go.
> And that's how it's been... I can see the deterioration over the last year.
> (Mother re son, emotional over-involvement (EOI) over-protection)

> I actually wanted to tell her I love her.
> I had fantasies of buying her a home...
> ... wanting to be some sort of Angel and save her.
> (Staff re client, evidence of EOI)

> Every one has their snapping point. Michael can push anyone way beyond that. If Michael's obnoxious it's no good, because I get uptight and it's a vicious circle.
> (Mother re son, generalised criticism, hostility)

> He just goes on and on. It's irritating. He knows how to do it, but he doesn't do it.
> (Staff re client, criticism)

> His shattered life can be mended... we have always been close.
> (Mother re son, warmth)

> I feel comfortable with her, being very friendly and our relationship being very equal.
> (Staff re client, warmth)

> I feel very positive towards him.
> (Staff re client, warmth)

THE IMPACT OF CARE IN SCHIZOPHRENIA

We have well-documented evidence from the 1950s that care giving in SMI has a clear and measurable impact on family members (Kuipers 1993; Tessler and Gamache 1994). Specifically, relatives are likely to have increased levels of worry and strain, face a wide range of emotional responses, have reduced social networks with the resulting problems of isolation and stigma, and find that dealing with disruptive behaviour and negative symptoms such as social withdrawal is most problematic.

We also know that carers need a range of services to enable them to maintain a caring role. They consistently ask for information, which does not in itself change outcomes, but has high face validity, improves optimism and helps carers engage in later intervention programmes (Cozolino et al., 1988; Tarrier et al., 1988; Lam 1991). Giving information at times of high need and its associated high stress levels is itself problematic, as very little will be remembered. Information needs to be personally relevant, to be understood , and its emotional impact has to be considered. While there is no documented best method of doing this, a variety of written material is now available and clinical experience suggests that staff should aim to have several meetings, to answer any questions from carers, to be prepared to repeat information, and be able to admit it when they do not know the answers.

Emotional support is probably the least well defined but the most important need to meet for carers. Even after many years, family carers' may still be in the initial stages of shock and denial. All carers will face a wide range of emotional reactions from grief, guilt, anger and rejection to worry and hopelessness. Such emotional states need to be normalised for the family, and specific problems that arise negotiated. Relative groups are a particularly effective way to deal with these issues (Kuipers and Westall 1992).

Practical support, such as help with finances, accommodation or day care is easier to provide than emotional support (MacCarthy et al., 1989). However, some kind of problem solving for practical difficulties is also indicated. Dealing with the symptoms and behaviour problems which are perceived as most difficult by carers, such as negative symptoms and disruptive behaviour, is crucial both in terms of being responsive to carers' needs and in being able to offer relevant help. Problems need to be specified, broken down into small and potentially manageable steps, and negotiated within the family system so that solutions are not imposed. There is now a considerable literature on effective methods for achieving this (e.g. Falloon 1985; Anderson et al., 1986; Barrowclough and Tarrier 1992; Kuipers et al., 1992).

The other area of practical help is respite, which is a well-documented requirement but one still more commonly provided for the elderly than for the severely mentally ill. In most areas now the responsibility for this provision has passed from health to social services, and is more frequently offered as part of local charitable initiatives. Thus access to it remains fortuitous rather than as a response to undoubted need. This is despite its preventative effects and likely cost-effectiveness, in that planned respite is likely to prevent a later crisis, which is usually disruptive for the client and the family and expensive in terms of days in hospital.

Finally, carers need continuity of services through all stages of the life cycle, as care is likely to continue for many years. Even community teams are not always able to provide this, as both organisational and staff changes militate against it. Nevertheless, within a team it may be possible to offer some continuity, at least in terms of a particular family's history, access to local services, and feeling that at least some team members are familiar faces.

THE QUALITY OF THE RELATIONSHIP BETWEEN CLIENT AND CARER

Initial reactions to the demands of caring for someone with psychosis are likely to range from bewilderment, anxiety and denial through to unrealistic (i.e. uninformed) expectations both about recovery and a client's role performance. It is typical for a carer to be extremely worried, find it very hard to obtain appropriate or understandable information, and not to understand why a relative is reacting so unusually. When ordinary attempts to cope with the situation, such as discussion or prompting, are ineffective, then carers frequently find themselves feeling frustrated and irritated by the problems. This can quickly lead to criticism both of the behaviours and also of the person, who is then blamed for the difficulties.

Alternatively, carers may know that "something" is wrong, and try to compensate for the perceived impairments. They may try to "look after" the client and take over social roles such as budgeting or housework, in the same way that all of us do when a relative is seen as unwell. While this reaction is perfectly valid in the short term, and usually helps to sort out temporary incapacity, it is only useful in acute phases of the illness. In the long term, if both carer and client become fixed into this pattern, various problems typically arise. These can include a loss of adult independence in the client, who loses skills and responsibilities, and may become like a child in the family again. In carers there are usually feelings of exhaustion and burden, and often there is emotional over-involvement and over-protection with all aspects of the client's life. This can be perceived as intrusive and inappropriate by the adult son or daughter, and often leads to arguments.

Both criticism and emotional over-involvement are key components of the measure of family attitudes called expressed emotion (EE) (Leff and Vaughn; 1985, Kuipers 1994). Ratings of critical comments (CC), EOI, warmth (W) and positive remarks (PR) are made from the CFI, which is a tape-recorded inverview with a carer (see quotes noted earlier). Of these CC and EOI are most predictive and more than 6 CCs and/or 3 out of 5 for EOI make for a rating of high EE in a carer. EE is now well established as a robust predictor of outcome in schizophrenia. Kavanagh (1992) reviewed 26 prospective studies and found that 9 month relapse rates for patients returning to live with families rated as high in EE were 48%, and those for returning to low EE settings were 21%. Bebbington and Kuipers (1994) used aggregated data from 25 studies (N=1346) and found 9 month relapse rates to be 50% for those returning to high-EE families and 21% for low-EE relatives. We also found no differences in relapse rates for gender, and that high contact with a low-EE relative (> 35 hours a week) was protective. Finally we were able to show that EE and medication were both independently related to relapse.

LINKS BETWEEN EE AND BURDEN RESEARCH

Despite the fact that research on EE and the impact of care on relatives both started in the 1950s, and both consider family reactions to living with schizophrenia, the research has been conducted in parallel with remarkably little crossover. Studies which look at both areas are only beginning to be published (e.g. Jackson et al. 1990). Smith et al. (1993), investigated 49 relatives of those with schizophrenia, and found that carers with high levels of EE reported higher levels of disturbed behaviour in clients, more subjective burden and less (perceived) effective coping. Scazufca and Kuipers (1996) investigated 67 relatives (50 key relatives) of 50 patients with a current diagnosis of schizophrenia. We found that relatives with high EE had significantly higher mean scores for their burden of care than low EE family members, and perceived more deficits in patient functioning. Both patient social behaviour and symptomatology were independent of the EE rating. We also found that relatives in higher contact with the patient had higher burden scores, and that most carers were women, as in other care-giving research. Finally, we found that relatives who had a job were more likely to be low EE.

When we compared coping strategies in the two groups, both low- and high-EE carers used "problem focused" and "seek social support", but high EE carers also used "avoidance" more frequently.

Thus although low-EE relatives still felt the burden of care, they perceived the difficulties as less problematic, and seemed not to use avoidance as a way of trying to cope.

This confirmatory finding has implications both for understanding the measure of EE and for services. If we accept that EE and burden are related we can define EE as an assessment of the quality of the relationship, based on the appraisal of problems. In other words, both EE and burden in relatives are more dependent on appraisal of a client's problems than on actual deficits in client behaviour.

These results emphasise not only that the impact of caring can be assessed in different ways, but also that there may be new ways to intervene in family settings. For instance, services might be able to use "burden" as an indication of family need, and target intervention more specifically at obviously "burdened" carers.

OPTIMAL STAFF RELATIONSHIPS

Another strand of research has extended the range of carers investigated. It is obvious that carers of the SMI are not always relatives, but may be staff such as hostel workers, CPN's, neighbours, or even other users of the mental health system. Staff in community settings are likely to have to deal with similar problematic behaviour, such as negative symptoms, and socially disruptive behaviour, may not always be trained, and may be relatively isolated in local houses rather than in a large institution. On the other hand they do have holidays, work does ostensibly finish at the end of the shift, and if things are too difficult they may have the option of finding another job; all aspects that are unlikely to be available to relative carers.

We hypothesised that both sorts of carers might share similarities in their attitudes to clients and in the range of emotional responses they felt, such as those measured by EE. There was a small amount of evidence for this in the literature. Watts (1988) used a modified version of the Camberwell Family Interview (CFI) with staff and found a range of high and low EE ratings about clients. Herzog (1992) found that 65% of staff on a psychiatric ward had high EE attitudes to one or more patients. A recent study by Siol and Stark (1995) has shown that one third of both therapists and parents of those diagnosed as having an acute schizophrenic illness were rated as having a high EE attitude towards them.

In our research, we looked at 35 key workers, in hostels or in teams, of 61 clients with long-term SMI. 43% of staff had more than 6 critical comments about at least one client using a modified version of the CFI. They also found the same behaviour problematic; socially embarrassing, disruptive behaviour and negative symptoms. While staff with a high EE relationship found prompting frustrating, and overlooked a client's perspective, low EE relationships were characterised by being able to set limits effectively (not being irritated by the slow speed of any progress), and most importantly by being able to be warm about some aspect of the client's behaviour or personality (Moore et al., 1992a and b: Moore and Kuipers 1992; Kuipers and Moore 1995).

For instance a staff member in a high-EE relationship with a particularly difficult client, said: "He's obscene sometimes... I don't have much time for him, he doesn't appeal to me".

However, another staff member in a low EE relationship said about the *same* difficult client: "He was inappropriate and sexually deviant, but it helps to focus on his strengths... he's one of those people you can laugh and joke with... he's done so well...he's not difficult when you get to know him."

This emphasises the importance of coping styles in staff–client relationships and shows that even very challenging patients can be seen to have positive features and thus can be worked with constructively.

A recent study on case management (Oliver and Kuipers 1996) replicated this finding and showed that a majority of key workers had a high-EE relationship with at least one client. This study suggests that the quality of key workers' relationships when clients live in the community may be both more intense and more stressful than has been thought previously.

Finally, one of the reasons for looking at EE in staff–client relationships is to see if it predicts outcome in the same way that it does for families of those with schizophrenia. Ball et al., (1992) found poorer outcome for clients in a naturalistic study of a hostel characterized by high-EE management, rather than a "low-EE" hostel. Snyder et al., (1994), in the USA found that critical attitudes in staff were associated with a poorer quality of life for residents. Although both of these studies are small, it does look as if there is some tentative evidence for poorer outcome for clients in high-EE settings, even if carers are staff rather than relatives.

Interventions

The evidence on the efficiency of family intervention in schizophrenia is now well documented and suggests that it is possible to improve the quality of relationships for carers and clients and that this also improves outcome. Interventions have all offered family psychoeducation and support and most have also attempted some kind of skill or communication training for relatives (Anderson and Adams 1996).

A recent paper found that even 8 years after family intervention, positive effects were still apparent (Tarrier and Barrowclough 1995). The successful intervention studies that are well known (Leff et al., 1982; Falloon et al., 1982; Anderson et al., 1986; Tarrier et al., 1988) have recently been supplemented. Randolph et al., (1994) used a random controlled trial (RCT) on 41 patients and their families and they showed beneficial effects for both low- and high-EE families and significantly reduced exacerbation in the first year, for families in behavioural family management, compared to standard care. Xiong et al., (1994), in China, did an RCT with 63 patients, where education, monthly family visits and family group sessions were compared to standard care. Over the next 12 months, those in family treatment had a 33% relapse rate, and those in standard care 60%. The family group were also less hospitalised, had better social functioning and relatives were less burdened. Zhang et al., (1994) completed a random controlled trial of 78 male patients with schizophrenia. 39 of them were offered multiple family, clinic-based psychoeducation, including individual and group sessions, every one to 3 months compared to 39 "customary care", control patients who were offered counselling and symptom management. After the 18 month intervention, those with family education and support had a better outcome. Thus interventions have involved different research groups and been effective in different cultures.

Outcome measures for family intervention

Penn and Mueser (1996) have recently reviewed the 12 family intervention studies so far published. The main outcome measure used in studies is always patient relapse, usually in the 9 to 12 months after intervention has started. Measuring relapse in psychosis remains problematic because many patients have continuous symptomatology which never remits. Thus, most judgements of relapse rely on decisions about "exacerbation" of symptomatology. In early studies this was mainly done using versions of standardised diagnostic system such as the Present State Examination (PSE) (Wing 1974). Later studies have also used the Brief Psychiatric Rating Scale (BPRS) (Overall and Gorham, 1962) as an indicator of symptom change. Hospital admission is discredited as a measure of symptomatic difficulties or relapse, because of its relationship to social problems (such as homelessness) and local political issues such as availability of hospital beds. Some studies therefore use days in hospital as an indication of severity, but more convincingly as a way of assessing the cost of an intervention (Falloon et al., 1982, 1985). Measuring outcome in terms of relapse shows that there are clear benefits for long-term family intervention which "reduces patients' vulnerability to relapse over 1 to 2 years" (Penn and Mueser 1996, p. 611). Typically, relapse rates for the family intervention decrease to less than 20%, 9 months after returning home, compared to a standardised 50% for high-EE families receiving standard care, including medication.

Relapse is of course only one rather narrow, clinical aspect of good outcome. Fewer studies have looked at other dimensions of recovery, such as patient's social functioning, but when it is examined, positive effects have been found (Hogarty et al., 1988; Falloon et al., 1985; Barrowclough and Tarrier 1990; Xiong et al., 1994).

Relatively few studies have been interested in the effects of family intervention on carers as well as clients, (Falloon and Pederson 1985; Kottgen et al., 1984; McCarthy et al., 1989; Xiong et al., 1994), and improvements have only been seen with psychoeducational approaches. More studies have looked at reducing burden in family carers when they are offered short-term educational input, but this has been separated from looking at patient outcome (e.g. Smith and Birchwood 1987; Abromowitz and Coursey 1989). However some short-term benefits have been shown, in terms of improving knowledge, and increasing optimism in such carers.

Finally, Falloon et al., (1982) looked at family functioning and improved problem solving in those who had received family interventions rather than individual treatment. Other studies have been able to reduce levels of EE (e.g. Leff et al., 1982, 1990) but most studies have used EE as a marker for difficulties, and it has not been used routinely as an outcome measure (Tarrier et al., 1988; Falloon et al., 1985).

The studies indicate that family intervention improves outcome, both for clients and carers, (Penn and Mueser 1996). Anderson and Adams (1996) go further and call family interventions in schizophrenia "an effective but underused treatment". This raises issues of implementation which will be discussed later. An underresearched issue is the criteria for the minimum amount of family treatment that can effect a treatment response (Penn and Mueser 1996). Several studies have compared different versions of family intervention (eg. Leff et al., 1990, Zastowny et al., 1992, McFarlane et al.,

1995), but no strong evidence has emerged for the efficacy of one type over another; both versions do well. However, psychodynamic approaches do not seem helpful (Köttgen et al., 1984), and short term treatment (less than 3 months) is also less likely to show benefits. In contrast, among studies with at least 9 months of treatment, only 2/10 "failed to show a beneficial effect on relapse" (Penn and Mueser 1996, p. 609).

The elements of family intervention that appear, at present, to deliver benefit, involve the following. Firstly, psychoeducation, normally over several sessions and including both discussion and written material. Secondly there has to be some focus on problem solving for the immediate day to day difficulties that families face, and some help in negotiation and in improving communication skills. Thirdly emotional processing which includes some cognitive reappraisal and normalising of even extreme emotions is a necessary and long-term intervention for all carers. Finally, all the studies include attempts to offer optimal medication to clients. Manuals describing in detail the approaches used by all the original research groups are now available (Falloon 1985, Anderson et al., 1986; Kuipers et al., 1992; Barrowclough and Tarrier 1992).

There have been no published studies of interventions for staff carers. Measuring outcome here is likely to involve both indications of staff stress and aspects such as burnout (e.g. Maslach Burnout Inventory, Maslach and Jackson 1986), as well as client symptomatology and social functioning. A pilot study by Baxter and Leff did investigate EE in five community care hostels and adapted a training course from the Thorn nurse training initiative (Kuipers et al., 1995) for staff caring for hostel residents. For all hostels a minimum of 25% of staff had at least one high-EE relationship, and negative symptoms in clients were a main problem area. Results of the training course are only indicative at this stage. Nevertheless, it seems likely that training that focuses on pertinent problems for staff in residential settings (e.g. a client not getting out of bed in the morning), which aims to increase staff knowledge about SMI and expand their coping repertoire, would be both appropriate and cost-effective in reducing crises and improving staff morale, and might also improve clients' quality of life.

Implications for services

We now have reasonably good evidence on how to promote recovery from SMI in a variety of community settings, particularly family homes. We also have some evidence on optimal therapeutic relationships for staff dealing with clients with SMI who can make unusual and high demands on both sets of carers; i.e. the importance of a positive, warm relationship with a client, despite residual problems. Such relationships appear to foster realistic progress, improve self esteem in clients and give carers some satisfaction.

As might be expected, both family and staff carers share a number of needs that services should aim to meet in order to enable care to continue.

1. *Education or Information.* Families and staff carers need information about SMI, both its positive and negative symptoms, in order to understand and attribute client behaviour more realistically, widen their reportoire of coping skills, and prevent them from "blaming a client for problems".

2. *Problem solving/coping skills.* Carers need a range of coping skills that foster negotiation and not confrontation between carer and client, focus on breaking problems down into manageable and achievable stages and enable both carer and client to experience and appreciate success or progress, rather than "failure".

3. *Awareness of emotional issues including processing of difficult, negative emotions, by reappraisal and normalising.* Staff may be less overtly aware of these issues than families, who frequently express a wide range of emotions from anger to guilt and grief.
   For staff, supervision and an ability to focus on positives in relationships with clients appears to be helpful, as is a safe place in which to ventilate negative emotions such as anger or distress. Multidisciplinary teams should provide this supportive environment, when staff have the SMI as their main client group.

4. *Optimal medication for clients, including discussion of side effects.* This latter is now a requirement, as laid out in the Health of the Nation guidelines.

5. *Family carers need respite occasionally, and long-term support over the life cycle.* The problems associated with a diagnosis of schizophrenia may continue for many years. Staff carers are likely to need team support for long term problems in community care, because key working on case management makes high demands on staff in terms of levels of responsibility (Muijen et al., 1994) high staff input (McCrone et al., 1994) and high case loads. Teams may well need to consider how to offer appropriate training, supervision and collaborative working to reduce the negative effects of such potentially demanding work (Kuipers and Moore 1995; Oliver and Kuipers 1996; Prosser et al., 1996).

Conclusion

In the long term it is going to be necessary to find ways of introducing such services routinely if client recovery is to be maximised and if family burden and staff burnout are to be minimised. Despite the empirical findings, translating the routine application of them into practice remains problematic. Anderson and Adams comment "It is tempting to speculate that the current status of family intervention programmes for treating people with schizophrenia might be different it they attracted the research resources and marketing prowess associated with drug treatments, or the political will associated with case management" (1996, p. 505). We do know that it is *possible* to intervene, in ways that are cost effective, prevent crisis, and minimise residual disability in clients, reduce burden in family carers and probably reduce stress in staff carers. The remaining challenge of implementation is more difficult. Possibly, organising guidelines for practice, including the optimal timing of treatment applications (Penn and Mueser 1996) would be a way forward.

Even in a severe and potentially disabling condition such as schizophrenia, it is feasible to support carers so that they can continue to provide and enjoy more positive relationships with the clients they may work or live with. We now have clear evidence that such relationships also promote recovery and minimise residual problems. In order to maintain care in the community for the foreseeable future, the services required to support both staff and family carers need to be built into community mental health teams as a priority.

REFERENCES

Abramowitz, I.A. and Coursey, R.D. (1989) Impact of an educational support group on family participants who take care of their schizophrenic relatives. *J. Consulting and Clinical Psychology*, **57**, 232–236.

Anderson, C., Reisi, D. and Hogarty, G.E. (1986) *Schizophrenia and the Family: a Practical Guide*. New York: Guilford Press.

Anderson, J. and Adams, C. (1996) Family intervention in schizophrenia: *British Medical J.*, **313**, 505–506.

Ball, R.A., Moore, E. and Kuipers, L. (1992) EE in community care facilities: a comparison of patient outcome in a 9 month follow-up of two residential hostels. *Soc. Psychiatry Psychiatr. Epidemiol*, **27**, 35–39

Barrowclough, C. and Tarrier, N. (1990) Social functioning of schizophrenic patients: 1 the effects of EE and family intervention. *Soc Psychiatry Psychiatr. Epidemiol*, **25**, 125–129.

Barrowclough, C. and Tarrier, N. (1992) *Families of Schizophrenia Patients: Cognitive Behavioural Intervention*. Chapman and Hall, London.

Bebbington, P.E. and Kuipers, L. (1994) The predictive utility of Expressed Emotion in schizophrenia: an aggregate analysis. *Psychological Medicine*, **24**, 707–718.

Cozolino, L.J. et al., (1988) The impact of education on relatives varying in levels of EE. *Schizophrenia Bull*, **14**, 675–686.

Falloon, I.R.H. (1985) *Family Management of Schizophrenia*. Baltimore, MD: Johns Hopkins Press.

Falloon, I.R.H. and Pederson, J. (1985) Family management in the prevention of morbidity of schizophrenia. Adjustment of the family unit, *Brit. J. Psychiatry*, **147**, 156–163.

Falloon, I.R.H., Boyd, J.L., McGill, C.W., Razini, J., Moss, H.B. and Gilderman, A.M. (1982) Family management in the prevention of exacerbations of schizophrenia. A controlled study. *N.Engl. J. Med*, **306**, 1437–1440.

Falloon, I.R.H., Boyd, J.L., McGill, C.W., Williamson, M., Razani, J., Moss, H.B., Gilderman, A.M. and Simpson, G.M. (1985) Family management in the prevention of morbidity of schizophrenia. Clinical outcome of a two year longitudinal study. *Arc. Gen. Psychiatry*, **42**, pp. 887–896.

Herzog, T. (1992) Nurses, patients and relatives: a study of family patterns on psychiatric wards. In *Family Intervention in Schizophrenia: Experiences and Orientations in Europe*, C.L. Cazzullo and G. Invernizzi (eds.). ARS, Milan.

Hogarty, G.E., McEvoy, J.P., Munetz, M., Di Barry, A.L., Baitone, P., Cather, R., Coolery, S.J., Ulrich, R.F., Carter, M. and Madonia, M.J. (1988) Dose of fluphenazine, family expressed emotion and outcome in schizophrenia: Results of a 2 year controlled study. *Arch. Gen. Psychiatry*, **45**, 797–805.

Jackson, H.T., Smith, N. and McGorry, P. (1990) Relationship between EE and family burden in psychotic disorders: an exploratory study. *Acta Psychiatr. Scand.*, **82**, 243–249.

Kavanagh, D.J. (1992) Recent developments in Expressed Emotion and schizophrenia. *Br. J. Psychiatry*, **160**, 601–620.

Köttgen, G., Sonnichsen, I. Mollenhauer, K. and Jurth, R. (1984) Group therapy with the families of schizophrenic patients: results of the Hamburg CFI study: III *Int. J. Family Psychiatry*, **5**, 84–94.

Kuipers, L. (1993) Family burden in schizophrenia: implications for services. *Soc Psychiatry Psychiatr Epidemiol*, **28**, 207–210.

Kuipers, E. and Moore, E. (1995) Expressed Emotion and staff client relationships. *Int. J. Mental Health*, **24**, 3, 13–26.

Kuipers, L. and Westall, J. (1992) The role of facilitated relative groups and voluntary self help groups. In: *Principles of Social Psychiatry*, D. Bhugra and J. Leff (eds.) Blackwell, London.

Kuipers, L., Leff, J. and Lam, D. (1992) *Family Work for Schizophrenia: a Practical Guide*. Gaskell, London.

Kuipers, E., Leff, J., Lam, D. and Gamble, C. (1995) *Family Work for Schizophrenia: a Training Manual*. Available from the authors.

Lam, D. (1991) Psychosocial family intervention in schizophrenia: a review of empirical studies. *Psychol. Med.*, **21**, 423–441.

Leff, J. and Vaughn, C. (1985) *Expressed Emotion in Families*. Guilford, London.

Leff, J., Kuipers, L., Berkowitz, R., Eberlein Treis, R. and Sturgeon, D. (1982) A controlled trial of social intervention in the families of schizophrenic patients. *Br. J. Psychiatry*, **141**, 121–134.

Leff, J., Berkowitz, R., Sharit, V., Strahlan, A., Glass, I. and Vaughan, C. (1990) A trial of family therapy versus a relatives group for schizophrenia: a two year follow up. *Brit. J. Psychiatry*, **157**, 571–577.

MacCarthy, B., Lesage, A., Brewin, C.R., Brugha, T.S., Manger, S. and Wing, J.K. (1989) Needs for care among the relatives of long-term users of day-care. *Psychol. Med.*, **19**, 725–736.

McCrone, P., Beecham, J. and Knapp, M. (1994) Community Psychiatric Teams; cost effectiveness of intensive support versus generic care. *Brit. J. Psychiatry*, **165**, 218–221.

McFarlane, W. R., Lukens, E., Link, B., Dushay, R., Deakins, S. A., Newmark, M., Dunne, E.J., Haren, B. and Toran, J. (1995) Multiple-family groups and psychoeducation in the treatment of schizophrenia. *Arch. Gen. Psychiatry*, **52**, 679–687.

Maslach, C. and Jackson, S.E. (1986) *Maslach Burnout Inventory Manual*, 2nd edition. Consulting Psychologists Press, Palo Alto.

Moore, E. and Kuipers, E. (1992) Behavioural correlates of EE in staff patient interaction. *Soc Psychiatry Psychiatr Epidemiol*, **27**, 298–303.

Moore, E., Ball, R.A. and Kuipers, L. (1992a) Expressed Emotion in staff working with the long-term adult mentally ill. *Br. J. Psychiatry*, **161**, 802–808.

Moore, E., Kuipers, L. and Ball, R. (1992b) Staff patient relationships in the case of the long-term mentally ill: a content analysis of EE interviews, *Soc Psychiatry Psychiatr Epidemiol*, **27**, 28–34.

Muijen, M., Cooney, M., Strathdee, G., Bell, R. and Hudson, A. (1994) Community Psychiatric Nurse Teams: Intensive support versus generic care. *Brit. J. Psychiatry*, **165**, 211–217.

Oliver, N. and Kuipers, E. (1996) Stress and its relationship to Expressed Emotion in community mental health workers. *Int. J. Soc Psychiatry*, **42**, 150–159.

Overall, J.E. and Gosham, D. R. (1962) The brief psychiatric rating scale. *Psychological Reports*, **10**, 799–812.

Penn, D. and Mueser, K. (1996) Research update on the psychosocial treatment of schizophrenia. *Am. J. Psychiatry*, **153**, 607–617.

Prosser, D., Johnson, S., Kuipers, E., Smukler, G., Bebbington, P. and Thornicroft, G. (1996) Mental health burnout and job satisfaction among hospital and community based mental health staff. *Brit. J. Psychiatry*, **169**, 334–337.

Randolph, E.T., Eth, S., Glynn, S., Paz, G., Leong, G., Shaner, A., Strachan, A., VanVort, W., Escobar, J. and Liberman, R. (1994) Behavioural family management in schizophrenia: outcome of a clinic based intervention. *Brit. J. Psychiatry*, 164, 501–506.

Scazufca, M., Kuipers, E. (1996) Links between Expressed Emotion, burden and coping in relatives of those suffering from schizophrenia. *Brit. J. Psychiatry*, 168, 580–587.

Siol, T. and Stark, F.M. (1995) Therapists and parents interacting with schizophrenic patients. *Int. J. Mental Health*, **24**, 3, 3–12.

Smith, J. and Birchwood, M.J. (1987) Specific and non specific effects of educational intervention with families living with a schizophrenic relative. *Brit. J. Psychiatry*, **150**, 645–652.

Smith, J., Birchwood, M., Cochrane, R., George, S. (1993) The needs of high and low expressed emotion families: a normative approach. *Soc. Psychiatry Psychiat. Epidemiol*, **28**, 11–16.

Snyder, K.S., Wallace, C.J., Moe, K. and Liberman, R.P. (1994) EE by residential care operators' and residents' symptoms and quality of life. *Hosp Community Psychiatry*, **45**, 1141–1143.

Tarrier, N. and Barrowclough, C. (1995) Family Intervention in schizophrenia and their long term outcomes. *Int. J. Mental Health*, **24**, 3, 38–53.

Tarrier, N., Barrowclough, C., Vaughn, C., Bamrah, J.S., Porceddu, K., Watts, S., Freeman, H. (1988) The community management of schizophrenia: a controlled trial of a behavioural intervention with families to reduce relapse. *Br. J. Psychiatry*, **165**, 532–542.

Tessler, R. and Gamache, G. (1994) Continuity of care, resident and family burden in Ohio. *Millbank Quarterly*, **72**, 149–169.

Watts, S. (1988) A descriptive investigation of the incidence of high EE in staff working with schizophrenic patients in a hospital setting. Unpublished dissertation for the BPS Diploma in Clinical Psychology.

Wing, J.K., Cooper, J.E. and Sartorius, N. (1974) *The Measurement and Classification of Psychiatric Symptoms*. Cambridge University Press, Cambridge.

Xiong, W., Phillips, M., Hu, X., Wang, R., Dai, Q., Kleinman, J. and Kleinman, A. (1994) Family based intervention for schizophrenic patients in China: a randomised controlled trial. *Brit. J. Psychiatry*, **165**, 239–247.

Zastowny, T. R., Lehrman, A. F., Cole, R. E. and Kane, C. (1992) Family management of schizophrenia: a comparison of behavioural and supportive family treatment. *Psychiatric Quarterly*, **63**, 159–186.

Zhang, M., Wang, M., Li, J. and Phillips, M.R. (1994) Randomised control trial of family intervention for 78 first episode male schizophrenic patients: an 18 month study in Suzhou, Jiangsu. *Brit. J. Psychiatry*, **165**, 96–102.

Chapter 12

TRAINING AND DISSEMINATION: RESEARCH TO PRACTICE IN INNOVATIVE PSYCHOSOCIAL TREATMENTS FOR SCHIZOPHRENIA

Nicholas Tarrier, Gillian Haddock and Christine Barrowclough

INTRODUCTION

The question of how to improve mental health services is enigmatic. In theory, research should provide information about which new treatments are efficacious. These should then be disseminated into clinical practice and services be organised or configured to accommodate them and facilitate their delivery. However, the "provision of mental health services bears little relation to research" whereas "psychiatry incorporates many commonly used treatments whose comparative effectiveness is equivocal at best". (Anderson and Adams, 1996). Why are empirically validated treatments for people with severe mental illness not becoming widely available while less well-supported treatments remain common practice?

Until quite recently, treatments for severe mental illness such as schizophrenia were thought of as being solely a biological preserve,

Outcome and Innovation in Psychological Treatment of Schizophrenia. Edited by T. Wykes, N. Tarrier and S. Lewis.
© 1998 John Wiley & Sons Ltd

although over the last decade, there have been very positive advances in the development of non-drug, or psychosocial treatments. Despite these developments, psychosocial treatments are rarely provided as routine within mental health services. What then is necessary for these research-validated treatments to become established in clinical practice and be available to those who would benefit from them? There may be a number of barriers to this process, such as: a lack of a partnership between researcher and clinician (Goldfried and Wolfe, 1996; Barlow, 1996); absence of appropriate knowledge and/or clinical skills within the relevant workforce (Lancashire et al., 1996); or a characteristic of the organisation, institution or workplace in constraining such new developments (Bernstein, 1982; Corrigan and McCracken, 1995a,b). To progress from innovation to practice it is necessary that new treatments be perceived as clinically relevant; that the new ways of working are empirically validated; that the treatments are meeting prioritised needs and that they can be taught in a way that is accessible enough for staff to readily and faithfully acquire the knowledge and skills (Liberman and Eckman, 1989; Goldfried and Wolfe, 1996).

In this chapter we will review briefly the recent innovations in psychosocial treatments of psychotic disorders and the issues surrounding their dissemination into routine clinical practice. We will specifically deal with the area of training of professional staff as a method of dissemination and we will concentrate mainly on the work of the Manchester group with which the current authors have been mainly involved.

RECENT DEVELOPMENTS IN PSYCHOSOCIAL TREATMENTS OF SCHIZOPHRENIA

The recent and considerable interest in non-drug treatments for psychotic disorders has been the product of a number of different influences such as the wider acceptance of the vulnerability–stress model of schizophrenia, the research on Expressed Emotion of relatives and its effect on the course of schizophrenia, the failure of medication to totally eradicate psychotic symptoms or prevent relapse and a general rise in the consumer movement in mental health and a desire for more needs-led services (Tarrier and Barrowclough, 1990). Psychosocial treatments can be divided into three general categories which have a separate set of clinical procedures and aims. These are: (1) family intervention; (2) cognitive–behaviour therapy for psychotic symptoms; and (3) early signs monitoring and early intervention. Each of these will be reviewed briefly.

Family intervention

Family interventions found much of their initial impetus in the research on Expressed Emotion (EE) in which studies consistently reported that patients who returned to live with relatives rated as high on EE had a much greater relapse rate than those who returned to live with relatives assessed as low EE (Kavanagh, 1992). It was reasoned that, if EE, which was assumed to reflect the behaviour of the relative towards the patient, could be changed through intervention, then the risk of relapse would be reduced. Interventions were designed by a number of groups independently with the aim of reducing stress in the home environment. These interventions, although differing in some aspects, have many common features, such as, including an educational component to provide the family with information about schizophrenia, adopting a practical problem-oriented approach, and assisting the family to cope better with the difficulties of living with a family member who has schizophrenia.

Rigorous controlled trials of family interventions have been carried out (see Mari and Streiner, 1994; Penn and Mueser, 1996 for reviews). Typically, these studies recruited families while the patient was experiencing an acute episode and the intervention commenced at hospital discharge and continued over a nine to twelve month follow-up period with the principal aim of preventing relapse. Relapse rates were then compared between families who received the family intervention as well as routine care with those who received routine care alone. Routine care included the use of prophylactic medication. The consistent finding of these clinical trials was that relapse rates were significantly reduced by family intervention over the follow-up period. A summary of the results of family intervention studies is presented in Table 12.1. Some trials have also investigated the maintenance effects of the interventions by assessing patients at extended follow-up periods. These studies have demonstrated that there is good evidence that after two years there is still a significant reduction in relapse rates for those receiving family intervention compared to control treatments (Falloon et al., 1985). In our own trial in Salford, patients were followed up at five and eight years and, although relapses do accumulate in all groups over this period, they were still significantly lower in the group who had received a nine-month family intervention compared to the appropriate control group even after this extended period of time (Tarrier et al., 1994)

The effects of family interventions on other outcomes besides relapse are less clear. There was some evidence from the studies by Falloon and colleagues and Tarrier and Barrowclough and colleagues that significant but modest improvements in patient's social functioning can be achieved in the short term and reductions in the level of burden of a key relative (Falloon et al., 1985; Tarrier, 1996). These two studies also reported rather crude health economic analyses which indicated that family interventions result in a financial saving.

In summary, there is good and consistent evidence from methodologically sound clinical trials that family intervention in conjunction with prophylactic medication reduces relapse rates in

Table 12.1 Controlled studies Comparing Family Intervention With Standard Treatment for Patients With Schizophrenia (Modified from Penn & Mueser, 1996)

Study	Treatment conditions	N	Type of family intervention	Frequency and duration of treatment	Relapse
Kottgen et al. 1984	Family intervention, high expressed emotion Customary care, high expressed emotion Customary care, low expressed emotion	15 14 20	Psychodynamic: separate groups for patients and relatives	Weekly or monthly up to 2 years	2 years: family intervention equal to customary care for families with either high or low expressed emotion
Falloon et al. 1982,1985	Behavioural family therapy Individual m/ment	18 18	Home-based behavioural family	Weekly for 3 months biweekly for 6 months monthly for 15 months	2 years: behavioural family therapy better thsan individual management
Leff et al. 1982, 1985	Family intervention Customary care	12 12	Psychoeducation to help relatives with high expressed emotion model coping of low expressed emotion relatives	Biweekly for relatives groups for 9 months	2 years: family intervention better that customary care
Tarrier et al. 1988, 1989, 1994	Behavioural family therapy enactive Behavioural family therapy symbolic Education only Customary care	16 16 25 20	Behavioural family therapy comprising stress management + training in goal setting	3 stress management and 8 goal-setting sessions over 9 months	2 years: behavioural family therapy better than education or customary care; education and customary care equal
Vaughan et al. 1992	Single-family psycho-education and support Customary care	18 18	Psychoeducation	10 weekly sessions	9 months: single-family eduaction and support equal to customary care
Mingyuan et al. 1993	Multiple-family psycho-education and support Customary care	2076 1016	Clinic-based lectures and discussions	10 lectures and 3 discussion groups over 12 months	1 year: multiple family education and support better than customary care
Randolph et al. 1994	Behavioural family Customary care	21 18	Clinic-based behavioural family therapy	Weekly for 3 months biweekly for 3 months biweekly for 6 months	2 years: behavioural family therapy better than customary care
Xiong et al. 1994	Behavioural family therapy Customary care	34 29	Clinic-based psychoeducation, skills training, medication/symptom management	Bimonthly for 3 months family sessions for 2 years (plus individual sessions with family members and patients): maintenance sessions every 2–3 months	18 months: behavioural family therapy better than customary care

Study	Treatment conditions	N	Type of family intervention	Frequency and duration of treatment	Relapse
Zhang et al. 1994	Multiple and single family psychoeducation and support Customary care	39 39	Multiple-family clinic-based psychoeducation counselling, medication/symptom management	Individual and group counselling sessions every 1–3 months for 18 months	18 months: family education and support better than customary care
Telles et al. 1995	Behavioural family management Individual case management	– –	Clinic-based behavioural family management	Weekly for 6 months, every 2 weeks for 3 months, monthly for 3 months	12 months: for total group conditions equal; for "poorly acculturated[b] patients, individual management better for "highly acculturated" patients, conditions equal
Leff et al. 1990	Multiple-family psycho-education and support Single-family psycho-education and support	11 12	Multiple-family groups in the clinic; single family sessions at home	Biweekly for 9 months, varying amounts afterward	2 years: conditions equal
Zastowny et al 1992	Behavioural family therapy Single-family psycho-education and support	13 17	Hospital-based behavioural family therapy; hospital based single-family psychoeducationand advice on handling common problems	Weekly for 4 months, monthly for 12 months	16 months: conditions equal
McFarlane et al. 1995	Multiple-family psycho-education and support Single-family psycho-education and support	83 89	Multiple-family groups or single family sessions in the clinic	Biweekly sessions for 2 years	2 years: multiple family conditions better than single family condition
Schooler et al. 1997	Applied family management Supportive family management	157 156	Applied management comprising home-based behavioural family therapy sessions plus supportive family management comprising clinic-based multiple family groups	Applied family management: behavioural family therapy weekly for 3 months, biweekly for 6 months, and monthly for 3–6 months plus concurrent monthly supportive family management for 24–28 months; supportive family management monthly for 24–28 months	2 years: conditions equal

schizophrenia at least in the short and medium term. There is also some evidence to suggest benefits on a wider range of outcomes. Despite this, in a recent editorial in the *British Medical Journal*, family interventions for schizophrenia were described as "an effective but underused treatment" (Anderson and Adams, 1996). The authors emphasised the utility of systematic reviews of the literature which employed predefined methodological criteria and meta-analysis (Cochrane Schizophrenia Group module of the Cochrane Database of Systematic Reviews; Mari and Streiner, 1996) The conclusions were that family interventions reduce schizophrenic relapse and rehospitalisation, and reduce the costs of services; however, despite this accepted evidence of the effectiveness of family interventions, the availability of this treatment remains poor.

Cognitive–behavioural therapy for psychotic symptoms

Although a number of case studies and case series have been published over the last few decades on the use of various cognitive and behavioural interventions in the treatment of hallucinations and delusions, it was not until the late 1980s that there was a real interest in research into the efficacy of cognitive–behavioural treatments for psychotic disorders (see Haddock and Slade, 1996 et al., 1997 for reviews). These treatments were initially developed to help patients suffering from chronic psychotic conditions, mainly schizophrenia, and who were experiencing persistent delusions and hallucinations despite neuroleptic medication.

Kingdon and Turkington (1991) described the successful use of cognitive therapy with a large case series of psychotic patients which included both chronic and acutely ill patients. In Liverpool an approach termed *focusing* was developed to treat hallucinations and compared with distraction in a small controlled trial (Haddock et al., 1996). Clinical benefit was indicated for both treatments. In Manchester, Tarrier and colleagues developed *coping strategy enhancement* as a method of teaching patients to improve their natural coping processes to reduce positive symptoms and the negative emotions that resulted. In a controlled trial, *coping strategy enhancement* was compared with *problem solving* for chronic patients who had experienced psychotic symptoms for at least six months despite medication without further improvement. Both treatment groups showed significant reductions in these symptoms although there was evidence that improvement in delusions and anxiety were greater in patients who received *coping strategy enhancement* (Tarrier et al., 1993). In London, Garety and Kuipers and colleagues developed a comprehensive cognitive–behavioural approach which significantly reduced residual positive psychotic symptoms (Garety et al., 1994).

So far these studies have produced considerable interest and optimism and there appears to be a consistent finding that psychotic and affective symptoms can be reduced using cognitive–behavioural treatments, although their impact on reducing negative symptoms or improving social functioning has been negligible. Currently, three large controlled trials are approaching completion in the UK, these are of Kuipers and colleagues in London, Tarrier and colleagues in Manchester and Turkington and colleagues in Newcastle, and these will shed further light on the effectiveness of CBT in the treatment of chronic and persistent psychotic symptoms. However, at this present time what evidence there is has accrued from case studies and case series or small, usually open, controlled trials. The evidence for individual cognitive–behavioural treatments is therefore currently much weaker than for family interventions.

More recently, there has also been interest as to whether cognitive–behavioural treatments could be effective with patients suffering an acute psychotic episode. The aim of treatment in the majority of studies evaluating CBT published so far has been to treat persistent symptoms which have not been effectively treated with medication. In contrast, the aim with acutely ill patients is to speed recovery and discharge and, as secondary aim to delay or prevent further relapse. In a recent study, cognitive therapy was shown to result in a 25–50% reduction in recovery time in schizophrenic patients with acute psychosis following an intensive inpatient individual and family intervention (Drury et al., 1996b). At nine month follow-up, 5% of the cognitive therapy group showed moderate to severe residual symptoms compared to 56% of the control group (Drury, Birchwood, Cochrane and MacMillan, 1996a). This is an exciting and encouraging preliminary study, although the results need to be interpreted with caution given that assessment was neither blind nor independent.

To further evaluate the effects of cognitive–behaviour therapy used during an acute episode a multi-site trial of cognitive–behaviour therapy for recent onset schizophrenia, termed the *Socrates* trial (Lewis et al., 1996) is currently under way in Liverpool, Manchester and Nottinghamshire. The study aims to evaluate whether cognitive–behaviour therapy and routine care is superior to supportive counselling and to routine care and routine care alone in speeding recovery and preventing subsequent relapse in recent onset schizophrenic day or inpatients experiencing an acute psychotic episode.

Early intervention

There has been considerable enthusiasm for the general principle of early intervention in psychosis. The form of interventions has generally been focused on three main areas: early intervention by providing services mainly focused in primary care (for example the Buckingham project; Falloon et al., 1996); early intervention in the course of the disorder by focusing on providing intensive services for patients with recent onset psychosis (for example, the Early Psychosis Prevention and Intervention Centre project in Melbourne; McGorry et al., 1996 and the Socrates study described above); and early intervention focused on detecting the onset of prodromal signs in patients prone to recurrence of their psychotic illness (for example, Birchwood et al., 1989). The latter intervention is based on the principle that patients have identifiable individual and characteristic relapse signatures which precede the onset of an acute relapse of their psychotic illness. Helping patients and families to identify and monitor these early signs of relapse can help them to identify when a relapse is imminent and to elicit treatment more speedily. There is some evidence that identifying relapse in its prodromal stage and providing pharmacological treatment can reduce the severity of a subsequent relapse and reduce rehospitalisation rates (Birchwood, 1996). A similar approach has been used with manic-depressive patients and has been demonstrated to be effective in two cases (Perry et al., 1995). A randomised controlled trial of this approach is near completion. This is an encouraging set of preliminary results which require further investigation, although there are a number of practical difficulties which make this type of intervention difficult, including the unpredictable nature of relapse and the short duration of most prodromal periods (Birchwood, 1996). The possibility that a psychological intervention could be implemented to prevent relapse during the prodromal period is very attractive although, as yet, unproven.

Despite the obvious progress in empirically validated research, these treatments are not becoming widely available and less well-supported treatments remain common practice. Anderson and Adams (1996), in their recent paper on family interventions, implied that there are powerful influences which determine changes in clinical practice other than empirical evidence. They suggested that if family intervention programmes for treating people with schizophrenia attracted the research resources and marketing prowess associated with drug treatments, or the political will behind the acceptance of case management, despite little evidence for effectiveness, then practice would follow research rather more quickly.

DISSEMINATION AND TRAINING IN PSYCHIATRIC REHABILITATION

Dissemination of effective clinical skills through traditional methods such as publications and professional meetings may have limited impact upon practitioners. There is little evidence that attendance at professional meetings or short educational courses has resulted in any change in clinical practice or services (Liberman and Eckman, 1989). However, there is considerable evidence to suggest that the acquisition of clinical skills requires active and practical training rather than lecture style didactic teaching. Studies which have attempted to teach specific behavioural skills to "front-line staff", usually nurses, have reported some success in the acquisition of these skills (e.g. Liberman et al., 1982; Milne, 1984). Nevertheless, these studies identify as considerable problems a high drop-out from training and poor implementation of the skills acquired. There is also an associated issue of which are the appropriate outcome measures that should be used to evaluate such training? Should they be they related to knowledge gained, skills acquired, number of staff trained, implementation, clinical outcome on the target patient population, or some characteristic of the service or organisation?

Bernstein, in her influential 1982 conceptual review of training in behavioural methods, suggested a functional ecobehavioural framework for investigating training effectiveness in which a behavioural analytic approach was integrated into a perspective which had social and ecological validity (Bernstein, 1982). She was interested in the dissemination of skills in behaviour modification in general but many of the points she made have relevance to the topic of this chapter. The traditional methods used for producing change in an individual patient have been to train the staff who have contact with that patient. Thus, the questions of interest would be how to best to teach the use of behavioural change skills and how to maintain the use or generalisation of those skills. The result of this type of approach is to ignore the interaction with various ecological systems which facilitate or inhibit the use of these skills. These are difficulties which are still faced in the area of staff training today and have been incompletely addressed. Bernstein proposed a model that would enhance the delivery of behavioural skills, termed the *Behavioural Service Delivery Model*. By examining the function of various roles through how they interacted with different parts of the ecological system, functions such as "programme implementor", "programme designer" and "trouble shooter/resource provider" could be described and assigned. These different functions would not necessarily correspond with different individuals. The important aspect of this approach is that the system could be addressed at different levels so as to maximise the implementation of the programme. Dissemination of a particular procedure would be more probable if it were possible to negotiate access through the various systems. Thus, to deliver a new psychological treatment to a patient suffering from psychosis requires not just the ability to deliver that treatment but also the ability to negotiate with those who will benefit from the treatment and those who work within the mental health service at all levels.

A similar theme can be seen in the writing of Corrigan and colleagues (Corrigan and McCracken, 1995a,b) who distinguish between an educational and an organisations model of staff development. They provide evidence that skills based on social learning principles can be successfully taught to staff in psychiatric rehabilitation settings but that follow-up studies indicate that organisational barriers impede their introduction and maintenance. They have proposed a set of organisational development strategies to overcome these barriers. Although these strategies are geared towards changing the organisation as a whole, the main point of Corrigan's group is to change the practice of clinical teams. They suggest that this is best assured by conducting training with the whole psychiatric team, and argue that this will be most successful if the training focuses on methods which staff perceive to be relevant to their clinical goals.

TRAINING IN PSYCHOSOCIAL INTERVENTIONS

There has been a long tradition in Manchester of developing programmes for training staff in behavioural methods and in evaluating the effectiveness of such programmes. For example, the Hester Adrian Research Centre developed the Education for the Developmentally Young (EDY) project to train educational psychologists to train teachers of people with learning disabilities in behavioural methods as a means of disseminating the behavioural approach (McBrien and Foxton, 1982). Similarly, Barrowclough and Fleming developed packages for training staff working with elderly people (Barrowclough and Fleming, 1986a) and undertook evaluation of such training methods (Barrowclough and Fleming, 1986b). From this training tradition, and the growing interest in psychosocial treatments generated from treatment trials such as the family intervention study carried out in Salford in the 1980s, an interest and a demand for training in the area of severe mental illness began to grow. This resulted in the development of training programmes of psychosocial interventions for mental health professional staff in Manchester and North West England.

The Preston Project

The first training programme originating from the Manchester team was developed to provide skills in family interventions to social workers in Preston (Tarrier et al., 1988). Experience had suggested that although the "one-off workshop" may be a useful way of creating interest in a new therapeutic approach, it would be ineffective in disseminating clinical skills and in changing clinical practice. Thus, to maximise the acquisition of family intervention skills by the trainees the training programme was based on clinical supervision of case work. The initial training consisted of five one-day workshops over a six-week period, with one and a half days of follow-up sessions over the subsequent two months and ten days over the subsequent nine months, concluding with a two-day summary workshop. A number of conditions were requested before trainees enrolled on the course:

1. that each participant had a co-worker from the same workplace, so that all interventions were carried out in pairs;

2. that there be agreement from the managers of each trainee pair that the course case work be given high priority so that adequate time could be given to carry out the family intervention, hence avoiding the problem of pressure of work not allowing sufficient time for the intervention;
3. that each trainee pair should have identified and attempted to engage a patient suffering from schizophrenia and their relative prior to the commencement of training;
4. that each trainee pair informed their professional colleagues about the nature of the intervention so as to facilitate their support for their work. This was considered especially important in the case of the consultant psychiatrist.

These were attempts to begin to address some of the organisational difficulties that impede dissemination.

The content of the training course was based on the Salford Family Intervention programme (see Barrowclough and Tarrier, 1992) and followed a modular structure which involved didactic teaching followed by continuous supervised practice. Training began with background material and was followed by instruction in the use of assessments with patients and families. Subsequent teaching modules consisted of providing education and knowledge about schizophrenia, stress management, coping skills and goal setting with relatives and patients. Following each individual session of didactic teaching, trainees were required to apply the methods learnt with "real" patients and families and present case material for supervision and feedback. Each module was taught through instruction and role play but considerable attention was given to the trainees presenting their case work and to using the larger trainee group as a process whereby issues and problems were discussed so as to generate solutions to these problems. No formal evaluation of the training was carried out but written feedback from trainees was generally very positive and families indicated that they had been helped and received benefit from the new approach being used by their social workers. We were sufficiently satisfied with the training course and the feedback that had been received to regard this as a good model for training programmes.

The Manchester community psychiatric nurse training programmes

Brooker and Butterworth in the Department of Nursing at the University of Manchester set up two training programmes of family interventions that were carefully evaluated. They were concerned about what they viewed as the drift by community psychiatric nurses (CPNs) away from working with patients with serious mental illness towards treating patients with much more minor and transient conditions within a primary care setting. They reasoned that one of the causes of this drift was the feeling among CPNs that there was little psychotherapeutically that could be done for patients with schizophrenia and that their training equipped them more adequately to provide services to patients with less severe mental health problems (Brooker, 1990). Thus, it was argued that helping CPNs to acquire skills in family interventions might motivate CPNs to return to working with patients with schizophrenia and would provide an intervention that would have a direct impact on the course of the disorder (Brooker and Butterworth, 1993).

In Brooker's first study (Brooker et al., 1992), nine CPNs were selected onto the training course. Each CPN was matched with a colleague at the same workplace on a number of variables including age, gender, length of experience as a CPN and post-basic training undertaken. The matched CPNs acted as a control group in a quasi-experimental design. All CPNs received training in carrying out assessments with severely mentally ill patients but only the experimental group received training in family interventions. Each CPN aimed to recruit three schizophrenic patients and their families into the study for which they would act as a key worker. Initially, 87% of the target number of 54 families were recruited; however, 17 families dropped out before the one-year follow-up. The 30 families who completed the trial represented 64% of the original sample. Comparison of the sample with that of other English family intervention studies indicated that these numbers were comparable. The study drop-outs had significantly more admissions and days in hospital than the study completers. Comparison between the patients of the experimental and those of the control CPNs did not reveal significant differences in demographic or clinical variables nor were there differences between characteristics of their relatives. The training programme was delivered by Tarrier and Barrowclough and followed a similar but extended version of the Preston training programme.

The patients in the experimental group showed significant improvements on depression, anxiety, delusions and retardation as assessed using the KGV scale (a measure for assessing symptoms in chronic psychotic patients; Krawiecka et al., 1977) at post-treatment and one-year follow-up. Control patients showed a significant improvement in symptoms at post-treatment only. There were significant improvements in social functioning which were maintained at follow-up in the experimental group patients but no change in the control group patients. Comparisons between patients on medication dosage and admissions to hospital indicated no difference between the groups. Comparisons of variables associated with the relatives indicated that there were significant improvements in the relatives' satisfaction with the patient's personal functioning, improvements in the relatives' mental health as measured by the General Health Questionnaire (GHQ, Goldberg and Hillier, 1978), which could be considered a measure of subjective burden of care, and improvements in a measure of consumer satisfaction with services. No significant changes were found in any of these measures in families treated by the control CPNs. Interestingly, on the consumer satisfaction measure, improvements in the following items were demonstrated in relatives managed by the experimental CPNs: practical advice given; information provided about the illness; coordination of services; and the attitude of professionals towards the family. The relatives treated by the control CPNs did not indicate an increase in their satisfaction with these topics but they did indicate a significant decrease in their satisfaction with the emotional support provided by the CPNs. Although this study is not without its statistical and methodological problems, such as lack of random allocation and lack of independent assessments, it did provide encouraging support for the possibility that training staff in family interventions would result in measurable benefits in outcome for both patient and their relatives sustained over a reasonable period of time.

In a second study, Brooker and colleagues (Brooker et al., 1994) adopted a prospective quasi-experimental design in which each CPN acted as their own control. Ten CPNs were selected onto the training course of which two subsequently dropped out. Each CPN aimed to identify three experimental families and three control families. Initially a sample of 60 families was anticipated but with the loss of two CPNs to training the potential sample size was reduced to 48. Forty-one families (85% of the target sample) were recruited to the trial of which 34 (83%) remained in the study until the twelve month follow-up. A within-subject design was used so that patients were assessed and then managed "as usual" by the CPN for six months to provide a baseline period. After six months baseline the experimental group received family intervention while the control group continued to receive treatment as usual. After the study period of twelve months the control group were then offered family intervention. Of the 24 control families, one had dropped out before the end of the twelve-month study period and 15 of the remainder took up the offer of family intervention. The remaining eight constituted a control subgroup who never received family intervention. There were no significant differences between the control and experimental patients or their relatives at pre-treatment. The training was organised by Falloon and his colleagues and followed their manual (Falloon et al., 1984). It consisted of organising household meetings, family education, communication training, and family problem solving. In a similar way to the first trial, the training course was oriented towards acquisition of clinical skills which were taught through role play and clinical supervision.

The results indicated that during the baseline period there were no changes in positive or negative symptoms of psychosis. The experimental group showed a significant reduction of positive and negative symptoms over the time that they received family intervention. Similarly, the control group showed no change over the first twelve months of the study but those families who accepted family intervention at twelve months showed a significant decrease in both positive and negative symptoms at 12-month follow-up. A similar pattern was seen in improvements in the measure of social functioning. The patients from families in both the experimental group and from the control group who went on to receive family intervention showed a dramatic decrease in the mean number of days in hospital when the periods of no family intervention were compared to the periods of family intervention (experimental group: no-family intervention 18.4 days, family intervention 1.8 days; control group: no-family intervention 24.2, family intervention 3.1 days). In contrast, the control subgroup who did not receive family intervention showed a marked increase in mean days in hospital (23.5 days to 73.5 days). It could be argued that the latter group was highly self-selected and their poor outcome owed more to some characteristic of treatment refusers rather than solely as a result of not receiving a family intervention. The poor outcome in this group of treatment refusers closely resembles those reported for treatment refusers in other family intervention studies (Tarrier, 1991).

This second study of Brooker and colleagues also suffers some of the methodological problems of the first, in that there was neither blind nor independent assessment of patients or relatives, and families were not randomly allocated to treatment. Moreover, in this second study it was assumed that CPNs would treat the control families in the usual manner while they were learning and implementing new treatments with the experimental families, assuming that there would be no transfer of benefit to the control families. Notwithstanding these difficulties, the second study largely replicated the results of the first study. There were benefits for both patients and their relatives as a result of receiving treatment from appropriately trained CPNs and the outcomes validated the training programmes of Tarrier and Barrowclough and Falloon which, despite both being behavioural interventions, differed in a number of ways.

The New South Wales study

It is worth examining a similar study carried out in Australia by Kavanagh and his colleagues (Kavanagh et al., 1993) which had a very different outcome. Kavanagh trained mental health workers in the Sydney area in a cognitive–behavioural approach to family intervention. However, despite considerable effort by the training team the training appeared to have little impact upon clinical practice and few of the trainees actually attempted to engage families for any length of time. The trainees received didactic and workshop training of approximately 30–35 hours duration after which they were asked to participate in a controlled evaluation of family intervention by acting as trial therapists. Initially, 160 therapists received training but only 44 of these elected to take part in the treatment trial and 28 of these saw only one family. In fact, 57% of the families in the study were seen by six therapists. Therapists reported particular difficulty in integrating the family work with their other duties and interests. In an evaluation of the training programme, only 4% of the sample reported that their knowledge of cognitive–behavioural approaches was a significant problem, but in a written test, most therapists failed to demonstrate even the minimum recall of the material they had been taught (Kavanagh et al., 1993). The authors reported that in families who received an intervention, 13% of the patients had experienced a marked exacerbation of symptoms compared to 27% in the group who received only an individual intervention. Nevertheless, they concluded "as a demonstration that the structured family intervention could be disseminated into routine community health practice, the project clearly was of limited success."

Apart from the possible differences in attitude and practice between Manchester and New South Wales there are two potential reasons why the training programme of Kavanagh and colleagues yielded such poor results compared to the comparative success of Brooker and colleagues. Successful training requires continuity and progressive clinical supervision, time-limited didactic and workshop teaching is unlikely to result in skill acquisition in the absence of guided practice. It is probable that without supervision within a structured teaching programme trainees will very quickly abandon the new approach, failing either to acquire the skill or not perceiving it as priority for meeting important clinical goals. The second important factor is the necessity for management commitment for the training and practice of the new approach. In Kavanagh's programme there appears to have been little in the way of management commitment to the re-organisation of workloads so that family intervention could be given a high priority. It appears that for most trained therapists in this study family work was just one more activity that had to compete in an already overloaded schedule. It is perhaps not surprising that very few therapists attempted to implement what they had been taught without management prioritising the family work, and clinical supervision to shape their practice.

The Thorn initiative nurse-training project

In 1991, the Sir Jules Thorn Charitable Trust approached Dr Jim Birley about the possibility of supporting specialist mental health nurse training similar to that provided for Macmillan nurses in palliative care. Birley approached colleagues in London and Manchester who had been actively involved in psychosocial intervention research and training and a combined steering committee was organised to oversee the development of a training programme at the two sites. The broad aim of the project was to train CPNs in problem-oriented psychosocial and psychological interventions with the seriously mentally ill. The project was funded by the Trust for three years and sub-committees to cover the development of the curriculum and to carry out an evaluation of the effectiveness of the training were constituted. The content of the course followed a broadly similar content at both sites with the reflection of local strengths and interests. At the end of the three year period funding was secured from health services sources and the training had received considerable interest both nationally and internationally. There was also considerable interest from other professional groups besides nursing and since 1994 the training has become open to trainees of other professional backgrounds. In the following section the Thorn training at Manchester will be described in greater detail.

Thorn training in Manchester

The University of Manchester Thorn training consists of a 1-year diploma course which covers three main subject areas: case management and assessment, behavioural family interventions and individual psychological management of symptoms. Trainees receive thirty six whole days formal teaching over the year and carry out an equivalent number of days in clinical practice with selected clients who have a severe mental illness and their families. Working with, and being supervised on, these clinical cases is an integral part of the course. The first module (case management) consists of: literature and government legislation surrounding case management; an up-to-date review of the literature relating to schizophrenia and other forms of serious mental illness; training in assessment of the multiple needs of psychotic patients and their families and monitoring of medication and side effects.

The behavioural family intervention training follows the case management module. It provides a thorough grounding in the literature relating to the influence of the family on the course of serious mental illness and helps trainees to identify the needs of families and patients who would benefit from intervention. Trainees are provided with skills to effectively assess families and patients and to plan and carry out interventions aimed to reduce family stress and to reduce the risk of relapse. Interventions are carried out with at least two families per trainee pair with supervision from course leaders. The individual psychological management of the psychotic symptoms module, which runs concurrently with the family module, provides a thorough grounding in the literature relating to individual cognitive and behavioural interventions for people with enduring psychotic symptoms. Trainees are taught to assess and monitor psychotic symptoms and to plan and implement interventions to reduce the distress, disruption and severity of these symptoms as well as implement strategies to facilitate early intervention. Again, supervision is provided by the course leaders, who are a clinical psychologist and a community psychiatric nurse.

Additional teaching and advice is provided by a multi-disciplinary teaching team which includes a combination of academic and clinical staff from the following professional backgrounds: clinical psychology, pharmacy, community nursing, social work and psychiatry.

The Thorn training has been subject to a rigorous evaluation of trainee and patient outcome. Initial results showed that trainees increased their knowledge and skills during training and patient outcome improved following the Thorn intervention in terms of positive, negative and affective symptoms and social functioning (Lancashire et al., 1996). Nevertheless, this evaluation is limited in that the patients were not randomly allocated to a comparison intervention group with which to compare outcome and the evaluation was not independent or blind. An independent evaluation is in progress. Despite these limitations, the study has confirmed the findings of earlier training programmes, that is, mental health professionals can acquire the skills necessary to provide cognitive–behavioural family and individual interventions which can produce significant benefits for patients and families and ultimately to services. As earlier training programmes found poor dissemination and generalisation into services, the Thorn programme was designed to maximise these using a number of strategies. In order to encourage generalisation into trainees ordinary working practice, only those who had written managerial support for their application for training were accepted. This was to ensure that the services were prepared to allow the practice of the approaches and were aware of the changes in practice which would be required. In addition, trainees were accepted onto the programme only if they could attend with another colleague at the same time. This was designed to encourage peer support and to facilitate co-working. During training, trainees were also encourage to address the problem of generalisation and to problem-solve strategies to help them to implement the interventions and to continue to receive local relevant clinical supervision when their formal Thorn training was finished.

In order to increase the dissemination of the Thorn training, an advanced training module was developed designed to provide skills in training and clinical supervision. Trainees who performed well on the diploma programme were invited onto this programme so that they could be instrumental in encouraging and providing local training programmes in their own sites. This has resulted in a small number of mini-Thorn courses being set up by ex-Thorn trainees which are being run with the collaboration of the University of Manchester. These initiatives provide introductory training courses for staff in their own places of work. In addition, trainees are encouraged to continue to liaise with the Thorn team at the University of Manchester after their training in order to maximise continued sharing of information, knowledge and support. A regular conference and meetings are also set up with ex-Thorn trainees to encourage continued support for the approaches.

TRAINING IN SITU

There are considerable advantages of formal and structured training courses such as Thorn, including disseminating research into clinical practice and creating a better trained and relevantly skilled workforce. However, there are also a number of weaknesses in this mode of training where the majority of the teaching takes place away from the work place. Not least of these is that staff receiving training have to leave their work place to attend the training. It is argued that any loss of trainee input in the short term is balanced by the long-term gain of better-trained personnel who will be able to implement interventions that will improve clinical and social outcomes and reduce service costs. However, although the trained personnel have increased skills there may be impediments to their implementing the skills: for example, following a change in job or an increase in seniority resulting in more administration and less clinical time.

An alternative method of dissemination is to investigate the patient and carer needs rather than the needs of the general workforce. We are currently carrying out an evaluation of this method of dissemination in Manchester (Tarrier et al., 1995). The project attempts to address the general question of whether empirically validated family interventions can be delivered in a service setting. Can research be translated into practice? The project aims to assess the psychosocial needs of families of schizophrenic patients and to appraise how far these needs are being met by existing services and to identify the shortfall. To achieve this, Barrowclough and colleagues (Barrowclough et al., 1996) have developed a computerised method of assessing psychosocial needs in carers of schizophrenic patients. Once needs have been identified an intervention can be delivered mainly through existing key workers who receive appropriate training, through supervision, personal instruction and workshops. Thus, training in specific skills is provided to meet the individual needs of a patient and carer with the assumption that these will generalise. This is in contrast to structured training programmes such as Thorn which work from the general to the specific. We are currently carrying out a randomised controlled trial of this individualised training approach.

CONCLUSIONS

Questions of how best to translate research into clinical practice in the area of severe mental illness are likely to be with us for a long time although it is an issue which will attract increasing importance and attention. The issues are clearly difficult to resolve. We have attempted to discuss how to improve mental health services to patients who have psychotic disorders by making available to them new innovative psychosocial treatments. This discussion has raised concerns as to whether these treatments have been validated sufficiently, whether they are a priority, what is the best way to teach them, how should training be organised, how should training be assessed and evaluated and how should they be considered good value for money? At the present time our understanding on these topics is patchy and the methodology for investigating them underdeveloped. However, the continuing priority for services for patients with severe mental illness together with the development of new treatment strategies means that attempts to overcome these problems will continue.

REFERENCES

Anderson, J. and Adams, C. (1996) Family interventions in schizophrenia: An effective but underused treatment. *British Medical Journal*, **313**, 505.

Barlow, D.H. (1996) Health care policy, psychotherapy research and the future of psychotherapy. *American Psychologist*, **51**, 1050–1058.

Barrowclough, C. and Fleming, I. (1986a) *Goal Planning with Elderly People. How to make plans to meet an individual's needs: A manual of instruction*. Manchester, Manchester University Press.

Barrowclough, C. and Fleming, I. (1986b) Training direct care staff in goal planning with elderly people. *Behavioural Psychotherapy*, **14**, 192–209.

Barrowclough, C. and Tarrier, N. (1992) *Families of Schizophrenic Patients: Cognitive Behavioural Interventions*. London, Chapman and Hall.

Barrowclough, C., Marshall, M., Lockwood, A., Quinn, J. and Sellwood, W. (1997) Assessing relatives needs for psychosocial interventions in schizophrenia: a relatives version of the Cardinal Needs Schedule (RCNS). *Psychological Medicine*, in press.

Bernstein, G. (1982) Training behavioural change agents: A conceptual review. *Behavior Therapy*, **13**, 1–23.

Birchwood, M. (1996) Early intervention in psychotic relapse. In, Haddock, G. and Slade, P. (eds), *Cognitive–behavioural Interventions for Psychotic Disorders*. London, Routledge.

Birchwood, M., Smith, J., Macmillan, F., Hogg, B., Prasad, R., Harvey, C. and Bering, S. (1989) Predicting relapse in schizophrenia: the development and implementation of an early signs monitoring system using patients and families as observers, a preliminary investigation. *Psychological Medicine*, **19**, 649–656.

Brooker, C. (1990) A description of clients nursed by community psychiatric nurses while attending ENB clinical course number 811: a clarification of current role. *Journal of Advanced Nursing*, **15**, 155–166.

Brooker, C. and Butterworth, A. (1993) Training in psychosocial intervention: the impact on the role of community psychiatric nurses. *Journal of Advanced Nursing*, **18**, 583–590.

Brooker, C., Tarrier, N., Barrowclough, C., Butterworth, A. and Goldberg, D. (1992) Training community psychiatric nurses for psychosocial intervention: report of a pilot study. *British Journal of Psychiatry*, **160**, 836–844.

Brooker, C., Falloon, I., Butterworth, A., Goldberg, D., Graham-Hole, V. and Hillier, V. (1994) The outcome of training community psychiatric nurses to deliver psychosocial intervention. *British Journal of Psychiatry*, **165**, 222–230.

Corrigan, P.W. and McCracken, S.G. (1995a) Psychiatric rehabilitation and staff development: Educational and organisational models. *Clinical Psychology Review*, **15**, 699–719.

Corrigan, P.W. and McCracken, S.G. (1995b) Refocusing the training of psychiatric rehabilitation staff. *Psychiatric Services*, **46**, 1172–1177.

Drury, V., Birchwood, M., Cochrane, R. and MacMillan, F. (1996a) Cognitive therapy and recovery from acute psychosis: a controlled trial. I. Impact on psychotic symptoms. *British Journal of Psychiatry*, **169**, 593–601.

Drury, V., Birchwood, M., Cochrane, R. and MacMillan, F. (1996b) Cognitive therapy and recovery from acute psychosis: a controlled trial. II. Impact on recovery time. *British Journal of Psychiatry*, **169**, 602–607.

Falloon, I.R.H., Boyd, J.L., McGill, C.W., Razani, J., Moss, H.B. and Gilderman, A.M. (1982) Family management in the prevention of exacerbations of schizophrenia. *New England Journal of medicine*, **306**, 1437–1440.

Falloon, I., Boyd, J. and McGill, C. (1984) *The Family Care of Schizophrenia*. London, Guilford.

Falloon, I.R.H., Boyd, J.L., McGill, C.W., Williamson, M., Razini, J., Moss, H.B., Gilderman, A.M. and Simson G.M. (1985) Family management in the prevention of morbidity in schizophrenia: Clinical outcome of a 2 year longitudinal study. *Archives of General Psychiatry*, **42**, 887–896.

Falloon, I., Kydd, R., Coverdale, J. and Laidlaw, T. (1996) Early detection and intervention for initial episodes of schizophrenia. *Schizophrenia Bulletin*, **22**, 271–282

Garety, P., Kuipers, L., Fowler, D., Chamberlain, F. and Dunn, G. (1994) Cognitive-behaviour therapy for drug resistant psychosis. *British Journal of Medical Psychology*, **67**, 259–271.

Goldberg, D. and Hillier, V. (1978) A scaled version of the General Health Questionnaire. *Psychological Medicine*, **9**, 139–146.

Goldfried, M.R. and Wolfe, B.E. (1996) Psychotherapy practice and research, repairing a strained alliance. *American Psychologist*, **51**, 1007–1016.

Haddock, G. and Slade, P.D. (1996) *Cognitive–behavioural Interventions for Psychotic Disorders*. London, Routledge.

Haddock, G., Bentall, R.P. and Slade, P.D. (1996) Psychological treatment of auditory hallucinations: focusing or distraction? In, Haddock, G. and Slade, P.D. (eds.) *Cognitive–behavioural Interventions for Psychotic Disorders*. London, Routledge.

Haddock, G., Tarrier, N., Spaulding, W., Yusupoff, L., Kinney, C. and McCarthy, E. (1997) Individual cognitive–behavioural therapy in the treatment of hallucinations and delusions: a review *Clinical Psycology Review* (in press).

Kavanagh, D. (1992) Recent developments in expressed emotion and schizophrenia. *British Journal of Psychiatry*, **160**, 601–620.

Kavanagh, D., Clark, D., Piatkowska, O., O'Halloran, P., Manicasvasagar, V., Rosen, A. and Tennant, C. (1993) Application of cognitive–behavioural family interventions in multi-disciplinary teams: What can the matter be? *Australian Psychologist*, **28**, 1–8.

Kingdon, D. and Turkington, D. (1991) Preliminary reports: the use of cognitive behaviour therapy and a normalising rationale in schizophrenia. *Journal of Nervous and Mental Disease*, **179**, 207–211.

Kottgen, C., Soinnichesen, I., Mollenhauer, K. and Jurth, R. (1984) Results of the Hamburg Camberwell Family Interview study, I-III. *International Journal of Family Psychiatry*, **5**, 61–94.

Krawiecka, M., Goldberg . D. and Vaughan, M. (1977) A standardised psychiatric assessment scale for chronic psychotic patients. *Acta Psychiatrica Scandinavica*, **55**, 299–308.

Lancashire, S., Haddock, G., Tarrier, N., Baguley, I., Butterworth, C.A. and Brooker, C. (1996) The impact of training community psychiatric nurses to use psychosocial interventions with people who have severe mental health problems. *Psychiatric Services*, **48**, 39–41.

Leff, J.P., Kuipers, L., Berkowitz, R., Eberlein-Fries, R. and Sturgeon, D. (1982) A controlled trial of intervention with families of schizophrenic patients. *British Journal of Psychiatry*, **141**, 121–134.

Leff, J.P., Kuipers, L. and Sturgeon, D. (1985) A controlled trial of social intervention in the families of schizophrenic patients. *British Journal of Psychiatry*, **146**, 594–600.

Leff, J.P., Berkowitz, R., Shavit, A., Strachan, A., Glass, I. and Vaughn, C.E. (1990) A trial of family therapy versus relatives' groups for schizophrenia. *British Journal of Psychiatry*, **157**, 571–577.

Lewis, S., Tarrier, N., Haddock, G., Bentall, R., Kinderman, P. and Kingdon, D. (1996) *A multicentre, randomised controlled trial of cognitive–behaviour therapy in early schizophrenia*. Medical Research Council funded grant (number #G9519373).

Liberman, R.P. and Eckman, T. (1989) Dissemination of skills training modules to psychiatric facilities. Overcoming obstacles to the utilisation of a rehabilitation innovation. *British Journal of Psychiatry*, **155** (suppl. 5), 117–122.

Liberman, R.P., Eckman, T. Kuehnel, T., Rosenstein, J. and Kuehnel, J. (1982) Dissemination of new behaviour therapy programs to community mental health programs. *American Journal of Psychiatry*, **139**, 224–226.

McBrien, J. and Foxton, T. (1982). *Education for the Developmentally Young (EDY) training manual*. Manchester, Manchester University Press.

McFarlane, W.R., Lukens, E., Link, B., Dushay, R., Deakins, S.A., Newmark, M., Dunne, E.J., Horen, B. and Toran, J. (1995) Multiple family groups and psychoeducation in the treatment of schizophrenia. *Archives of General Psychiatry*, **52**(8), 679–687.

McGorry, P., Edwards, J., Mihalopoulos, C., Harrigan, S. and Jackson, H. (1996) EPPIC: An evolving system of early detection and optimal management. *Schizophrenia Bulletin*, **22**, 305–326.

Mari, J.J. and Streiner, D. (1994) An overview of family interventions and relapse on schizophrenia: meta-analysis of research findings. *Psychological Medicine*, **24**, 565–578.

Mari, J.J. and Streiner, D. (1996) The effects of family intervention on those with schizophrenia. In, Adams, C., Anderson. J., Mari, J.J. (eds), *Schizophrenia module, Cochrane Database of Systematic Reviews*. London, Cochrane Library.

Milne, D. (1984) The development and evaluation of a structured learning format introduction to behaviour therapy for psychiatric nurses. *British Journal of Clinical Psychology*, **23**, 175–185.

Mingyuan, Z., Heqin, Y., Chengde, Y., Jianlin, Y., Qingfeng, Y., Peijun, C., Lianfang, G., Jizhong, Y., Guangya, Q., Zhen, W., Zhen, W., Jianhua, C., Minghua, S., Junshan, H., Longlin, W., Yi, Z., Buoying, Z., Orley, G. and Gittleman, M. (1993) Effectiveness of psycheducation of relatives of schizophrenic patients: a prospective cohort study in five cities of China. *International Journal of Mental Health*, **22**, 47–59.

Penn, D.L. and Mueser, K.T. (1996) Research update on the psychosocial treatment of schizophrenia. *American Journal of Psychiatry*, **153**, 607–617.

Perry, A., Tarrier, N. and Morris, R (1995) Identification of prodromal signs and symptoms and early intervention in manic depressive psychosis: two case examples. *Behavioural and Cognitive Psychotherapy*, **23**, 399–409.

Randolph, E.T., Eth, S., Glynn, S.M., Paz, G.G., Shaner, A.L., Strachan, A., Van Vort, W., Escobar, J.I. and Liberman, R.P. (1994) Behavioural family management in schizophrenia: Outcome of a clinic based intervention. *British Journal of Psychiatry*, **164**, 501–506.

Schooler, N.R., Keith, S.J., Severe, J.B., Matthews, S.M., Bellack, A.S., Glick, I.D., Hargreaves, W.A., Kane, J.M., Ninan, P.T., Frances, A., Jacobs, M., Lieberman, J.A., Mance, R., Simpson, G.M. and Woerner, M.G. (1997) Relapse and rehospitalisation during maintenace treatment of schizophrenia. The effects of dose reduction and family treatment. *Archives of General Psychiatry*, **54**, 453–463.

Tarrier, N. (1991) Some aspects of family interventions in schizophrenia: I. Adherence to intervention programmes. *British Journal of Psychiatry*, **159**, 475–480.

Tarrier, N. (1996) A psychological approach to the management of schizophrenia. In, Moscarelli, M., Rupp, A. and Sartorius, N. (eds), *Handbook of Mental Health Economics and Health Policy*, Volume 1. *Schizophrenia*. Chichester, Wiley.

Tarrier, N. and Barrowclough, C. (1990) Mental health services and new research in England: Implications for the community management of schizophrenia. In Kales, A., Talbot, J. and Stefanis, C. (eds), *Recent Advances in Schizophrenia*. New York, Springer-Verlag.

Tarrier, N., Barrowclough, C. and D'Ambrosio, P. (1988) A training programme in psychosocial intervention with families with a schizophrenic member. *The Behavioural Psychotherapist*, **27**, 2–4.

Tarrier, N., Barrowclough, C., Vaughn, C.E., Bamrah, J.S., Porceddu, K., Watts, S. and Freeman, H. (1989) The community management of schizophrenia: A controlled trial of a behavioural intervention with families to reduce relapse: a 2 year follow-up. *British Journal of Psychiatry*, **154**, 625–628.

Tarrier, N., Barrowclough, C. and Lewis, S (1995) *A Novel Family Support and Psychoeducational Service in Schizophrenia: Effectiveness and Training*. NHS Executive North West, Innovation Development Fund grant.

Tarrier, N., Beckett, R., Harwood, S., Baker, A., Yusupoff, L. and Ugarteburu, I. (1993) A trial of two cognitive–behavioural methods of treating drug resistant psychotic symptoms in schizophrenic patients. I Outcome. *British Journal of Psychiatry*, **162**, 524–532.

Tarrier, N., Barrowclough, C., Porceddu, K. and Fitzpatrick, E. (1994) The Salford Family Intervention Project for schizophrenic relapse prevention: five and eight year accumulating relapses. *British Journal of Psychiatry*, **165**, 829–832.

Telles, C., Karno, M., Mintz, J., Paz, G., Arias, M., Tucker, D. and Lopez, S. (1995) Immigrant families coping with schizophrenia. Behavioural family intervention vs. case management with a low income Spanish speaking population. *British Journal of Psychiatry*, **167**, 473–479.

Vaughan, K., Doyle, M., McConaghy, N., Blaszczynski, A., Foz, A. and Tarrier, N. (1992) The Sydney intervention trial: a controlled trial of relatives' counselling to reduce schizophrenic relapse. *Social Psychiatry and Psychiatric Epidemiology*, **27**, 16–21.

Xiong, W., Phillips, M.R., Hu, X., Wang, R., Dai, Q. and Kleiman, A. (1994) Family based intervention for schizophrenic patients in China: A randomised controlled trial. *British Journal of Psychiatry*, **165**, 239–247.

Zastowny, T.R., Lehman, A.F., Cole, R.E. and Kane, C. (1992) Family management of schizophrenia: a comparison of behavioral and supportive family treatment. *Psychiatry Q*, **63**(2), 159–186.

Zhang, M., Wang, M., Li, J. and Phillips, M.R. (1994) Randomised control trial family intervention for 78 first episode male schizophrenic patients: an 18 month study in Suzhou, Japan. *British Journal of Psychiatry*, **65** (supplement 24), 96–102.

Chapter 13

OUTCOME AND COSTS OF PSYCHOLOGICAL THERAPIES IN SCHIZOPHRENIA

H. Brenner and M. Pfammatter

INTRODUCTION

This chapter, rather than reporting on new developments, will take a step backwards in order to cast a critical eye over a scientific and clinical field which has been also the centre of our own work. We will examine replicated research evidence. Effective treatments must modify at least one of the hypothetical constructs presumed to influence outcome, according to the diathesis–stress model of schizophrenia: (1) biological vulnerability, (2) environmental stress, (3) coping skills, or (4) social competence (cf. Bellack and Mueser, 1993; Liberman, 1994). The question is, whether, how and to what extent this holds true for psychological interventions.

Psychological treatments can be roughly classified in respect of their focus (e.g. family, individual, group, organisation), setting (e.g. hospital, community), mode (e.g. cognitive–behavioural versus psychodynamic, insight-oriented) and with regard to their objectives (symptom reduction,

Outcome and Innovation in Psychological Treatment of Schizophrenia. Edited by T. Wykes,
N. Tarrier and S. Lewis.
© 1998 John Wiley & Sons Ltd

alteration in the expressed emotion (EE) status etc.). Here, we examine cognitive behavioural treatment modes.

Cognitive behavioural family therapy

No other group of psychological treatments of schizophrenia has been so intensively investigated in the last 15 years as has cognitive–behavioural family therapy. Since 1990 several longitudinal studies on the clinical effectiveness of this treatment approach have been published (Falloon et al., 1985; Hogarty et al., 1986, 1991; Leff et al., 1982, 1985, 1989, 1990; Tarrier et al., 1988, 1989; Randolph et al., 1994; Xiong et al., 1994; Telles et al., 1995). Four renowned groups in the United States and England have made important contributions to this development. In each case they carried out prospective controlled studies with a two-year follow-up investigation on the efficacy of family therapeutic interventions (Leff et al., 1982, 1985; Falloon et al., 1985; Hogarty et al., 1986, 1991; Tarrier et al., 1988, 1989). A central role was assigned to the now well-known concept of "expressed emotion" (EE), which attempts to assess and operationalise the emotional atmosphere of interactions between the patient and his or her relatives or carers.

Despite some differences in conceptualisation and the actual therapeutic procedures, these family interventions show several common characteristics. All were carried out in the context of community psychiatric care on the basis of optimal neuroleptic treatment in schizophrenic patients who had recently been discharged from the hospital, either with remission from an acute exacerbation or a first episode of the disorder, or stabilized at the level of slight persistent symptoms. Because of the suspected correlation between EE status and the rate of relapse, only families with a raised EE status (Camberwell Family Interview, CFI) were included in these studies. The most important criterion for the clinical efficacy of family therapy in these investigations was the achievement, in addition to the effect of neuroleptic treatment, of lower relapse rates through an improvement of problem–solving skills and a reduction of family tensions using cognitive–behavioural interventions. The relevant results are summarised in Table 13.1.

Falloon et al., (1985) investigated the efficacy of their approach when compared with supportive individual therapy aiming at improving the patient's social adjustment. Tarrier et al., (1988) compared behavioural family therapy with routine treatment available by community psychiatric care and with a purely psychoeducational programme. In the Hogarty et al., (1986) study, four conditions regarding their efficacy on relapse prevention were compared with one another: (a) family therapy; (b) patient-oriented training of social skills; (c) a combination of these two treatment conditions and (d) a supporting neuroleptic control condition.

Table 13.1 Relapse rates in family therapy

Study	Intervention	N	Relapses (%)/p follow-up 9–12 months	24 months
Leff et al.	Family intervention	12	9	20
(1985, 1982)	Routine treatment	12	50	78
Falloon et al.	Family intervention	18	6	17
(1986, 1991)	Individual treatment	18	44	83
Hogarty et al.	Family intervention	21	19	29
(1986, 1991)	Social skills training	20	20	50
	Combined intervention	20	0	25
	Pharmacotherapy	29	38	62
Tarrier et al.	Family intervention	25	12	33
(1988, 1989)	Psychoeducation	14	43	57
	Routine treatment	15	53	60

Leff et al., (1985) investigated the efficacy of family therapy in comparison with a standard form of neuroleptic treatment without any additional interventions besides assessments for the symptomatic and EE-status. The Tarrier et al., (1989) study provided further follow-up data while in the other studies family therapy interventions continued during the entire two-year follow-ups, albeit with largely decreasing frequency.

The results of the comparison of the rates of relapse between the different treatment conditions show significant advantages in favour of the family therapy conditions, at least for the first 9–12 months. The complete absence of relapse in the combined treatment condition in the study of Hogarty et al., (1986)—social skills training and family therapy—is difficult to explain and the theoretical model of Liberman (1994) might be helpful in this respect. In this model, "personal" protective factors in the form of enhanced individual coping skills (here social skills training), combined with environmental protective factors associated with the improved family "problem-solving" ability (here family treatment) decreases both the intrinsic vulnerability of the patient and his environmental stress. The effect of a reduced rate of relapse is sustained in all studies also in the follow-up after 24 months despite a significant increase of the relapses in the second year of study. The hypothetical relationship between EE status, relapse and chronicity is not unidirectional in nature, as shown by the fact that there was a proportion of patients also in the control groups in whom the high EE status of the relatives changes in the direction of low EE status, but who nevertheless show a greater rate of relapse than the patients in experimental groups. Besides this, a rise of the EE level was found also in routinely treated families with low EE status. Such a rise was not shown in the relatives with low EE status who were offered psychoeducative treatment in addition to routine care. These results show the danger in considering families of low EE status as being free of treatment-relevant problems.

In further work, Randolph et al., (1994) and Xiong et al., (1994) presented two further controlled studies on the efficacy of family therapy employing a treatment approach similar to that of Falloon and co-workers. These studies confirmed in the main the previous results regarding lower relapse rates, shorter in-patient treatment and improved social integration compared with standard care. Another recent study, by Telles et al., (1995), is the only one in which the cognitive–behavioural family therapy approach does not appear to be superior. However, this study was different from the other ones in the following points: (a) the patients were exclusively Spanish–American immigrants and (b) only one small group of relatives displayed a high EE level. Cultural and statistical effects may thus have contributed to the lower efficacy of family therapy, underscoring the likely importance of cultural factors in therapeutic interventions. Other studies of family therapy have compared the treatment of individual families using the approach of Falloon et al., (1985) with the relatives' or family groups approach (Linszen, 1995; Schooler et al., 1995). No significant differences were found between family therapy and relatives' groups, but the relapse rates were on the whole quite low, possibly attributable to the comprehensive treatment concepts used (e.g. case management), raising the possibility of ceiling effects. In addition, these studies incorporated various psychopharmacological interventions (such as the standard treatment, low dosage and interval therapy), whereby the standard approach proved superior in comparison with the others. According to McFarlane et al., (1990, 1995), interventions with groups of several families were superior to an individual family approach. Here again, the relapse rates were very low and comparable with the ones of those earlier studies.

In contrast with the impressive results of the effects of long-term family interventions, only modest improvements in social functioning, with no lowering of relapse rates, were recorded in several studies on the efficacy of short-term family interventions, i.e. those lasting less than two months. Such interventions had basically a purely psychoeducational direction (cf. Bellack and Mueser, 1993; Birchwood, Smith and Cochrane, 1992). An exception seems to be the psychoeducational crisis-oriented approach by Goldstein et al., (1978). These authors reported an intervention, which was the only one to achieve better results in respect of relapse prevention as well compared with the standard treatment (Glick et al., 1985, 1990; Vaughan et al., 1992). Seen as a whole, however, the studies showed that the relatives of schizophrenic patients can achieve a considerable amount of knowledge about the illness, and that this acquired knowledge leads to a less negative attitude and increased confidence regarding the ability to cope with the illness, as well as to a lowering of the level of anxiety and strain on the family. Also improvements in the patients' social functioning were reported in some studies. Thus, education seems to be a necessary component in relapse prevention programmes, but not as a sole treatment in itself. Long-term therapeutic benefits emerge when education is combined with stress-reducing, problem-solving interventions (e.g. Smith and Birchwood, 1987; Birchwood et al., 1992; Hahlweg et al., 1989; Tarrier et al., 1988, 1989). While there is a clear administrative and fiscal appeal for more limited treatment interventions, it seems that sustained clinical effort and support are required before many families can process, integrate and effectively apply newly acquired information.

In the present economic climate, the proof of clinical efficacy of a treatment approach is not sufficient for it to become established in current care practice. Proof must also be provided of the possibility of cost-effective integration of the new approach into the system of care provision. In pursuing this goal Tarrier, Lowson and Barrowclough (1991) examined the excess costs which were incurred by their family intervention after nine months. Only the direct costs were calculated (see Table 13.2). Their results showed that the additional costs due to the family therapy were more than compensated for, largely due to the decline in days of (re)hospitalisation. The question remains as to whether these savings will be sustained over time, since at the time of the second follow-up the relapse rate for the family intervention, while still significantly below that of the control

Table 13.2   Cost-effectiveness of family therapy

Study	Costs	Treatment	
Cardin, McGill and Falloon (1986)	Over 12 months	Family intervention (N = 18) costs/person	Individual therapy (N = 18) costs/person
	Total treatment costs	$6 475	$8 273
	Indirect costs	$2 405	$2 634
	Total costs	$8 880	$10 907
Tarrier, Lowson and Barrowclough (1991)	Over 9 months	Family intervention (N = 25) costs/person	Routine treatment (N = 25) costs/person
	Hospital care	$104	$830
	Day care	$545	$392
	Outpatient treatment	$522	$581
	Total costs	$1 171	$1 803

condition, had risen significantly. Cardin, McGill and Falloon (1985) came to a similar result for the family therapy approach of Falloon et al. (1985). In this study, too, the savings were predominantly a result of reduced demand for in-patient care and crisis intervention for the patients in the family condition (see Table 13.2).

These results are confirmed by a recent study on the cost effectiveness of a two-year psychoeducational family treatment programme for schizophrenic adolescents by Rund and colleagues in Oslo (Rund et al., 1994). The treatment programme included parent seminars, family therapy sessions, problem-solving sessions and advice to the key people in the patient's social network. In comparison with a standard reference treatment this programme was more effective as measured by relapse, and more cost-effective (measured by direct treatment costs) during a two-year treatment period. Similar results were reported by Held (1993): in a two-year intervention study comparing again the family therapy approach of Falloon et al., (1985) with a standard treatment condition he found a cost reduction ranging from one quarter to one third in favour of family therapy.

Overall, it can be said that cognitive–behaviourally oriented family therapy shows positive effects with regard to (1) reducing relapse and rehospitalisation rates; (2) reduction in the burden on the family, and possibly (3) an improvement in the social competence of the patient. These effects appear to be attributable to the specific content of this approach (mainly the EE status of the family) and the specific therapeutic procedures (structured, task-oriented, active co-operation of the patient and his or her reference persons, pragmatic introduction to, and specific practice of, a more efficient coping with real-life difficulties), especially since a controlled study on the effectiveness of a psychodynamically oriented family therapy showed no such successes (Köttgen et al., 1984). The precise mechanisms of change are, however, largely unknown. This prevents a more specifically goal-oriented procedure, matched to the situational conditions and the requirements of the individual family, and makes it impossible to achieve an ongoing assessment as to how far the goals of the therapy are being achieved. The lack of knowledge about the change mechanisms can also be attributed to the still inadequate differentiation of the EE construct which underlies the various treatment approaches. The importance of erroneous attributions and beliefs or of the role of unprocessed grief and feelings of loss on the part of the family members etc., for the development of a specific family atmosphere, need to be investigated. Another open question is the extent to which cognitive–behavioural-oriented family interventions achieve their effects by means of improved medication compliance. This seems to play an important part, but is unlikely to account for all the effect, since even with clear compliance there are significant differences which still remain in the outcome variables between experimental and control groups.

Perhaps the most important open question of all, however, is how long the therapeutic effect persists after the end of treatment. The findings cited above do not allow for any definitive conclusions to be drawn, since, with the exception of the study of Tarrier et al., (1988, 1989), there are no good follow-up data available. The available data indicate that, in the second year, the number of episodes of florid symptoms again rises; an indication that family intervention does not necessarily prevent relapse, but only postpones it. In this context, the predominantly chronic nature of schizophrenic disorders needs to be taken into account. Family therapy, in a similar way to treatment with medication, is given rather intermittently in the longer term, and is possibly best thought of as a continuing intervention. A further problem is presented by the considerable number of families which do not respond to family therapy, or which break off treatment after a short time, ranging up to one third (Smith and Birchwood, 1990; Tarrier, 1991). Patients whose family members break off the intervention seem to have an increased risk of relapse. In any event, we need to get away from the tendency of seeing the family affected as a problem family, and move towards a view of the family as an involved and aware partner in the therapeutic treatment of the schizophrenic family member. Failure to educate and engage patients and their caregivers in a long-term informed therapeutic alliance can result in non-compliance with essential antipsychotic medication, with psychosocial treatments, and with supportive services (Smith and Birchwood, 1990).

TRAINING OF SOCIAL SKILLS

The protective shield of a tolerant, supportive, not over-demanding, family environment is only one of a number of factors that protect against the damaging effects of stress on the course and outcome of schizophrenia. Another factor is the advancement and extension of a vulnerable persons's personal resources, such as the strengthening of self-confidence as well as increasing of his coping ability and social competence. Schizophrenic people suffer from a number of social deficits resulting in reduced social networks. Deficits in social behaviour increase the probability of critical and hostile reactions by the relatives and by the wider social environment and thus carry with them the risk of stress-laden interactions. Thus, inadequate social functioning in schizophrenia has far-reaching implications for the course and the prognosis of the illness. Change can be an important protective factor in the fragile equation of stress and vulnerability (cf. Liberman, 1994).

The development of sophisticated approaches to the training of social skills has occurred during the past 15 to 20 years. Their efficacy has been investigated in a series of individual case studies and in a number of controlled ones (Bellack et al., 1984; Hogarty et al., 1986, 1991; Wallace and Liberman, 1985; Wallace et al., 1992; Liberman, Mueser and Wallace, 1986; Eckman et al., 1992). Despite various methodological deficiencies there appears a relatively consistent pattern in this research (c.f. Halford and Hayes, 1991; Liberman, 1994; Liberman et al., 1993, 1994; Bellack and Mueser, 1993). Table 13.3 summarises the results of three classical controlled studies carried out in the 1980s (Bellack et al., 1984; Wallace and Liberman, 1985; Hogarty et al., 1986, 1991).

In their study, Bellack et al. (1984) compared a three-month group social skills training programme lasting a total of 36 hours and combined with a day clinic programme, with the efficacy of individual standard care at the day clinic. Pre–post comparisons as well as the results of a six-month follow-up showed a significant improvement of the patients' social skills measured by self-evaluation questionnaires and role-play sessions. No such improvements were recorded in the control group. Both groups however reported improvements in various measures of general functioning and psychopathology. Less encouraging was the efficacy of the two conditions in respect to relapse rates defined as rehospitalisations: both treatment groups experienced a relapse rate of almost 50% by the end of the year following treatment.

Wallace and Liberman (1985) compared the effects of social skills training in a group setting based on in-patient psychiatric care with a so-called holistic treatment. Both therapy methods were carried out over a period of nine weeks and included daily group sessions and weekly behaviourally-

Table 13.3 Rehospitalisation or relapse rates in social skills training (SST)

Study	Intervention	N	Rehospitalisations/ Relapses (%) follow-up	
			9–12 months	24 months
			Rehospitalisations	
Bellack et al. (1984)	Social skills training	29	48	
	Day hospital programme	12	50	
			Relapses	
Wallace and Liberman (1985)	Social skills training	14	21	50
	Holistic health therapy	14	50	79
Hogarty et al. (1986, 1991)	Social skills training	20	20	50
	Family intervention	21	19	29
	Combination	20	0	25
	Pharmacotherapy only	29	38	62

oriented family therapy sessions. The results show that the patients in the social skills training group acquired significantly more social skills, including long-term ones. Also the differences in favour of social skills training increased over the course of the follow-up. In addition, there was evidence that acquired skills were being generalised and transferred onto situations outside the treatment setting. The persons undergoing training of social skills spent considerably less time as in-patients two years after discharge than the patients undergoing the holistic regimen. However, even though certain advantages in respect of relapse and rehospitalisation rates were observed in the two years followed up for the social skills training programme, the differences were not significant.

In the study of Hogarty et al. (1986, 1991)—as mentioned earlier—the relapse rate was found to be markedly lower after the first year of treatment for both the family therapy and the social skills training, as well as for the two interventions combined, than was the case in the control group condition with neuroleptic treatment only. This effect was less pronounced, as we have seen, at the time of the two-year follow-up for the family therapy condition and it had almost disappeared in the social skills training group. Nonetheless, there was still a slight advantage after two years in favour of social skills training when compared with the control group undergoing medication treatment only.

Taken together, the results of these studies, as well as of a meta-analysis evaluation of various outcome dimensions (Benton and Schroeder, 1990), show that schizophrenic patients acquire and maintain a number of instrumental and social skills through social skills training and generalise or adapt them to a modest degree to "natural" situations. In addition, patients regard themselves as more self-confident and less socially apprehensive after the training. On the other hand, training seems only moderately to influence the general level of functioning, in particular when the latter is investigated more broadly than on behavioural dimensions alone. The generalising effect seems to depend on the complexity of the social situation and the relevant skills to enable an adequate adjustment to it (Bellack and Mueser, 1993; Liberman, 1994). Generalisation is enhanced when patients are encouraged to use the skills they have learned in training sessions in their natural environment—and when they are reinforced by their peers, relatives and caregivers for employing their skills (Liberman, 1994). However, it is precisely the encouragement of correctly acquired social skills that is so difficult to realize in the "natural" social environment. For how long the new skills persist seems to depend on the duration of training. If the training programme lasts less than two to three months, and if the sessions are conducted less frequently than once every other week, the likelihood that the skills will be maintained over a longer period of time diminishes. In addition, during an episode of pronounced symptomatology only some additional skills are acquired and then only with great difficulty, and severely ill patients acquire fewer skills, more slowly (Bellack and Mueser, 1993).

It is important to note that training of social skills can lead to the patient being discharged from hospital earlier. Despite the small size of samples used to evaluate data on hospital discharges, the effect of a higher discharge rate seems to be stable. Also, a modest yet significant effect regarding reduction of relapses through training of social skills can be regarded as confirmed. This effect seems however to appear only after a therapy period lasting at least 3–12 months and it is not very marked (cf. Benton and Schroeder, 1990). However, explicit cost-effectiveness studies on social skills training are lacking. Whether training of social skills proves to be as successful from the point of view of cost-effectiveness as behavioural family therapy is questionable, especially if one considers that the bulk of cost savings is attributable to the significantly lower costs of rehospitalisation—an effect that is much weaker in skills training. In addition, we must ask whether the therapy results achieved under costly laboratory conditions in terms of time and personnel can be repeated in the context of routine psychiatric care.

Relevant to this, Liberman et al. (1993) have devised a transferable, comprehensive skills training programme divided into individual modules. These modules make up a comprehensive training package which includes several key areas of social functioning. The effective application of these modules in various treatment settings and service delivery systems has been demonstrated in a number of empirical studies (Liberman and Eckman, 1989; Wallace et al., 1992; Eckman et al., 1992). This is in line with our own experiences regarding the successful implementation of the Integrated Psychological Therapy Programme in very different treatment settings throughout the German-speaking countries (Brenner et al., 1992, 1994).

An important issue for further investigation is the question of the key process mechanisms of skills training. Our ignorance of these mechanisms and the corresponding processes of change hinders the development of specific procedures to be tailored to the individual needs, deficits, goals, as well as strengths of individual patients. This is of central importance in a cost-effective integration of social skills training in psychiatric routine treatment. Research also needs to identify patient characteristics predictive of response to interventions of varying intensity, duration, and content so that cost effectiveness of service delivery can be optimised.

COGNITIVE REMEDIATION

Schizophrenic patients suffer from a number of information-processing disorders which can hinder the acquisition, generalisation, maintenance and utilisation of social skills and may lead to a heightened susceptibility to stress. From a systemic point of view, information-processing disorders are regarded as moderating factors in the positive feedback loops between neurobiological and micro- and macro-social processes. According to this concept, neurobiologic anomalies, cognitive dysfunctions and deficits in social functioning are mutually dependent on one another (Brenner, 1989). Thus, cognitive remediation of these disorders could possibly become yet another starting point of effective, cost-efficient, cognitive–behavioural interventions and it has indeed come under the scrutiny of therapy researchers in past years (Spring and Ravdin, 1992; Liberman and Green, 1992; Brenner et al., 1987, 1992; Hogarty and Flesher, 1992; Bellack, 1992; Bellack and Mueser, 1993; Green, 1993). Regarding the starting point of cognitive remediation, it seems useful to differentiate between various forms of cognitive dysfunctions at least along two dimensions. Thus distinction should be made between, on the one hand, elementary information-processing deficits versus those of higher-order processes, and on the other hand, primary versus secondary cognitive dysfunctions. The approaches and aims of cognitive remediation depend further on the theoretical models of information processing (e.g. a capacity model versus a step model).

Whether these deficits are immutable or open to change is a central issue. In recent years various computer-based training procedures have been developed, employing a wide range of tasks such as the Continuous Performance Test (CPT; Rosvold et al., 1956) and the Span of Apprehension Test (SAT; Asarnow, Granholm and Sherman, 1991) on a more elementary level of information processing, and the Wisconsin Card Sorting Test (WCST; Heaton, 1981) on a more complex level of processing. The studies varied in the methods, study designs and measures used. However, one robust finding is that various training procedures indeed lead to an improvement in information-processing dysfunctions. The question as to the duration of these effects of treatment remains unanswered. Also, questions about the generalization of such improvements to the more practical everyday aspects of problem solving and to the general level of social functioning as well as questions about differentiated indication and about specificity of effects remain open, despite of promising results in this respect as reported by Green (1993), Delahunty, Morice and Frost (1993) and Spaulding et al., (1996). In addition, individual studies have shown that very seriously handicapped schizophrenic subjects respond poorly to treatment while at the same time less handicapped subgroups in out-patient care performed as well as control groups. These results suggest that cognitive deficits are not remediated in the narrow sense, rather they seem to be compensated for.

The Integrated Psychological Therapy programme (IPT) developed by Brenner et al., (1992, 1994) is based on the assumption that dysfunctions at lower functional levels lead to dysfunctions at higher levels, which in consequence influence the lower levels again. Such mutual interdependence can be described as two vicious circles. Elementary cognitive disorders disrupt higher-level cognitive processes, which leads to a continuing cognitive dysfunction. This cognitive dysfunction increases the risk of the subject being exposed to social stressors and diminish at the same time his or her ability to cope with these stressors. The corresponding arousal again leads to an increase of information-processing disorders. The combination of these two vicious circles accounts for the onset of symptoms, the diminution of social functioning, and the mechanisms by which these dysfunctions are maintained in the absence of observable causal factors. Treatment programmes that strive to break these noxious feedback loops must address both the cognitive and the social dysfunctions that continue to expose the individual to stress (Brenner et al., 1992). Accordingly, the IPT consists of five subprogrammes in which there is a gradual shift of therapeutic emphasis from cognitive processes towards social skills, but which also stress the permanent interplay that exists between cognitive and social factors. The clinical efficacy of IPT and its individual subprogrammes have been tested in a number of controlled studies at different institutions and in different treatment settings (hospital, out-patient services). One study included an eighteen months follow-up assessment and showed significantly lower rehospitalisation rates and significantly greater improvements in the level of social functioning in the experimental condition compared with two control conditions (Brenner et al., 1987). However, it is difficult to pinpoint the effect mechanisms of IPT. Positive effects are seen in more elementary cognitive deficits, while the effects on complex cognitive dysfunctions, as well as on the general level of social functioning, are obscured perhaps due to the results of the mixed interventions in the later subprogrammes (Brenner et al., 1994; Liberman and Green, 1992).

In the light of the present findings it is not clear at what level and how broadly cognitive remediation should be addressed and which specific information-processing disorders should be targeted with cognitive treatment programmes. It seems possible that the cognitive deficits that contribute to the onset of psychosis (and presumably also lead to subsequent relapses) are different from the deficits that restrict the social and occupational functioning of the patients (Green, 1993). Such differentiation of cognitive dysfunctions would have important implications for cognitive remediation procedures. In addition, it seems that motivational, emotional, interpersonal and socio-cultural aspects should also be taken into account in understanding the interactions between information processing and overt behaviour—as should elements of the theory of action. This would mean an important step toward bridging the gaps in the underlying theoretical concepts. In view of this spectrum of open questions it is not yet possible to give a final evaluation of the effectiveness of cognitive remediation. Also, questions of whether and how such programmes could be cost-effectively integrated into comprehensive treatment programmes—and how they should be combined with neuroleptic medication and other cognitive–behavioural interventions—are still to be answered.

COGNITIVE–BEHAVIOURAL TREATMENT OF PERSISTENT POSITIVE SYMPTOMS

Despite significant advances in pharmacotherapy, a considerable number of schizophrenic patients still suffer from persistent positive symptoms. This problem is often accompanied by stress, fear, and depression, and also leads to widespread restrictions in social and employment competence, as well as in the general quality of life of schizophrenic people and their relatives. The cognitive–behavioural methods which have been used for the treatment of persistent positive symptoms can be characterised on the basis of their theoretical background and their differing focal points of attention, and divided into operant procedures, stimulus control procedures, cognitive procedures, and self-control or self-management procedures. In this regard, a trend can be identified away from the operant methods towards cognitive procedures and self-control procedures (Vauth and Stieglitz, 1993). The efficacy of the procedures applied is examined mostly in descriptions of individual clinical cases, less often in controlled individual case studies or non-controlled group research, and rarely by means of randomised group designs (cf. Vauth and Stieglitz, 1993; Tarrier et al., 1993a).

Following the emphasis in recent research we confine ourselves here to cognitive procedures and self-control or self-management procedures. Cognitive procedures for the treatment of persisting positive symptoms need to be distinguished from the cognitive training programmes for the remediation of information-processing dysfunctions. Their goal is to modify the experience of, or ability to cope with, consciously processed thoughts, conceptualisations, beliefs, and perceptions. More especially, they approach the treatment of symptoms from the assumption that these are based on a distortion of what might be termed "normal" thought processes (Birchwood and Shepherd, 1992; Tarrier, 1992). By means of non-confrontational reality-testing procedures, Socratic dialogue, and other disputation techniques, the attempt is made to modify these distorted styles of thinking and faulty attributions or beliefs, and interventions usually are focused not on the faulty perceptions themselves, but on their strength of proof. In a series of individual case studies and non-controlled group studies significant success has been achieved with regard to changing abnormal ways of thinking, or reducing them in frequency and strength.

Of particular interest in this context is the work of Chadwick and Lowe

(1990, 1994). Starting from an elaborated cognitive model for the development of delusions, they employed two kinds of cognitive interventions designed to change or weaken delusive ideas: a "verbal challenge" method and an "empirical reality testing" method. The efficacy of these interventions was tested in a number of single-case studies administering the two interventions in reversed order, and using a multiple baseline design and a between-subject comparison in out-patients with at least two years of continually experiencing delusions. They found encouraging results with regard to the strength of adherence to the individual delusions and to the degree of preoccupation with them as well as to accompanying anxiety and depression.

A different approach uses either self-control or self-management techniques. The theoretical background of this line of intervention largely is based on the self-regulation model by Kanfer (cf. Kanfer, Reinecker and Schmelzer, 1991) or the concept of self-efficacy by Bandura (1977). The self-control or self-management techniques do not primarily aim at the treatment of persistent positive symptomatology. Rather, the patient learns better to cope with it. Thus, the practice of self-control strategies aims to optimise the generalisation and efficiency of self-control strategies, and it does so by letting the patient "manage" his or her own process of change while the therapist mainly assists (Vauth and Stieglitz, 1993). The patient is thus trained in a number of strategies designed to bring positive symptoms under control, should they emerge. One of these is the technique of thought stopping. However, a number of studies has shown the technique to be rather ineffective, and the use of coping strategies seems to be much more promising. Suitable treatment techniques aim at the acquisition of different individual coping techniques on the basis of the patient's already existing coping strategies.

The best example here is the treatment programme developed by Tarrier et al. (1993a), who called their approach "Coping Strategy Enhancement" (CSE). CSE involves a detailed analysis of symptoms, of the antecedent conditions and consequences, the selection of adequate coping strategies from the existent coping resources of individual patients to manage the various symptoms and the exercising of these coping techniques in simulated situations or—in the event that positive symptoms emerge during a therapy session—in vivo. Most important are the following coping strategies, singly or in combination, tailored to the specific needs and resources of the patients: (1) cognitive strategies (e.g. attention switching, attention narrowing, self-instruction); (2) behavioural strategies (e.g. increasing solitary activities, increasing social interactions, social disengagement, reality testing); (3) strategies to produce physiological changes (such as relaxation, exercise).

The efficacy of CSE has been investigated in a randomised group study which compared the experimental condition with a problem-solving treatment approach. Schizophrenic patients displaying therapy-resistant psychotic symptoms and treated as out-patients were randomly assigned either to the experimental CSE group or to the problem-solving group. 50% of the patients in both treatment groups were then placed on a waiting list. The treatment lasted five weeks in either case. The main results of this study are summarised in Table 13.4 and show significant improvements with regard to the number of positive symptoms as well as a reduction of accompanying fear, a decrease in preoccupation, conviction and interference from symptoms, i.e. symptom severity. However, no significant positive effects were found with regard to depression, negative symptoms and psychosocial functioning.

In summary, we can conclude that a number of cognitive–behavioural methods appear to be effective in the treatment of persisting positive symptomatology. This is particularly true for the two approaches mentioned last, i.e. the cognitive intervention methods and the self-control and self-management techniques. However, the findings are neither uniform from the point of view of treatment procedures, nor well-founded due to methodological inadequacies of a large percentage of the evaluation studies. Again, many questions still have to be answered. There are questions on the generalisability and duration of therapy effects, the comparative efficacy and specificity of the various elements of treatment, and the predictions of treatment response. Other questions concern treatment planning and organisation, duration of treatment, efficacy of booster sessions, combination with other treatment methods and the setting

Table 13.4 Effects of Coping Strategy Enhancement (CSE)

NUMBER OF POSITIVE SYMPTOMS Study	Treatment	N	Pre-treatment	Mean scores. Post-treatment	N	follow-up (at 6 months)
Tarrier et al. 1993a	Coping strategy enhancement	15	5	2.83	12	2.08
	Problem solving	12	2.8	2.46	11	1.82
	Waiting list	14	3.54	3.77	—	—
SYMPTOM SEVERITY Study	Treatment	N	Pre-treatment	Mean scores (sd). Post-treatment	N	follow-up (at 6 months)
Tarrier et al. 1993a	Coping strategy enhancement	15	20.8	9.8	12	7.58
	Problem solving	12	10.17	8.0	11	5.55
	Waiting list	14	14.54	14.5	—	—

within which such interventions should be carried out. At present, the findings addressing these questions are inconsistent. The results of Tarrier et al. (1993b) seem not to offer strong support to the assumption that a generalisation of effects of coping training on general psychopathology and on the psychosocial adjustment takes place. The increase in social functioning which was found in three successfully treated hallucinating patients and reported in the study by Chadwick and Lowe (1994) is more hopeful.

FINAL REMARKS ON COST-EFFECTIVENESS

Some general aspects deserve particular attention at the end of this review. Davies and Drummond (1994) have shown that in a calculation of the direct and indirect costs of schizophrenia in Great Britain, 97% of the direct costs were incurred by less than half of the patients. This shows that statements about the average costs per patient carry less weight particularly with regard to this disorder, due to its heterogeneous nature in terms of course and outcome. If, for example, half of the approximately 10% of patients who today need long-term hospitalisation or long-term treatment in intensive community programmes could be helped to the extent that routine treatment in predominantly community-based services was sufficient then according to this calculation almost 40% of the treatment costs incurred by schizophrenia could be saved. With regard to this disorder, the contention by Goldberg (1991) applies in particular, that "more expensive treatments may sometimes be cheaper for society". Undoubtedly, however, it is psychological therapies which, in cases of a chronic course of the disorder, help to create the preconditions for reintegration into the community and for patients to remain there, able to live more independent lives.

Cost effectiveness already has become an important theme and it is likely to dominate the treatment sector in the years ahead, since it seems an unavoidable fact that the resources available in the future will not be sufficient to provide patients with all the available treatments, especially those resulting only in a slight degree of improvement in their health and well-being. The principle practised hitherto, of separating the consideration of the need from the consideration of the resources called upon for them, will become a more and more untenable position. Treatment costs for a specific group of patients or for a specific treatment procedure call for resources which, as a consequence, are then no longer available for other patients or therapies. It is likely that, in this context, it will be the more cost-intensive psychological treatments and psychotherapies which will come under increasing pressure to justify themselves.

Considerations of cost-effectiveness will therefore become an imperative for researchers as well as for clinicians in the area of psychological therapy procedures. The costs and benefits of these procedures, and their acceptability, need to be judged alongside other forms of treatment, such as drug treatment. We must ensure, by increasing our research efforts, that our patients continue in future to benefit from the use of effective professionally conducted psychological therapies despite economic constraints.

REFERENCES

Asarnow, R.F., Granholm, E. and Sherman, T. (1991) Span of apprehension in schizophrenia. In S.R. Steinhaauer, J.H. Gruzelier and J. Zubin (eds) *Handbook of Schizophrenia*, Vol. 5: *Neuropsychology, Psychophysiology and Information Processing*, Amsterdam, Elsevier Science Publisher BV, pp. 335–370.

Bandura, A. (1977) Self-efficacy: Toward a unifying theory of behavioral change, *Psychological Review*, **84**, 191–215.

Bellack, A.S. (1992) Cognitive rehabilitation for schizophrenia: Is it possible? Is it necessary? *Schizophrenia Bulletin*, **18**, 43–50.

Bellack, A.S. and Mueser, K.T. (1993) Psychosocial treatment for schizophrenia, *Schizophrenia Bulletin*, **19**, 317–336.

Bellack, A.E., Turner, S.M., Hersen, M. and Luber, R.F. (1984) An examination of the efficacy of social skills training for chronic schizophrenic patients, *Hospital and Community Psychiatry*, **35**, 1023–1028.

Benton, M.K. and Schroeder, H.E. (1990) Social skills training with schizophrenics: A meta-analytic evaluation, *Journal of Consulting and Clinical Psychology*, **58**, 741–747.

Birchwood, M. and Shepherd, G. (1992) Controversies and growing points in cognitive–behavioural interventions for people with schizophrenia, *Behavioural Psychotherapy*, **20**, 305–342.

Birchwood, M., Smith, J. and Cochrane, R. (1992) Specific and non-specific effects of educational intervention for families living with schizophrenia. A comparison of three methods, *British Journal of Psychiatry*, **160**, 804–814.

Brenner, H.D. (1989) The treatment of basic psychological dysfunctions from a systemic point of view, *British Journal of Psychiatry*, **155** (suppl. 5), 74–83.

Brenner, H.D., Hodel, B., Kube, G. and Roder, V. (1987) Kognitive Therapie bei Schizophrenen: Problemanalyse und empirische Ergebnisse, *Nervenarzt*, **58**, 72–83.

Brenner, H.D., Hodel, B. Roder, V. and Corrigan, P. (1992) Treatment of cognitive dysfunctions and behavioral deficits in schizophrenia, *Schizophrenia Bulletin*, **18**, 21–25.

Brenner, H.D., Roder, V., Hodel., B. and Kienzle, N. (1994) *Integrated Psychological Therapy for Schizophrenic Patients* (IPT), Seattle, Hogrefe and Huber.

Cardin, V.A., McGill, C.W. and Falloon, I.R.H. (1986) An economic analysis: Costs, benefits and effectiveness. In I.R.H. Falloon IRH (ed) *Family Management of Schizophrenia*, Baltimore, Johns Hopkins University Press, pp. 115–123.

Chadwick, P.D.J. and Lowe, C.F. (1990) Measurement and modification of delusional beliefs, *Journal of Consulting and Clinical Psychology*, **58**, 225–232.

Chadwick, P.D.J. and Lowe, C.F. (1994) A cognitive approach to measuring and modifying delusions, *Behaviour Research and Therapy*, **32**, 355–367.

Davies, L.M. and Drummond, M.F. (1994) Economics and schizophrenia: The real cost, *British Journal of Psychiatry*, **165** (suppl. 25), 18–21.

Delahunty, A., Morice, R. and Frost, B. (1993) Specific cognitive flexibility rehabilitation in schizophrenia, *Psychological Medicine*, **23**, 221–227.

Eckman, T.A., Wirshing, W.C., Marder, S.R., Liberman, R.P., Johnston-Cronk, K., Zimmermann, K. and Mintz, J. (1992) Technique for training schizophrenic patients in illness self-management: A controlled trial, *American Journal of Psychiatry*, **149**, 1549– 1555.

Falloon, I.R.H., Boyd, J.L., McGill, C.W., Williamson, M., Razani, J., Moss, H.B., Gilderman, A.M. and Simpson, G.M. (1985) Family management in the prevention of morbidity of schizophrenia. Clinical outcome of a two-year longitudinal study, *Archives of General psychiatry*, **42**, 887–896.

Glick, I., Clarkin, J., Spencer, J., Haas, G., Lewis, A., Peyser, J., De-Mane, N., Good-Ellis, M., Harris, E. and Lestelle, V. (1985) A controlled evaluation of inpatient family intervention: I. Preliminary results of a 6-month follow-up, *Archives of General Psychiatry*, **46**, 882–886.

Glick, I., Spencer, J., Clarkin, J., Haas, G., Lewis, A., Peyser, J., De-Mane, N., Good-Ellis, M., Harris, E. and Lastelle, V. (1990) A randomized clinical trial of inpatient family intervention: IV. Follow-up results for subjects with schizophrenia, *Schizophrenia Research*, **3**, 187–200.

Goldberg, D. (1991) Cost-effectiveness studies in the treatment of schizophrenia: A review, *Schizophrenia Bulletin*, **17**, 453–459.

Goldstein, M., Rodnick, E., Evans, J., May, P. and Steinberg, M. (1978) Drug and family therapy in the aftercare of acute schizophrenics, *Archives of General Psychiatry*, **35**, 1169–1177.

Green, M.F. (1993) Cognitive remediation in schizophrenia: Is it time yet? *American Journal of Psychiatry*, **150**, 178–187.

Hahlweg, K., Feinstein, E., Müueller, U. and Dose, M. (1989) Family management programmes for schizophrenic patients. Prevention of relapse and modification of familial communication patterns, *British Journal of Psychiatry*, **155** (suppl. 5), 112–116.

Halford, W.K. and Hayes, R. (1991) Psychological rehabilitation of chronic schizophrenic patients: Recent findings on social skills training and family education, *Clinical psychological Review*, **11**, 23–44.

Heaton, R.K. (1981) *Wisconsin Card Sorting Test Manual*, Odessa, FL, Psychological Assessment Resources.

Held, T. (1993) Ambulante Familienintervention rechnet sich für Arzt und Patient. Kosten durch Prophylaxe minimiert, *Fortschritte der Medizin*, **111** (suppl. 147), 7–10.

Hogarty, G.E. and Flesher, S. (1992) Cognitive remediation in schizophrenia: Proceed ... with caution! *Schizophrenia Bulletin*, **18**, 51–57.

Hogarty, G.E., Anderson, C.M., Reiss, D.J., Kornblith, S.J., Greenwald, D.P., Javna, C.D. and Madonia, M.J. The EPICS Research Group (1986) Family psychoeducation, social skills training, and maintenance chemotherapy in the aftercare treatment of schizophrenia. I. One-year effects of a controlled study on relapse and expressed emotion, *Archives of General Psychiatry*, 43, 633–642.

Hogarty, G.E., Anderson, C.M., Reiss, D.J., Kornblith, S.J., Greenwald, D.P., Ulrich, R.F. and Carter, M. The EPICS Research Group (1991) Family psychoeducation, social skills training, and maintenance chemotherapy in the aftercare treatment of schizophrenia. II. Two-year effects of a controlled study on relapse and adjustment, *Archives of General Psychiatry*, **48**, 340–347.

Kanfer, F.H., Reinecker, H. and Schmelzer, D. (1991) *Selbstmanagement Therapie*, Berlin, Springer Verlag.

Köttgen, C., Sonnichsen, I., Mollenhauer, K. and Jurth, R. (1984) Group therapy with families of schizophrenic patients: Results of the Hamburg Camberwell-Family Interview Study III, *International Journal of Family Psychiatry*, **5**, 83–94.

Leff, J., Kuipers, L., Berkowitz, R., Eberlein-Vries, R. and Sturgeon, D. (1982) A controlled trial of social intervention in the families of schizophrenic patients, *British Journal of Psychiatry*, **141**, 121–134.

Leff, J., Kuipers, L., Berkowitz, R. and Sturgeon, D. (1985) A controlled trial of social intervention in the families of schizophrenic patients: Two year follow-up, *British Journal of Psychiatry*, **146**, 594–600.

Leff, J., Berkowitz, R., Shavit, N., Strachan, A., Glass, I. and Vaughn, C. (1989) A trial of family therapy v. a relatives group for schizophrenia, *British Journal of Psychiatry*, **154**, 58–66.

Leff, J., Berkowitz, R., Shavit, N., Strachan, A., Glass, I. and Vaughn, C. (1990) A trial of family therapy versus a relatives' group for schizophrenia. Two-year follow-up, *British Journal of Psychiatry*, **157**, 571–577.

Liberman, R.P. (1994) psychosocial treatments for schizophrenia, *Psychiatry*, **57**, 104–114.

Liberman, R.P. and Eckman, T.A. (1989) Dissemination of skills training modules to psychiatric facilities. Overcoming obstacles to the utilisation of a rehabilitation innovation, *British Journal of psychiatry*, **155** (suppl. 5), 117–122.

Liberman, R.P. and Green, M.F. (1992) Whither cognitive behavioral therapy for schizophrenia? *Schizophrenia Bulletin*, **18**, 27–35.

Liberman, R.P., Mueser, K.T. and Wallace, C.J. (1986) Social skills training for schizophrenic individuals at risk for relapse, *American Journal of Psychiatry*, **143**, 523–526.

Liberman, R.P., Wallace, C.J., Blackwell, G., McKain, S. and Eckman, T.A. (1993) Training social and independent living skills: Applications and impact in chronic schizophrenia. In J. Cottraux, P. Legeron and E. Mollard (eds), *Annual Series of European Research in Behavior Therapy: Which Psychotherapies in Year 2000?* Amsterdam, Swets and Zeitlinger, pp. 65–85.

Liberman, R.P., Kopelowicz, A. and Young, A.S. (1994) Biobehavioral treatment and rehabilitation of schizophrenia, *Behavior Therapy*, **25**, 89–107.

Linszen, D. (1995) *The Amsterdam Study of Family Intervention*, paper presented at the World Congress of Behavioural and Cognitive Therapies, Copenhagen, Abstractvolume, p. 108.

McFarlane, W.R. (1990) Multiple family groups and the treatment of schizophrenia. In M.I. Merz, S.J. Keith and J.P. Docherty (eds) *Psychosocial Treatment of Schizophrenia*, New York, Elsevier, pp. 167–190.

McFarlane, W.R., Lukens, E., Link, B., Dushay, R., Deakins, S.A., Newmark, M.A., Dunne, E.J., Horen, B. and Toran, J. (1995) Multi-family groups and psychoeducation in the treatment of schizophrenia, *Archives of General Psychiatry*, **52**, 679–687.

Randolph, E.T., Eth, S., Glynn, S., Paz, G., Leong, G.B., Shaner, A.L., Strachan, A., Van Wort, W., Excobar, J.I. and Liberman, R.P. (1994) Behavioural family management in schizophrenia: Outcome of a clinic-based intervention, *British Journal of Psychiatry*, **164**, 501–506.

Rosvold, H.E., Mirsky, A.F., Sarason, I., Bransome, E.D., Jr. and Beck, L.H. (1956) A continuous performance test of brain damage, *Journal of Consulting Psychology*, **20**, 343–350.

Rund, B.R., Moe, L.C., Sollien, T., Fjell, A., Borchgrevink, T., Hallert, M. and Naess, P.O. (1994) The Psychosis Project: An efficiency study of a psychoeducational treatment programme for schizophrenic adolescents, *Acta Psychiatrica Scandinavica*, **89**, 211–218.

Schooler, N.R., Keith, S.J., Severe, J.B., Matthews, S.M., Bellack, A.S., Glick, I.D., Hargreaves, W.A., Kane, J.M., Ninan, P.T., Frances, A., Jacobs, M., Lieberman, J.A., Mance, R., Simpson, G.M. and Woerner, M.G. (1995) Relapse and rehospitalization during maintenance treatment of schizophrenia: The effects of dose reduction and family treatment, *Archives of General Psychiatry*, **54**, 453–463.

Smith, J. and Birchwood, M. (1987) Specific and non-specific effects of educational intervention with families living with a schizophrenic relative. *British Journal of Psychiatry*, **150**, 645–652.

Smith, J. and Birchwood, M. (1990) Relatives and patients in the management of schizophrenia. The development of a service model, *British Journal of Psychiatry*, **156**, 654–660.

Spaulding, W., Reed, D., Elting, D., Sullivan, M. and Penn, D. (1996) Kognitive Veränderung im Verlauf der psychiatrischen Rehabilitation. In W. Böker and H.D. Brenner (eds) *Integrative Therapie der Schizophrenie*, Bern, Verlag Hans Huber, pp. 156–169.

Spring, B.J. and Ravdin, L. (1992) Cognitive remediation in schizophrenia: Should we attempt it? *Schizophrenia Bulletin*, **18**, 15–20.

Tarrier, N. (1991) Some aspects of family interventions in schizophrenia. I: Adherence to intervention programmes, *British Journal of Psychiatry*, **159**, 475–480.

Tarrier, N. (1992) Psychological treatment of positive schizophrenic symptoms. In D.J. Kavanagh (ed.) *Schizophrenia: An Overview and Practical Handbook*, London, Chapman and Hall, pp. 356–373.

Tarrier, N., Barrowclough, C., Vaughn, C., Bamrah, J.S., Porceddu, K., Watts, S. and Freeman, H. (1988) The community management of schizophrenia. A controlled trial of a behavioural intervention with families to reduce relapse, *British Journal of Psychiatry*, **153**, 532–542.

Tarrier, N., Barrowclough, C., Vaughn, C., Bamrah, J.S., Porceddu, K., Watts, S. and Freeman, H. (1989) Community management of schizophrenia. A two-year follow-up of a behavioural intervention with families, *British Journal of Psychiatry*, **154**, 625–628.

Tarrier, N., Lowson, K. and Barrowclough, C. (1991) Some aspects of family interventions in schizophrenia. II. Financial considerations, *British Journal of Psychiatry*, **159**, 481–484.

Tarrier, N., Beckett, R., Harwood, S., Baker, A., Yusupoff, L. and Ugarteburu, I. (1993a) A trial of two cognitive–behavioural methods of treating drug-resistant residual psychotic symptoms in schizophrenia patients: I. Outcome, *British Journal of Psychiatry*, **162**, 524–532.

Tarrier, N., Sharpe, L., Beckett, R., Harwood, S., Baker, A. and Yusopoff, L. (1993b) A trial of two cognitive behavioural methods of treating drug-resistant residual psychotic symptoms in schizophrenia patients: II. Treatment-specific changes in coping and problem-solving skills, *Social Psychiatry and Psychiatric Epidemiology*, **28**, 5–10.

Telles, C., Karro, M., Mintz, J., Paz, G., Arias, M., Tucker, D. and Lopez, S. (1995) Immigrant families coping with schizophrenia: Behavioral family intervention vs. case management with a low-income Spanish-speaking population, *British Journal of Psychiatry*, **167**, 473– 479.

Vaughan, K., Doyle, M., McConaghy, N., Blaszczynski, A., Fox, A. and Tarrier, N. (1992) The Sydney intervention trial: A controlled trial of relatives' counselling to reduce schizophrenic relapse, *Social Psychiatry and Psychiatric Epidemiology*, **27**, 16–21.

Vauth, R. and Stieglitz, R.D. (1993) Psychologische Interventionsmöglichkeiten bei persistierendem Wahn und persistierenden akustischen Halluzinationen bei schizophrenen Patienten, *Psychiatrische Praxis*, **20**, 211–217.

Wallace, C.J. and Liberman, R.P. (1985) Social skills training for patients with schizophrenia: A controlled clinical trial, *Psychiatry Research*, **15**, 239–247.

Wallace, C.J., Liberman, R.P., McKain, S.J., Blackwell, G. and Eckman, T.A. (1992)

Effectiveness and replicability of modules for teaching social and instrumental skills to the severely mentally ill, *American Journal of Psychiatry*, **149**, 654–658.

Xiong, W., Phillips, M.R., Hu, X., Ruiwen, W., Dai, Q., Kleinman, J. and Kleinman, A. (1994) Family based intervention for schizophrenic patients in China: A randomised controlled trial, *British Journal of Psychiatry*, **165**, 239–247.

Chapter 14

ECONOMIC EVALUATION OF PSYCHOLOGICAL TREATMENTS FOR SCHIZOPHRENIA

Martin Knapp and Andrew Healey

INTRODUCTION

A recently completed review of psychotherapy services in the UK's National Health Service raised a host of issues. In its coverage of the field, including reviews of relevant research, it reached predictable conclusions about the availability of economic evidence, but offered welcome encouragement:

> True economic appraisals of psychotherapy [psychological interventions, more generally] are rare ... Economic evaluation of psychotherapeutic treatment should be a priority. Further research is needed to assess the cost-effectiveness of alternative methods of treatment. (National Health Service Executive, 1996a, pp 8, 12).

Why has so little economic evidence on psychological interventions accumulated? And what are the positive contributions which economics is expected to make to their development? These are two of the questions

Outcome and Innovation in Psychological Treatment of Schizophrenia. Edited by T. Wykes, N. Tarrier and S. Lewis.
© 1998 John Wiley & Sons Ltd

addressed in this chapter, with illustrations drawn from both the economics and the clinical literatures. We shall also address some background questions concerning the economic consequences of schizophrenia: the implications of the illness for sufferers and their families are presently generating new interest in the economic evaluation of alternative treatments. Consequently, many treatment modes, both pharmacological and psychological, new and old, widely employed and more specialist, are today being scrutinised in research which is beginning to add an economic dimension.

We start the chapter with a discussion of the broad economic implications of schizophrenia, drawing on British and other evidence. The scale of these economic consequences helps to explain why many health care and other agencies have sought evidence from economic evaluations. However, there are other sources of demand, which we discuss under "The demands for economic evaluations", each of them stemming from the fundamental economic problem of scarcity. When resources are scarce, choices have to be made. If we allocate more resources to psychological interventions we automatically give up the opportunity of using them on other welfare-enhancing activities, be they opportunities forgone in the health care sector, the broader public sector or the economy in general.

The prevalence of scarcity necessitates choice—how to make the best use of available resources (such as hospital in-patient beds or hours of psychotherapy treatment)—and economics has tended to focus on a few central criteria for choice, particularly efficiency and equity. The aims of the various modes of economic evaluation—the most common of which are cost-effectiveness, cost-benefit and cost-utility analyses—are to compare the efficiency of alternative treatments, systems and arrangements of care, and to provide insights into the distribution of costs and benefits falling on different individuals, groups and agencies, and the equity of those distributions. These evaluative methods are explained and illustrated under "Economic evaluation". There are, however, relatively few completed evaluations for psychological interventions—or for mental health services generally—and the Section "The supply response from economics" briefly discusses why this might be so. In the concluding section we examine the prospects for integrating economic with other evidence in the psychological treatment of schizophrenia. There is undoubtedly a need for more economic evaluations, but they must achieve adequate standards in their design and execution if they are to make valued contributions to the planning and delivery of services.

THE ECONOMIC CONSEQUENCES OF SCHIZOPHRENIA

The considerable and persistent personal and social consequences of schizophrenia are well known: the chronicity of the illness and its impact on cognition, health, functioning and quality of life leave many sufferers and their families with devastated lives. They often face many costs, perhaps as large in aggregate as the more direct and more immediately measurable costs borne by those agencies caring for people with schizophrenia in hospital or in community settings. These clinical, personal, family and social implications of schizophrenia have been discussed in earlier chapters. The consequences can clearly be far-reaching in individual and social terms, but they can also be enormously burdensome in economic terms (Knapp, 1997).

The costs of schizophrenia fall to the individual patient, his or her family and other caregivers, the health care system and to the wider society. Some of these costs are directly connected to the care and treatment of people with schizophrenia, whilst others are more indirect, perhaps long-term and often almost hidden from observation. These wide-ranging economic consequences need to be recognised in policy discussions, professional practice and empirical research, as is now becoming more common. It is also becoming recognised that we cannot afford to overlook the forces which erect or dismantle economic hurdles in the way of effective coordinated care. For example the fragmented nature of care systems and the pressures of cost containment in many countries are encouraging "cost shifting": one agency or stakeholder has greater opportunity and greater incentive to reduce their own expenditure by limiting the volume or range of treatment they provide, but in so doing they may—unwittingly or otherwise—increase levels of expenditure in other parts of the care system or by patients and their families. The problem of cost shifting is not solved by economic evaluation, but such evaluations can shed light on some of the underlying issues and incentives.

Patient costs

To the individual patient with schizophrenia, as we know, the consequences of the illness can be far-reaching and long-term. (For example, Mason et al., 1996, recently reported no amelioration or deterioration trends for a sample of first-episode schizophrenia cases even over a 13-year period.) The illness strikes at interpersonal relationships, making it more difficult for sufferers to initiate and maintain meaningful close friendships and other relationships. Social participation levels are low. Self-care and related capabilities can also be damaged, making it hard for sufferers to carry out or maintain what are widely regarded as the normal activities of daily living. People with schizophrenia find it hard to get paid employment and to keep it, which directly affects their income, limits the size of their social networks, and may lower their self-esteem and social status. The illness often damages other aspects of quality of life, such as sexual functioning and performance, and also length of life, as people with schizophrenia have a higher risk of mortality. Each of these personal consequences can be seen as a personal cost, although most are unlikely to be expressed in monetary terms (Davies and Drummond, 1994).

Caregiver costs

It is widely recognised that schizophrenia often needs substantial informal caregiver support by families, friends, neighbours or volunteer helpers, particularly if public sector expenditure cuts mean the withdrawal or limitation of services. However, many of the costs of caregiver support are difficult to observe. It is not always necessary for the purposes of economic evaluation that family or caregiver burden should be quantified in monetary terms, but when (necessarily crude) estimates have been made they have generally shown the costs to be sizeable (McGuire, 1991). For instance, Rice et al., (1990) estimated that just the time costs of caregiver support for people with schizophrenia in the US amounted to $2.5 billion a year.

There may be direct costs for families incurred by the need to pay for some treatment or support services, but the indirect costs associated with the effects on family routine and relationships, work and leisure opportunities, mental and physical health, distress, stigma and guilt are likely to be much more substantial (Schene et al., 1994). These broader and longer-term impacts on caregiver quality of life and health were recognised in the reforms introduced by the 1990 National Health Service and Community Care Act in the UK, even if subsequent practical action has done relatively little to compensate for them.

Health care costs

Health care treatment and support costs are the most direct and most easily identified economic consequences of schizophrenia. These include expenditures on in-patient hospitalisation, out-patient services, day treatment, accident and emergency services, the various community mental health services, and primary care. Within these services, some proportion of expenditure—usually a rather modest proportion—will be accounted for by psychological treatments, and another modest proportion by medications and associated laboratory and diagnostic tests.

An interesting report, *Burdens of Disease*, from the UK National Health Service Executive (1996c) offers some unique indicators, at the national level, of health care expenditure patterns by diagnostic group. Schizophrenia (defined by ICD-9 criteria) accounted for only 0.05% of primary care expenditure in England in 1992/93, and other non-organic psychoses (codes 296–299) accounted for 0.45%. Together these two diagnostic categories were responsible for 1.07% of total pharmaceutical expenditure in the same year. However, their contributions to hospital in-patient spending were the most considerable. Again for England in 1992/93, schizophrenia patients accounted for 5.37% of in-patient expenditure, and people with other non-organic psychoses 2.42%. These percentages equated to annual expenditure of £652 million and £294 million, respectively. Only two other diagnostic groups (learning disability and stroke) made larger contributions to total in-patient expenditure. In out-patient settings, the treatment of people with schizophrenia represented 0.04% of total activity in expenditure terms, and other non-organic psychoses 0.53%.

These high costs of in-patient care arise because a large proportion of people with schizophrenia are readmitted to hospital after relapsing, that is after their first episode. Most secondary health care is still dominated by in-patient treatment, so that it should be no surprise that people suffering their *first* episode of such a major illness as schizophrenia should find themselves admitted.

Other social costs

Over and above the personal, family and direct treatment consequences of schizophrenia are the additional costs to the wider society. Of course "society" in its broadest sense bears all of those costs mentioned above—those falling to patients, caregivers and the health care system—as well as certain other direct care costs falling outside the health care system, particularly those associated with social care (social welfare) services, special housing, criminal justice services and social security or income support. With the movement away from hospital-based treatment in many countries to care in community settings, these non-health care agencies are coming to play increasingly important roles. For example, if we look at specialist residential accommodation for people with mental health problems in England we see that voluntary and private organisations have become major providers (Lelliott et al., 1996).

There are indirect social costs associated with fears that psychiatric patients living in the community might be a danger to themselves or to others. Violent incidents involving schizophrenia sufferers in the UK have, for example, attracted a great deal of media attention amid concerns about personal safety (Audit Commission, 1994).

Aggregating these patient, caregiver, health care and social costs would not be straightforward. This is because different elements are calculated from different data bases (and different assumptive bases, in fact), because many of the necessary data are not available, and simply because many of the indirect costs are conceptually very difficult to express in money terms. The usual approach to demonstrating this overall economic impact of schizophrenia or another disease or disorder is to offer cost-of-illness estimates. For the USA, for example, Rice et al., (1990) estimated a total cost-of-illness of $38 billion. Of this total, direct health care treatments accounted for 53%; indirect costs of lost income and premature mortality 37%; and other costs (social welfare, criminal justice and so on) 10%. Caution should always be exercised with cost-of-illness estimates, particularly when they range so widely into the difficult territory of indirect costs. They tend to underestimate the value of life lost and not to value morbidity (other than earnings loss), and they tend not to "net out" the benefits of earlier death (such as non-use of health services). Moreover, such estimates are of no help if one's primary concern is the evaluation of different treatment (Drummond, 1992).

There is no equivalent cost-of-illness figure for the UK. Davies and Drummond (1994) suggested a total cost of £310 million, using the usual "top-down" approach, but this is now recognised to be a substantial underestimate (Knapp, 1997). Kavanagh et al., (1995) built "bottom-up" up estimates of the direct costs of schizophrenia care falling to all public, voluntary and private agencies in 1994, and also the direct costs falling to families and sufferers themselves, insofar as they could be identified. Together these amounted to £1905 million for the identified 109 000 people in England being treated for schizophrenia but obviously exclude employment and mortality effects and all of the indirect costs.

THE DEMANDS FOR ECONOMIC EVALUATIONS

As we shall argue below, the demands for economic insights—and especially the demands for economic evaluations—have many different roots, some common to all mental health problems, and some specific to schizophrenia. If we concentrate on schizophrenia and its treatment, can we identify the underlying needs for these economic insights? How do they get expression in today's health care systems?

Scarcity and choice

We should remember the fundamental economic problem of scarcity. Economics starts with recognition of the widespread prevalence of scarcity: there are too few resources relative to needs or demands. To the economist, demand is a need or desire for something (such as health care) which is backed by the willingness (and ability) to pay for it. Different people and different parts of society would be likely to hold different views as to what constitutes a "need", but there is usually held to be a gap between the level of need for a service and the level of demand: many needs go untreated. Certainly most people working in the mental health care systems of European and North American countries, and certainly in less developed countries, would be likely to argue that there are not enough resources available for the treatment of schizophrenia. The recent National Health Service Executive (1996b) report for example, commented on the apparent shortages of psychological therapists. From an economic viewpoint such judgements can only be made with reference to how much people (patients, families and society in general) value treatment of schizophrenia (as reflected in their willingness to pay) relative to the cost of its provision.

A survey by the National Schizophrenia Fellowship (based on a postal survey of "social/community psychiatrist" members of the Royal College of Psychiatrists in 1995) produced results which illustrated that prices were influencing prescribing patterns for antipsychotic drugs:

> Although relatively high numbers of psychiatrists felt that cost was a factor which affected the use of atypical drugs, especially clozapine, far fewer translated this into the actual practice of formal limiting. However, a small but significant number of psychiatrists are limited in their use of these two new neuroleptics, and the number who are [limited in this way] indicated that rationing does exist, even though levels of prescription appear to be comparatively low (Hogman, 1996, p.20).

Psychological therapies are also argued to be scarce relative to the number of schizophrenia patients who might benefit from them. It has been suggested, for example, that too many CPNs are spending less time on seriously mentally ill patients and more on less serious neuroses and affective disorders, and despite evidence on the effectiveness of family interventions (see below) few patients have access to them.

Scarcity has brought about a choice, which could be contentious, but there is little point in seeking to apportion blame for it because scarcity is fundamentally endemic. There have never been and there never will be enough resources to meet all of society's needs or wants. Of course, it is quite legitimate to argue that action or inaction by one part of society has *exacerbated* the problem of scarcity, but in one form or another the problem will always be there. One branch of economics has focused particularly on understanding how choices in the face of scarcity are and can be made so that criteria such as efficiency and equity are achieved. For example, the aims and focus of health economics are to describe, evaluate, understand and guide the workings of public and private decision-making so as to improve the efficiency of policies that impact upon people's health (how resources are deployed so as to effect people's health-related wellbeing), and to advise on the distributional and equity implications of policies and practices. In fact, economic evaluations can address a number of choice criteria, the most common of which are economy, effectiveness, efficiency and equity (see Table 14.1). These criteria are not necessarily competitive or mutually exclusive although in practice it is often the case that trade-offs have to be made between them.

Table 14.1 Criteria for choice

Economy	• … is the saving of resources; cutting costs.
	• The pursuit of economy requires detailed costs data …
	• … but ignores the impact on patients or families (the outcomes).
	• The economy criterion underpins the simplest of economic evaluations (cost-offset and cost minimisation analyses).
Effectiveness	• … is the achievement of improvements in outcome.
	• The pursuit of effectiveness requires data on changes in health status, symptomatology, quality of life, etc …
	• … but pays no regard to costs.
	• Economic evaluations base effectiveness measures on standard instruments for assessing psychopathology, behaviour, social functioning, quality of life; or on unidimensional ("utility") measures (see text).
Efficiency	• … is the reduction of the cost of achieving a specified level of effectiveness, or the improvement of the outcomes achieved from a fixed budget.
	• More broadly, it is the allocation of resources to maximum social advantage.
	• The concept of efficiency combines information on resources (cost) and effectiveness.
	• Some of the controversy around the pursuit of efficiency stems from usage of the term as a euphemism for "cheap". This is incorrect.
	• Efficiency can sometimes be promoted by spending more, not less, because improved outcomes may outweigh the additional costs.
Equity	• … is justice or fairness in the allocation or distribution of resources or outcomes. Whether an allocation is equitable is to be judged by decision-makers, *not* economists.
	• Like efficiency, it usually needs information on both resources and their effects.
	• Equity is not the same as equality (except in special cases).
	• Targeting services on needs is one example of adopting an equity criterion.

Growing pressures of scarcity

The Office for Population Censuses and Statistics has recently published summary results from a set of psychiatric morbidity surveys which reveal many things about mental illness in Britain, including the quite high levels of untreated morbidity of psychosis (Meltzer et al., 1995). As the risks of developing mental illness become more apparent and better understood, claims on resources (whether valid or otherwise) for preventive and treatment strategies are likely to intensify.

Less direct in their impact on the perceived scarcity of treatment resources are the rising expectations of mental health patients, their families and society generally.

Patient demands for new pharmaceutical drugs could be higher simply because they are new, but those people who must take medications are well aware of the side-effects and quite naturally will want to try new compounds which have fewer such deleterious consequences. Side-effect problems with conventional ("typical") antipsychotics are a major contributory factor in patient-non-adherence with medication regimes (McPhillips and Sensky, Chapter 9 of this volume). In the circumstances it is perfectly understandable if patients or families question clinicians' decisions to deny them access to these or other new drugs. Unfortunately, the new (atypical) antipsychotics have far higher prices than conventional drugs—perhaps 50 to 100 times higher—which has led directly to rationing of their usage as pharmacy departments try to keep within their budgets (Hogman, 1996). There are also new demands for psychological treatments either as alternatives or as adjuncts to medication. Given the long course of some psychological interventions, it is not surprising that these changing demands for treatments have been accompanied by requests for their closer evaluation, including their *economic* evaluation.

The various forces discussed above generate "latent" demands for economic data and evaluations. After a time, these latent demands may become manifest: they may change from underlying trends into *expressed demands*. In understanding the relevance of these needs and demands for economic evaluations it is helpful first to examine how far it is feasible or sensible to rely on market forces to allocate resources.

Expressed demands for economic evaluations

The main reason for the growth of what has become known as "managed care" in the US has been the rapid escalation of the costs of mental health care falling to employers and other payers. Managed care in mental health contexts "includes (i) benefit limits, cost sharing and pricing approaches; (ii) organizational arrangements; and (iii) case management techniques". Much of the recent debate about managed care in the US has centred on the need to monitor the activities of private (for-profit) providers who have latterly taken a larger market share of both in-patient and other services (Friedman and Kutash, 1994). Questions have been raised about supplier-induced demand and quality monitoring. Managed care itself raises numerous practical and ethical issues, particularly the influence which cost should have on clinical decision-making. Some, such as Sabin (1994) take the view that the clinician not only has a duty to the individual patient to prescribe the most efficacious treatment but also a responsibility to the community of taxpayers to pursue efficiency in the broader provision of care. Managed care arrangements may lead to the withdrawal of funding for psychological treatments (Austad and Berman, 1991; Trad, 1992; Hargreaves et al., 1997)

Cost awareness, which is at the heart of many of the challenges posed by managed care, has been seen as an ethical duty for doctors in the British NHS for some time. A much-quoted British Medical Association (1988) statement included the principle that "it is the doctor's ethical duty to use the most economic and efficacious treatment available". In this UK context, it is now readily acknowledged that economic data are needed to inform, structure and monitor the contracts drawn up between purchasers and providers of services. At one level the degree of direct management in the NHS has lessened, with the movement from a "command and control" hierarchy to quasi-markets, and with patterns of provision and utilisation more obviously determined locally and with greater opportunities for patient influence. At the same time, with the tremendous push from the NHS Executive (nationally) towards evidence-based medicine and the growth and extension of general practice fundholding with clear budget limits (effectively the equivalent of mini-health maintenance organisations in the US system), there are arguably more economic factors now intervening in the doctor-patient relationship.

Currently there are two dominant concerns around psychological interventions in the UK National Health Service. The first concern is that fears have been raised about the fate of psychological therapies in the developing internal markets, because purchasers may undervalue their role and contributions (Fahy and Wessely, 1993; McGrath, 1994; National Health Service Executive, 1996b). The growth in counselling and psychotherapy services in the private sector and the attendant dangers of under-regulation identified above suggests a need for regulator involvement outside quasi-public sector markets, whether by government or by professional bodies. The second concern is that the rapid growth of "counselling" in primary care has been subject to so little research, not just whether it makes efficient use of scarce primary care resources, but fundamentally whether it is in fact effective (Sibbald, 1996).

This move to evidence-based purchasing of treatments is well and good, but it is natural for pharmaceutical companies to use cost-effectiveness evidence in helping to sell their drugs to clinicians and formularies. By contrast, psychological therapies have no obvious "product champions" to fight their corner, nor are they separately identified, approved or marketed (Hargreaves et al., 1997; Anderson and Adams, 1996). In addition, treatment–outcome links can be difficult to discern. These various factors could disadvantage psychological vis-à-vis pharmacological interventions as health care budget-holders and other decision-makers become more cost-conscious. The "psychological treatment community", or the government would be advised to ensure that psychological treatments come under similar evaluative review. If they are found to be "cost-ineffective" there could be a case for limiting their use: if their cost-effectiveness is demonstrated, there could be an argument for advocating their more widespread adoption in appropriate clinical areas.

Beyond issues of service organisation and how to spend budgets, economics can at the least address broader issues relating to the appropriate use of mental health care. Questions such as "How much should be spent on psychological interventions?" are value-laden, but should not be avoided. Unfortunately, the information necessary to address questions of this kind is hard to obtain. In reality, of course, funding levels are determined politically, but there ought to be a place for evidence-based support for those and other decisions.

THE SUPPLY RESPONSE FROM ECONOMICS

The response from economics to these latent and expressed needs has been limited. Although the needs-related and resource-related pressures described earlier have been around for a long time, and although requests for evaluations have also been voiced for some years—at least in relation to some areas of practice and policy (such as hospital closure)—comparatively few economic evaluations have been completed. Certainly there have been very few completed evaluations of psychological interventions which include an economic component (we could identify barely a dozen UK studies in our review work for the National Health Service Executive, 1996b) although a number are now under way. Others have lamented this dearth of economic evidence (e.g. Krupnick and Pincus, 1992):

One can suggest various reasons for this low supply response: a lack of economic expertise and interest among economists, a dearth of suitable and relevant data, and a lack of incentives for service providers and purchasers to seek economic insights. Seven nested "hypotheses' can be put forward for this situation, drawn from suggestions some years ago by the UK health economist Alan Williams. They still have validity today.

One can suggest:

1. Policy-makers or decision-makers at various tiers in key agencies do not believe or recognise economic problems as being researchable.
2. They do, but do not want to know what the economic problems or possibilities might be.
3. They would like to know about economics, but cannot wait.
4. They are willing to wait, but the research commissioning process is just not up to it.
5. The research commissioning process is fine, but the research community in general has better (i.e. more enjoyable) things to do than economic studies.
6. The research community in general would be delighted to do economic

studies, but cannot find any economists interested enough (or congenial enough) to take on board as colleagues to do the work.
7. Economic studies, even when carried out, are written up so incomprehensibly that policy-makers and decision-makers could not respond sensibly to them even if they wanted to, so they have become disillusioned.

Each of these "hypotheses' might draw some support if we look for economic research on psychological interventions in any number of countries, and especially in relation to schizophrenia. There *are* economic evaluations of these interventions, some of them rather good, but they have almost all been conducted in the USA. Miller et al., (1997) provide an excellent up-to-date review of many of these studies and the issues they raise. The situation in the UK offers a contrast. The evidence of the last few years for example, would suggest that the first four of Williams' seven hypotheses should now be rejected, although for many years this was not the case. Research commissioning today by the Department of Health (and the National Health Service Executive within it) and relevant boards of the Medical Research Council now almost always includes a request for the economic dimension in the health services research which they fund.

Universally, the real difficulties would appear to rest with the last three hypotheses (5 to 7), for the supply of health economics expertise has not been able to keep pace with the demand. Within the health economics profession, mental health services research appears to have attracted relatively few people and most of those have confined their attentions to drug trials, partly because psychological treatments lack a strong constituency of funded support of the kind offered by drug companies, and partly because some of these treatments are inherently difficult to evaluate. Nevertheless, there are certainly now a few interesting economic evaluations of psychological interventions. The next section introduces and illustrates the most widely used evaluative methods in this context.

ECONOMIC EVALUATION

Economic evaluations seek to measure and compare the costs and outcomes of alternative treatments, practices or policies. Costs and (especially) outcomes can be conceptualised and measured in different ways, so that these evaluations come in four main varieties, each with different data demands, and each with different uses and possibilities.

Modes of evaluation

The three most useful and common modes of economic evaluation are cost–effectiveness analysis, cost–benefit analysis and cost-utility analysis.

(Drummond et al., 1997, review these methods in the broad health economics context; while Kavanagh and Stewart, 1995, describe and illustrate these technique in mental health settings. Healey and Knapp, 1997, discuss some of the methodological issues which now face research in this area.) These modes of evaluation have some common elements, particularly in relation to cost definition and measurement, but they differ in two main respects: they measure outcomes using different techniques (Table 14.2), and consequently they address slightly different policy or practice questions. (Two other modes of evaluation—cost-offset and cost-minimisation analyses—do not measure outcomes. As we noted earlier, cost-of-illness or burden-of-illness studies are not evaluations as such, although they are increasingly common preludes to cost-effectiveness or other analyses. They calculate all direct and indirect costs resulting from an illness.)

Cost–benefit analysis (CBA) is unique in that it addresses the extent to which a particular course of action, such as a new form of pharmacological or psychological therapy, is socially worthwhile. More specifically, it addresses questions like "How much should we spend on specific interventions (if anything)?", or more globally, "How much of the nation's resources should be allocated to mental health care?" In a CBA all costs and benefits are valued in the same units—usually in terms of money—and can thus be directly compared. The simple comparison of "costs incurred" with "costs saved" is not a CBA but a cost-offset analysis. Conducting proper cost–benefit analyses is particularly rare because of the difficulty of valuing benefits in monetary terms.

Cost-effectiveness analysis (CEA) is concerned with ensuring that resources allocated to the treatment of schizophrenia or to another activity are used to maximum effect. CEA is usually employed to help decision-makers choose between alternative interventions available to or aimed at specific patient groups: If two treatments for acute schizophrenia cost equal amounts, which provides the greater benefits? Or if two treatments are equally beneficial in terms of patient or population impact, which is the less costly? Where CEAs have been conducted in the mental health field they have tended to use batteries of functional and symptom-based outcome measures of the kind familiar to clinical evaluators from their own studies.

Table 14.2 Modes of economic evaluation

Mode of evaluation	Cost measurement	Outcome measurement
Cost-minimisation, cost-offset	comprehensive	not measured
Cost-effectiveness	comprehensive	clinical scales
Cost-benefit	comprehensive	monetary values
Cost-utility	comprehensive	utility (e.g. QALYs)

The newest mode of economic evaluation, *cost-utility analysis* (CUA), is similar to CEA with the important exception that it measures and then *values* the impact of an intervention on a patient's health-related quality of life as well as the cost of achieving that improvement. The value of health improvement from a treatment is measured in conflated units of "utility", in contrast to CBA which uses monetary values. CUAs avoid the potential ambiguities with multidimensional outcomes in CEAs, and can be applied to choices across a range of treatments or diagnoses: they can compare one clinical area to a quite distinct other area. If properly conducted, they could compare antipsychotic treatment of schizophrenia with kidney dialysis or chemotherapy or osteopathy for lower back pain. The most common value measure of health outcomes used in CUAs is the quality-adjusted life-year (QALY). Despite their inherent attractiveness, and their growing use across a wide span of health care contexts, CUAs have rarely been conducted in schizophrenia evaluations.

Conducting an economic evaluation

Generally, and for ease of execution, an economic evaluation should have the same broad design (criteria for eligibility, intervention modes quasi-experimental approach, sample sizes) as the design chosen for the main clinical evaluation to which it is likely to be attached. It should employ the same data collection points, and should span a similar period of time. There are unlikely to be strong reasons for adopting a different design in relation to each of these methodological considerations, except for sample size. To achieve enough power to test some economic hypotheses might require a large sample, but currently there is little evidence upon which to base this argument.

It is helpful to distinguish six main stages to an economic evaluation (Table 14.3). These stages are described in more detail in, for example, Knapp and Beecham (1996). To aid the discussion of methods, these stages will be described by going through an economic evaluation of "compliance therapy" linked to the trial conducted by Kemp et al., (1996). As noted earlier, the costs of schizophrenia relapse, stemming from lack of treatment efficacy and (very often) non-compliance, can be especially high and long-

Table 14.3 Six stages of cost-effectiveness evaluation

1. Define the alternative treatments or services to be evaluated
2. List the outcomes and costs to be covered by the evaluation
3. Quantify and value the outcomes and costs for each alternative
4. Compare the costs and outcomes between alternatives
5. Conduct sensitivity analyses and maybe qualify or revise the findings
6. Examine the distributional implications, and draw conclusions

term. Consequently, health care decision-makers need to evaluate carefully any new treatments which promise to tackle one or both of these root problems.

Define the alternatives to be evaluated

The first task in any evaluation—economic or clinical—must be to clarify the question to be addressed: What is the purpose of the study? All evaluations are comparative, whether they compare two or more alternative policies or modes of intervention, two or more groups of people or localities, or a single group of people before and after an intervention. It is obviously imperative from the outset that the alternatives being compared are agreed. It is also necessary to choose the research design, and there have been numerous discussions as to the usefulness of the randomised controlled design when evaluating psychological interventions (Fonagy and Higgitt, 1989; Parry, 1992). At this point, therefore, the decision has to be taken as to the mode of evaluation to be employed.

Another important decision to take at this early stage is the evaluative *perspective* to be adopted. From whose perspective are the alternative treatments to be compared? Is the focus to be on the health care system, or on all health and social care agencies, so that the perspective to employ in the costing is similarly narrow? Or is a patient or family perspective to be employed? Or a societal perspective? These are not trivial differences, partly because the breadth of the costing and the breadth of the outcome assessment are both linked to the perspective (see below), and partly because the policy or practice significance of the findings could be rather different. In their systematic review of family interventions, for example, Mari and Streiner conclude that six or seven families need to be treated in order to prevent one schizophrenic relapse over a one-year follow-up period. They suggest that "this cost/benefit balance may be acceptable to the families of those with schizophrenia, but not so attractive to providers and managers of care" (1994, p.8).

In the "compliance therapy" evaluation the comparison was to be made between a routinely-employed counselling approach and a new cognitive–behavioural intervention for improving medication compliance in patients with a psychotic illness. As we have seen, non-compliance (or non-adherence) has particular importance in mental health care practice (and policy) given the debilitating consequences of relapse and its attendant costs. The economic evaluation builds on a randomised controlled trial which has had encouraging results (Kemp et al., 1996). Patients were followed for up to 18 months after randomisation, with outcome assessments at baseline, 6, 12 and 18 months, and cost measures (retrospectively) at the same time points. The economic evaluation is a cost-effectiveness analysis.

List the outcomes and costs

The second evaluative stage is to draw up a comprehensive list of all relevant cost and outcome dimensions, even if it is expected that some dimensions need not be measured (because a narrower perspective is to be adopted) or might subsequently prove impossible to measure in practice. In this way, the full breadth of the possible resource and effectiveness impacts of the alternative treatments can be drawn to the attention of decision-makers, agencies in service delivery networks, researchers and others, even if there are no data for some of those impacts. For example, very few completed evaluations have been able to obtain adequate measures of the costs borne by families, yet a substantial number of mentally ill people are financially dependent on their families.

The decision was taken in the "compliance therapy" study to attempt as broad a costing as possible, covering health, social care, specialist accommodation, criminal justice and other direct costs. In fact, both interventions—standard counselling and the new therapeutic intervention—were expected to have identical (narrow) resource implications, but other services may have been used in different combinations and at different levels, particularly in the latter part of the research period, so a comprehensive costing was important. Family (caregiver) costs were not measured in monetary terms. Outcomes were measured by Kemp et al., (1996) so as to cover major psychiatric symptoms, social functioning, insight, attitudes to medication, extra-pyramidal symptoms, and compliance.

Quantify and value the outcomes and costs

The third stage in an economic evaluation is the measurement or quantification of each of the costs and outcomes. On the outcome side of the evaluation, the research task will clearly depend on the evaluative technique to be employed. Both clinical (symptom-based) and functional (social role functioning) outcomes should be included (Krupnick and Pincus, 1992). Clinical scales for assessing outcomes are discussed in other chapters of this book, and would form the basis of a CEA. If a cost–benefit analysis is to be undertaken, these effects or outcomes would also need to be valued in monetary terms. We have already noted how difficult it would be to attach monetary values to most mental health outcomes, although some studies have used employment earnings as a (single and generally inadequate) benefit indicator. In a cost–utility analysis a single, unidimensional indicator of "utility" would need to be constructed. The most commonly used such measure is the QALY, but the instruments currently used for QALY assessment and comparison across specialties and diagnostic groups are not immediately applicable for mental health research. Recent QALY-type methodological advances in research on people with schizophrenia might eventually help (Revicki et al., 1996).

Cost measurement is probably easier, but unfortunately still not straightforward. Cost measures are most usefully based on service utilisation data obtained for each sample member. Service utilisation data can be collected using an instrument such as the Client Service Receipt Inventory (CSRI) (Beecham and Knapp, 1992). Costs are then attached to each service or element of support in turn, using the best available estimates of *long-run marginal opportunity cost*. In this procedure, "marginal" refers to the addition to total cost attributable to the inclusion of one more user, and "opportunity cost" refers to the opportunities forgone by not using a resource in its best alternative use, which is the conventional economics definition. The short-run average revenue cost plus appropriately measured capital and overhead elements is usually likely to be close enough to the long-run marginal cost for most services, and it is conventionally taken as the cost estimate for empirical work in economic evaluations. Hargreaves et al., (1997) offer an excellent account of how costings can be undertaken in the US. For the UK there is an annual compendium of many such unit cost measures, ranging across the most important services and based on sound empirical research (Netten and Dennett, 1996.)

Compare the costs and outcomes
The fourth stage is to compare the costs and outcomes. Comparisons between the alternatives being evaluated are made in relation to both costs and outcomes after whatever summation is possible. (In cost–benefit studies, the costs of a treatment or policy can be compared directly with its benefits, and cost–benefit differences or ratios can then be compared between alternative treatments or policies to see which offers the greatest net benefits to the health service or to society.) Difficulties can arise when costs and outcomes are distributed over time in different patterns: for example, costs may be incurred early, but outcomes may not accrue until rather later. The usual procedure is to discount future costs and outcomes back to a present value before making comparisons, using a suitable procedure to weight future costs and outcomes less highly than current costs and outcomes.

The most common practice in a cost-effectiveness analysis is to calculate average costs for each of the samples and compare them with the outcomes, and then to conclude that the option with lowest cost per given level of outcome is the most desirable (on the grounds of efficiency in the use of resources). Some CEAs endeavour to rely on a single (dominant) outcome in order to ease this comparison—perhaps the mortality rate, or improvement in positive symptoms—but it is generally more relevant (as a guide to policy or practice) to use multidimensional outcome measures. Complications will then arise if there is improvement along some outcome dimensions but deterioration along others, and/or because the cost and outcome comparisons may point to different preferred solutions: treatment A may be more effective than treatment B, but also more expensive. In these circumstances the role of the economic evaluator is to present all relevant findings about A and B to those policy-makers or practitioners whose task it is to make decisions. In turn, the latter will need to weigh up the clinical, social or political importance of those findings.

It is too early to give the results of the compliance therapy economic evaluation, but we will be retaining all of the outcome dimensions throughout the economic evaluation. It would be possible to focus on one dimension—say compliance itself—for the purposes of computing cost-effectiveness ("cost-compliance") ratios, but one must be careful not to miss important other dimensions. The study has no utility (QALY) or monetary benefit measures.

Examine the sensitivity of the findings

The fifth stage is to examine how sensitive are the findings to the assumptions that inevitably have to be made in the course of any evaluation. The stage can therefore also check the assumptions made in all previous calculations in case error or bias has crept in.

Examine the distributional implications and draw conclusions

The last stage is to draw conclusions from the evaluation. If, as is usually the case, the primary purpose of an economic evaluation is to examine efficiency, this final stage should also explore how equitable or fair is the distribution of the burden of costs and the enjoyment of outcomes which would follow if each of the alternative treatments or services was implemented. One treatment may be the more cost-effective (efficient) of two alternatives, but it may leave patients or their families bearing a much higher cost burden. If this treatment was to be more widely adopted it may therefore be necessary to find a way to compensate patients and families for their extra costs, not only on the grounds of equity, but also because these costs may create a disincentive for them to continue with treatment

Completed economic evaluations

In order to be efficient a new treatment mode should not have to demonstrate that it is less costly than current or alternative modes, but it should be able to demonstrate that any increase in costs (compared to its closest alternative) is at least matched by increased effectiveness (better patient or family outcomes). As we have argued above, given the breadth of both outcome and resource consequences of schizophrenia and its treatment, an evaluation of comparative efficiency ought to be broad for the network of potential associations between concepts and events to be mapped.

The narrowest direct costs of treating schizophrenia—on the left-hand side of Table 14.1—are the expenditures on drugs, psychological therapies and other mental health care supports and services. The treatments are provided in the hope that they have a direct impact on patient and caregiver health and quality of life, as reflected in the standard dimensionality of outcomes: the positive and negative symptoms of schizophrenia, personal and family functioning, social interactions, subjective quality of life, satisfaction with services, caregiver burden, societal impacts, and so on (Lehman et al., 1995). Set against the range of concepts and dimensions summarised by Table 14.1, completed evaluations currently to be found in the published literature are rather pale imitations. Few evaluations—economic or otherwise—employ measures which cover all outcome dimensions, none of the economic evaluations measures costs comprehensively or for anything other than a short duration, and it is very rare to find comparisons between alternative modes (or combinations) or treatments which get to the heart of the decisions which individual health care professionals face on a daily basis. These failings apply almost as much in relation to pharmacological interventions as they do to psychological treatments. For example, the available economic evidence on clozapine and risperidene is mostly observational and conjectural, very little economic data coming from randomised controlled trials (see Meltzer 1996). However, the active marketing of the new atypical antipsychotics threatens to widen that margin considerably in the next few years with the reporting of findings from a number of new prospective trials.

Most of the completed economics research on psychological interventions appear to have concentrated on family interventions. A recent systematic review by the new Cochrane Collaboration Schizophrenia Review Group 1994 "confirms what mental health researchers have suspected for some time—that such interventions reduce relapse rates, rehospitalisation, and costs of treatment and also increase compliance with medication" (Anderson and Adams, 1996, p. 505). In fact, the cost result is not perhaps as unequivocal as this *BMJ* editorial claimed, for the three family intervention studies which included an economic dimension are, in some respects, methodologically flawed (Cardin et al., 1986; Tarrier et al., 1991; Xiong et al., 1994). The same must be said about a fourth study, by Rund et al., (1994). None of the four is especially weak, for the cost component of each is integrated into a sound and relevant randomised trial. Moreover, each has important contributions to make to our understanding of family interventions. Caution is however suggested because sample sizes are sometimes small (casting doubt on statistical power; see Gray et al., 1997), cost measures are sometimes quite narrow (largely confined to direct health care costs) and cost–outcome linkages are not explored as thoroughly as might have been warranted by the reported variations in both costs and outcomes within samples.

Notwithstanding these limitations, Tarrier et al., (1991) report the direct cost implications of behavioural family therapy and a psycoeducational programme, both within routine community-based care, finding that the family intervention reduces direct costs by 27% over 9 months. Rund et al., (1994) in their study of adolescents with schizophrenia, found that the family intervention package was more effective and less costly than the comparator standard treatment. The two other published family intervention studies with an economic dimension measured a wider range of resource implications. The well-known family therapy study by Falloon and colleagues and the more recent study in a family educational support programme both found improved effectiveness and lower costs compared to standard treatment. Both also found lower unemployment rates (Cardin et al., 1986).

There appear to have been no economic evaluations of other psychological interventions. However, as Brenner and Pfammater show in their chapter in this volume, some trials have found that hospitalisation rates can be reduced or durations shortened with social skills training or cognitive therapy, which may be indicative of cost reductions were the latter to be properly assessed. The dearth of economic evaluations of individual psychological therapies is partly a supply problem (as discussed above under "The supply response from economics") and partly an almost inevitable corollary of the small number of evaluations of any orientation (as witnessed by other chapters in this book; and see Scott and Dixon, 1995; Kuipers, 1996; Roth and Fonagy, 1996). At least one randomised trial is currently under way which includes an economic component (which is being undertaken at CEMH). This is a trial, organised from the Charing Cross and Westminster Medical School, comparing cognitive behavioural therapy with a psycho-educational intervention for improving compliance with medication regimes.

CONCLUSIONS

Although they were writing about psychotherapy research across all psychiatric diagnostic groups (and, indeed in relation to somatic disorders), the authors of an American review article could just as well have been commenting specifically on schizophrenia when they concluded:

> The existing data on the cost-effectiveness of psychotherapy indicate that (1) little current research activity relates to this area; (2) previous studies have been narrow in scope, are few in number, and have had substantial methodological limitations; and (3) important design and measurement issues need to be carefully considered (Krupnick and Pincus, 1992, p.1303)

Schizophrenia has a major impact on the quality of life of sufferers and its broader impacts on families and on the wider society are well known if perhaps less thoroughly documented. The majority of sufferers require long-term treatment and support, and there are depressingly regular media stories about violent incidents involving people with the illness. The costs of schizophrenia, broadly defined, consequently loom large not just from the perspectives of health care decision-makers and governments, but also to sufferers and their families and to a great many other people with only indirect experience. As we have argued, there is increasing recognition that economics can offer conceptual frameworks, relevant data and interpretations which can inform decision-makers' choices in the face of resource scarcity.

The supply response from economics has been low, not least because few mental health researchers until quite recently have sought to include an economic dimension in their evaluations. As other chapters of this book make plain, there is considerable variety in the range of psychological interventions available (in principle) to treat people with schizophrenia. This variety should be remembered when trying to tease out the implications of available evidence, economic or otherwise. There is perhaps too great a readiness to generalise from a single study whose patient population, intervention type, treatment length, therapist characteristics and treatment setting are particular to one context (Krupnick and Pincus, 1992). In addition, there is the pervasive difficulty of trying to generalise from research settings to the "real world" of everyday practice, a difficulty which is obviously not peculiar to economic research.

If the right extrapolations and generalisations are made, economic evidence could greatly assist in policy formulation, practice decisions and service planning. But it is important to recognise that economic appraisal—even when cost and outcomes are well-measured—is an *aid* to decision making and not a *substitute* for it. Other factors will and must influence the planning and delivery of treatment services. Economic evaluation can be used to identify the trade-offs between the efficient use of resources and the pursuit of other objectives. For example, if psychotherapy is less cost-effective among certain socio-economic, demographic or diagnostic groups, evidence can be presented to the decision-maker that highlights the cost-effectiveness and distributional implications of alternative courses of action.

However and wherever economic evaluations of psychological interventions are to be located in the decision-making structure, it is clear that if they are to make valued contributions to decisions as to the utilisation of scarce resources, it is vital that the qualities of the economic data and the evaluative methodology are carefully scrutinised. This is not to put a dampener on ongoing research, but both to caution those non-economists who might over-enthusiastically build on the findings of inadequate research and to remind those economists active in schizophrenia research of the need to maintain the highest standards in what is such an important area of health care provision.

REFERENCES

Anderson J. and Adams C. (1996) Family interventions in schizophrenia (editorial), *British Medical Journal*, **313**, 505–506.

Audit Commission (1994) *Finding a Place*, HMSO, London.

Austad, C.S. and Berman, W.H. (1991) *Psychotherapy in Managed Health Care*, American Psychologial Association, Washington DC.

Beecham, J.K. and Knapp, M.R.K. (1992) Costing psychiatric interventions, in G. Thornicroft, C. Brewin and J. Wing, *Measuring Mental Health Needs*, Oxford University Press, Oxford.

British Medical Association (1988) *Philosophy and Practice of Medical Ethics*, BMA, London.

Cardin, V.A., McGill, C.W. and Falloon, I.R.H. (1986) An economic analysis: costs, benefits and effectiveness, in I.R.H. Falloon (ed.) *Family Management of Schizophrenia*, Johns Hopkins University, Baltimore.

Cochrane Collaboration Schizophrenia Review Group (1994) Schizophrenia and the Cochrane Collaboration, *Schizophrenia Research*, **13**, 185–188.

Davies, L.M. and Drummond, M.F. (1994) Economics and schizophrenia: the real cost, *British Journal of Psychiatry*, **165** (supplement 25), 18–21.

Drummond, M.F. (1992) Cost-of-illness studies: a major headache? *PharmacoEconomics*, **2**, 1–4.

Drummond, M.F., Stoddart, G.L. and Torrance, G.W. (1997) *Methods for the Economic Evaluation of Health Care Programmes*, Oxford Medical Publications, Oxford.

Fahy, T. and Wessely S. (1993) Should purchasers pay for psychotherapy? (Editorial) *British Medical Journal*, **307**, 576–577.

Fonagy, P and Higgitt, A (1989) Evaluating the performance of departments of psychotherapy, *Psychoanalytic Psychotherapy*, **4**, 121–153.

Friedman, R.M. and Kutesh, K. (1994) Challenges for child and adolescent mental health, *Health Affairs*, **11**, 125–136.

Gray, A., Marshall, M., Lockwood, A., et al. (1997) Problems in conducting economic evaluations alongside clinical trials: lessons from a study of case management for people with mental disorders, *British Journal of Psychiatry*, **170**, 47–52.

Hargreaves, W.A., Shumway, M. and Hu T.-W. (1997) Measuring psychotherapy cost and effectiveness, in N. Miller, K. Magruder and A. Rupp (eds) *The Cost-Effectivness of Psychotherapy: A Guide for Practitioners, Researchers and Policymakers*, John Wiley, New York.

Healey A. and Knapp, M.R.J. (1997) Economic evaluation of mental health service and treatment initiatives, in C. Brooker and J. Repper (eds) *Serious Mental Health Problems in the Community*, Baillière Tindall, London.

Hogman, G. (1996) *Is Cost a Factor?* National Schizophrenia Fellowship, London.

Kavanagh, S. and Stewart, A. (1995) Economic evaluations of mental health care: modes and methods, in M.R.J. Knapp (ed.) *The Economic Evaluation of Mental Health Care*, Arena, Aldershot.

Kavanagh, S., Opit, L., Knapp, M.R.J. and Beecham, J. (1995) Schizophrenia: shifting the balance of care, *Social Psychiatry and Psychiatric Epidemiology*, **30**, 206–212.

Kemp, R., Hayward, P., Applewhaite, G., Everitt, B. and David A. (1996) Compliance therapy in psychotic patients: a randomised controlled trial, *British Medical Journal*, **312**, 345–349.

Knapp, M. and Beecham, J. (1996) Programme-level and system-level health economics, in H.C. Knudsen and G. Thornicroft, *Mental Health Service Evaluation*, Cambridge University Press, Cambridge.

Knapp, M.R.J. and Healey, A. (1997) Psychotherapy: individual differences in costs and outcomes, in N.Miller, K. Magruger and A. Rupp (editors), *The Cost-*

Effectiveness of Psychotherapy: A Guide for Practitioners, Researchers and Policymaker, John Wiley, New York and Chichester.

Knapp, M.R.J. (1997) Costs of schizophrenia, *British Journal of Psychiatry,* **171,** 509–518.

Krupnick, H.K. and Pincus, A.A. (1992) The cost-effectiveness of psychotherapy: a plan for research, *American Journal of Psychiatry,* **149,** 1295–1305.

Kuipers, E. (1996) The management of difficult-to-treat patients with schizophrenia, using non-drug-therapy, *British Journal of Psychiatry,* **169** (supplement 31), 41–51.

Lehman, A.F., Thompson, J.W., Dixon, L.B. and Scott, J.E. (1995) Schizophrenia: treatment outcomes research—editors' introduction, *Schizophrenia Bulletin,* **21,** 561–566.

Lelliott, P., Audini, B., Knapp, M.R.J. and Chisholm, D. (1996) The mental health residential care study I: classification of facilities and description of residents, *British Journal of Psychiatry,* **169,** 139–147.

McGuire, T.G. (1991) Measuring the economic costs of schizophrenia, *Schizophrenia Bulletin,* **17,** 375–388.

McGrath, G. (1994) Economic aspects of psychotherapy, *Current Opinion in Psychiatry,* **17,** 241–244.

Mari, J.J. and Streiner, D.L. (1994) An overview of family interventions and relapson schizophrenia: meta analysis of research findings, *Psychological Medicine,* **24,** 565–578.

Mason, P., Harrison, G., Glazebrook, C., Medley, I. and Croudace, T. (1996) The course of schizophrenia over 13 years, *British Journal of Psychiatry,* 169, 580–586.

Meltzer H.Y. (1996) Cost-effectiveness of clozapine treatment, *Journal of Clinical Psychiatry,* Monograph Series, **16,** 16–17.

Meltzer, H., Gill, B., Petticrew, M. and Hinds, K. (1995) *The Prevalence of Psychiatric Morbidity among Adults Living in Private Households,* Office of Population Census and Surveys, London.

Miller, N., Magruder, K. and Rupp, A. (eds) (1997) *Psychotherapy: Costs and Benefits,* National Institute for Health, Washington DC.

National Health Service Executive (1996a) *NHS Psychotherapy Services in England. Summary of Strategic Policy,* NHSE, London.

National Health Service Executive (1996b) *NHS Psychotherapy Services in England. Review of Strategic Policy,* NHSE, London.

National Health Service Executive (1996c) *Burdens of Disease. A Discussion Document,* NHSE, London.

Netten, A. and Dennett, J. (1996) *Unit Costs of Health and Social Care 1996,* Personal Social Services Research Unit, University of Kent at Canterbury.

Parry G. (1992) Improving psychotherapy services: applications of research audit and evaluation, *British Journal of Clinical Psychology,* 31, 3–19.

Revicki, D.A., Shakespeare, A. and Kind, P. (1996) *International Clinical Psychopharmacology,* **11,** 101–108.

Rice, D.P., Kelman, S., Miller, L.S. et al., (1990) *The Economic Costs of Alcohol and Drug Abuse and Mental Illness: 1985.* DHHS Pub. No. (ADM) 90–1694, National Institute of Mental Health, Rockville, MD.

Roth, A.D. and Fonagy, P. (1996) *What Works for Whom? A Critical Review of Psychotherapy Research,* Guilford Press, New York.

Rund, B.R., Moe, L.C., Sollien, T., Fjell, A., Borchgrevink, T., Hallert, M. and Naess, P.O. (1994) The psychosis project—an efficiency study of a psychoeducational treatment for schizophrenic adolescents, *Acta Psychiatrica Scandinavica,* **89,** 211–218.

Sasbin, J.E. (1994) A credo for ethical managed care in mental health practice, *Hospital and Community Psychiatry,* **45,** 859–86.

Schene, A.H., Tessler, R.C. and Gamache, G.M. (1994) Instruments measuring family or caregiver burden in severe mental illness, *Social Psychiatry and Psychiatric Epidemiology*, **28**, 11–16.

Scott, J.E. and Dixon, L.B. (1995) Psychological interventions for schizophrenia, *Schizophrenia Bulletin*, **21**, 621–630.

Sibbald, B. (1996) *The Role of Counsellors in General Practice*, Royal College of General Practitioners, London.

Tarrier, N.,Lowson, K., Barrowclough, C. (1991) Some aspects of family interventions in schizophrenia. II. Financial considerations, *British Journal of Psychiatry*, **159**, 481–484.

Trad, P.V. (1992) Will the health care crisis sabotage the practice of psychotherapy? (Editorial), *American Journal of Psychiatry*, **46**, 499–500.

Xiong, W., Phillips, M.R., Hu, X., Wang, R., Dai, Q., Kleinman, J. and Kleinman, A. (1994) Family-based intervention for schizophrenic patients in China: a randomised controlled trial, *British Journal of Psychiatry*, **165**, 239–247.

INDEX

acceptance   91–2
acute psychosis   5, 6
 cognitive behaviour therapy   221
adherence   172–3
affect
 assessment   104–5
 see also anxiety; depression
age, choice of therapy and   6
age of onset   43–4
 social adjustment outcomes and
  193, 194
akathisia   165
akinesia   165
alcohol misuse, compliance and
 165–6
anger   64
antipsychotic drugs   20–1, 180
 adverse effects   164–5, 187
 cognitive effects   181
 compliance, *see* compliance
 depot preparations   169–70
 depression as dysphoric response
  83–4
 economic issues   265, 267
 low-dose therapy, with skills
  training   187–96
 optimal therapy   209, 210
  with behavioural therapy   182–7
  regimens   164
anxiety
 assessment   104–5
 cognitive behaviour therapy   64, 66,
  72–3
 psychosis   72–3, 74
Appraisal of Problems Measure   110,
 114
Asberger's syndrome   134
Assessment of Interpersonal Problem-

Solving (AIPS)   150, 152
Assessment of Involuntary Movement
 Scale (AIMS)   185
attention
 Cowan's model   27, 28
 deficits   18–19, 122, 123–4
Attitudes to Medication (ATM) scale
 168
attributional style
 abnormal biases   36, 124–8
 cognitive deficits affecting   134–6
 in depression   125, 133
 early environmental effects
  133–4
 in obsessional psychosis   69
 in paranoid patients   3, 125–8
 parental   133–4
 self-representations and   131–2
 therapeutic modification   137–8
Attributional Style Questionnaire
 (ASQ)   125, 127, 132
attrition, sample   11, 106–7
autism   134–5

basal ganglia   155, 156
Beck, A.T.   59–60, 61
Beck Depression Inventory   111, 114,
 115
befriending control group   67
Behavioural Science Delivery Model
 223
behavioural skills training
 vs supportive group psychotherapy
  187–96
 see also social skills training
behavioural syndromes   74
behavioural therapy, and optimal drug
 therapy   182–7

beliefs
  analysis of 104
  delusional *vs* normal 120
  modification therapy 136–7
Beliefs about Voices Questionnaire
  (BAVQ) 51–2, 89, 104
Bentall, Richard 33, 35–6
biobehavioural therapy 179–96
  outpatients 187–96
  treatment refractory patients 182–7
biopsychosocial intervention 181
blame, self- 125, 131
Bleuler, Eugene 19, 20
blindness, study participants 107
BMDP 5V 108, 111
Brief Psychiatric Rating Scale (BPRS)
  46–7, 55
  biobehavioural therapy evaluation
    184, 191
  cognitive behaviour therapy
    evaluation 111, 114, 115
  cognitive remediation evaluation
    152, 153
  family intervention evaluation 208
burnout 209

Camberwell Family Interview (CFI)
  201–2, 206
cannabis 71
Capgras delusion 121
carers 201–11
  burden on 205, 217
  compliance and 168
  costs of schizophrenia 262
  education 171, 210
  effects of family intervention 208
  impact on 202–3
  interventions aimed at 7
  needs 202–3, 209–10
  outcome assessment 53
  relationships with client 204,
    205–11
  see also family; staff
catastrophising 66
central executive module 27, 28
choice
  criteria for 265, 266
  and scarcity 264–5
clients, *see* patients
Client Service Receipt Inventory
  (CSRI) 275
Clinical Global Impression scale (CGI)
  55

biobehavioural therapy evaluation
  183, 184–5
Clinical Research Center for
  Schizophrenia and Psychiatric
  Rehabilitation 181
clinical themes/subgroups 68–74
Cochrane Collaboration Schizophrenia
  Review Group 220, 277
coercion 169, 173
COGLAB tasks 153
cognitive appraisal 89–95
  psychotic illness 91–5
  symptoms 89–91
Cognitive Assessment of Voices
  Schedule (CAV) 89
cognitive behaviour therapy (CBT)
  9–11, 59–76, 249–52
  compliance management 60, 66, 72,
    171–2
  delusions, *see* delusions, cognitive
    behaviour therapy
  efficacy 249–51
  evaluation 101–16
    measurement issues 102–6
    methodological issues 106–9
    pilot study 106, 109–16
  family, *see* family intervention
  follow-up study (Kingdon) 67–76
    clinical subgroups 74
    clinical themes 68–74
    patterns of illness 74–6
  goals 109–10
  hallucinations, *see* hallucinations,
    cognitive behaviour therapy
  pilot study (Garety *et al*) 106,
    109–16
    goals/assessment measures
      109–10
    measures 110–11
    outcome 112
    participants 112–13
    results 113–14
    statistical analysis 111–12
    therapy 113
    timing of assessments 110
  pilot study (Kingdon) 61–7
    control befriending group 67
    results 67
    treatment techniques 61–6
  rationale 20–1
  recent innovations 220–1
  styles and methods 10, 59–61, 249
  targets 36–7

cognitive deconstruction 96
cognitive neuropsychological
  abnormalities 17–21, 247
  antipsychotic medication and 181
  attributional biases and 134–6
  compliance and 164
  role in delusions, *see* delusions,
    cognitive origins
  3-factor view 154–5
  see also information-processing
    abnormalities
cognitive remediation 9, 11, 60–1,
  145–57, 246–9
  individual differences and treatment
    mechanisms 154–6
  mechanisms of effect 146–7
  Nebraska IPT study project 148–54
    assessment/treatment procedures
    151–2
    experimental design 149–50
    outcome measures 150–1
    results 152–4
  outcome methodology and 147–8
cognitive therapy, depression in
  psychosis 96
community care 169, 263
community psychiatric nurses (CPNs)
  access of patients to 265
  Manchester training programmes
    225–8
  Thorn training projects 229–31
Community Transition Program (CTP)
  149–50, 151
compliance 161–73
  assessment 162–3
  definition 162
  determinants 163–8
    carers and family 168
    environment 164
    illness 163–4
    medical team 166
    medication 164–5
    patients 166–8
    substance misuse 71–2, 165–6
  interventions to enhance 168–72
    cognitive behaviour therapy 60,
      66, 72, 171–2
    economic evaluation 273, 274
    family interventions 242–3
    legal/coercive methods 169
    medication regime 169–70
    psychoeducation 170–1
  vs adherence 172–3

Comprehensive Psychopathological
  Rating Scale (CPRS) 49, 61, 67
computer crash analogy 155
confrontation, avoiding 62
consent, informed 107
continuity of services 203
Continuous Performance Test (CPT)
  247
  3–7 memory load (3–7 CPT) 31–2
  degraded stimulus 30, 31
control, locus of, *see* locus of control
control groups
  cognitive behaviour therapy 67,
    107
  cognitive remediation 149
coping strategies, carers 205, 206
coping strategy enhancement (CSE)
  60, 220, 250
  for carers 210
  efficacy 250–1
cost(s)
  caregiver 262
  health care 262–3
  marginal 275
  opportunity 275
  patient 261–2
  of schizophrenia 45, 260–4
  social 263–4
cost–benefit analysis (CBA) 271
cost-effectiveness 12, 252–3
  analysis (CEA) 271, 272–6
  family intervention 241–2, 277–8
  social skills training 246, 278
cost–utility analysis (CUA) 272
Cotard delusion 123
CPNs, *see* community psychiatric
  nurses
critical collaborative analysis
  technique 65
critical comments 202, 204, 206
cultural differences 44, 240

data
  missing 106–7
  presentation/analysis 107–8
delusions 17, 119–39
  affective components 105
  analysis of beliefs about 104
  changing conceptualisation 103,
    105
  cognitive behaviour therapy 59–60,
    62–4, 73, 74, 113–16, 136–9

cognitive origins   33–4, 36, 121–8
  aetiological speculations   132–6
  attributional abnormalities   124–8
  probabilistic reasoning deficits
    122–3
  selective information processing
    biases   123–4
content   105
grandiose   73
as meaningful phenomena   120
multi-dimensional approach
  103–4, 116
as perceptual abnormalities   120–1
persecutory (paranoid)   3, 119
  cognitive model   128–32
  cognitive origins   36, 121–8
denial   91, 92
depot preparations   169–70
depression   81–96
  assessment   104–5
  attributional style   125, 133
  cognitive behaviour therapy   64, 66,
    114–16
  postschizophrenic   82
  in psychosis   82–6
    cognitive approach   89–95
    as diagnostic mistake   85
    as dysphoric response to
      neuroleptics   83–4
    as intrinsic component   82–3
    prevalence   82
    as reaction to psychosis   85–6
    suicide risk   87–8
  vs negative symptoms   48
  vs schizophrenia   20, 81
  see also suicide
developing countries   44
diagnosis
  depression in schizophrenia   85
  schizophrenia   1–3, 43–4
Diagnostic and Statistical Manual fourth
  edition (DSMIV)   44
diaries, self-report   53, 74
dissemination
  research results   13, 215–16
  treatment skills   12, 222–32
distraction techniques   60
dopamine dysregulation   32, 155–6
drop-outs, study   11, 106–7
drug abuse   23, 71
  compliance and   71–2, 165–6
drug-related psychosis   71–2, 74
Dysfunctional Attitudes Scale (DAS)
  130

dysphoria, neuroleptic-induced   83–4,
  165
dystonias, acute   165

early interventions   5–6, 221–2
Early Psychosis Prevention and
  Intervention Centre   222
economic evaluations   259–79
  completed studies   276–8
  conducting   272–6
  demands for   264–9
  methods   270–2
  reasons for low number   269–70
economy   266
education
  carers   171, 210
  patient, to enhance compliance   170
  see also psychoeducation
Education for the Developmentally
  Young (EDY) project   224
effectiveness   266
efficiency   266
emotion, expressed, see expressed
  emotion
emotional over-involvement (EOI)
  202, 204
emotional processing   209
emotional Stroop task   123, 124, 130
emotional support   203
entrapment   93–5, 96
environmental factors
  compliance   164
  early, attributional style and   133–4
environmental stressors   6–8, 22, 23,
  122
  extreme sensitivity   73
epidemiology of schizophrenia   43–4
equity   266
ethical aspects, economic evaluations
  268
ethnosemantic beliefs   91–3
exacerbations, psychotic
  in family intervention studies   208
  social skills training and   193–5
  see also relapse
expert therapists   12
exposure techniques   71
expressed emotion (EE)   7, 134, 204
  compliance and   168
  components   204
  interventions   207, 216–17
  links with burden to carers   205
  modification   72, 208, 238–41

in staff relationships 206–7, 209
"extended leave" 169
extrapyramidal side-effects 165, 187

face recognition 121
family
  benefits of staff training 226–7
  burden 205, 217
  compliance and 168
  costs of schizophrenia 262
  education 10, 171
  effects of family intervention 208
  expressed emotion see expressed
    emotion
  impact on 202–3
  outcome assessment 53
  see also carers; parents
family intervention (therapy) 7, 10,
  216–20
  components 209
  cost-effectiveness 241–2, 277–8
  drug-related psychosis 72
  duration of effects 243
  efficacy 207
  outcome and costs 238–43
  outcome measures 207–9
  staff training programmes 224–31
  underutilisation 220
  see also psychoeducation
fluphenazine 187–96
focusing 60, 71, 220
Frith, Christopher 33, 34–5

gender differences 43
General Health Questionnaire (GHQ)
  226–7
general practitioners 166
genetic susceptibility 23
Global Assessment of Function (GAF)
  Scale 54, 55
Global Assessment Scale (GAS) 54,
  55
goal-directedness, lack of 19–20
group psychotherapy 9–10
  supportive (SGP), vs behavioural
    skills training 187–96

Hallucination Interview Schedule
  (HIS) 52
hallucinations 17
  affective components 105
  analysis of beliefs about 104
  changing conceptualisation 103, 105

cognitive appraisal 89–90
cognitive behaviour therapy 60, 63,
  65–6, 69–71, 73, 220
  content 105
  Hemsley–Gray hypothesis 33–4
  multi-dimensional approaches 104
  obsessional 69
hallucinogenic drugs 71
haloperidol (HPL) 182–7
Health Belief Model (HBM) 167, 168
health care costs 262–3
Health of the Nation Outcome Scales
  (HoNOS) 54, 55
"Hearing Voices" movement 60
Hemsley–Gray cognitive model 32–4
hippocampus 32
hopelessness 88, 96
hospital
  admissions 208
  days in 208, 246
hostel workers 205–6, 209
humiliation 93–5, 96
Hustig and Hafner Hallucinations
  Assessment 111

identity, in psychotic illness 91–2, 95
Idiosyncratic Prodromal Scale (IPS)
  190
Idiosyncratic Target Symptom Scale
  183
individual differences, treatment
  mechanisms and 154–6
individual therapies 7, 12, 278
"inference chaining" technique 62, 73
information, for carers 202–3, 210
information-processing abnormalities
  17–21, 247
  Bentall hypothesis 33, 35–6
  British vs American theories 37
  cognitive remediation and 153
  Frith hypothesis 33, 34–5
  Hemsley–Gray hypothesis 32–4
  role in delusions, see delusions,
    cognitive origins
  selective biases 123–4
  as targets for intervention 36–7
  treatment approaches 20–1
  UCLA Clinical Research Center
    concept 29–32, 33
  see also cognitive neuropsychological
    abnormalities
information-processing models

information-processing models
(continued)
    Cowan   26–9, 30
    Houk and Wise   156
insight, impaired   172–3
Insight scale   110
Integrated Psychological Therapy
    (IPT)   9, 60–1, 148, 246
    efficacy   247–8
    mechanisms of effects   154
    Nebraska study project   148–54
Internal, Personal and Situational
    Attributions Questionnaire (IPSAQ)
    127–8, 131
International Classification of
    Diseases, tenth revision (ICD10)
    44, 61
intrauterine environment   23
IPT, see Integrated Psychological
    Therapy

Jaspers, K.   120

KGV (Psychiatric Assessment Scale)
    49–50, 55, 226
Kraepelin, Emil   18–19

labelling theory   91–2
learning
    reinforcement   155–6
    verbal   26
legal coercion   169
liability factors, see vulnerability
    factors
Life Skills Profile   111
locus of control   92–3
    early influences   133–4
    in paranoid patients   127
    loss   93–5

Maher, B.A.   120–1
managed care   267–8
Manchester
    community psychiatric nurse
        training programmes   225–8
    Thorn training project   230–1
Maudsley Assessment of Delusions
    Schedule (MADS)   10, 50–1
    cognitive behaviour therapy
        evaluation   104, 114
medical team, role in compliance   166
Medication Management Module   171
memory

cognitive remediation and   153
    Cowan's model   26–7, 28
    in paranoid patients   124
    processing deficits   31–3
meta-analysis   103
methodological issues   11
    cognitive behaviour therapy studies
        106–9
    cognitive remediation studies
        147–8
misidentification, delusional   121
missing data   106–7

Nebraska IPT study project, see
    cognitive remediation, Nebraska IPT
    study project
negative symptoms   18
    assessment scales   48–9
    cognitive behaviour therapy   63, 66
    cognitive origins   30
    compliance and   164
neurocognitive abnormalities, see
    information-processing
    abnormalities
neurodevelopmental factors   23
neuroleptic drugs, see antipsychotic
    drugs
neuroleptic-induced deficit syndrome
    (NIDS)   165
New South Wales, staff training
    programme   228–9
non-compliance, see compliance
nurses, community psychiatric, see
    community psychiatric nurses

obsession, definition   69
obsessional psychosis   69–71, 74
outcome (in schizophrenia)   44–5
outcome measurement   43–55
    affect and self-esteem   104–5
    analysis of beliefs/thinking
        processes   104
    changing concepts of key symptoms
        103, 105
    cognitive behaviour therapy   102–6
    content of delusions/hallucinations
        105
    multi-dimensional approaches
        103–4
outcome measures   2–3, 10–11, 45–53
    choice   11, 102–3, 106
    cognitive behaviour therapy
        110–11

cognitive remediation study 150–1
cost-effectiveness analysis 274–5
family intervention 207–9
global 54–5
reliability, validity and relevance 45
over-protection 202, 204

paranoid patients
attributional style 3, 125–8
cognitive behaviour therapy 138–9
cognitive model of delusions 128–32
selective information processing biases 123–4
see also delusions, persecutory
parasuicide 86, 87
parents
attributional style 133–4
expressed emotion, *see* expressed emotion
representations of clients 130
patients
costs of schizophrenia 261–2
education, to enhance compliance 170
factors affecting compliance 166–8
preferences 13
relationships with carers 204, 205–7
perception 27
abnormalities 17–18, 120–1
deficits in early processing 30–1
subtle changes 20
persecutory delusions, *see* delusions, persecutory
Personal Beliefs about Illness Questionnaire (PBIQ) 92–3
Personal Questionnaire Rapid Scaling Technique (PQRST) 52–3
Personal Questionnaires 111
phases of schizophrenia 4–6
Positive and Negative Syndrome Scale (PANSS) 48–9, 55, 152
positive remarks 204
positive symptoms 17–18
assessment scales 47–9
cognitive origins 33–4, 35–6
see also delusions; hallucinations; information-processing abnormalities
postschizophrenic depression 82
practical support 203

preferences, clients' 13
prefrontal cortex 32
Present State Examination (PSE) 103, 110, 208
Preston training project 224–5
probabilistic reasoning deficits 122–3
problem solving skills 9, 60
for carers 203, 210
effects of family intervention 208
training 209, 220
prodromal period (initial) 5, 6
prodromes (further exacerbations) 6
early detection 222
prognostic factors 46
Psychiatric Assessment Scale (KGV) 49–50, 55, 226
psychodynamic theories 3–4
psychoeducation 10, 209
cost-effectiveness 242
efficacy 240–1
to enhance compliance 170–1
psychological factors, compliance 167–8
psychological treatments
background to development 1–6
choice 8–11
cost-effectiveness, *see* cost-effectiveness
economic evaluation 259–79
future research issues 12–13
implementation 13
methodological issues 11
outcome and costs 237–53
psychological themes 3–4
targets 6–8
vs biobehavioural therapy 180–1
psychosocial treatments
dissemination and training 222–32
innovative 215–33
recent developments 216–22
psychotherapeutic model 92, 93
Psychotic symptom rating scales (PSYRATS) 51

quality-adjusted life years (QALY) 272, 274
quality of life assessment 53
questioning, Socratic 62–4

random-effects models 108, 111
randomised controlled trials 106–9
clinical/statistical significance 108–9

data presentation/analysis   107–8
sample attrition/missing data
   106–7
rapport   62
rate-limiting factors   26
Rating of Medical Influences (ROMI)
   scale   168
reality-testing techniques   59, 62, 65,
   69
reasoning deficits, probabilistic   122–3
recovery   5
regression models   111–12
relapse   5
   cognitive remediation and   248
   compliance with medication and
      161
   detecting early signs   222
   in family intervention studies
      207–8, 217, 239
   social skills training and   244–5
   see also exacerbations, psychotic
relatives, *see* family
relaxation tapes   62
reliability, outcome measures   45
Research Diagnostic Criteria (RDC)
   44
residential accommodation   263
respite   203, 210
risperidone   181
Rosenberg Self-Esteem Scale   110

Salford Family Intervention
   programme   225
sample
   attrition   11, 106–7
   representativeness   11
SAS PROC MIXED   108
Scale for the Assessment of Negative
   Symptoms (SANS)   48
Scale for the Assessment of Positive
   Symptoms (SAPS)   47–8
Scale for the Assessment of Thought,
   Language and Communication
   (TLC)   152
scarcity
   and choice   264–5
   growing pressures   266–7
schizo-affective disorder   82
schizophreniform disorder   44
self-blame   125, 131
self-concept, in paranoid patients
   128, 130
self-control strategies   250

Self-Discrepancy Theory (SDT)   128–9
self-esteem   93
   cognitive behaviour therapy and
      64
   in depression   125
   in paranoid patients   128
self-image   92
self-regulatory model   167, 250
self-representations
   paranoid patients   128–9, 130
   relationship to attributions   131–2
sensitivity disorder   73–4
services
   carer needs and   209–10
   for carers   202–3
   outcome measures   53
sexual dysfunction   165
sheltered environments   7
significance, clinical/statistical   108–9
Social Adjustment Scale (SAS) II   191,
   192
Social Avoidance and Distress Scale
   111
social costs   263–4
social functioning   5, 6, 243
   assessment   53
   cognitive remediation and   248
   in family intervention studies   208,
      217, 240–1
   prediction of treatment effects   193
   social skills training and   192, 194
   staff training programmes and   226
social skills training (SST)   9, 243–6
   cognitive remediation and   152
   cost-effectiveness   246, 278
   duration of effects   245–6
   efficacy   243–6
   evaluation   150
   vs supportive group psychotherapy
      187–96
sociodemographic factors, compliance
   166–7
Socrates study   76, 221, 222
Socratic questioning   62–4
Span of Apprehension Test (SAT)
   247
   COGLAB   153
   forced-choice   30, 31
speech
   disorganized   18
   thought-disordered   64–5
staff
   expressed emotion   206–7, 209

interventions for   7, 209
relationships with clients   205–7
training   13, 215–16, 222–32
    in situ   232
    Manchester CPN programmes
        225–8
    New South Wales study   228–9
    Preston project   224–5
    Thorn nurse-training project
        229–31
statistical analysis   107–8, 111–12
statistical significance   108–9
stress
    role in hallucinations   65
    staff   209
stressors, environmental, see
    environmental stressors
stress-vulnerability models, see
    vulnerability-stress models
substance misuse, compliance and
    165–6
suicidal ideation   66, 88
suicide   6, 86–9, 95–6
    escape theory   96
    precursors   87–9
    predicting   87
    prevalence   86–7
summary statistics   107–8
support, for carers   203, 210
supportive group psychotherapy
    (SGP), vs behavioural skills training
    187–96
symptoms (of schizophrenia)
    17–18
    assessment   2–3
    cognitive appraisal   89–91
    cognitive behaviour therapy, see
        cognitive behaviour therapy
    diversity   2
    individual approach   2
    instruments to measure severity
        50–3
    multi-dimensional approaches
        103–4
    negative, see negative symptoms
    positive, see positive symptoms

temporal variation   5
systematic reviews   220

team, medical, role in compliance   166
Theory of Mind (ToM) deficits   134–6
Thorn Nurse Training Scheme   12,
    229–31
thought
    disorder, cognitive behaviour
        therapy   63, 64–5, 69–71
    processes, analysis   104
    stopping   250
threat-related information, abnormal
    attention to   123, 124
3-factor view of schizophrenic
    cognition   154–5
training, staff, see staff, training
treatment refractory patients,
    biobehavioural therapy   182–7

UCLA Clinical Research Center
    29–32

validity
    concepts of schizophrenia   44
    outcome measures   45
violent incidents   263
visual masking   30, 31
vocational functioning   5
voices
    cognitive appraisal   89–90
    cognitive behaviour therapy   65–6
    see also hallucinations
vulnerability factors   6, 21–6, 122
    information-processing   29–36
    mediating   24–6, 33, 34, 35, 36
    stable   23–4, 25, 26, 33
vulnerability-stress models   21, 22,
    122
    cognitive behaviour therapy and
        61–2, 73

warmth   202, 204
Williams, Alan   269–70
Wisconsin Card Sorting Test (WCST)
    247

Related titles of interest...

Cognitive Analytic Therapy for Borderline Personality Disorder

Anthony Ryle

The interventions illustrated in this book have been used to treat outpatients for 15 years, and results indicate that treatments can achieve clinically significant changes in the course of 16-4 sessions in a substantial proportion of patients.

0-471-97617-2   206pp   1997   Hardback
0-471-97618-0   206pp   1997   Paperback

Cognitive Behaviour Therapy for Psychosis

Theory and Practice

David Fowler, Philippa Garety and Elizabeth Kuipers

Focuses on the four main problems presented by people with psychosis: emotional disturbance; psychotic symptoms like delusions and bizarre beliefs; social disabilities; and relapse risk.

0471 93980 3   212pp   1995   Hardback
0471 95618 X   212pp   1995   Paperback

Psychological Management of Schizophrenia

Edited by Max Birchwood and Nicholas Tarrier

Offers a practical guide for mental health professionals wanting to develop and enhance their skills in new treatment approaches.

0471 95056 4   176pp   1994   Paperback

Cognitive Therapy for Delusions, Voices and Paranoia

Paul Chadwick, Max Birchwood and Peter Trower

Guides professionals towards a better practice by treating the individual symptoms of delusions, voices and paranoia, rather than by the categorization of schizophrenia.

0-471-93888-2   230pp   1996   Hardback
0-471-96173-6   230pp   1996   Paperbac